The Rich Don't Always Win

The Rich Don't Always Win

THE FORGOTTEN TRIUMPH OVER PLUTOCRACY THAT CREATED THE AMERICAN MIDDLE CLASS, 1900–1970

SAM PIZZIGATI

Seven Stories Press

NEW YORK

Seven Stories Press
140 Watts Street
New York, NY 10013
www.sevenstories.com

College professors may order examination copies of Seven Stories Press titles for a free six-month trial period. To order, visit http://www.seven-stories.com/textbook or send a fax on school letterhead to (212) 226-1411.

Book design by Elizabeth DeLong

Library of Congress Cataloging-in-Publication Data

Pizzigati, Sam.
  The rich don't always win : the forgotten triumph over plutocracy that created the American middle class, 1900/1970 / Sam Pizzigati. -- 1st ed.
      p. cm.
  Includes bibliographical references and index.
  ISBN 978-1-60980-434-3 (pbk.)
  1.   Wealth--United States--History--20th century. 2.   Middle class--United States--History--20th century. 3.   Equality--United States--History--20th century. 4.   United States--Economic condi-tions--20th century. 5.   United States--Social conditions--20th century. I. Title.
  HC110.W4P59 2012
  305.5'509730904--dc23

                                    2012037428

Printed in the United States

9 8 7 6 5 4 3 2 1

For Pablo Saul and Bianca Xitlaly

CONTENTS

PREFACE

We Americans today consume most of our history from pop culture, from television and movies—and even ceremonies at Major League ballparks. Our popular culture teaches and preaches that the United States vanquished three terrible dangers back in the twentieth century: We beat Hitler and the Nazis. We beat the Russians and the commies. And we beat racial bigotry, thanks to heroes like Jackie Robinson.

But one vanquished threat to our twentieth century domestic tranquility gets precious little play in our popular culture, virtually no mention whatsoever: Over the first half of the twentieth century, we beat back plutocracy, rule by the rich.

I grew up in the 1950s on Long Island, right in the middle of the new America this victory over plutocracy created. My classmates and I took America's new middle class for granted. And why not? We hadn't struggled to create a society where average families enjoyed security and comfort. We didn't know—or appreciate—how long and difficult that struggle had been.

In my case, that appreciation would finally come in the early 1970s when I started working as a labor journalist. I encountered in that work all sorts of old-timers. I still remember many of them. Len De Caux had turned seventy by the time I met him. He had immigrated to the United States as a young man in 1921 and had himself become a labor journalist. He covered union campaigns through the labor movement's darkest days and then, in the late 1930s, edited the union paper that chronicled labor's greatest upsurge. De Caux knew many of the political celebrities of those turbulent times. But he helped me understand that I owed my comfortable world to the struggles and sacrifices of *average* Americans.

As did Pat Tobin, a veteran activist who was representing the West Coast longshoremen's union in Washington, DC, when I first met him. Tobin had been a poor Irish kid in 1934 San Francisco when a dockworker walkout turned into a citywide general strike. He never forgot those heady days. I kept in touch with Tobin after he retired at the start of the Reagan era. I loved listening to his stories, even the second and third time around. They gave me a sense of a time when working Americans by the millions saw the nation's awesomely affluent as more pathetic than powerful. I've learned from those stories, and I've tried to bring their sensibilities into these pages.

I've also learned a great deal from historians of my own generation, scholars who grew up in the same era I did and have devoted their careers to keeping alive our forgotten past. Historians like Joshua Freeman and Alan Brinkley take us back to a not-so-distant time when ordinary Americans felt ever so deeply that if they just kept working and struggling together, they could change their lives for the better.

I've done some digging on my own as well, into old newspapers and memoirs and boxed-up personal papers. I didn't go looking for blockbuster deep dark secrets. I searched instead for overlooked episodes from our past that might help explain the smashing triumph over plutocracy we today so desperately need to repeat. I found some.

I do believe my grandfather would have liked this book. He helped make this history. A poor immigrant teenager from Italy a little over a century ago, a chauffeur for the rich in the 1920s, a Socialist Party organizer against the rich in the 1930s, the proprietor of a gas station in the 1950s—my grandfather saw it all. Unfortunately, I never knew enough back then to ask him about it. I should have.

We should always ask.

Sam Pizzigati
Kensington, Maryland
July 2012

INTRODUCTION

In 1952, one of America's most beloved social historians set out to write the story of the tumultuous first half of the twentieth century. Frederick Lewis Allen, the influential editor of *Harper's* magazine, would call his book *The Big Change*. Allen wanted to describe the awesome transformation that he personally—and Americans collectively—had witnessed since 1900. He certainly had plenty to write about.

Back in 1900, Americans lived without airplanes and automobiles, without TV and radio, without high-rises and suburbs. No Americans laughed and cried with family and friends at local movie theaters when the twentieth century dawned, or stuffed clothes into washing machines. Hardly anyone—outside the nation's most southerly climes—even ate fresh fruit in the winter.

So what did Frederick Lewis Allen, amid all these colossal changes, end up citing as the twentieth century's single most important change of all? Simply put: equality.

"Of all the contrasts between American life in 1900 and half a century or more later," Allen wrote, "perhaps the most significant is in the distance between rich and poor."[1]

Over the century's first half, the popular historian marveled, the mansions and estates of "the rich and fashionable" had become museums and hospitals and college campuses. The super rich, an overbearing presence in America circa 1900, had essentially disappeared.

All sorts of midcentury observers celebrated that disappearance. Stuart Chase, a MIT-trained engineer and a nationally respected social critic since the 1920s, began a 1968 memoir by noting that he had lived through an "era of shattering change." How shattering?

"I can remember as a small boy," wrote the then eighty-year-old

1

Chase, "the first electric light installed in my grandfather's house in New England, and the first automobile on the street outside, and I have recently watched on television a space capsule with men aboard coming down on target in the ocean."[2]

Yet for Stuart Chase, as for Frederick Lewis Allen, the technological miracles of their new midcentury age paled against America's remarkable economic transformation, "the achievement of an economy of abundance, an affluent society, where for the first time in history poor people are in a minority."[3] And rich people? Their "gracious plantations, estates, and mansions," Chase related, had gone "up for sale to innkeepers and rest homes, if not carved into subdivisions."[4]

The grand rich who had somehow managed to dodge the subdivisions, the *New Yorker* writer Kenneth Lamott observed in 1969, amount to archaic "survivals" from "an earlier epoch," nothing more, "not men of our own time" and unquestionably "not the men of the future."[5] The fortunes of these remaining wealthy, Lamott added, have the same long-range prospects as "sand castles that stand against an incoming tide."[6]

Lamott and other observers were not experiencing some social mirage. America had indeed become more equal. In 1928, before the Great Depression, America's most affluent 1 percent were taking in nearly one of every four dollars in national income. By the early 1950s, they were grabbing a mere one dollar in ten.[7] The contrast higher up America's economic summit ran even starker. In 1928, nearly half the income the nation's top 1 percent collected settled in the pockets of the top 1 percent's top tenth. This top 0.1 percent of Americans—in effect, the richest one of every thousand—pulled in nearly 12 percent of the nation's income in the late 1920s. The comparable share for 1953's top one in a thousand: just 3 percent.

The shape of America's income distribution, Columbia University sociologist C. Wright Mills would note in 1956, had become "less a pyramid with a flat base than a fat diamond with a bulging middle."[8]

What explained this middle-class bulge, this massive tilt away from the top? One of midcentury America's most eminent economists, Simon Kuznets, saw the nation's growing equality as a natural consequence of economic maturation. Any industrializing society, Kuznets argued in his 1955 American Economic Association presidential address, will see income divides widen dramatically as industrializing upsets "long-established pre-industrial economic and social institutions."⁹ But those divides, Kuznets believed, will always narrow as societies stabilize and mature.

The takeaway from Kuznets for America's midcentury lay public: In the United States, we've outgrown those barbaric robber-baron gaps between rich and poor. We really don't have to worry much about inequality anymore. Those vast fortunes, those grandiose mansions and estates, have left us—and they're never coming back.

"Never" would last about a generation. By 1985, the year the Nobel Prize–winning Simon Kuznets died, American economists had begun tracking an entirely new phenomenon: A mature, developed economy—our economy—was growing markedly more unequal.

This growing inequality would continue into the 1990s and then, early in the new twenty-first century, would pick up even more momentum. America's most affluent had once again become a super rich. By 2007, on the eve of the Great Recession, the nation's top 1 percent was raking in 23.5 percent of the nation's income. Back in 1928, on the eve of the Great Depression, this top 1 percent share grabbed a nearly identical 23.9 percent.¹⁰

We had become since midcentury a different nation, a staggeringly unequal nation. In 2007, the four hundred American taxpayers with the highest incomes averaged an incredible $344.8 million each, the equivalent of over $1 million of income per day, assuming they took Sundays off.¹¹ In 1955, the nation's top four hundred had averaged, in dollars inflation-adjusted to 2007 levels, only $12.8 million each.¹²

Shall we put some human faces—some rich human faces—on this stunning surge of dollars to America's economic upper reaches? In 1954, George Romney became the chief executive of American Motors, the maker of the mighty little Rambler, the first successful American compact car. Romney would go on to become one of the nation's most celebrated CEOs. By 1968, he had emerged as a top contender for the GOP presidential nomination. Thanks to this presidential bid, we know exactly how much George Romney earned over his high-profile CEO years. His tax returns, voluntarily released to *Look* magazine, revealed that Romney had been averaging about $275,000 a year as the American Motors top executive, the inflation-adjusted equivalent of less than $2 million in 2008, the year Mitt Romney, George's son, made *his* first bid for the Republican presidential nomination.¹³

Mitt hadn't followed his father into the car business. He chose instead to wheel and deal his way to fortune, as a private-equity executive. That fortune came. Mitt's fourteen years as the CEO of Bain Capital, the *New York Times* reported late in 2007, had left him with a personal net worth near $350 million.[14] Mitt's father George would have had to work over two hundred years, after taxes and living expenses, to amass a fortune that size.

The super rich of our early twenty-first century have no trouble rationalizing their good fortune. They consider their megamillions a just reward for their free-market success. By succeeding, their story goes, they create jobs and fill bellies. Any move to share the wealth of the fabulously wealthy, their flacks assure us, would be downright silly— and fail to redistribute anything except disappointment. Anyone who argues otherwise deserves our society's deepest contempt.

Among cheerleaders for grand fortune, this contempt has a long-standing—and bipartisan—political history.

"Soaking the rich," as Representative William Robert Wood, the chairman of the Republican National Congressional Committee, opined in a 1925 address, "has been a favorite pastime of political charlatans since the dawn of history."

"Heavy taxes upon the man of wealth and upon corporations," Wood added, "strangle business, act as a deadweight to commerce, and slow down the wheels of Industry," leaving hard times for all, poor included, "the logical and inevitable result."[15]

Senator Joseph Robinson from Arkansas, the Democratic Party's Senate floor leader in the Great Depression's early days, would echo the Republican Wood.

"In my humble opinion," the powerful Democrat told reporters in 1931, "taxes should not be levied for the purpose of distributing wealth or reducing fortune, but solely with the view of obtaining revenue. Taxation on any other principle approaches confiscation."

The year Robinson made that comment, wealthy taxpayers faced a 25 percent federal tax on income over $100,000. Robinson could not envision the top tax rate on any income of the wealthy ever safely going higher.

"It is generally understood," he explained, "that there is a limit to the rate which may be imposed without discouraging investment and production."[16]

The middle decades of the twentieth century would prove Senator Robinson and his fellow friends of fortune embarrassingly mistaken.

Levels of "investment and production" would remain robust, even record-breaking, throughout the decades right after World War II—at the same time the top federal tax rate hovered around 90 percent, well over triple the 25 percent top rate Robinson considered the prudent tax-the-rich "limit."

No wealthy taxpayers after World War II, to be sure, ever actually paid 90 percent of their *total* income in taxes. Midcentury America's stunningly high tax rates only applied to dollars *above* specified income thresholds. In 1961, for instance, a married couple's income over $400,000 faced a 91 percent tax rate. On income below that figure, tax rates declined steadily, from 90 percent on dollars between $300,000 and $400,000 to 20 percent on any income under $4,000 left over after standard deductions.[17] And the rich, then as now, also enjoyed a variety of tax code loopholes that lowered their actual paid tax rate further still.

But America's midcentury rich, even with these loopholes, paid a substantial share of their total incomes in federal tax. In 1961, the taxpayers who filed the nation's four hundred highest-income returns reported, in today's dollars, an average $14 million in income. They paid, on average, 42.4 percent of this $14 million in federal income tax.[18] Let's give this figure some perspective: In the Great Recession year of 2009, the most recent year with IRS figures, our top four hundred averaged $202.4 million in income and paid just 19.9 percent of that in federal income tax.[19] In other words, after adjusting for inflation, today's top four hundred are taking home nearly fifteen times *more* income than their wealthy counterparts a half century ago and paying over two times *less* of their income in federal tax.

In American political life today, no major national political leader is advocating that we double current federal tax rates on our nation's megarich. No top elected leader is even advocating that we raise taxes on the rich by as much as a half. Those higher tax rates that wealthy Americans paid back in the 1950s and 1960s have receded into history's hoary mist. Our economy would surely tank, our contemporary conventional wisdom holds, if our rich faced tax rates as stratospherically high as 90 percent.

But America's economy did not tank back at midcentury. America's economy did just fine, especially for average Americans. In the 1950s, these average Americans became something the world had never before seen, a mass middle class. They lived in a society where a majority of the population could afford comfort and security.

Before World War II, these basics had belonged only to those who worked in traditional middle-class occupations. Doctors, lawyers, shopkeepers, clergy, and the like occupied a narrow demographic strata between the rich at America's economic summit and the vast mass of Americans in the economic basement. This poor majority had virtually no discretionary income. Most of the dollars these Americans earned went for food and shelter, for elemental survival.

Families in the early twentieth century's relatively small middle class, by contrast with the poor majority, could afford to take vacations. They could eat at restaurants. Their children had college as a viable option. They had ample and regular leisure time. They had enough savings set aside to ensure a somewhat comfortable old age. Most Americans before the 1940s enjoyed none of these middle-class comforts. Their labor enriched the already rich, not their own families. That injustice, that inequality, simply seemed the way things had always been. And always would be.

In the late 1930s few Americans knew life at the summit of their distinctly unequal nation more intimately than Herbert Claiborne Pell Jr. The blue-blood Pell could trace his family—and its fortune—back a dozen generations. Pell had turned sixteen in 1900 and spent a good chunk of that landmark year on grand tour in Europe, a standard rite of passage for young men of his age and means. In 1938, Pell would look back on his formative years for an essay in the *North American Review*, the nation's most venerable literary magazine.

"I can remember going to a ball in New York given in a private house where at supper three hundred people were each given a perfectly prepared wild duck and the entire meal from soup to ice-cream was made in the house," he wrote. "Such things were not rare in those days."[20]

But such things, Pell predicted, would be exceedingly rare in the new age he saw coming. Pell, by then a diplomat and a former congressman, would deem it "mere madness to imagine that we will be able to maintain a society with the enormous difference between the poor and the rich that has existed." In the future, he predicted, the "more prosperous" Americans would only be able to maintain their "material comfort" by moving "rapidly" to raise the living standards of the poor.

"This cannot be done," he warned his comfortable readers, "without the sacrifice of some personal and private luxuries."

But that sacrifice, Pell immediately added, would be well worth any discomfort the well heeled might have to endure. A "more equal distribution" of society's wealth "will make for a higher outlook on life."

"Life in a few years will be a different thing from what it is or has been," Pell advised. "People anxious to shine before their friends will find that they cannot do it with champagne, yachts, or seven-course dinners."

America would one day help the world realize an "increased happiness for mankind," he concluded, but only if our leaders moved "to promote the distribution of material products far more widely than they have ever been distributed in the past."

Pell wrote these words nearly a decade into the Great Depression. At that time, few of Pell's fellow rich shared his preference for greater equality. And not many Americans, at any income level, shared Pell's optimism about the "increased happiness" he saw ahead. Depression had come to seem a permanent fixture of modern American economic life. Yet Pell's prediction for a more equal, stronger, happier America would largely come true—and within a single generation.

How could such a fundamental transformation ever take place so quickly? Some thoughtful observers would later credit this phenomenal social shift to the jolt that World War II gave the US economy. This costly conflict, coming right on the heels of the Great Depression, knocked America's wealthy off their stride—and left previously inconceivable political options, like heavy taxes on the rich, both conceivable and unavoidably necessary.

But great shocks to an unequal social system, we now know, don't automatically translate into setbacks for society's wealthiest. We Americans have experienced shocks aplenty since the twenty-first century began: deadly terrorist attacks, trillion-dollar wars, and the greatest financial crash since the Great Depression. Yet we have become less equal as a nation, not more. In fact, we have become a nation that almost exactly mirrors the America that existed before Frederick Lewis Allen's "big change," a nation where average families struggle for security while the wealthy bob and weave their way to ever-greater fortune.

So where does that leave us? If the sheer shock of Great Depression followed by global war didn't generate Allen's big change, then what did?

These pages will posit that a movement engineered this enormous change, a movement of men and women of varied political stripes and economic backgrounds that took root in the early 1900s. The activists behind this movement shared little more than revulsion at the concentrated wealth and power they saw amassing all around them. They would struggle over half a century to clip that wealth and limit that power. In the 1940s and 1950s, they triumphed.

Depression and world war certainly did create an opportunity for greater equality. But we as a nation had the capacity to seize that opportunity only because America's egalitarians had battled, decade after decade, to place and keep before us a compelling vision of a more equal—a better—society. The United States would never become a truly decent society, this vision held, so long as some Americans had too little and others too much. A good society had to both level up the poor and level down the rich. If we wanted decency, we had to attack inequality at both ends. We had to challenge, as famed newspaper publisher Joseph Pulitzer would put it in 1907, both "predatory poverty" *and* "predatory plutocracy."[21]

Millions of Americans over the first half of the twentieth century would take this vision to heart. And out of the street protest and legislative action this vision animated, as economist Robert Kuttner points out, would come a set of "equalizing institutions that moderated the tendency of a laissez-faire economy to produce an income distribution of extremes."[22] These institutions would be "equalizing" at full blast by midcentury: Social Security and unemployment compensation, FHA loans and banking regulation, the Tennessee Valley Authority and statewide networks of public colleges and universities. All these institutions and more helped fashion a new middle-class America. But two particular institutions would stand out in importance and impact.

The first of this mighty institutional pair: a system of steeply graduated progressive tax rates that placed the lion's share of the tax burden on those most able to bear it. The second: a vital trade union presence in workplaces all across the United States. The tax system bankrolled the public services that enabled entry into America's new mass middle class. The union presence forced employers to share the wealth the postwar economy was creating. Together, complementing each other, unions and progressive taxes prevented the accumulation of private fortunes powerful enough to sabotage the nation's new middle-class order.

This egalitarian triumph would not be confined to the United States. Dominant middle classes would emerge in the mid-twentieth century throughout the world, in Japan, Canada, and all over Europe. But the United States led the way. We set the pace on standards for social decency. Not anymore. By nearly every major benchmark, from life expectancy to social mobility, the United States today ranks substantially behind every other major developed nation. In much of Europe, details global social analyst Steven Hill, average families enjoy paid leave after the birth of a child, free university education, and cash payments for home caregivers of the elderly, all luxuries almost nonexistent in the United States.[23]

Hill lectures widely in Europe. On one recent tour, he found himself talking with an Austrian in the picture-book city of Salzburg.[24]

"I wonder if you can even imagine," the Austrian asked him, "what it must be like to live in a country where every person has health care. And a decent retirement. And day care, parental leave, and sick leave, education, vacation, job retraining. For every plumber, carpenter, taxi driver, waitress, executive, sales clerk, scientist, musician, poet, nurse, of all ages, income, race, sex, whatever, not worrying about those basic arrangements."

"In America, you are so rich," the exasperated Austrian continued. "Why don't you have these things for your people?"

We ought to feel even more exasperated than that Austrian. We remain a fabulously rich nation. Our overall economic output has doubled over the last thirty years.[25] Yet our middle-class families are reeling, and our numbers of desperately poor families are rising. In California, once our middle-class holy land, prisons account for a greater share of the state budget than higher education.[26]

What went wrong? We have let ourselves become unconscionably unequal.

A half century ago, we shared our wealth and prospered in the sharing. This sharing slowed in the 1970s and then stopped in the 1980s. Wealth has been cascading into our nation's most privileged pockets ever since.

In 1970, a new teacher in the New York City public schools took home only $2,000 a year less than a starting lawyer on Wall Street. Four decades later, that starting lawyer is averaging, says a McKinsey business consulting group study, $115,000 more than that new teacher.[27]

The titans of Wall Street who keep that lawyer's palms greased are, in the meantime, amassing fortunes that have no historical precedent. In 2001, a top Wall Street trade journal began tracking the annual earnings of hedge fund managers. These managers run what amount to mutual funds open only to extremely wealthy investors. They typically charge these investors a 2 percent fee on the invested dollars they manage and claim an additional 20 percent of any investment profits they generate.

In 2002, a hedge fund manager needed to make $30 million to enter the ranks of the industry's twenty-five most lavishly compensated executives.[28] By 2010, the entry level for the hedge fund top twenty-five had leaped to $210 million. All combined, the top twenty-five grabbed $2.8 billion in 2003. In 2007, the year before the financial industry meltdown, the top twenty-five walked off with $22.3 billion, an average of nearly $900 million each. That average would dip to under $500 million in 2008, but quickly bounced back. In 2010, a year that saw unemployment in the double digits, the hedge fund industry's top twenty-five executives averaged $882.8 million.

Most of America's rich, not just hedge fund managers, have bounced back rather neatly from the Great Recession. In 1962, notes Economic Policy Institute analyst Sylvia Allegretto, the wealthiest 1 percent of American households held 125 times more "net worth"—assets minus debts—than the typical American household. In 2009, that gap between top and typical reached 225 times "the highest ratio on record."[29]

America's rich have never been richer in the lifetime of any American now living, or more dominant politically. Our pundits seldom play up this dominance. They tend instead to prattle endlessly about gridlock. But the rich never seem to have much of a problem getting our allegedly gridlocked political system to swing sprightly into action.

Back in 2003, for instance, pharmaceutical industry CEOs were charging so much for prescription drugs that senior citizens simply couldn't afford to buy them. The Big Pharma CEO solution to this dilemma: have the federal government give seniors tax dollars to buy drugs, ban Medicare from negotiating for lower drug prices, and prevent Americans from importing lower-cost drugs from Canada or anywhere else. Lawmakers considered this package a swell idea. They passed it.

In 2005, banks and credit card companies needed a similar political fix. Average Americans couldn't afford to pay off the stiff rates the financial industry was charging on loans and credit card debt. They were declaring bankruptcy at record rates and denying banks usurious interest in the process. The financial industry's better idea: have

Congress make bankruptcy harder for average Americans to declare. To Congress, this seemed another swell notion. The gridlocked waters parted. Bankruptcy "reform" became law.

But the swellest idea of all—from America's rich and powerful—would come three years later. In 2008, the financial industry deregulation that Wall Street had shoved through Congress a decade earlier would trigger a financial industry collapse that crushed two Wall Street banking giants out of existence and threatened to wipe out a good chunk of the remaining survivors. The industry's preferred solution: a taxpayer bailout that would keep Wall Street above water and let average homeowners drown. Congress would give Wall Street's bankers almost everything they demanded. By 2010, high-finance bonuses and corporate profits were running back at pre-collapse levels. Mainstream economists would hail the rebound as the end of the Great Recession.

"Making the richest people richer is not a recovery," riposted progressive political commentator Jim Hightower. "It's a robbery."[30]

Robbery would turn into extortion in 2010's final days when congressional Republicans demanded a two-year extension of the tax cuts for wealthy taxpayers originally enacted in 2001 and 2003 in exchange for a one-year extension of federal supplemental unemployment benefits. Democrats in Congress, prodded along by President Obama, agreed. We had no choice, the deal's Democratic supporters explained. We had to protect the jobless.

But the jobless would soon see that protection shredded. Early in 2011, Michigan lawmakers voted to slash the length of time any jobless person could receive unemployment checks from twenty-six weeks to twenty.[31] In Florida, lawmakers pushed for a twelve-week limit.[32] The wealthy, meanwhile, would enjoy the December bargain's full benefits. For taxpayers making over $1 million a year, the deal would mean an average $2,686 a week in personal tax savings.[33] The maximum weekly unemployment check in Michigan: $362.

In the middle of all this disheartening deal making on Capitol Hill, journalist William Greider—a close observer of the games rich people play ever since he covered the Reagan White House for the *Washington Post* in the early 1980s—asked a friend what she made of "the current mess in Washington."

"Whatever the issue," she responded, "the rich guys win."[34]

But they don't. Not always. The rich guys didn't win the epic struggle that consumed the first half of the twentieth century. Average

Americans won. They triumphed over plutocracy. The pages ahead will tell their story.

That tale begins on the eve of the twentieth century, at the moment of plutocracy's greatest triumph. In 1900, America's plutocrats finally seemed to have everything under control. We'll explore the savagely unequal world these plutocrats fashioned as they consolidated their power—and expanded their fortunes—at the expense of average Americans.

The pushback from these average Americans would come swiftly. We'll look at how and why the opposition to grand concentrations of private wealth gained ever-increasing momentum in the years before World War I. Then we'll turn to the war itself, a global conflict that both buttressed the assault against plutocracy and undercut it. We'll trace this turbulent trajectory through the war years and into the 1920s, a decade of resurgent plutocratic privilege that would drive America into economic cataclysm.

Out of the resulting devastation would emerge in the 1930s still another grand charge against plutocratic power. We'll delve into the strategies and the psyches of those who waged class-war battle during the Great Depression years. We'll detail how they ultimately fell short until still another world war opened new opportunities for challenging America's wealthy more profoundly than ever before.

In the aftermath of World War II, average Americans seized these new opportunities. They shaped a postwar world where the rich no longer held the nation's economy—or polity—in a vise grip. These average Americans would have help from an unexpected source: an appreciable number of the rich themselves. We'll introduce these egalitarian affluent and probe behind their commitment to a much more equal America.

That more equal America, a middle-class America, would rise up from a foundation built by trade unions and progressive taxes. We'll profile the new lives America's emerging middle class would build upon this foundation. We'll render this new middle-class America in all its glory—and all its internal contradictions. We'll show how these contradictions would eventually crack America's middle-class base and usher in what would become an astonishingly thorough plutocratic restoration.

And what if this restoration lingers, if our rich keep getting richer? What then for America? Our story will end with these questions—and some answers that the history in these pages seems to so strongly suggest.

Chapter One

PLUTOCRACY TRIUMPHANT

In the 1890s, millions of Americans revolted against politics as usual. They rose up against what they called "plutocracy," the rule of the money lords who had come to dominate both of the nation's major political parties. These Americans created their own political party, and this new People's Party—the Populists, as the party would become known—contested elections across the South and the West. Populist candidates ran to win, not just to register a protest. And many did win in elections throughout 1892 and 1894. Populists were soon serving as local officeholders, state lawmakers, governors, representatives to Congress, and even US senators.

In 1896, the Populists would aim higher still. The Democrats gave their presidential nod that year to a former member of Congress, a young firebrand from Nebraska who had first won national attention when he led a congressional charge for a tax on high incomes. The Populists would make this candidate, William Jennings Bryan, their nominee as well, and that choice set the stage for America's most pivotal presidential election since the Civil War. On the one side, the nation's fabulously wealthy, the titans of the greatest industrial empires the world had ever seen. On the other, average Americans, workers and farmers who had spent the last quarter century struggling against those empires at the ballot box, on picket lines, in pitched battles against private strikebreaker armies.

The Populists felt they could win this historic election. The plutocrats felt they could not afford to lose. In October 1896, just weeks before the balloting, future US Secretary of State John Hay wrote from his home in Cleveland that local men of property actually feared they would be hanging from lampposts after Election Day if Bryan emerged the winner.[1]

To stave off this impending doom, America's wealthy would open up their wallets as never before. Total spending on the 1896 presidential campaign would more than quadruple the level of spending on any other presidential race over the next eleven decades. In 2008, just over a dime of every $1,000 Americans spent for goods and services—our gross domestic product—went for presidential campaign expenses. In 1896, presidential campaign outlays made up sixty cents of every $1,000 in America's GDP.[2] And over 90 percent of that campaign cash aimed to promote the election of the candidate plutocrats saw as their savior, the Republican William McKinley.

McKinley did win. William Jennings Bryan polled well enough to keep the popular vote close, but McKinley swept the North and cruised to a comfortable electoral college majority. The nation's plutocrats, Senator Richard Pettigrew from South Dakota would later lament, "put up many millions to purchase and corrupt the voters of the country and to defeat Bryan, so that they could go along with their work of concentrating in the hands of a few the result of the toil of the American people."[3]

America's rich had simply overwhelmed the Populists. They spent record millions. The mostly rural Populists had no millions to spend. In the wake of their crushing 1896 defeat, they had no future. The People's Party crumbled. Almost totally. Almost overnight.

For America's wealthy, a glorious new century now beckoned. Men of awesome means felt themselves poised to fashion an America of freedom everlasting—for men of awesome means. All that remained would be a few political mopping-up operations. But these operations would be important. The plutocrats had a message to send: The guardians of America's natural economic order wanted the nation to know they would no longer tolerate any political misbehavior. Those brash enough to misbehave would suffer the consequences. Men of means would reach out from their Wall Street redoubts and smite these foolish souls down, anywhere they might be. Even South Dakota.

Senator Richard Pettigrew had lived in South Dakota since 1869, before statehood. He had helped survey the territory for the federal government, then opened a law practice and became the state's first member of the US Senate in 1889. The son of abolitionists, Pettigrew came to Washington as a proud Republican. But he broke with his party in 1896. He could not stand the moneymen behind McKinley. After McKinley's nomination, Pettigrew led a convention walkout of renegade Republicans and went on to campaign energetically for Bryan.[4]

After McKinley's victory, Pettigrew soldiered on against the triumphant plutocrats. In the Senate, he assailed the great railroad "combinations" that "were robbing the government as well as the people of the United States." The railroads, Pettigrew documented, were renting mail cars to Uncle Sam for $6,000 a year, twice what the cars cost them to buy, and making tens of millions more swapping the nearly worthless desert scrubland they owned for highly coveted public domain acres.[5] The legislation Pettigrew introduced to keep federal lands "from getting into the grip of the few" would go nowhere in the 1898 Senate session.[6] The South Dakotan expected as much. His years in the Senate had convinced him that "power over American public life, whether economic, social, or political, rested in the hands of the rich."[7]

Those rich would now silence Richard Pettigrew. Mark Hanna, the Ohio industrialist who had masterminded McKinley's electoral victory, would see to it. Hanna had been the chairman of the Republican National Committee during the 1896 campaign, then entered the US Senate the next year. From his new Senate perch, Hanna moved to make Pettigrew an object lesson. He would erase the last of the irritating resistance leftover from 1896. He would complete the plutocratic triumph.

In 1900, with Pettigrew up for reelection to a third Senate term, Hanna raised a $500,000 war chest to defeat the Republican renegade—an enormous sum in a state with fewer than a hundred thousand voters. Most of Hanna's campaign cash came from the railroads, as did "trunkfuls of blank passes" for free train trips that South Dakota's Republican State Committee passed out liberally throughout the campaign. Hanna left nothing to chance. He even personally stumped the sparsely settled South Dakota himself on a special train the railroads had thoughtfully made available. His free-flowing cash, meanwhile, turned local bankers into a vote-buying network. Farmers coming into town for provisions would be escorted into bank offices, handed a few bills, and promised a few more if Pettigrew lost the county's support.[8]

Months before the election, Hanna had dispatched political operatives into South Dakota to gauge Pettigrew's popularity. Their survey work found the incumbent comfortably ahead. By Election Day, Hanna had purchased himself a majority. Pettigrew lost decisively. The incumbent senator never saw the defeat coming.

"I had underestimated the resources of the business interests," Pettigrew would reflect back years later, "overestimated the possibilities of ordinary human nature."

Mainstream Republican and Democratic Party politicos had spent the decades after the Civil War abjectly kowtowing to those "business interests." Their election campaigns had shunted aside real issues— economic exploitation, for one—and instead cynically exploited the nation's racial, religious, and regional animosities. The Populists had refused to play that game. They focused their fire on America's vast gap between those who live "in splendid mansions, in gorgeous palaces" and "the great masses, the toilers of the nation."

"The rapid concentration of wealth in the hands of a few," as Milford Wriarson Howard, a Populist congressman from Alabama, had written in 1895, "is the most alarming sign of the times and unless speedily checked portends the decay of our national greatness."[9]

The Populists advanced real reforms to break up that concentration. They called for a tax on America's highest incomes, monopoly-busting moves to break up industrial empires, and public ownership of the railroads, then the nation's most powerful corporations. And the Populists even dared, in the Deep South, to challenge the racism that kept impoverished black and white farmers divided and weak. That South and the prairie lands of the West would generate most of the Populist ballot-box success. But plutocracy in the closing years of the nineteenth century had faced challenges from other regions as well.

Out of California came Henry George, a journalist turned economic theorist. George's immensely popular 1879 book, *Progress and Poverty*, would inspire two decades of "wholesome discontent" against wealth's concentration.[10]

"So long as all the increased wealth which modern progress brings goes but to build up great fortunes, to increase luxury and make sharper the contrast between the House of Have and the House of Want," George would write in his masterwork, "progress is not real and cannot be permanent."[11]

The answer Henry George offered? Consider land and other natural resources gifts of nature that belong to us all.[12] Tax away the "unearned increment" landowners reap when social forces and speculation drive up the value of their property. This "single-tax" prescription would appeal to Americans by the millions. In 1886, workingmen in New York City drafted George to run for mayor on a third-party ticket. He did well enough to outpoll the Republican in the race, a young up-and-comer by the name of Theodore Roosevelt.

Two years later, another visionary would build on Henry George's inspiration with a utopian novel that would eventually outsell every secular book of the entire nineteenth century save *Uncle Tom's Cabin*. This 1888 volume, *Looking Backward*, imagined an affluent Bostonian waking up to find himself in the year 2000, amid an America that had become an amazingly bountiful—and equal—society. The author: Edward Bellamy, the frail journalist son of a New England Baptist minister. Bellamy's novel, reformer John Reed would write a few years later, "took the masses whom George had set to thinking by storm."

Both George and Bellamy, Reed added, took as their subject "the inequality of condition which divided mankind into a few rich and many poor." George had his single tax as the remedy. Bellamy favored "nationalizing, and publicly operating the aggregate of productive land and capital in the interest and on the account of all."[13]

By 1896, Henry George was preparing for another New York mayoral bid, and "nationalist clubs" dedicated to Bellamy's vision had begun springing up across the country. But George died in 1897. Over a hundred thousand admirers marched in his funeral procession. Bellamy died the next year.[14] The pushback against the great American greed grab had lost its two most compelling thinkers.

America's men of property now rushed to consolidate their political dominance. With the Populists defeated and the most celebrated radical economic thinkers of the age departed, the lavishly propertied faced no opposition with any chance of imminent success. But just to make sure, they changed the rules.

By 1900, in state after state, lawmakers beholden to grand fortune had locked into place structural changes in the electoral process that would prevent any resurgence of the unpleasantness the rich had experienced in the nineteenth century's last decade. The Populists had scored much of their state and local electoral success by "fusing" with Republicans in the Democratic Party–dominated South and with Democrats in the Republican-dominated West. The fused parties nominated the same candidates, who then ran on both the Populist and allied major-party lines. State lawmakers made this fusion illegal in all but a handful of states. Two different parties would no longer be able to run the same candidate on more than one ballot line and have that candidate's votes on the two lines combined.

In the South, elites also worked to codify white supremacy and keep poor whites and blacks forever divided. They unleashed, notes historian Alan Dawley, "a many-pronged affair of lynching, disfranchisement, Jim Crow statutes, and paranoia"—an onslaught dedicated to "halting the tentative steps toward interracial collaboration that posed such a threat to planters and industrialists."[15]

America's wealthy and powerful, with these structural finishing touches, had now teed up the nation's economy for the grandest accumulation of private fortune in human history. Nothing now stood in their way. Not the Populists. Not dissenting economic thinkers bold enough to capture the public imagination. Not ornery lawmakers like Richard Pettigrew.

And certainly not taxes.

Congress had levied an income tax in 1894, a relatively minor nuisance that placed a 2 percent tax on all income over $4,000, an income level high enough at the time to ensure that only the richest 2 percent or so of Americans would face any income tax liability. But the Supreme Court took pity on those inconvenienced rich and deemed the new levy unconstitutional in 1895. By 1900, almost all federal revenue was coming from taxes that disproportionately burdened the poor.[16] High "protective tariffs"—federal levies on imports—raised prices on basic consumer goods. Federal excise taxes raised prices on alcohol and tobacco, the only two daily "luxuries" working people could afford.

At the local level, all property owners, extremely rich ones included, did pay a property tax. But the traditional property tax only applied to real estate. Property in other forms went totally tax-free.[17] Farmers faced property taxes on their land. Financiers faced no tax at all on the Wall Street securities that filled their safe-deposit boxes.

With no taxes on income and levies on only one category of property, grand fortunes in the new twentieth century could continue to multiply unencumbered and at the same dazzling pace the nation's financially favored had first set during the Civil War years. The United States had hosted, of course, exceedingly wealthy people before the Civil War. The word "millionaire" traces all the way back to 1843, the year obituary writers needed a label to convey the immensity of the fortune banker and tobacco king Peter Lorillard had left behind.[18] But few pre–Civil War deep pockets would ever amass much more than a single million. America's real rich would not appear until after Fort Sumter.

The shooting war that began at Fort Sumter created almost overnight what America had never had: a huge national market for mass-produced goods. In 1861, at the First Battle of Bull Run, only thirty-seven thousand troops were wearing Union blue. By 1865, over two million men had taken up arms for the Union. All these soldiers needed to be outfitted and transported. New factories would do the outfitting. New railroad lines would do the transporting. By the war's end, a broad array of new and expanded local businesses had the capacity to market goods well beyond their local borders.

This new reality ushered in far more lucrative opportunities for grand fortune than had ever existed. In America's pre–Civil War marketplace, men of commerce faced limits on the quantity of product they could sell—and the quantity of profit they could reap. In the new national market the Civil War opened, quantities and profits seemed limitless. With a national market soon stretching from sea to shining sea, stupendous fortune awaited any "captains of industry" able to grab significant market share. And grab they did—by any means necessary. They grabbed from government. The railroad giants swallowed up 155 million acres of land grants from various public authorities. In Minnesota alone, these gifts would total an area twice the size of Massachusetts.[19] They grabbed from workers, violently suppressing those who objected, sometimes with police, sometimes with private thugs. And they grabbed from any business competitor they met in the marketplace, in a relentless commercial cavalcade of industrial espionage, bribery, and cutthroat pricing.[20]

All the grabbing would pay enormous dividends. In 1861, America's grandest fortune topped out at about $15 million. By 1900, analysts were placing the value of John D. Rockefeller's oil dynasty at somewhere between $300 and $400 million. Steel king Andrew Carnegie held a net worth of equal grandeur.[21]

Inflation accounted for little of this huge surge in net worth. Prices hardly changed at all in the decades after the Civil War. But America did. And the Rockefellers and the Carnegies, by means fair and foul, exploited every opportunity that change created. In the new 1900s, America's defeated and depleted ranks of reformers expected to see more of the same. More new markets. More corporate scrambling to dominate these markets. More swindles at worker, consumer, and taxpayer expense.

The biggest new market would soon emerge out of America's urban explosion. Immigrants from foreign lands—and America's farmlands—were packing the nation's cities. By 1910, city dwellers had come to make up nearly half the nation's population. An incredible one-tenth of the entire nation lived within the city limits of just three cities alone, New York, Philadelphia, and Chicago.[22] All of America's newly overstuffed cities, big and small alike, needed to move and warm and light their ever-denser populations. Private corporations rushed in to deliver these services. Municipalities showered down franchises worth hundreds of millions of dollars for street railways, gas lines, electricity, and telephones.[23] In some cities, companies bid honestly against each other to win the lucrative franchises. In most, honesty would not be among the bidding criteria. Private utility companies passed politicians kickbacks. Politicians passed utilities monopoly pricing power—and signed franchise agreements that locked down exorbitant phone and gas and light rates for years to come.

"In no other way," historian Otis Pease would later note, "can wealth be obtained so easily."[24]

Well, maybe one other way: insurance.

American families on the farm had always had their land to fall back on when times turned hard. They could raise their own food and get by without much cash. In rural America, "store-bought" bread— or clothes, for that matter—had always been novelties.[25] In America's rapidly growing cities, working families had no safety net beyond their paychecks. If those paychecks stopped coming, the results could be catastrophic since government did nothing to help average Americans make up for the loss of a job or, even worse, the sudden loss of a loved one. Into that void raced a massive new life insurance industry.

Small businessmen and those Americans fortunate enough to have a regular salary bought "whole life" policies that guaranteed their families a sense of security should they die unexpectedly. And should they live, the cash value these whole life policies built up over time could provide welcome and badly needed income for retirement. Average American workers couldn't take advantage of this whole life insurance. They couldn't afford the annual or quarterly premiums that whole life policies required. For these workers, insurance companies had a different product, "term life" policies that would continue in effect only as long as policyholders kept paying the tiny weekly premiums, as low as twenty-five cents per week.[26] But workers who lost their jobs couldn't afford even that quarter. They would lose their coverage and have absolutely nothing to show for their previous premium payments, since term life policies built up no cash value. Only one in twelve of the insurance industry's term life policies ever had to pay a benefit.

Overall, forty cents of every premium dollar the insurance companies collected went into insurance company salaries, commissions, and stock dividends. By 1905, the nation's ninety "chartered legal reserve insurance firms" held three times as much in assets as the nation's over five thousand banks, and the industry's three largest insurers—the Equitable, the Mutual, and New York Life—held almost half the industry's asset base. The big three's top executives were riding a veritable money machine. The Mutual's president spent $12,000, the equivalent of more than a quarter million today, on a single office rug.[27]

A new breed of journalists—"muckrakers," as they came to be called—would chronicle these sorts of depredations as the early 1900s unfolded, exhaustively illustrating "the methods of the spoliators engaged in perpetual schemes of deception and plunder."[28] The great French novelist Honoré de Balzac had once opined that a crime lurked behind every great fortune. Muckraker tales would confirm his suspicion. America's rich, "these devotees to the Faith of Greed," muckraking author William Vickroy Marshall thundered in 1909, "are in the eyes of the moral law, if not in that of the criminal law, villains a hundredfold more perfidious and deserving of punishment than are the most bloodthirsty anarchists or howling bomb throwers."[29]

That same year, Gustavus Myers, a journalist famed for his exposé of the New York Tammany Hall political ring, produced a massive three-volume industry-by-industry compendium of this moral and legal criminality, with mind-numbing detail that aimed to explain the "accelerated concentration of immense wealth" Americans now found pressing down so heavily upon them.[30] But America's immensely wealthy, other more subtle observers realized, hadn't just broken the law. They had changed the law, rewritten the rules that govern how America's capitalist economy operates—and, with that rewriting opened the door to a ferocious amassing of wealth that dwarfed the thievery of the post–Civil War robber baron years.

The businesses the robber barons created had typically operated as closely held corporations or partnerships. In effect, the founders of these companies owned the entire business, sometimes with family, friends, and close associates. If these companies needed money, notes financial historian Lawrence Mitchell, "they dipped into their earnings, went to the bank, or sold bonds."[31] Few of them sold stock in their enterprises to raise capital. New York's stock market played a distinctly second-tier role in this "founder capitalism."

That would suddenly change in the 1890s. In a few short years, as Lawrence Mitchell observes, the stock market evolved from a "disruptive game, played by a few professionals and thrill-seeking amateurs that from time to time erupted into a major frenzy," into American capitalism's new "genetic material."[32] American corporations, as originally constituted in the decades after the Civil War, manufactured products and offered services. To prosper, they needed to sell more of what they made and brought to market. The new corporation that leaped onto the scene in the late 1890s existed, by contrast, to sell shares of stock, not products—stock, explains Mitchell, "that would make its promoters and financiers rich."[33]

None of this would have been possible without changes in America's economic rules. Traditional corporate law had prohibited one corporation from buying and holding stock in another. In 1889, New Jersey enacted legislation that invited corporations to buy and hold as much stock in other companies as they pleased. By 1896, companies could do even more: They could use their own stock to buy up other companies. These stock swaps, notes historian Mitchell, left "the matter of price entirely within the discretion of corporate directors," a subtle and incredibly lucrative alteration.

In earlier times, any enterprise issuing shares of stock had to take into account the actual hard value of the enterprise's assets, in much the same way that borrowers have traditionally had to present collateral when they go after a bank loan. If a borrower wants $10,000, the traditional banker will want to see collateral worth that same $10,000 in case the borrower defaults on the loan. The new corporate order that New Jersey introduced severed this link between real assets and share value. Wheelers and dealers of companies could do their own asset valuing, and they had, as Mitchell points out, "almost irresistible incentives to put high values on the assets they were buying."

"The more they valued their assets, the higher the amount of capital they could justify and the more stock they could issue," he explains. "The more stock they could issue, the more stock they could take for themselves. And the more they could take for themselves, the more they could sell on the market for cash."[34]

These wheelers and dealers only needed one other piece in place to realize their windfalls: a stock market flush with cash. And that would come in 1896 with McKinley's White House triumph. The elimination of those pesky Populists from the political scene sent a surge of confidence throughout Wall Street. Interest rates dropped. Investors could now much more cheaply access what would come to be called "other people's money." Still more investible cash would come from the growing global demand for US grain. Higher prices for American agricultural commodities nurtured new strata of wealthy investors looking for investment outlets. Wall Street's finest would graciously provide them. In 1897, they began underwriting a gigantic merger wave that would sweep the economy.[35]

The sweeper-in-chief would be J. Pierpont Morgan, Wall Street's most powerful financier. Morgan had begun his career in high finance with $5 million and a transatlantic network of business contacts that his banker father had left him.[36] By the end of 1901, the younger Morgan had combined under his new US Steel corporate umbrella "213 different manufacturing plants and transportation companies, 41 mines, 1,000 miles of private railroad, 112 ore vessels, and 78 blast furnaces, as well as the world's largest coke, coal, and ore holdings."[37] This massive industrial empire held 60 percent of America's entire productive capacity in basic and finished steel.

The tangible assets that went into the new US Steel—the plants, the mines, the railroads, and all the rest—held a hard value of $676 million. Morgan "capitalized" the entire enterprise at $1.4 billion, over twice that amount. He created for investors, in effect, over $700 million out of thin air. For his own investment banking operation, Morgan took 1.3 million shares in US Steel as a fee for putting the giant steel combination together—and then unloaded those shares onto the stock market for a sweet $62.5 million, clearing the equivalent of about $1.65 billion in today's dollars.[38]

Giant "trusts" like US Steel would soon be rising up all across America's economic landscape. DuPont held over 70 percent of the chemical market, International Harvester the same mastery over farm machinery.[39] The "trusts," one 1905 report concluded, held a fifth of the nation's wealth, with no more than sixty men, analysts estimated, controlling this entire vast block of power.[40] Five years into the new century, the great merger wave had washed away over 2,200 independent companies.[41] The same wave left behind a host of colossal individual fortunes. Andrew Carnegie sold his steel businesses into US Steel in 1901 and retired from active business life with $226 million from the sale, enough to make him, at least for the moment, the richest man in the world.[42]

John D. Rockefeller had gone into the merger wave already enormously wealthy. One 1895 estimate had put his total fortune at $125 million, or more than the total assessed property wealth at the time in seven US states and territories.[43] The mergers would eventually make Rockefeller even wealthier than Carnegie. By 1913, analysts were putting his total net worth at $1 billion.

A more rigorous appraisal of individual American wealth—by a federal commission in 1915—would conclude that the United States held 1,598 personal fortunes large enough to yield an income over $100,000 per year, or at least $2.2 million today.[44] Some forty-four families, the commission added, were collecting over $1 million a year in income, over $22 million in today's dollars.[45]

These dollar totals, even after adjusting for inflation, hardly do justice to the vast purchasing power that the megawealthy had at their disposal a century ago. The typical New York family of means owned a residence in Manhattan, a summer home in Newport, Rhode Island, and a country retreat either up the Hudson Valley or out on Long Island's "Gold Coast." Frederick Vanderbilt, the grandson of the mid-nineteenth-century's richest man, had his Hudson Valley mansion completed in 1898.[46] The fifty-four-room mansion boasted walls and ceilings that Swiss craftsmen had carved out of Russian walnut and mahogany from Santo Domingo. Nearly two dozen servants labored in Vanderbilt's mansion. Another forty kept up the surrounding grounds.

Servant staffs of up to sixty would not be uncommon at the era's finest country houses, counting gardeners, chauffeurs, and grooms.[47] The rich needed these huge staffs in part to prepare and serve huge meals. A standard millionaire menu would feature ten courses: oysters, soup, fish, entrée, roast, second entrée, salad, dessert, fruit, and candy.[48] The most memorable meals would come with accessories. In 1914, jewelry heir and designer Louis Comfort Tiffany hosted a "Peacock Feast" for one hundred and fifty "men of genius" at his Laurelton Hall, an eighty-four-room Long Island manse tucked amid six hundred impeccably manicured acres. The festivities opened with a parade of young women wearing the flowing robes of ancient Greece and carrying succulent fair on silver platters. The first young woman in the parade, dressed as the goddess Juno, sashayed in with an "exquisitely barbaric" headdress that featured a real peacock's head.[49]

Visitors to Louis Tiffany's Laurelton Hall may have included financier Otto Kahn, a patron of the arts who in 1917 completed his own colossal Long Island country estate. Kahn's mansion rose on an artificial hill specially constructed to bring his 126-room French chateau–style castle ninety feet above sea level. The estate's 443 acres had everything from an eighteen-hole private golf course to a racetrack and its own airstrip. Local townspeople thought Kahn had lions too. An understandable bit of confusion: The basement "cages" the locals thought they glimpsed actually served as wind tunnels. Kahn's architects had these twenty-foot-wide units installed for natural air conditioning.[50]

Kahn reigned over the New York cultural scene as chairman of the New York Metropolitan Opera, and Caruso sang in his Gold Coast ballroom. Other rich of the era had somewhat more plebeian tastes. In 1910, for the heavyweight "fight of the century" between Jack Johnson and James Jeffries, promoters organized a special train to ferry one hundred well-heeled passengers from New York to Reno, Nevada.[51] The cost of one ticket for the excursion amounted to more than the average American could earn over three years of labor.

Newspapers of the day regularly chronicled this plutocratic excess. The rich welcomed the chroniclers. They would share the menus of their feasts, the lists of precious gifts their newly married progeny received at their weddings. One maverick turn-of-the-century economist, Thorstein Veblen, would give this phenomenon a lasting label: "conspicuous consumption."[52] For the rich, Veblen wrote, public displays of lavish living had a social purpose. They served as a "manifestation of dominance."

Conspicuous consumption would reach its early-twentieth-century pinnacle in the 1912 maiden voyage of the RMS *Titanic*. About two hundred families traveled first class, and, suggests one commentator, "never again would established wealth be so blatantly displayed."[53] The first-class travelers would have hundreds of ship stewards at their beck and call, not to mention the small army of handmaids, valets, nurses, and nannies they brought for the voyage. The richest man aboard, John Jacob Astor IV, wore at one reception a lace jacket that set him back, in today's dollars, about $20,000. Astor went down with the ship, one of 118 men in first class who perished.[54] For America's rich, the disaster would be a tragedy of epic proportions, a rare reminder that even the most fortunate might someday find themselves shivering, soaked, and frightened in the cold.

Millions of John Jacob Astor's fellow Americans shivered on a regular basis, without having to ever suffer the trauma of shipwreck. In 1903, one of these often-shivering Americans wrote a letter to President Theodore Roosevelt.[55] Mrs. Cy J. Cremler lived with her husband, three young children, and sixty-five-year-old mother in a small rented house on the outskirts of Washington, DC. Mrs. Cremler had read, she wrote the president, that the average manufacturing laborer was making less than $450 per year. Her family, she continued, must be doing better than average. Her husband had made $459 the previous year from a $1.50 daily wage.

Mrs. Cremler explained in her letter that she had asked her oldest daughter to "keep an exact account" of family expenditures over the past year, "to see that we did not run in debt." She shared that accounting in her letter. The Cremlers spent, to the penny, $460.75. Most of that, $328, went for food, "a fraction less than 90 cents per day—15 cents for each of six persons, or not quite 5 cents a meal." The Cremlers did try to shave that average meal price down below a nickel. But they couldn't. Noted Mrs. Cremler's letter: "A cup of bread and milk for one of the children is more than that." The rent for the Cremler's three-room house—not three bedrooms, but three rooms—ate up most of the rest of the family's budget.

"Of course we are badly cramped for space," Mrs. Cremler related. "There must be a bed in each room. Fortunately we have not much other furniture."

The family did have one stove, "an old broken concern that was second hand when we got it." In the winter, Mrs. Cremler wrote, "my mother lies abed considerable of the time to keep warm and give those of us a chance at the fire." The previous winter, Mrs. Cremler herself had come down with pneumonia, from "getting my feet wet while wearing unmended shoes and sitting in a cold room." She had been "sick for a fortnight." Thankfully, her husband had not had his work "interrupted by sickness," a miracle in and of itself. Mr. Cremler "walked to his work every morning, even through the rain, without spending a cent for street car tickets."

Her God-fearing family, Mrs. Cremler's letter acknowledged, had "not been to church this year, for we will not occupy anybody else's pew, nor the pauper pew, and sit like a bump on a log when the contribution plate is pushed under our noses." The family had also "not gone out on picnics, nor excursions, nor attended any entertainment of any kind."

"How could we?" Mrs. Cremler asked. "Few slaves on a southern plantation ever worked harder, or had less in the way of amusement or recreation in the course of the year, than we."

How many American families endured hardships this unrelenting in the early 1900s? One economist, Henry Laurens Call, endeavored to catalog the nation's entire population by level of privilege in an American Association for the Advancement of Science paper he delivered just after Christmas in 1906. Only "the one-thousandth part of our population can be said to be enormously rich," Call estimated, with those living in merely "comfortable circumstances" making up, overall, "perhaps the one-twentieth part" of the nation. America's remaining 95 percent, Call told his Columbia College audience, "cannot be said to live other than a precarious existence; compelled to depend upon their day's labor for life itself, and if the right to toil be denied them, brought face to face with actual want."[56]

"A sad spectacle this, under any circumstances," Call lamented. "Viewed in connection with our enormous wealth production, and the billionaire fortunes of the day, it is an infamous spectacle!"

This "infamous spectacle" haunted some of the more sensitive among America's financially successful, Louis Brandeis among them. Brandeis had become America's wealthiest commercial lawyer. In 1912, two months before the *Titanic* went down, he found himself addressing an audience at the Ethical Culture Meeting House in his home city of Boston. He spoke that evening of life in the nation's great steel mills. The Associated Charities of Pittsburgh, Brandeis noted, had recently investigated "what it costs for a family consisting of husband, wife, and three children, not to live, but barely to subsist."

"If the common laborers in the steel industry were to work twelve hours a day for 365 days a year," Brandeis told his audience, "they would be unable to earn even that minimum amount."[57]

Another wealthy and troubled attorney, Amos Pinchot of New York, would later that year observe that the steel industry actually promenaded as "one of the more humane trusts."[58] How can we attach a label of humanity, Pinchot wondered, to an industry "of enormous profit making" that works its laborers seventy-two hours a week, eighteen more than the maximum allowed in England's steel mills?

The most ambitious effort to chronicle America's early-twentieth-century economic inhumanity would come from a federal panel known as the Commission on Industrial Relations. Two of the country's most celebrated social workers, Chicago's Jane Addams and New

York's Lillian Wald, had asked President William Howard Taft in 1911 to appoint an official federal commission that could "gauge the breakdown" of the nation's industrial economy.[59] Taft dithered. The panel would not take final shape until two years later, under President Woodrow Wilson, and the commission's staffers would spend two more years conducting hearings in all the nation's big cities. They took testimony from employers, trade union and civic leaders, clergy, doctors, efficiency engineers, economists, bankers, corporate directors, and ordinary "workingmen and working women."

In August 1915, commission research director Basil Manly presented the staff's "findings of fact, conclusions, and recommendations."[60] This staff report related that "the very least that a family of five persons can live upon in anything approaching decency is $700." America's highest-paid wage-earners—railroad engineers and skilled craftsmen like glassblowers—could annually take home as much as $2,000, enough to bring "a fair living for a family of moderate size, education of the children through high school, a small insurance policy, a bit put by for a rainy day—and nothing more." But occupations that can bring a "fair living," the commission staff added, amount to "but a handful compared to the mass of the workers." Only one-tenth of male factory and mine workers eighteen years of age and older "earn more than $20 a week." Two-thirds to three-fourths were making less than fifteen dollars—and as many as one-third were taking home less than ten dollars per week, or around $500 a year.

Women were making substantially less. Weekly wages in factories, stores, and laundries seldom inched over eight dollars. Nearly one-half of women workers labored for weekly paychecks less than six dollars. What does a wage this low, the commission report asked, mean to America's young employed women? The report had an answer:

> To the girl it means that every penny must be counted, every normal desire stifled, and each basic necessity of life barely satisfied by the sacrifice of some other necessity. If more food must be had than is given with 15 cent dinners, it must be bought with what should go for clothes; if there is need for a new waist to replace the old one at which the forewoman has glanced reproachfully or at which the girls have giggled, there can be no lunches for a week and dinners must cost five cents less each day. Always too the

room must be paid for, and back of it lies the certainty
that with slack seasons will come lay-offs and discharges.

And then came the children. Every American child, the commission report observed, ought to be receiving at least a grammar school
education. Only one-third did. Only one-tenth finished high school.

"Those who leave are almost entirely the children of the workers, who, as soon as they reach working age," the commission report
continued, "are thrown, immature, ill-trained, and with no practical
knowledge, into the complexities of industrial life."

By "working age," the commission investigators meant the age
a child could literally begin to perform useful labor. In some industries, that could be age ten, or even younger. The wages these children
brought home may have been America's cruelest joke. Indeed, the
commission staff concluded, the dollars children earned did not
matter in the end because "all experience has shown" that the wages
fathers earn get "reduced by about the amount that the children earn."
In those industries "where women and children can be largely uti-
lized," the commission found, men's wages run "extremely low."

Other blue-ribbon panels and commissions would deepen the por-
trait of poverty the Industrial Commission painted. The New York
Factory Investigating Commission found 13,268 tenements "licensed
for home manufacturing." In each of these tenements, as many as
fifty apartments would have entire families laboring on piecework of
various sorts, with five or six people each working at least five hours
daily. The average daily net proceeds from this labor: forty cents for
an entire family.[61]

Tenements—five- to seven-story apartment buildings, jammed
onto lots typically only twenty-five feet wide—filled New York. Over
two-thirds of the city's population of 3.4 million lived in crowded,
dark apartments. Only four of the fourteen rooms on each tenement
floor received direct light and air, and three or four families usually
filled the fourteen rooms. The "bedrooms" amounted to closets, barely
big enough for a bed. Contemporaries considered these tenements
"centers of disease, poverty, vice and crime, where it is a marvel, not
that some children grow up to be thieves, drunkards, and prostitutes,
but that so many should ever grow up to be decent and self-respect-
ing."[62]

Workplaces beyond the tenement walls offered no safe harbor. The
"sandhogs" who blasted the tunnels that would connect Manhattan

to New Jersey and Long Island, notes historian Glenn Altschuler, regularly rushed to escape flooding passageways "and, all too often, collapsed from 'the bends' soon after they returned to the apparent safety of the sidewalks of New York."[63] Sewing machine operators, the tireless researcher Florence Kelley found, had their eyes "used up" after sewing machine stitch speed more than doubled between 1899 and 1905.[64] A 1915 study of dockworkers by sociologist Charles Barnes "authenticated 309 longshore accidents on the Manhattan waterfront, 96 of them fatal, in a single year."[65] Danger lurked in workplaces far beyond Manhattan. In Midwestern steel plants, a 1910 study disclosed, 15 percent of Slavic immigrants suffered a serious injury every year.[66] In Pennsylvania's Allegheny County, steel industry accidents claimed five hundred lives a year.[67]

The railroads would be a particularly dangerous place to work. Between 1890 and 1917, computes one recent historical accounting, "158,000 mechanics and laborers were killed in repair shops and round-houses, another 72,000 workers on the tracks, and close to 2 million were injured."[68] One enterprising journalist dove into the railroad accident records to demonstrate that the bloody 1894 national railroad strike actually saved worker lives. Railroad accident casualties in the two years before the strike, the journalist showed, averaged three thousand per month. The strike idled a fifth of the nation's railroads for half a month. If those railroads had operated that half-month, three hundred workers would have likely perished. The strike left only a hundred workers killed or wounded.[69]

Strike and die. Work and die. By the early 1900s, the deck seemed totally stacked against working people. And the turn-of-the-century merger wave only made matters worse. The Reverend Washington Gladden, a Congregational pastor who served on the city council in Columbus, Ohio, saw the "great consolidations of business" as a corporate move to keep labor forever tamed. Workers, Gladden noted in a 1905 lecture, had cause to "regard those huge combinations of capital with grave suspicion."[70] Giant merged corporations, he explained, could easily shut down "mills and furnaces" where workers struck for higher wages and shorter hours, and transfer their production to other mills and furnaces.

"That is not," Gladden added, "a very farsighted policy, but we have had abundant proof, of late, that men at the head of great affairs are not always farsighted; the narrowness and lack of sagacity which they sometimes exhibit are very conspicuous."

How conspicuous? America's men of "great affairs" opposed any and all legislation meant to lighten life's burdens on working people. Their lavish campaign contributions to lawmakers usually ensured these reform proposals a dim future. The United States Senate, wrote the nationally renowned Kansas newspaper editor William Allen White, has become a "millionaires' club" where senators represent "principalities and powers in business," one legislating for the Union Pacific Railway, another for the New York Central, "still another the insurance interests of New York and New Jersey."[71] Ordinary voters seemed powerless against these perversions of democracy. US senators a century ago didn't even have to stand for election. State legislators, not the general electorate, voted them in, as the US Constitution stipulated.

Theoretically at least, state legislators answered to the people. But huge swatches of the American people could not vote. Women had no vote. Black men in the South largely had no vote thanks to new poll taxes, literacy tests, and residency rules that also struck substantial numbers of poor whites off the voting rolls. Overall turnout in Virginia dropped from 59.6 percent of potential voters in 1900 to 27.7 percent in 1904.[72] Many immigrants had no vote either. In 1910, one of every seven adult males living in the United States rated as a non-naturalized immigrant and could not cast a ballot.[73]

Amazingly, despite all the campaign cash and election rigging, legislation that sought to even the economic playing field occasionally did become law. In these rare cases America's rich could always count on their robed brethren. State and federal courts routinely ruled reform laws unconstitutional. Judges struck down legislation that forced employers to pay wages on a timely basis. They refused to allow regulations that defined the situations where employers could be held liable for workplace injuries. They allowed employers to blacklist union-friendly workers and deny them gainful employment.[74]

Other laws of the land would become, upon judicial review, reverse images of the original legislative intent. The Fourteenth Amendment, a measure intended to protect the rights of African Americans, evolved "into an outright prohibition on state regulation of the market to protect wage earners," notes historian Alan Dawley.[75] The 1890 Sherman Antitrust Act, never much more than a symbolic sop to angry farmers in the first place, would enable judges to routinely issue injunctions—court orders—to stop strikes and other acts of labor resistance.[76] Unions and their allies, courts ruled, could not conduct consumer boycotts against intransigent employers or even circulate lists of such intransigents.[77]

Even court rulings that ostensibly went against corporate interests could leave the rich and powerful smiling. In 1911, for instance, the US Supreme Court agreed that John D. Rockefeller's massive Standard Oil violated the Sherman Act. But the high court's take on that act rendered the legislation essentially toothless. Only "unreasonable" restraints of trade, the court ruled, violated federal law—an interpretation that gave judges the authority to declare some combinations "reasonable" and off-limits to antitrust action.[78]

Amid these unrelentingly rich people–friendly political dynamics, the ebb and flow of daily commerce could not help but enrich the already rich. But no one knew exactly how wealthy the wealthy were becoming. The federal government only counted people, not dollars. Richard Pettigrew, while still a senator from South Dakota, had worked to broaden the Census Bureau mission. In his first Senate year he secured an amendment to the 1890 census bill that required enumerators "to ascertain the distribution of wealth through an inquiry into farms, homes, and mortgages." Later, in 1898, Pettigrew used data from that enumeration to charge that four thousand families, just 0.03 percent of the population, held 20 percent of the nation's aggregate wealth.[79]

Before his 1900 election defeat, Pettigrew tried to get the first census of the new century to include a much more in-depth tally of who held the nation's wealth.

"The question as to what becomes of what the toilers of the land produce, whether it goes to them or is taken from them by special privileges, and accumulated in the hands of a very few people," Pettigrew told his Senate colleagues, "is a very important one and reaches ultimately the question of the preservation of free institutions."[80]

His colleagues, by and large, paid no attention. Meanwhile, other statisticians went scrounging for additional data. Dr. Charles B. Spahr used New York State surrogate court data on inheritances to estimate that America's richest 1 percent owned just over half the nation's wealth. His data covered the same basic timeframe as the 1890 census and seemed to roughly match up with Pettigrew's figures.[81]

Henry Laurens Call, in his 1906 American Association for the Advancement of Science presentation, used Spahr's research as a starting point. Given the enormous concentration of wealth since 1890, Call calculated that the nation's richest 1 percent might at that moment be holding as much as 90 percent of the nation's treasure.[82] Call's figures caused enough of a sensation for the dour *New York Times* to round up some contrary opinion, since, as the *Times* noted, "if the statements recently made in this city by Henry Laurens Call before the American Association for the Advancement of Science are true, the concentration of wealth in this country has reached such a pitch that the most radical measures might well be invoked."[83]

But the chief expert the *Times* put forward, Columbia sociologist Franklin Giddings, did not fully cooperate.

"It ought to be understood that we do not know, in any scientific sense of the word 'know,' what the concentration of wealth in the United States is," Giddings told the *Times*. "Everything that is printed or spoken on the subject is inference more or less probably."[84]

Other attempts at quantifying the nation's wealth distribution would soon follow. John Spargo, a British socialist writer who had moved to the United States in 1901, used occupational data from the 1900 census to argue that just under 1 percent of those gainfully employed held just over 70 percent of the nation's total wealth.[85] Willford King, a conservative University of Wisconsin statistician, had set out to rebut the claims coming from socialists like Spargo. But the numbers he found would give him pause. As of 1910, he concluded in a 1915 report, the nation's richest 2 percent seemed to be holding as much as 60 percent of the nation's wealth, the poorest 65 percent, only 5 percent.[86]

Had America's workers, asked the Commission on Industrial Relations staff report soon after King's numbers became public, "received a fair share of the enormous increase in wealth which has taken place in this country?" The answer had to be "emphatically" no. If the nation had "a reasonably equitable division of wealth," their report concluded, the "entire population" would be able to "occupy the position of comfort and security which we characterize as Middle Class."

The reaction to America's economic divide from the Industrial Relations Commission's chairman, Missouri attorney Frank Walsh, would not be as restrained. In a supplemental statement to the staff report, Chairman Walsh passionately vented his anger. America's great "inherited fortunes," he charged, "automatically treble and multiply in volume" while average Americans toil up to twelve hours a day. "From childhood to the grave," Walsh continued, average Americans "dwell in the shadow of a fear that their only resource—their opportunity to toil—will be taken from them, through accident, illness, the caprice of a foreman, or the fortunes of industry." Average American families, he raged, find their babies "snuffed out by bad air in cheap lodgings," their fathers and husbands "maimed in accidents."[87]

Walsh's rage surprised no one. By 1915, all sorts of Americans were giving voice to similar passion. Even a president of the United States.

"We have been proud of our industrial achievements," Woodrow Wilson proclaimed in his 1913 inaugural, "but we have hitherto not stopped thoughtfully enough to count the human cost, the cost of lives snuffed out, of energies overtaxed and broken, the fearful physical and spiritual cost to the men and women and children upon whom the dead weight and burden of it all has fallen pitilessly the years through."

"The great Government we loved has too often been made use of for private and selfish purposes," intoned Wilson, "and those who used it had forgotten the people."[88]

The selfish Americans Wilson condemned couldn't care less about "the people." At one hearing, Industrial Relations Commission chairman Frank Walsh had asked the great J. Pierpont Morgan "to what extent are the directors of corporations responsible for the labor conditions existing in the industries in which they are the directing power?"

"Not at all I should say," Morgan replied.[89]

Business success, the captains of industry and their Wall Street enablers believed, reflected a necessary survival of the fittest. If we helped the losers in that struggle, how would they ever learn? How would the human race ever progress?

"Let the buyer beware; that covers the whole business," announced Henry O. Havemeyer, the president of the American Sugar Refining Company. "You cannot wet nurse people from the time they are born until the time they die. They have got to wade in and get stuck, and that is the way men are educated and cultivated."[90]

Employers, magazine editor Norman Hapgood would later recall, "used to tell me that higher wages and shorter hours would merely be spent in drink." And if lawmakers were to hold corporations liable for industrial accidents, employers warned Hapgood, employees would go and have "their legs cut off on purpose."[91]

James J. Hill, the chairman of the Great Northern Railway, took every opportunity to blast the foolishness that would upset the genius of the nation's "natural" economic order. He saw "waste, idleness, and rising wages all interrelated to one another, now as cause and now as effect," and considered "the modern theory that you can safely tax the wealthy" as "just as obnoxious as the medieval theory that you can safely oppress or kill the poor."[92] In a 1909 newspaper interview, Hill, then worth over $2 billion in today's dollars, blamed the high cost of living on the extravagance of the American people.

"He was asked," the newspaper story related, "how the American people as a whole could be very extravagant on an average wage of $437 a year, which is the wage that the census of 1900 revealed." Extravagance, Hill harrumphed, clearly constituted a "relative" phenomenon. America's workers, like everyone else, should practice "thrift and economy." At the time Hill lived in a five-floor Minnesota mansion that featured thirteen bathrooms, twenty-two fireplaces, sixteen crystal chandeliers, and a hundred-foot-long reception hall.

The "vast majority" of America's most privileged, New York attorney Amos Pinchot would write in 1912, believed as James J. Hill believed.[93]

"They naturally desire to bequeath the advantages of wealth to their children, and their children's children," Pinchot observed. "They believe that the only way to do this is to hold to the old order, and oppose the new. Any change—and progress—may be the opening wedge to slit the rock of privilege upon which they stand. They must ward off progress at all costs."

The wealthy, Pinchot concluded, "will not listen to reason." They stand "firmly opposed to a distribution of wealth which will be a little more comfortable for the country." They "have failed in the first duty of citizenship; they have neglected to think enough."[94]

But other Americans like Amos Pinchot were thinking. They found themselves repulsed by the smug bromides they heard from the Carnegies and Hills. They saw their democracy sliding away, sinking down the ever-deeper crevice that separated America's plutocrats from everyone else. These Americans would challenge the plutocracy that ruled them. They would fight to end it. Some even thought they might succeed.

Chapter Two

ENTER A NEW OPPOSITION

In early 1912, the city of Schenectady held a somewhat odd pair of distinctions. This upstate New York locale hosted both one of the most powerful corporations in the entire United States and a mayor who belonged to the Socialist Party. In that strange duality, David Nelke saw opportunity. Nelke edited a rabidly antisocialist magazine. His magazine needed money, and General Electric, Schenectady's corporate pride and joy, obviously had plenty of it. On a February day in 1912, editor Nelke journeyed to General Electric to ask GE president Charles A. Coffin for his support.

Nelke had every reason to believe that this support would be forthcoming. Schenectady Mayor George Lunn, after all, was advancing an aggressive socialist agenda. He was demanding the municipal ownership of all Schenectady's public utilities. He was moving to have the city provide free medical and dental care, and even start selling ice, coal, and groceries.[1] A corporate leader as distinguished as Charles A. Coffin, Nelke must have figured, would surely appreciate the clear and present danger.

But the GE president kept Nelke waiting, and the moment the GE top executive finally did appear, he offered no pleasantries. Coffin instead "began roaring" about the antisocialist diatribes in Nelke's magazine. Mayor Lunn, Coffin pronounced, may well be the best mayor Schenectady had ever had. Your magazine, Coffin told Nelke as he ushered him out the door, was "simply tearing down socialism" and offering nothing in the way of needed reform.[2]

What might David Nelke have been thinking as Charles Coffin gave him the bum's rush? Did he suddenly fear for the future? Did he see a red tide overtaking America? Was he wondering how men of property and good sense could ever possibly prevail if some of their number—men like Charles Coffin—were so outrageously breaking ranks?

A century ago, in 1912, men like David Nelke fervently believed in property rights and order. That same year, by contrast, most Americans fervently believed in the absolute necessity of change and reform. And the ranks of these change-minded Americans even encompassed, as David Nelke learned on his disappointing day in Schenectady, men of property and considerable power.

A ruling rich, in whatever era they may rule, need more than sheer might and money to get their way. They need those below them to trust in them. By 1912, few Americans trusted the rich and powerful. The claims that the nation's plutocratic elite had so long advanced— the notion, most notably, that grand fortunes represent grand victories for the human race, a "survival of the fittest" that all Americans ought to welcome and celebrate—had come to ring preposterously hollow, even among some of the rich and powerful themselves. Most Americans, a decade into the new century, did not see a social order poised for progress or even survival. They saw a nation rotting at the core, and they saw at that core massive concentrations of private wealth that someday, if left unchecked, might even destroy the nation.

"The distribution of the accumulated earnings of the great working masses," as US Senator Albert Cummins from Iowa would posit, "is the burning issue of the day—the great question which overshadows every other problem in America."[3]

This "problem of distribution," the Republican Cummins believed, "will wreck the American republic, if the republic ever is wrecked." And that wrecking, in the early 1900s, seemed a real possibility. "Comparatively few men," Cummins lamented, "now virtually control the necessities of life." And history taught what such narrow control inevitably brings.

"Ancient Persia died when 2 percent of the people owned all the land and kept most of its products," a *New York Times* writer reminded readers in 1909 after interviewing railroad mogul James J. Hill. "Rome went down when 1,800 men owned what was then all of the known world."[4]

Would James J. Hill and his fellow plutocrats now bring down America? Men like Albert Cummins would not sit back and let that happen. They joined with men and women across the political spectrum and placed before the American people a vision of an alternate

future. That vision, in their own time, would not sweep away plutocracy. America's rich proved resilient and ruthless in defense of their
privilege. They survived the new century's opening decades, their fortunes and power largely intact. But the pre–World War I struggles
against plutocracy did hone the ideas and the strategies that would
eventually bring plutocracy down. The young men and women who
came of age amid these struggles would emerge in the 1930s as leaders
in their own right. They would apply the lessons they learned over the
century's early years and they would triumph. The young Americans
who took inspiration from the likes of the Republican Albert Cummins and the Socialist George Lunn would not leave the American
scene until the 1960s. The plutocracy of their youth, by that time, had
passed on too.

America's plutocrats, as the twentieth century dawned, never really saw
the challenge coming. They had, after all, crushed the Populists and
their angry agrarian revolt. In railroad yards and steel mills they had
beaten back veritable armies of striking industrial workers. Everyone
else in society who mattered in any way—the ministers, the attorneys,
the engineers, all the pillars of middle-class respectability—seemed
comfortable enough with America's plutocratic political order.

Louis Brandeis certainly counted among those pillars. The Boston
attorney came from eminently respectable stock. A Brandeis uncle
had delivered a nominating speech for Abraham Lincoln at the 1860
Republican convention.[5] His father had prospered as a Louisville
grain merchant. Young Louis seemed destined to add to his family's distinction. At Harvard, his intellectual brilliance and personal
integrity left a lasting impact on elders and peers alike. By 1890, many
considered the thirty-four-year-old Brandeis Boston's leading commercial lawyer. He was making $50,000 a year, a prodigious sum at
a time when most of the nation's lawyers would have felt themselves
enormously fortunate if they took home $5,000.[6]

Politically, the young and successful Brandeis remained conventional. He opposed William Jennings Bryan in 1896. McKinley and
the men around him, Brandeis believed, had the nation's best interests at heart. Brandeis certainly shared their underlying attitudes. The
nation, he noted in one lecture series, didn't need laws protecting
workers from long hours or substandard wages. Anyone who wanted
to work long hours ought to have the freedom to do so. Long hours

of work, Brandeis opined, probably pose no more danger to worker health "than the eating of mince pies by people with weak digestion."[7]

Ruling elites, whatever their epoch, need people like this young, respected—and clueless—Louis Brandeis. They can reign secure so long as these respectables remain content. But woe to these elites when respectables like Louis Brandeis start doubting the prevailing wisdom of their time. In the United States that doubt started gaining momentum after plutocracy's grand triumph in 1896. By the early 1900s appreciable numbers of professionals as distinguished as Louis Brandeis had come to believe that an unequal America was not working out—and never could.

"The rising resentment at plutocratic action will make itself severely felt," Brandeis would write his brother. "After all, we are living in a Democracy, and some way or other, the people will get back at power unduly concentrated, and there will be plenty of injustice in the process."[8]

Why did Brandeis and so many of his fellow professionals start doubting in the years after McKinley's 1896 triumph? The motivations—the pressures—varied. For Brandeis himself, a deep sensation of disgust likely played a role. The increasing inefficiency and corruption he encountered in his professional life and public service endeavors left him appalled. Brandeis believed in honesty and fair play, and many men of property, he discovered, simply didn't.

Brandeis had begun serving in "good government" groups around Boston almost as soon as he started practicing law.[9] He regularly volunteered his legal talents to local battles against wheelers and dealers and their shady maneuvers to gain and exploit local public service monopolies. These battles seemed to escalate year by year in significance. Brandeis would soon find himself investigating and litigating cases that involved his state's most powerful business interests. By the late 1890s, notes historian Melvin Urofsky, Brandeis was formulating "a coherent philosophy about the nature of American society, the relation of an industrial economy to political democracy, and the need to restrain bigness." Modern industrial America, Brandeis had come to believe, needed a distinctly more level playing field. Men of great property and influence could no longer be allowed to set their own rules and place the public in jeopardy.[10]

Only by daring to challenge great wealth could that public be protected, and his profession, Brandeis acknowledged, had largely failed in that task. America's lawyers, "instead of holding a position of independence between the wealthy and the people," have "allowed themselves to become an adjunct of the great corporations." They have, Brandeis concluded, "neglected their obligation to use their powers for the protection of the people."[11]

Other successful lawyers would follow Brandeis into confrontation with plutocracy. Samuel Untermyer, a wealthy New York corporate attorney, would become a tireless voice for regulating the stock market. He served as counsel to the congressional panel, the Pujo Committee, that went after the "money trust" in 1912 and 1913.[12] In Georgia, attorney John Reed began contemplating "the American situation" after writing a legal textbook. With that contemplation, he would later relate, "plutocracy began to startle and alarm him." Reed would eventually develop a political hierarchy of plutocratic corruption. Streetcar, lighting, heat, power, telephone, and other local utility companies run America's cities, he concluded. Steam railroads, telegraph, oil, liquor, and banking corporations dominate the states, and national banks and trusts—maintained by "unjust favors to a few"—govern the country.

"This supremacy of private corporations," Reed charged, "has degraded America from the proudest and highest place ever attained by democracy far below any other civilized nation in the depths of corrupt government."[13]

Other professionals found themselves doubting America's unequal economic order as they contemplated the nation's chronic economic instability. With wealth concentrating at the economy's summit, they realized, workers couldn't afford to buy what they were producing. So argued Washington Gladden, a Congregational pastor elected to Ohio's Columbus City Council in 1900.

"If the laborers are so poor that they can buy but little, then little is sold and little can be manufactured, and merchants and bankers fail and mill wheels stop and railroads go into receivers' hands and there is general depression," Gladden wrote five years later. "If capital deserves to prosper, capital must help labor to be prosperous: the contrary policy is not merely bad, it is stupid."[14]

Ever greater rewards for capital, plutocrats had assured the nation, would give America's captains of industry an incentive to forge ever more efficient industrial processes, and that efficiency would mean progress for society overall. But the rush after great wealth, skeptics began understanding, wasn't generating industrial progress. The rich weren't getting richer producing ever more efficiently. They were getting richer playing games with Wall Street securities, and America's

industrial know-how—the only real guarantor of national progress—was lagging significantly behind other industrial nations. The
US Steel trust that emerged in 1901, as Louis Brandeis noted, inherited "the most efficient steel makers in the world." But the US Steel
monopoly let this advantage go by the boards. Just ten years after
the massive merging that created the steel giant, America's premier
engineering journal declared the United States "five years behind
Germany in iron and steel metallurgy."[15]

Still other reformers began to distrust the enormous wealth of
America's upper class as they went about easing the suffering of
America's poor. These reformers contended that a culture that celebrated the rich as society's "fittest" would inevitably dismiss the poor
as unfit losers. No sane society, they argued, could afford to dismiss
anyone. No one made this case more powerfully than Jane Addams,
the nation's most famous advocate for society's "wretched refuse."
Addams had pioneered the "settlement house" movement, an effort
that had middle-class people "settle" in poverty-ravaged slums to
share their skills and culture. The greater the gap between rich and
poor, her settlement house experiences led Addams to realize, the
greater the peril for prosperous and poor alike.

Addams would illustrate this peril in a best-selling 1910 memoir
that shared the story of a comfortable Chicago widow she knew who
had "held herself quite aloof" from her immigrant neighbors. This
widow "could never be drawn into any of the public efforts to secure
a better code of tenement-house sanitation." The widow eventually
sent her two lovely daughters back East for college. One June the
two came home for summer holidays. They both somehow caught
typhoid fever, the tenement scourge. One daughter died.[16]

Typhoid could escape a poor neighborhood. The prosperous, so
long as they tolerated inequality, could never escape typhoid.

"The relationships of society are changing," social worker, lawyer, and urban reformer Frederick Howe, a Cleveland City Council
member, had noted a few years earlier in 1905. "We are being drawn
into an intimacy, a solidarity, which makes the welfare of one the
welfare of all."[17]

That conviction would resonate ever more widely as the 1900s wore on.

"In the long run," as by then former president Theodore Roosevelt
observed at an April 1912 appearance in Philadelphia, "this country
will not be a good place for any of us to live unless it is a reasonably
good place for all of us to live in."[18]

A deeply unequal America, reformers had become convinced, could never be that "reasonably good place." The chase after grand fortunes made grand miseries—"the evils of surplus wealth," as Columbia University philosopher Felix Adler dubbed them—inevitable. Adler then rated as one of America's most honored moral voices. He had founded the Society for Ethical Culture and chaired the National Child Labor Committee, the pioneering social justice campaign that worked to unshackle young children from workplace exploitation.

We have child labor, Adler told a 1907 Carnegie Hall audience, because employers can get rich employing it. That this labor must always pervert children's "physical, mental, and moral growth" meant nothing to these employers "as long as they got labor cheap." Elsewhere in the economy, Adler saw the same story. What could be more "utterly mean and contemptible," he would ask, than the corporate giants who fill their customers "with worthless stuffs and poisons in the adulteration of food products and drugs." And yet, he continued, "many fortunes had been built up upon such methods."[19]

Adler came out of the Jewish tradition, and his father served as the rabbi at one of New York's most important congregations. The young Adler did study to become a rabbi. But his passion for social justice led him into a lifelong search for moral teachings that could unite men and women of good will across religious lines.

Adler's passion for social justice stirred in other religious faiths as well. Out of America's Protestant denominations came the Social Gospel movement. Baptist minister Walter Rauschenbusch, an early Social Gospel movement leader, consistently deplored "the concentration of wealth in a few hands," notes one contemporary Baptist commentary on his legacy. Wealth meant to nations, Rauschenbusch would preach, what manure meant to farms. Spread evenly over the soil, manure enriches the whole. With manure concentrated in heaps, the land becomes "impoverished and nothing will grow."[20]

A Minnesota farmboy, John Ryan, would lead Catholics in the same Social Gospel direction. Ryan had grown up reading Henry George, the Gilded Age's most tireless crusader against inequality, and as a St. Paul seminary student in 1892 had voted for the Populist Party's first candidate for president. The Populist ticket that year held a personal attraction for Ryan: His fellow Minnesota Irish Catholic, Ignatius Donnelly, had written the preamble to that first Populist platform.

"The fruits of the toil of millions are badly stolen to build up colossal fortunes for a few, unprecedented in the history of mankind," Donnelly had written. "From the same prolific womb of governmental injustice we breed the two great classes—tramps and millionaires."[21]

The year before that platform appeared, Pope Leo XIII's landmark "labor encyclical," *Rerum Novarum*, had signaled church support for strategies that "give workers a stake in the appreciating wealth of industry."[22] Ryan, once ordained in 1898, would begin advocating for those strategies. His first major book, *A Living Wage* in 1906, would spurn "overly acquisitive and unregulated free market capitalism as economically unhealthy and morally bankrupt."[23]

But moral outrage at inequality only partially explains the intense hostility that so many reformers ultimately came to feel about the plutocracy that engulfed them. Many of these respected pillars of their communities most certainly—and sincerely—did despise the suffering they saw. But they also feared what might happen if those suffering ever erupted in rage. In 1871, within living memory, a revolutionary upheaval in France had left blood gushing through the streets of Paris. Bloody confrontations between labor and capital had also broken out all across the United States in the decades after the Civil War. Reformers knew this history. Could violent revolution now rend America's social fabric? Was the nation, as historian Paul Buhle has put it, "perched over a proletarian volcano"?[24] Could that volcano blow at any moment?

Everywhere reformers looked they seemed to see that eruption coming. A radical working class was once again rumbling. In 1905, a "Continental Congress" of this working class in Chicago gave birth to a fiery and uncompromising new union, the Industrial Workers of the World. Almost all of America's already established unions organized workers by trade and craft. The IWW called instead for "one big union." The "Wobblies," as they would be dubbed, believed in "direct action," not contracts. They would strike whenever justice demanded. If bosses came at them with thugs, they would not turn the other cheek. If need be, the Wobblies declared, they would fight back with sabotage.[25] In mining and labor camps, among the nation's most brutally exploited workers, this Wobbly message resonated powerfully.

"Card-carrying" IWW members, the US Commission on Industrial Relations would observe in 1915, number only a few thousand. But their spirit "permeates to a large extent enormous masses of workers, particularly among the unskilled and migratory laborers." And "entirely apart" from those who accept the IWW's "philosophy and creed" stand "numberless thousands of workers, skilled and unskilled, organized and unorganized, who feel bitterly that they and their fellows are being denied justice, economically, politically, and legally."[26]

What made the great Wobbly uprisings in places like Lawrence, Massachusetts, and Paterson, New Jersey—such a "living nightmare," to use historian Alan Dawley's phrase, for "executives everywhere"?[27] Certainly not the relatively modest demands of the strikers for higher wages and better working conditions. In and of themselves, these demands didn't particularly terrify employers. But the strikers themselves did. In these great Wobbly strike battles, America's immigrant hordes were coming together for the first time. The poor "huddled masses" from Southern and Eastern Europe were rising up—and united.

These new immigrants had started streaming into the United States in the 1890s. By 1911, the United States Immigration Commission was reporting that only one-fifth of newly arriving immigrants were coming from America's traditional immigrant homelands in Northern and Western Europe.[28] The new immigrants from Southern and Eastern Europe typically arrived unskilled and uneducated. They came divided by language, culture, and religion. Employers liked them that way. Unskilled, divided, illiterate populations could be more easily exploited. And they would be exploited, paid next to nothing, and stuffed into slums where nothing green ever grew.

These immigrants appeared, by most accounts, resigned to their fate, totally unable to comprehend the depth of their oppression. One Italian immigrant woman, Jane Addams recalled, came to a reception at a Chicago settlement house and found red roses decorating the affair. The immigrant woman, absolutely delighted to see the roses, expressed her surprise that the flowers had been "brought so fresh all the way from Italy." Oh, no, a settlement house staffer explained, the roses had been grown right there in America. That could not be, the Italian woman insisted. She "had lived in Chicago for six years and had never seen any roses."[29]

Now, a decade into the new century, these same culturally overwhelmed immigrants were mobilizing in massive strikes—twenty thousand garment workers in New York, over forty thousand more in Chicago. No employers, no Americans of means, had ever considered such mobilizations even a remote possibility.

In April 1911, one garment-worker organizer, the twenty-eight-year-old Rose Schneiderman, would capture the new immigrant spirit at a memorial for the 146 young women who had perished the month before when fire had ravaged their Manhattan blouse factory, the now infamous Triangle Fire. The workers had found themselves trapped when the fire broke out. The owners had locked a stairway escape route.

"What the woman who labors wants is the right to live, not simply exist," Schneiderman told the memorial for her union sisters. "The worker must have bread, but she must have roses, too."[30]

"We want bread and roses" would become the most memorable picket-line motto the next winter at the grandest strike of them all, in Lawrence, New England's mightiest industrial center. No labor struggle had ever shaken America more.

Half the population of Lawrence over age fourteen, more than forty thousand workers in all, toiled in the city's enormous wool and cotton mills. The millworkers typically earned less than ten dollars a week and routinely put over half their meager incomes into rent for their firetrap tenements. The workers subsisted, relates historian Joyce Kornbluh, on "bread, molasses, and beans." Over a third of them, one local doctor calculated, were dying before they reached twenty-five years of age.[31]

On January 11, 1911, Polish women weavers at one Lawrence cotton mill walked out to protest a missing thirty-two cents in their pay envelopes. The strike spread quickly, and workers soon called on the IWW for help. The top Wobbly organizer who rushed to the scene, the twenty-seven-year-old Joseph Ettor, spoke Italian, Polish, and English and could get by in Yiddish and Hungarian. He needed every one of those languages. The Lawrence workers spoke all of them and more. The Lawrence mill owners had sent recruiting agents out all over Europe. They figured that poor, uneducated immigrants wouldn't have either the smarts or the courage to make any trouble. They figured wrong. The striking Lawrence workers would brave martial law and police clubs. They would lose their leader, Joseph Ettor, to an arrest on bogus murder charges. But the immigrant workers and their spirited picket lines held firm and amazed the nation.

"The tired, gray crowds ebbing and flowing perpetually into the mills," reported labor journalist Mary Heaton Vorse, "had waked and opened their mouths to sing."

By the end of March, the strikers had won the wage increase and overtime pay they demanded. Textile wages would soon start rising throughout New England.

The IWW, as an organization, would not. The Wobblies would leave no lasting institutional presence in Lawrence, or Paterson, or any other site of their most dramatic clashes. They invested little energy in nurturing union organizational structures at the local level. They had their hearts set on a grander goal, general strikes that would topple the capitalist order and usher in worker control on every factory floor. Building local union structure required tedious attention to mundane detail. The Wobbly leading lights had little patience for that tedium.

But the era's great labor struggles, some Wobbly-led, some not, most definitely did leave a lasting impact on the psyche of strikers—and the nation. Those poor, uneducated immigrant masses had confounded the plutocrats. They had served notice that the nation's least powerful would be beasts of burden no more for anyone.

"Some day we will have the courage to rise up and strike back against these great 'giants' of industry," veteran labor organizer and IWW cofounder Mary Harris "Mother" Jones had predicted in 1910, "and then we will see that they weren't giants at all—they only seemed so because we were on our knees and they towered over us."[32]

The Mother Jones prediction seemed to be coming true. Immigrants had risen up off their knees to take on the corporate giants. And in the process they were changing how the privileged professionals who stood between them and those giants saw the world. Those respectables began appreciating not just the power of poor immigrants, but their humanity. And these professionals increasingly contrasted the humanity they found below their station with the inhumanity they felt pressing down from above.

Louis Brandeis, for instance, would find himself mediating labor struggles across the Northeast, and these interventions had him interacting closely, for the first time in his life, with organized workers.

"I am experiencing a growing conviction that the labor men are the most congenial company," Brandeis would note after negotiating one dispute in Syracuse. "The intense materialism and luxuriousness of most of our other people makes their company quite irksome."[33]

Those luxurious "other people"—America's rich—would face both an economic *and* political challenge from the nation's new immigrants. These immigrants didn't just bring their labor power to the United States. They brought radical ideas. Almost every ethnic group—the Jews, the Italians, the Finns—came with activists schooled in class struggle. In cities and towns across the United States, these immigrant radicals would help give America's emerging new Socialist Party a mass popular base.

A "Socialist Labor Party" had first appeared in the United States back in 1876, but this fledgling effort remained little more than a debating society for isolated handfuls of German immigrants who argued endlessly about Old World politics.[34] That wouldn't change until the 1890s when two new dynamics jumbled America's radical political calculus. The first: Fairly significant numbers of native-born Americans had begun moving to an explicitly socialist perspective. The second: Left-leaning immigrants were finally achieving political critical mass.

Eugene Victor Debs led the native-born. Debs had been a militant, if largely conventional, railway craft union leader since the 1870s. He had even served a term as a Democrat in the Indiana State Legislature. But Debs by the 1890s was exploring new approaches to labor struggle. In 1894, his new American Railway Union—a union organized industrially across craft lines—won a major strike against James J. Hill's Great Northern Railway, and then walked out nationally in support of workers who manufactured the Pullman railroad sleeping cars. Federal troops would break this ill-fated solidarity strike, and Debs would be jailed for violating a federal injunction.

In prison, Debs dug into the socialist classics and returned to society the next year committed to radical political action.[35] In 1896, Debs would support the Populist ticket. By 1900, he was running for president himself, as a Socialist. In 1901, he would join with immigrant leaders to fuse two different socialist groups into a new Socialist Party of the United States.

The activists in this new party brought contrasting strategic perspectives to the struggle against capitalism. Some like Milwaukee's Victor Berger, a German-born teacher and printer, concentrated on building ballot-box success at the municipal level and gaining influence within unions affiliated with the American Federation of Labor, the nation's largest labor network. Others like William "Big Bill" Haywood, a secretary-treasurer of the independent Western Federation of Miners, would go on to help create the IWW. Haywood's wing of the Socialist Party saw no future in Berger's "sewer socialism."

But these "left" and "right" wings of the new Socialist Party would not fly apart. The party operated throughout its first decade as a "big tent" for a wide variety of radicals. Everyone under that big tent agreed that workers needed to change the rules that ran the economy. That meant, above all else, attacking the vast accumulations of wealth

and power that had made those rules a hammer that pounded working people.

"Democracy and Plutocracy cannot continue to exist together in
the State," Debs had expounded in 1900. "Democracy must be given
new life or cease to be."[36]

Socialists would continually emphasize the peril in tolerating tow-
ering accumulations of private property. Before the Civil War, Socialist
writer Reginald Wright Kauffman noted, the nation's "richest private
estate" totaled no more than $7 million. The new century's richest
individual, John D. Rockefeller, had an estate worth "nearly one hundred times as much." In their "mad race for profits," Kauffman would
charge, Rockefeller and his fellow capitalists were sacrificing workers'
"physical, moral, and mental welfare" to their "own insatiable greed."[37]

"The wealth of the country was produced by labor," Massachusetts
Socialist James Carey echoed. "Capital itself produces nothing. Why
should those who produce everything have nothing, while those who
produce nothing have everything?"[38]

In the new "cooperative commonwealth" ahead, Socialists preached,
workers would finally stand tall as economic equals. They would
receive, Gene Debs forecast, "the full produce" of their labor.[39]

"I look into the future," he would write, "with absolute confidence."

That confidence did not seem at all misplaced. Socialist parties
in Europe were already making a significant impact. In Germany,
Europe's most economically dynamic nation, the socialist Social Democratic Party was becoming the single largest political party in the
Reichstag. And Europe's most illustrious socialist leaders, the Germans included, saw even greater promise for socialism in the United
States. Capitalism, these European socialists believed, had developed
far more extensively in the United States than anywhere else. So would
socialism. As August Bebel, the top German socialist, pronounced in
1907: "Americans will be the first to usher in a Socialist republic."[40]

In the early 1900s, the Socialist Party of the United States appeared
to be moving smartly toward that goal. Before his early 1904 death
from typhoid fever, Republican Party powerhouse Mark Hanna would
predict that socialism would be America's most significant issue by
1912.[41] Later in 1904, Debs would collect 420,000 votes for president as
the Socialist Party candidate, over quadruple his 1900 total.

Within the US labor movement, meanwhile, socialist ideas and
influence were also spreading. A resolution endorsing socialism came
close to passing at the 1902 AFL convention, falling by just a 4,897

to 4,171 margin.[42] Several major AFL unions—the United Mine Workers, the United Brewery Workers, the International Machinists Union, and the International Ladies Garment Workers Union—all had either socialist leaders or a large socialist presence.[43]

At the ballot box, Socialist Party candidates were scoring equally impressive successes. At the party's pre–World War I peak, almost twelve hundred socialists held local elected office.[44] Socialists served as mayors in cities from Schenectady to Milwaukee. Two Socialist Party leaders, Victor Berger from Milwaukee and Meyer London from New York's Lower East Side, would be elected to Congress. And the party's appeal would swell beyond city borders. In fact, as a percentage of total votes cast, the most impressive statewide Socialist Party vote tallies would come in Oklahoma, Nevada, Montana, Washington, and California. Oklahoma alone boasted twelve thousand dues-paying Socialist Party members, organized in 961 local chapters.[45]

These members—and many of their neighbors—voraciously consumed socialist media. The *Appeal to Reason*, an independent national socialist weekly out of Kansas, had a circulation of seven hundred thousand by 1912.[46] No weekly publication in the United States, and probably the world, enjoyed readership as wide. For special editions, the *Appeal* would print over four million copies and distribute them, coast to coast, with an "*Appeal* Army" of eighty thousand local volunteers.[47]

John Reed, a reform lawyer and decidedly not a socialist, would observe that the *Appeal* was attracting readers with "its stouthearted and uncompromising championship of the people against plutocracy."[48] Wherever those people went into motion, wherever "capitalist muck needed to be raked," Americans could count on finding *Appeal* reporters.[49] One *Appeal* editor gave writer Upton Sinclair the advance he needed to go research the meatpacking industry in Chicago, then serialized his resulting novel, *The Jungle*, in the *Appeal's* pages. Sinclair's horrific slaughterhouse descriptions, later published as a book, would shock the nation and inspire the 1908 federal legislation that created what eventually became the federal Food and Drug Administration.

Socialist newspaper publishing would extend far beyond the *Appeal*. In 1912 Americans could choose among five socialist dailies and 262 weeklies in English—and eight dailies and thirty-six weeklies in Yiddish, Italian, and nearly every other major language immigrants spoke in the nation's major urban centers.[50] The Socialist Party message spread deep into the heartland too. The St. Louis–based *National Rip Saw* had 150,000 readers. In Texas, halfway between Houston and

San Antonio, the Halletsville *Rebel* had twenty-six thousand.[51] *The Messenger*, the world's only African American magazine of "scientific radicalism," would reach a forty-three thousand circulation. Its editor, New York socialist A. Phillip Randolph, would decades later initiate the landmark 1963 civil rights movement March on Washington for Jobs and Freedom.[52]

These newspapers mattered. They passed from hand to hand and gave broad numbers of Americans a readily accessible alternative source of news and views. Not all readers of the socialist press would vote for Socialist Party candidates. But most all readers of socialist papers did encounter perspectives that fed a thoroughgoing skepticism of plutocratic aims and claims. The rich might have monopolies in coal and steel, but they had no monopoly over media. The socialist movement had an infrastructure. Plutocracy had a reason to worry.

Eugene Debs defined the Socialist Party as "first of all a political movement of the working class."[53] But Debs defined "working class" rather broadly.

"By the working class I mean all useful workers," he explained, "all who by the labor of their hands or the effort of their brains, or both in alliance, as they ought universally to be, increase the knowledge and add to the wealth of society."[54]

For Debs and most socialists, points out historian Otis Pease, the fundamental class divide fell between "those who produce and those who merely profit," the people on the one side, the plutocrats on the other.[55] That perspective left the Socialist Party front door open to professional men and women who had never set foot on a factory floor—and many walked right in, usually after years of activism in various other reform causes. Lena Morrow Lewis, the daughter of a Presbyterian minister, graduated from a college in New Jersey and joined the temperance movement, then went on to become active in the campaign for women's suffrage, and ended up as a Socialist Party organizer on the West Coast. Anna Louise Strong, an Oberlin College grad with a doctorate from the University of Chicago, started her career editing a Protestant weekly. She later won election to the Seattle school board as a good-government education reformer. By the eve of World War I, she had become a Socialist Party activist.[56]

But if some middle-class reformers saw the Socialist Party as the logical extension of their personal commitment to create a nobler nation, others saw socialism as a threat to the better America they hoped to help fashion. These respectables did not dispute the socialist indictment of America's industrial order. The socialists, as the influential editor Norman Hapgood acknowledged, offer a justifiable critique of "the terrible injustices of the present system." But "no honeyed words" from socialists, added Hapgood, "can disguise the inherent evils" of the "vast bureaucracy" that a socialist economic transformation would bring to America, an "over-government" that would go "against the deep-seated desire of men to work out their own destinies in a thousand different ways of their own devising."[57]

Hapgood and Louis Brandeis worked closely together. Both believed that a zest for economic competition came naturally to Americans. Socialism, they felt, would only gain converts in the United States if those "terrible injustices" socialists so rightfully railed against went unchecked. Only reform, and fundamental reform at that, could stop socialism. Those who promoted this fundamental reform seethed when plutocrats labeled their reform proposals "socialistic," or worse.

"The propositions I make," Theodore Roosevelt righteously declared in 1912, "constitute neither anarchy nor Socialism, but, on the contrary, a corrective to Socialism and an antidote to anarchy."[58]

Roosevelt would denounce the "dull purblind folly of the very rich man" who did not share his commitment to change. The rich man's "greed and arrogance," he charged, would nurture the growth of a Socialist Party "far more ominous than any Populist or similar movements of the past."[59]

For reformers like Roosevelt, the rich had become the problem. The "prevailing abuses and sins" that make reform necessary, Herbert Croly argued in his influential 1909 book, *The Promise of American Life*, all arise from "the prodigious concentration of wealth, and of the power exercised by wealth, in the hands of a few men." Croly's *Promise of American Life* called on reformers to strike out at the "roots" of this "existing concentration" and would become a veritable political guidebook for Theodore Roosevelt and his circle. America, Croly implored, needed to subordinate the "peculiar freedom" to become fabulously wealthy to a new "constructive national purpose." A new "nationalism" could defeat "socialism" if the government of the United States went about "making itself responsible for a morally and socially desirable distribution of wealth."[60]

Religious leaders worried about socialism's secular bent shared Croly's sense of urgency.

"The spread of Socialism is one of the phenomenal facts of the past decade," the Social Gospel leader Washington Gladden told a 1905 audience at New Jersey's Drew Theological Seminary. "Ten years ago it seemed a mere dream; today it is not merely a hope, but a strong expectation in the minds of millions."[61]

These millions included "thoughtful men" of the "educated classes." His conversations with them, Gladden noted, "reveal the presence of large numbers who regard Socialism as the goal toward which society is moving."[62] That movement would prove irreversible, Gladden added, if reform did not moderate "the cold, hard, haughty temper of the House of Have and the envy and hatred of the House of Want."

Social reform, agreed Catholic University's William Kerby, offered "the only effective defense against the Socialist crusade." Workers needed minimum-wage laws and the right to join unions. In fact, added Fall River Bishop William Stang in Massachusetts, workers needed social insurance against all the "reverses of life," everything from sickness to loss of work and old age, a "security of existence" that "would keep them from drifting into socialism."[63]

Mere charity from the rich, reformers believed, would never deliver this desperately needed security. America didn't need philanthropy from the wealthy. America needed an end to the exploitation that generated their vast wealth in the first place. Let the nation's economic surplus "come back to the people of the community in which it is created," urged Columbia University's Edward Devine, "not by gifts of libraries, galleries, technical schools and parks, but by the cessation of toil one day in seven and sixteen hours in the twenty-four, by the increase of wages, by the sparing of lives, by the prevention of accidents."[64]

Exploitation, reformers believed, created plutocratic wealth. Plutocratic wealth gave the wealthy the political power they needed to frustrate reform. The reform project, so long as America remained plutocratic, would forever be frustrated.

"We can have democracy in this country," as Louis Brandeis would put it, "or we can have great wealth concentrated in the hands of a few, but we can't have both."[65]

Just how to end that concentration would be a matter of continuing debate in the years that led up to World War I. As president, Theodore Roosevelt had initiated a widely publicized series of antitrust prosecutions against oil, tobacco, and agricultural machinery manufacturers before he left office in 1909. But the great "trustbuster" never did much, outside these showcase confrontations, to undo the great merger wave that had "trustified" America over the turn of the century. His administration's entire antitrust staff consisted of five attorneys and four stenographers.[66] By 1910, an out-of-office Roosevelt would no longer pay lip service to busting bigness. He had come to see "combinations in industry" as an economic inevitability that "cannot be repealed by political legislation."[67]

"The effort at prohibiting all combination has substantially failed," Roosevelt pronounced. "The way out lies not in attempting to prevent such combinations, but in completely controlling them in the interest of the public welfare."[68]

Reformers in the Brandeis circle disagreed. Big, they held, could never be beautiful. Beyond a certain size, businesses become inefficient and abusive—and too powerful to reign in with the sorts of regulation that Roosevelt's camp considered appropriate. The federal government, in this perspective, needed to concentrate on preventing concentrations of marketplace power. Government had to establish and enforce rules that kept the marketplace freely competitive.

"No regulated private monopoly of the capitalists," Brandeis confided to his wife Alice. "Either competition or State Socialism. Regulate competition, not monopoly, is my slogan."[69]

The socialists agreed in part with both Roosevelt and Brandeis. Like Roosevelt, they considered massive industrial combinations an inevitable consequence of capitalist economic relations. Like Brandeis, they considered the notion that these giants could be tamed with regulations a silly pipe dream. The socialist response: place the giant combinations under direct public control. Make them publicly run, socialized enterprises. How would this socializing take place? Socialists disagreed. Simply assume control of the trusts, the party's left advised.[70] Buy the trusts, the party's right countered.

Some on the socialist right would take pains to detail how such a purchase could take place. Hoping to win over apprehensive reformers, author and lecturer John Spargo explained that a democratically elected socialist government would first place a value on the assets of any trust to be socialized, then issue bonds "to all the shareholders in strict proportion to their holdings." Wealthy shareholders would collect income from these bonds for years to come, but over time, progressive taxation—annual income taxes, levies on inheritances—

would eat away at bondholder wealth "without inflicting injury or hardship upon any human being."[71]

All these perspectives—regulate monopoly or prevent it, reform or revolution—would be fiercely debated in the years before World War I. But the partisans of the various perspectives would rarely be fierce with each other. People simply shared, as historians have noted, too much "common ground."[72] Trade unionists, professionals, and shopkeepers all saw themselves as soldiers in the same war against plutocracy.

"On the one side were men of property and influence," Cleveland reformer Frederick Howe explained, "on the other the politicians, immigrants, workers, and persons of small means."[73]

The men of property, for their part, could never present a united front, and the dissenters in their own ranks, like Boston businessman Edward Filene, would capture the public imagination. Filene had turned an obscure women's specialty shop he inherited from his father into an innovative retail empire. True modern mass production, he believed, had to be production *for* masses of *people*, not production *of* masses of *goods*. Commercial success, Filene contended, rests ultimately on the average customer's power to purchase, and anyone in business with any brains, he argued, ought to be constantly seeking to expand that average purchasing power. Within his own enterprise, Filene bargained collectively with employees, instituted profit sharing, and put in place a then novel assortment of fringe benefits for workers. He would go on to found the modern American credit union movement and help launch the US Chamber of Commerce, an effort Filene undertook to encourage community-mindedness among business leaders.

Those business leaders who practiced the progressive creed Filene preached could win public plaudits. Those who thought they could play at progressivism and continue business as usual met with humiliation. In Chicago, Sears Roebuck president Julius Rosenwald certainly did. Rosenwald had built America's first truly national mail-order retailer, then became a renowned philanthropist and a trustee on the famed Hull House board. He also served on a 1910 city vice commission that ended up concluding that low wages were driving Chicago's young women into prostitution. But Sears Roebuck made no significant move to raise its wages in the aftermath of that 1910 report, and in 1913 another blue-ribbon panel on prostitution ended up grilling Rosenwald as a witness. His testimony would cause a sensation. "No connection," Rosenwald told the panel, existed between low wages and "the immorality of women and girls." But the panel's chairman would force Rosenwald to acknowledge that a major connection did exist between Sears profits and the company's low wages. In fact, the Sears president found himself admitting that his company "would be able to pay large stock dividends even if it gave employees a quarter of its profits."[74]

This public shaming would leave Rosenwald flailing about for some way to get back in the good graces of Chicago's reformers. Eventually, acting on a suggestion from a fellow Hull House trustee, Rosenwald established a profit-sharing plan that would evolve into one of Corporate America's most generous.

On the Hull House board and in countless other social settings, reformers and radicals, respectables and revolutionaries, would share stories and strategies, hopes and dreams. They interacted with each other. They inspired each other. Louis Brandeis counted Edward Filene as a client. Brandeis lectured at the New York Society for Ethical Culture that his brother-in-law, the philosopher Felix Adler, had founded.[75] Adler, an advocate for "an income tax graduated up to 100 percent on all income above that needed to supply all the comforts and true refinements of life,"[76] would be a frequent presence at the home of Edwin Seligman, the economist who gave academic legitimacy and public policy momentum to taxing the rich at progressively higher rates than everyone else.[77] Margaret Sanger, the courageous campaigner for birth control and sex education, would be a close friend of Big Bill Haywood, the Wobbly labor leader.[78] Haywood would one evening debate anarchists and socialists at the Manhattan apartment of banking heiress Mabel Dodge. Among the formally attired guests would be Amos Pinchot, the wealthy New York attorney close to Theodore Roosevelt, and Walter Lippmann, a former secretary to Schenectady's Socialist Party mayor.[79]

These heady times would stamp a powerful imprint on the young who grew up in them. On a Saturday in March 1911, thirty-year-old social worker Frances Perkins was visiting a friend in New York's Greenwich Village when she heard "sirens and screams" coming from the nearby Triangle Shirtwaist Factory. Perkins and her friend arrived at the scene just as trapped young workers had begun to jump to their deaths from the fire-engulfed upper floors of the ten-story factory building. Two decades later, Perkins would be the US secretary of labor. She would later call the Triangle tragedy "the day the New Deal began."[80]

Henry Wallace, the future secretary of agriculture in the same New Deal cabinet as Perkins, would be twenty-seven and living in

Iowa when his uncle Henry died a more peaceful death in February 1916. Uncle Henry, the nation's most widely read farm-belt editor, had championed the Midwest Republican agrarian insurgents, and President Theodore Roosevelt relied on him for counsel on all matters agricultural. His will, read to the young Henry and the rest of the Wallace clan, warned his flock to beware the temptation to chase after grand fortune. "Avoid all this," the will read. "Keep clean in speech, clear in mind, vigorous in body—and God will bless you."[81]

No good could come from grand accumulations of private wealth. The young would imbibe this message, over and over, from their egalitarian elders.

In 1915, the federal Commission on Industrial Relations concluded in its final report that America needed a national "readjustment" that would "reduce the swollen, unearned fortunes of those who have a superfluity" and "raise the underpaid masses to a level of decent and comfortable living."[82] This enormous task—the leveling down of the rich, the leveling up of the poor—would require action, reformers agreed, on a broad variety of fronts. Some progressives campaigned to have municipalities run their own street railways and gas and electric light companies. Placing these "natural monopolies" under public control, they argued, would result in savings for local consumers—and deny plutocrats an easy path to excessive riches and power. In this report, the commission would call for public control on an even broader scale. The Commission recommended abolition of "private ownership of coal mines" and a complete federal buyout of the private American Telephone and Telegraph Company.[83]

These calls for "socializing" private enterprises met with widespread approval within respectable reform circles, even among those skeptical about socialism. By 1915, most reformers had come to consider public ownership of selected industries a reasonable policy alternative. Social Gospel leader Washington Gladden even expected to see, in the not too distant future, public "collective industry existing side by side with private industries, and no hard and fast line dividing them."[84]

Other progressive campaigns concentrated on limiting the impact of plutocratic political power. Reformers pushed for bans on corporate contributions to political campaigns and new election rules that would enable voters to run detours around lawmakers beholden to plutocrats. Voters, progressives argued, needed the right to "recall" corrupted elected officials and vote down, in referendum balloting, any corrupt laws these lawmakers might pass. Voters also needed to be able to initiate their own laws. Finally, and perhaps most fundamentally, voters deserved the right to directly elect the members of the United States Senate.

State legislators had up until then always chosen US senators, as constitutionally mandated. The nation's wealthiest deeply appreciated this arrangement. A state legislative majority, after all, cost a good deal less to buy than a majority vote in a general election. And plutocrats bought with abandon, none more so than William Andrews Clark, the Montana copper mining mogul Mark Twain would later label "as rotten a human being as can be found anywhere under the flag."[85] In 1899, the Democrat Clark bribed enough Republican state legislators to get himself selected to the Senate, then bribed the grand jury convened to investigate the original bribery. In early 1900 the Senate would refuse to seat him. But later that year Clark would bankroll enough candidacies in state legislative races to get himself selected to the Senate once again, this time without having to bribe anyone.[86]

Clark served a full Senate term starting in 1901, and devoted himself to the counterattack against President Theodore Roosevelt's landmark moves to protect the nation's natural resources from corporate despoliation. Clark, a major despoiler himself, did his best to make life miserable for Gifford Pinchot, the first chief of the US Forest Service.

"Those who succeed us," Senator Clark would declare in the debate over creating a national forest system, "can well take care of themselves."

Conservationists like Gifford Pinchot, the older brother of activist New York attorney Amos Pinchot, would come to see their struggle to safeguard the environment as a struggle against plutocracy as well. Pinchot noted in a 1910 address that reformers dedicated to conservation believe "that all the people ought to get from our natural resources every advantage they can yield, both now and hereafter." But all the people would never enjoy these resources, continued Pinchot, "if the big fellows get an undue share of the wealth of the earth."[87]

Those "big fellows," progressives ultimately agreed, could only be tamed by government's most basic authority, the power to tax. "It is idle to say we are helpless," Louis Brandeis would put it. "By taxation bigness can be destroyed."[88] But which tax? Governments in the United States had, of course, been taxing one form of wealth—real estate property—for generations. This "property tax" worked "well enough," notes historian M. Susan Murnane, in an agricultural society where "visible taxable property seemed to approximate real economic power."[89] But traditional property taxes left the new fortunes of America's industrial age largely untouched.

Some reformers in the early 1900s pushed what they called a "progressive property tax." Charles Howell, an editor and prosecutor in Michigan, proposed amending the Constitution with "a direct, annual, national, individual, graduated property tax" on all "lands, cash, stocks, bonds, investment securities, and real and personal property." The first $100,000 worth of such property would face a .0005 percent tax rate, or fifty dollars of tax. That rate would rise by $100,000 increments all the way up to 100 percent. Howell considered his proposal a counterweight to "the illusive dreams of socialists." A progressive property tax would bring about "the inauguration, enforcement, and perpetuity of economic liberty."[90] Such a levy, like-minded reformer William Vickroy Marshall opined, would "end the domination of the trusts and monopolies by rendering it unprofitable to effect combinations of 'predatory' wealth."[91]

But most progressive interest in taxing property would revolve around the property the wealthy left behind at death. In the 1890s, a number of states had begun levying taxes on inheritances at rates that rose progressively higher as the size of the inheritance increased. By 1900, New York, Illinois, Michigan, and Wisconsin were all taxing inheritances at these "graduated" rates.[92] The federal government had had a modest inheritance tax in effect during the Civil War, and an inheritance levy would resurface in 1898 during the Spanish-American War. This second inheritance tax, enacted purely as an emergency revenue-raising measure, would not linger long past the war's end. By 1902, the federal government had no inheritance tax on the wealthy in place—and no income tax either, after the Supreme Court struck down as unconstitutional an income tax enacted in 1894.

In the wake of that Supreme Court ruling, advocacy for taxing the incomes of rich people shifted to the state level. In Wisconsin, "Fighting Bob" La Follette would become governor in 1900 running on a platform that decried "the encroachment of the powerful few upon the rights of the many." The Republican La Follette, notes historian Nancy Unger, considered the income tax "the only effective way to reach the invisible wealth of powerful parasites." A decade of local struggle later, Wisconsin and four other states would have income tax laws on the books.[93]

Meanwhile, in academia, a new generation of professional economists was making the case for tax policies that aimed to more equitably distribute the nation's tax burden. All citizens, argued Columbia University's Edwin Seligman and his colleagues, ought to contribute to government's upkeep based on their "ability to pay"—and the wealthy had a far greater ability to pay than the poor.[94] In the early 1900s the actual federal tax system in place had this "ability to pay" principle upside down. Between high tariffs on imported goods and excise taxes on alcohol and tobacco products, federal taxation was actively *widening* the nation's grand economic divide.

High tariffs had evolved into a matter of solemn political faith for Republican leaders in Congress. But other Republicans, most notably President Roosevelt, were moving in the opposite direction. In December 1906, five years into his presidency, the unpredictable TR would deliver a presidential address that totally startled his party's Brahmins and vindicated one wag's claim that the "two most extraordinary things in America" had to be "Niagara Falls and Theodore Roosevelt."[95]

"The National Government has long derived its chief revenue from a tariff on imports and from an internal or excise tax," the president noted. "In addition to these there is every reason why, when next our system of taxation is revised, the National Government should impose a graduated inheritance tax, and, if possible, a graduated income tax.[96]

No president had ever so explicitly endorsed the principle of progressive taxation. Roosevelt even advanced a philosophic rationale for his new tax-the-rich stance: "The man of great wealth owes a peculiar obligation to the State because he derives special advantages from the mere existence of government." We need, the president continued, "to distribute the burden of supporting the Government more equitably than at present." And the nation could do that distributing by placing "a constantly increasing burden on the inheritance of those swollen fortunes which it is certainly of no benefit to this country to perpetuate."

A half century later, Franklin Roosevelt's tax adviser Randolph Paul would look back at Theodore Roosevelt's 1906 tax speech and marvel. Teddy, Paul noted, was most certainly "airing unorthodox views about leveling off the inequalities of fortune prevailing in the country." Unorthodox, that is, for Washington, DC. Elsewhere in America, beyond Pennsylvania Avenue, tax-the-rich sentiment united radicals and respectable reformers more than any other cause.

Many of these reformers followed Roosevelt and emphasized the inheritance tax as a means to "mitigate" existing inequalities.

"The preservation intact of a fortune over a certain amount," Herbert Croly asserted in his 1909 *Promise of American Life*, "is not desirable either in the public or individual interest."[97]

The rich man, Croly explained, "cannot possibly spend his income save by a recourse to wild and demoralizing extravagance." And philanthropic good works, Croly added, in no way obviate the need for taxing grand fortune.

"If wealth, particularly when accumulated in large amounts, has a public function, and if its possession imposes a public duty," he noted, "a society is foolish to leave such a duty to the accidental good intentions of individuals."

Political developments overseas would reinforce the growing American support for progressive taxation. In Britain, Chancellor of the Exchequer David Lloyd George introduced a revolutionary "People's Budget" in 1909 that upped the already existing British inheritance tax and turned Britain's modest income tax into a graduated income levy that taxed income in the highest bracket at triple the rate on income in the lowest. Britain, Lloyd George pronounced, needed to place its tax "burdens on the broadest shoulders."

"There are many in the country blessed by providence with great wealth," he added, "and if there are amongst them men who grudge out of their riches a fair contribution towards the less fortunate of their fellow-countrymen, they are very shabby rich men."[98]

In the United States, the shabby rich men were losing ground, and they knew it. In 1907, a young Tennessee congressman, Cordell Hull, had introduced a federal income tax bill that went nowhere in the Republican-controlled Congress. But the Democrats would add an income tax constitutional amendment plank to their 1908 party platform—"to the end that wealth may bear its proportionate share of the burdens of the Federal Government"—and William Howard Taft, the 1908 Republican nominee, saw so much popular support for the Democratic Party position that he came out for an income tax, too. This support for taxing the rich stamped Taft as a reformer and helped cement his triumph in the November 1908 general election.

Once elected, Taft would let Republican leaders in Congress

maneuver to keep the tax status quo in place. These Brahmins agreed to a compromise with their progressive rivals. Under the terms of the deal, reformers would accept another round of high tariffs. The Brahmins would accept a moderate new tax on corporations and a move to place before the states a constitutional amendment supporting the income tax. This income tax amendment would need to gain approval from three-quarters of America's state legislatures to become the law of the land. Republican congressional leaders gave that outcome no possible chance.

Their confidence at first appeared well founded. In New York State, Wall Street's political base, the Republican assembly majority in Albany would crush the income tax amendment in three separate 1910 votes.[99] Any federal income levy, Republican income tax opponents argued, would constitute an unfair assault on New York, the home to more affluent citizens than any other state. New Yorkers, they claimed, would pay one-eighth of the nation's total income tax bill.[100]

Outside New York, income tax amendment opponents argued the exact opposite. A federal income tax, Kentucky Governor Augustus Willson asserted, would have no impact whatsoever on the nation's most affluent, the "Carnegies and Rockefellers and other multi-millionaires."

"Under our present system of taxation it is the mass of the people who bear the burden, not the multi-millionaires," the governor protested. "Under a Federal income tax the same condition would exist."[101]

The "Carnegies and Rockefellers," for their part, simply argued that the government had no business taxing their incomes.

"When a man has accumulated a sum of money within the law, that is to say, in the legally correct way," old John D. Rockefeller intoned, "the people no longer have any right to share in the earnings resulting from the accumulation."[102]

The people disagreed. In the 1910 elections, progressives swept to resounding victories. Democrats nationally won the House of Representatives for the first time in two decades, unseating forty-one conservative Republican incumbents.[103] In state after state, including New York, the Republicans lost legislative majorities. In state after state, the new majorities began endorsing the income tax amendment.

Any savvy political observer could now see clearly that the political momentum had shifted against plutocracy and the politicos who carried plutocracy's water. Progressives were charging ahead, and the nation's most ambitious political hopefuls were rushing to catch up with their charge. No one would rush any faster than Woodrow Wilson, the son of a Southern clergyman who had become president of Princeton University in 1902.

Before 1910, Wilson had nothing particularly progressive about him. In 1896, he had opposed the Populists and William Jennings Bryan. As late as 1908, notes historian Melvin Urofsky, Wilson was praising the trusts for "adding so enormously to the economy and efficiency of the nation's productive work" and condemning any government regulation of business as a slide down the slippery slope to socialism.[104] At his best, the moralistic Wilson could be a principled voice against individual political corruption. At his worst, he remained a bigot who welcomed the vicious new age of segregation that had emerged in the 1890s. At Princeton, Wilson steadfastly maintained the university's ban on admitting black students.[105] His 1902 book, *History of the American People*, would reveal an almost equally profound contempt for America's new immigrants. Italians, Hungarians, and Poles, Wilson wrote, had "neither skill nor energy nor any initiative of quick intelligence."[106]

But Wilson had enough "quick intelligence" of his own to realize he would never get anywhere in politics without progressive support. In 1910, Wilson ran for governor of New Jersey as a reformer and once in office actually did some reforming. His first year as governor would bring a series of progressive victories: a workman's compensation law to protect injured workers, a new commission to regulate public utilities, as well as a direct primary law and other political reforms.[107] As governor, Wilson also spoke out against the nation's "money monopoly," the "few men" in whose hands control of the nation's credit had "concentrated." Their "great undertakings," Wilson charged, "chill and check and destroy genuine economic freedom."[108]

Wilson's oratorical skills could give these charges compelling resonance. By word and deed, he now seemed to speak to the nation's reforming spirit. By the end of 1911, reform-minded Democratic Party insiders had come to view Wilson as prime presidential timber. He seemed a winner—and the upcoming 1912 election, top Democrats agreed, could be won.

Republicans had run the White House ever since the Civil War, except for two brief interludes under the conservative Democrat Grover Cleveland. Now they had split. The party establishment stood behind Theodore Roosevelt's handpicked successor, William Howard Taft. Wall Street had found President Taft a dependable figure. The party's progressive insurgents, by contrast, considered him little more than a plutocratic pawn.

This entire situation pained Ex-President Roosevelt. Teddy had left the United States for a triumphal world tour a month after Taft's March 1909 inauguration. He returned fourteen months later to find that his personal choice for the White House had essentially "cast his lot" with the Republican Party's most reactionary wing.[109] Taft had let the Brahmins call the shots in the tariff battle. Even more shockingly, Taft had even fired the Roosevelt administration's most widely admired champion of progressive values, US Forest Service chief Gifford Pinchot.

Angry Republican insurgents, Roosevelt feared, might do something rash. Angry voters might too. To avert these disasters, Roosevelt set out to heal his party. He embarked in the summer of 1910 on a cross-country tour that would have him enunciate progressive principles and campaign for the GOP candidates who espoused them. The subsequent public pressure, Roosevelt assumed, would force President Taft to beat a quick retreat from his rightward drift, allowing Roosevelt to then endorse Taft's reelection bid in 1912. Insurgents would fall in line behind TR's leadership, and the GOP's hold on the White House would be secure for another four years.[110]

The plan seemed to make good political sense, at least to Roosevelt, and on August 23, 1910, he left his Long Island home for a nineteen-day, fourteen-state marathon that would take him as far west as Colorado. The tour's most important engagement would come August 31 in Osawatomie, Kansas, where Roosevelt had an invitation to help dedicate the historic town's John Brown Memorial Park.[111] The grateful Kansans pulled out all the stops for Roosevelt, the "world's most popular citizen" after his global tour. By the appointed day, Osawatomie had never looked better: a new park, streets swept clear of debris, foul-smelling ditches covered over.

"We are ready for plutocrat and peasant," exulted one local editor, "to honor the ground where John Brown made his decisive stand for freedom."[112]

The plutocrats never did show, but average Kansans did. They started arriving the day before TR's scheduled appearance, in a driving rain, by foot and bicycle, motorcar and wagon. The rain, fortunately, stopped before the mud became too deep, and Roosevelt would have

open skies when he stepped up onto his podium—a kitchen table—
to begin his address before a crowd of thirty thousand. The "surging
throng," chronicles historian Robert La Forte, "continually cheered"
for the next hour and a half.

Roosevelt's address would outline a progressive vision for the 1912
Republican Party platform. TR covered all the progressive bases: Our
national resources, he pronounced, must not be "monopolized for the
benefit of the few." We must "prohibit the use of corporate funds
directly or indirectly for political purposes" and hold corporate officials "personally responsible when any corporation breaks the law."
Again and again, Roosevelt urged his cheering listeners to demand
state and national "restraint upon unfair money-getting." The absence
of that restraint, he noted, "has tended to create a small class of enormously wealthy and economically powerful men, whose chief object
is to hold and increase their power."

We should permit fortunes "to be gained," Roosevelt continued,
"only so long as the gaining represents benefit to the community." And
even those fortunes, Roosevelt added, needed to be checked because
the "really big fortune, the swollen fortune, by the mere fact of its size
acquires qualities" that "differentiate it in kind as well as in degree
from what is possessed by men of relatively small means," qualities
that help ensure the "political domination of money."

To check the growth and limit the power of these fortunes, Roosevelt called for a progressive income tax and an "inheritance tax on big
fortunes, properly safeguarded against evasion and increasing rapidly
in amount with the sizes of the estate." We need, Roosevelt roared,
to "destroy privilege." Ruin for our democracy will be "inevitable if
our national life brings us nothing better than swollen fortunes for
the few."

The assembled Kansans roared back their approval. Back East, apologists for grand fortune would be aghast. Editorial writers labeled the
speech "frankly socialistic." A later historian, George Mowry, would
call TR's talk, soon to be known as his "New Nationalism" address,
"the most radical speech ever given by an ex-President."[43]

Republican progressives would be jubilant, as well they should
have been. One of their own, Gifford Pinchot, had written the speech.
But Roosevelt would not rejoice in their jubilation. He apparently
never expected a conservative Republican reaction as negative as the
one he received. His grand plan was falling apart. His progressive
public pronouncements were deepening the party split. In the 1910

congressional elections, Republican progressives would largely hold their own. Conservatives would suffer crushing defeats. Roosevelt had hoped to unite and strengthen his party. His party, instead, now limped, deeply divided, into the 1912 presidential year.

After the 1910 elections, Roosevelt himself initially disavowed any interest in running against Taft in 1912, and Republican insurgents would rally instead around "Fighting Bob" La Follette from Wisconsin. But La Follette's candidacy would self-destruct early in 1912 at the annual banquet of the American magazine publishers association in Philadelphia. Woodrow Wilson spoke first and "held the eight hundred guests spell-bound."[114] Then an overtired La Follette, apparently distraught over an impending operation for his daughter, rose and began to attack the assembled media moguls in an incoherent address that lasted two-and-a-half embarrassing hours. La Follette didn't sit down until after midnight. By then the hall had emptied. La Follette would suspend his campaign the next day and go on sick leave. His 1912 presidential bid would never recover.

The Pinchot brothers, Gifford and Amos, and other top Republican progressives would now declare for Roosevelt, and the ex-president, under increasing pressure to save the party from Taft, officially announced his bid for the GOP nomination three weeks after La Follette's meltdown.

That bid would soon become an energetic candidacy against plutocracy. Americans, TR would tell a Carnegie Hall audience late in March 1912, "are today suffering from tyranny." A small minority "is grabbing our coal deposits," lurking "behind monopolistic trusts," and "battening in the sale of adulterated drugs."[115]

Roosevelt, Taft retorted before the Massachusetts GOP primary, was making "adroit appeals to discontent and class hatred."[116] Republican voters, to the party leadership's chagrin, found these appeals attractive. Roosevelt topped Taft handily in primary voting. But only a few states in 1912 were selecting convention delegates via primaries. State party machines would choose the bulk of the delegates to the Chicago 1912 GOP convention, and those state parties supported Taft. That June, in Chicago, the Republican Party would give Taft his renomination. The Roosevelt forces immediately bolted and announced a new Progressive Party.

"At present both the old parties are controlled by professional politicians in the interest of the privileged classes," candidate Roosevelt told the crowd gathered for the founding convention of the new party in August. "This is class government, and class government of a peculiarly unwholesome kind."[117]

"Our aim," TR promised, "is to promote prosperity and then see to its proper division."[118]

With the new Progressive Party up and running, the stage would now be set for plutocracy's political humiliation. Four substantial candidates would vie for the White House in the 1912 presidential election. Three of them—Roosevelt for the Progressive Party, Woodrow Wilson for the Democrats, and Eugene Debs for the Socialist Party—would make plutocracy, in one guise or another, their prime target.

Amos Pinchot, the new Progressive Party's chief communicator, would position Roosevelt's race at every opportunity as a campaign against plutocratic privilege. The American people, Pinchot would write in one broadside, had allowed "an uncontrolled industrial oligarchy to assume, and use for its own purposes, a tremendous and arrogant power." This plutocracy had the "power to rob the people by great tariffs" and the "power to drive little children to mines, factories, and sweat shops," the "power to dominate two great political parties," and the "power to monopolize the vast natural resources that are the source of our nation's wealth."[119]

"The Progressive Movement is radical because it has real problems to solve," Pinchot would continue. "It is a practical movement because it deals chiefly with a more just distribution of wealth, which is at the very bottom of the bread question in every land and age."

That same unjust distribution of wealth would figure large in the Democratic Party's 1912 campaign themes. The party platform would hit hard on Republican support for high tariffs. The problem with those tariffs? Explained the platform: "The high Republican tariff is the principal cause of the unequal distribution of wealth; it is a system of taxation which makes the rich richer and the poor poorer."[120]

But the Democrats had no coherent program to rival Roosevelt's "New Nationalism," and Wilson would be smart enough to realize he needed his own inspirational platform to gain national credibility as a reformer. Louis Brandeis gave him that credibility. The "New Freedom" that Brandeis supplied Wilson went after Roosevelt's stance on the great industrial monopolies. Roosevelt's Progressive Party, as Brandeis explained to Wilson, believed that private monopolies "should be made 'good' by regulation." The New Freedom, by contrast, holds "that competition can be and should be restored in those branches of industry in which it has been suppressed by the trusts." And "if at any future time monopoly should appear to be desirable in any branch of industry," Brandeis added, "the monopoly should be a public one— monopoly owned by the people and not by the capitalists."[121]

Wilson would never spell out to voters his "New Freedom" in any detail. But he did follow the basic outlines of the Brandeis script, emphasizing over and over the struggle against the plutocratic few.

"The government of the United States is not free," Wilson told a September campaign crowd in Columbus, Ohio, "because it takes its counsel with regard to the economic policy of the United States from a very limited group of persons; and so long as it takes its counsel from that limited group of persons it cannot serve the interests of the nation as a whole."[122]

"We are going to consult a great many people," Wilson told a Pittsburgh gathering the next month, "instead of a very few people."[123]

Wilson's "New Freedom" would be just enough to give progressive Democrats sufficient reason not to bolt to Roosevelt. Wilson might be vague, but he had full-throated support from Brandeis. That gave progressive Democrats all the reassurance they needed.

The fourth significant candidate in the race, Gene Debs, would be far more vivid than vague. Debs would vow in his acceptance speech to "tear up privilege by the roots."[124] In his first stump address, delivered in Chicago, he lashed out against "the plutocrats, the politicians, the bribe-givers, the ballot-box stuffers" and contrasted "the parasites in palaces and automobiles and honest workers in hovels and tramping the ties."[125]

The incumbent president Taft, meanwhile, knew he had no chance. He gave just two major speeches during the entire campaign. In the first, he positioned himself as the race's only upholder of economic orthodoxy. Roosevelt and Wilson, Taft charged, were foolishly attempting to legislate equality. Their proposals invited a "condition in which the rich are to be made reasonably poor and the poor reasonably rich by law."[126]

In the end, Taft would receive fewer than 3.5 million votes out of over fifteen million cast, less than a quarter of the total. The election victory went easily to Wilson, as expert political observers expected. Wilson only received 42 percent of the vote, but with Republicans split that would easily be enough. Roosevelt followed with 27 percent. Debs tallied just over nine hundred thousand votes, 6 percent of the total, well over double the Socialist Party vote four years earlier.

The Debs vote would actually be a disappointment to the Socialist camp. The Socialists had much higher hopes. But fierce internal battles between the party's right and left would prove major distractions. Roosevelt's Progressive Party, by championing an eight-hour day, a federal Department of Labor, and a host of other longstanding Socialist Party platform planks, also stole a good bit of the socialist thunder. A *Harper's Weekly* cartoon would capture the Socialist Party predicament. The cartoon featured an exasperated Gene Debs standing naked in a swimming hole while a grinning Theodore Roosevelt rushed away from the scene with a set of clothes labeled "Socialism" dangling over his shoulder.[127]

The newly elected president, Woodrow Wilson, had in no way led the popular surge against plutocracy in 1912. He merely rode the wave. The wave rolled on after November. Wilson kept riding.

The first piece of progressive business after the election would be ending plutocracy's free pass at tax time. In February 1913, Delaware became the last of the thirty-six states needed to ratify the income tax amendment to the Constitution. Congress now had the constitutional authority to tax the incomes of America's most affluent. By October, after House and Senate action, a historic new income tax had gone into effect. The new tax would burden only the affluent. No married couple earning less than $4,000 per year, the equivalent of about $90,000 today, would pay one cent in federal income tax. The greater the income above that threshold, the higher the tax rate.

This principle of "graduation" represented a victory for congressional progressives. Conservative Democrats had sought a "flat" rate for the new income tax. They wanted all income above the $4,000 threshold to face the same tax rate. Progressives argued for rates graduated steeply enough to start narrowing America's vast divide between the rich and everyone else. Representative Ira Copley, a progressive Republican from Illinois, called these steeply graduated rates "the best way of equalizing the opportunities which society in this country offers to certain men in securing more than their fair share of the benefits derived from the labors of other men."[128] Copley wanted graduated rates in the new federal income tax to top off at 68 percent.

The compromise that Congress eventually struck would give Copley and the progressives their graduated rates but at far lower levels than progressives felt essential. The first $16,000 over the $4,000 threshold would face a 1 percent federal tax rate. Taxpayers in the five tax brackets over $20,000 would pay that 1 percent plus a surtax that would rise up to 6 percent on income over $500,000. No millionaires in America, under the new income tax act, would pay over 7 percent of any income dollar in federal tax.

The first modern federal income tax, in other words, would have value more symbolic than real. The federal government at long last was finally taxing the rich, not just ordinary citizens. But the modest new federal income tax posed no danger to great fortune. America's richest would be inconvenienced, nothing more. Still, progressives could see advancement and even feel some pride. The rich, after all, had gone years without feeling any inconvenience.

This same pattern—a major reform, a minor result—would repeat over and over in Woodrow Wilson's early years as president. The new Federal Reserve System, created in 1913, would give the federal government a regulatory role over banking, but the new system would leave the big Wall Street banks in position to essentially control any major regulatory outcomes.[129] The new Federal Trade Commission had the power to issue cease and desist orders against monopolistic marketplace maneuvers. But the rulings of this new commission, as one historian notes, would be "subject to judicial review in courts that were well beyond the reach of the people's elected tribunes."[130] And the Clayton Antitrust Act of 1914—the Wilson administration's most acclaimed initiative against monopoly power—would most definitely expand the federal government's capacity to block corporate mergers and predatory pricing schemes. But the legislation in no way merited the "labor's *Magna Carta*" plaudits that AFL president Samuel Gompers gave it. Courts would continue to harass unions with injunctions, even with the Clayton Act in effect.

Louis Brandeis would later look back with some satisfaction on the early Wilson years. Woodrow Wilson, he felt strongly, had "changed the atmosphere" in Washington. The years 1913 and 1914, Brandeis believed, would be "the only time in recent American history when rich men had not had an undue influence with an administration."[131]

The influence of America's wealthy, while perhaps less "undue," did remain substantial. Wilson's New Freedom left untouched the basic structure of the new finance capitalism that had emerged in the 1890s. Wall Street would continue to operate, notes historian Lawrence Mitchell, as "an institution that facilitated the accumulation of wealth from speculation." Progressive lawmakers had introduced legislation before Wilson's election that would have significantly restricted this speculating. One bill would have permitted corporations to issue stock only "to finance legitimate revenue-generating industrial activities," a restriction that would have prevented Wall Street's movers and shakers from issuing stock solely to finance big-time speculative plays. But no bill along these lines would ever gain serious consideration. Business, notes Mitchell, would remain free "to organize, capitalize, and manage as it saw fit."[132] In the process, the incomes of America's business titans continued to rise. Between 1913 and 1916 the incomes of the nation's richest 0.01 percent nearly doubled.[133]

Yet progressives of various stripes still had cause for optimism. Public sentiment against plutocracy was continuing to build, and Wilson knew it. With his 1916 reelection bid looming, the president moved beyond his political comfort zone and began backing more aggressive legislation to protect Americans from plutocratic predation. Important legislation rushed through Congress in a torrent. The Kern-McGillicuddy Workingmen's Compensation Act gave federal workers disability insurance protection and gave states a model for protecting their own private and public sector workers. The Keating-Owen Child Labor Act banned in interstate commerce the sale of goods that corporations had exploited children to manufacture. By Election Day in 1916, notes historian Melvin Urofsky, Congress had essentially "enacted every important plank in the Progressive Party platform of 1912."[134]

The Supreme Court, to be sure, would later rule the Keating-Owen Act unconstitutional. But even here, on the Supreme Court front, progressives had reason to cheer. In January 1916, Wilson nominated America's most acclaimed progressive reformer, Louis Brandeis, for the nation's highest court. Progressives would be jubilant. Wilson, pronounced Republican insurgent Bob La Follette, "has rendered a great public service." The president, added Roosevelt supporter Amos Pinchot, had made a decision that took "courage."[135] Conservatives would be furious. Ex-president Taft denounced Brandeis as "a muckraker, an emotionalist for his own purposes, a socialist, prompted by jealousy," a man of "infinite cunning" and "much power for evil."[136]

"The real crime of which this man is guilty," countered Brandeis supporter Senator Thomas Walsh of Montana, "is that he has exposed the iniquities of men in high places in our financial system. He has not stood in awe of the majesty of wealth."[137]

Five months later, in June 1916, the Senate confirmed the Brandeis nomination. The reform tide had never risen higher, and even higher tides seemed to beckon. In the fall's election campaign, reformers would unite enthusiastically behind Wilson. Amos Pinchot had never before voted for a Democrat. But he would line up for Wilson's reelection campaign an all-star lineup of progressive celebrities that ranged from the philosopher John Dewey to America's most eminent rabbi, Stephen Wise. Americans needed Wilson in the White House, Pinchot told a rally of five thousand in Troy, New York, because "the bench and the bar of this country have taken the side of plutocracy and special privilege." Woodrow Wilson, Pinchot and his "Wilson Volunteers" would emphasize repeatedly, had taken on "the moneyed interests." Newspaper coverage of the progressive tour would hammer home the same theme. One headline for Rochester's daily *Democrat and Chronicle* read simply, "Wilson Fighting Wall Street."[138]

Meanwhile, at the state level, real socialists—as opposed to the variety conservatives charged Brandeis to be—were exploring unconventional electoral strategies and scoring surprising progressive triumphs. In 1915, North Dakota socialist activists broke away from the Socialist Party and formed a new "Nonpartisan League" that would battle *inside* the Republican Party to advance socialist demands. By the following April this new Nonpartisan League would have forty thousand North Dakotan members. Six months later, in the November 1916 elections, Nonpartisan League candidates would sweep to victory in statewide races, including the North Dakota gubernatorial contest, on a platform that called for a graduated income tax, a state-owned bank, and state ownership of flourmills and other industries that directly served farmers.[139]

Socialists were running and winning as Republicans. Republican progressives were cheering on to reelection a Democratic Party president who dared grace the Supreme Court with plutocracy's least favorite reformer. By the end of 1916, anything seemed possible. Greater progress against plutocracy seemed inevitable.

More gains would indeed come in the years ahead. But plutocracy would push back much more brutally than progressives had expected—or could withstand.

Chapter Three

WORLD WAR AND THE WEALTHY

On this spring evening, at New York's Park Avenue Hotel, polite society would not be particularly polite. Only three weeks earlier, on April 6, 1917, Congress had declared war on Germany, and now the grande dames of New York had gathered under the auspices of the Women's City Club to contemplate the grand question that declaration had left hanging. Namely, how would this war be financed?

Gentlemen and ladies of distinction filled the hotel ballroom. They all shared a rather significant stake in the evening's discussion. Together, they held a good many of the millions the nation needed to wage the new war. How would the nation get at those millions? By borrowing from men of wealth and their ladies? Or by taxing their millions away?

The Women's City Club had brought in two eminent speakers to enlighten the evening's three hundred guests. A banker and a reformer. But not just any banker and not just any reformer. The banker, Frank A. Vanderlip, had served nearly two decades earlier as the assistant US secretary of the treasury. Vanderlip had arranged the loans that bankrolled the Spanish-American War. He had gone on to become the president of the formidable National City Bank and ranked as Wall Street's most estimable financial statesman. In America's reform pantheon, New York attorney Amos Pinchot held an equally prominent place. Pinchot had been a prime mover behind Theodore Roosevelt's Progressive Party bid in 1912 and among Woodrow Wilson's most energetic champions in 1916. He was currently making headlines as chairman of the American War Finance Committee, a newly organized initiative that counted within its ranks many of America's leading reformers, everyone from Jane Addams to Rabbi Stephen Wise.

Vanderlip spoke first, and his presentation went well. Americans of means, the bank president noted, love their country. In its hour of need, they will most certainly come to its aid. They will, he had no doubt, buy government bonds in generous quantities. And every liberty bond they purchase will bring victory—and liberty for all—ever closer.

Amos Pinchot's remarks would go less smoothly. Fabian Franklin, a fiercely conservative editor at the New York *Evening Post*, began taunting Pinchot soon after he began speaking. Franklin's outburst, the *New York Times* would report, "evoked an uproar of laughter" at Pinchot's expense. The unruly "demonstration," the *Times* dispatch went on, reflected "a desire to rebuke" Pinchot for his insufficiently patriotic views.

Eventually, Pinchot regained the audience's attention. More trouble. He "appeared to convey the impression," the *Times* reported, "that the rich were not willing to do their share in the war." Cries of "No! No!" rang out from the ballroom. But Pinchot didn't flinch. The new war, he predicted, would not have broad support, and neither would the conscription of young Americans to do battle. Such a war "fought 3,000 miles away," Pinchot told his finely attired audience, "cannot be popular."

By this time, some listeners had started hissing. Over near Miss Belle da Costa Greene, the librarian at the magnificent J. Pierpont Morgan Library, several women were shouting that the war most definitely was popular. Poor Amos Pinchot, Yale class of 1897, at that point lost all sense of proper decorum.

"Well, I do not believe it is," he retorted to the angry matrons. "I have my own views."

The views of Amos Pinchot did not carry that April evening. "Diners, Angered, Rebuke Pinchot," as the *New York Times* headline blared the next morning.[1] But Pinchot's views would have far more impact in the years immediately ahead than Pinchot or his exceedingly hostile well-heeled audience could have ever imagined. The great global conflict would turn the US tax code—for the first time ever—into a hammer mighty enough to pound down plutocracy.

Just what, at root, did Amos Pinchot believe? Pinchot most certainly did not believe that any good could come from the horrible slaughter in Europe. Over the previous three years, ever since the European war's outbreak in August 1914, he had watched the slaughter slow the American reform movement's forward momentum. Instead of fighting plutocracy, progressives were battling among themselves over "preparedness."

Theodore Roosevelt, reform's most celebrated champion, had returned to his "big stick" jingo roots. By not preparing for war, the old warrior roared in 1915, America was following "a policy of supine inaction."[2] We were letting other nations push us around, sink our ships, bludgeon our friends. By 1916, Roosevelt had totally abandoned reform. In that year's presidential race, he refused to run on the Progressive Party ticket and supported instead the conventional Republican nominee, Charles Evans Hughes. Better a nonreform Republican than a weak-kneed Wilson. For his former reform allies who flocked to Wilson's camp, Roosevelt had nothing but contempt, and he did not hesitate to express it.

"When I spoke of the Progressive Party having a lunatic fringe," Roosevelt wrote Amos Pinchot after Pinchot announced his support for Wilson, "I specifically had you in mind."[3]

The belligerently prowar TR now found himself back in Wall Street's good graces. The biggest names in American finance and industry—Morgan, Rockefeller, Carnegie, Du Pont, Vanderbilt— had a definite self-interest in the European conflict. They had all been junior partners with British bankers for decades, enmeshed together in lucrative investment syndicates that chased windfalls from the Middle East to Latin America.[4] At the war's outbreak in 1914, Britain's movers and shakers had turned to their US business partners for financial support, and Wall Street had promptly invested $2 billion in the British war effort.[5] For America's privileged, a British defeat would certainly be an unpleasant turn of events. But these savvy privileged understood quite clearly that the vast majority of Americans had no stomach for entering the European war on anybody's side. The war camp would not openly push direct US entry into the war, but would instead push "preparedness." We must be prepared to defend our freedom.

Noninterventionists did push back against the rising war fever. The still-potent William Jennings Bryan wing of the Democratic Party would, for instance, pronounce the "preparedness hullabaloo" a "rich man's scare."[6] But the scaring only escalated as the European war wore on, particularly after more than one hundred Americans died in a German U-boat attack on the world's fastest passenger liner, the

Lusitania, in May 1915. The next March, the Mexican revolutionary Pancho Villa raided a New Mexico border town. The brief skirmish left eighteen US citizens dead. The world suddenly seemed a dangerous place. Preparedness seemed a prudent response.

In late summer 1916, a divided Congress approved President Woodrow Wilson's request for a costly military expansion, then set about debating how to pay for it. Tariffs had traditionally supplied a hefty chunk of federal receipts. But the tax reforms of recent years had lowered tariff rates, and the war's disruption of transatlantic trade had reduced tariff revenue even more. The federal government did have the new income tax in place. But the initial tax rates topped off at a mere 7 percent on income over $500,000 and remained much too low to generate appreciable revenue. President Wilson, for his part, was discouraging lawmakers from borrowing to foot the preparedness bill. The "industry of this generation," he stressed, "should pay the bills of this generation."[7]

Wilson's pressure gave lawmakers only two options, and their choice would mark a key turning point in the struggle against plutocracy. Lawmakers could finance Wilson's military expansion by taxing the rich, mainly by building upon the still fledgling federal progressive income tax. Or lawmakers could expand the nation's regressive federal consumption taxes. They could double down on "sin taxes" that targeted drinkers and smokers. They could push America down the road to a national sales tax, a course of action, suggests tax historian W. Elliot Brownlee, that might have shielded wealthy Americans from progressive taxation for generations.[8]

Mainstream Democrats in Congress weren't thinking generations in 1916. They had a general election looming that November. Average Americans, these lawmakers knew all too well, still hadn't warmed to the idea of entering the European conflict. These average Americans weren't going to be happy about paying higher prices on what they consumed to fund preparations for a war they did not want to fight, not when the wealthy were still bearing so light a share of the nation's tax burden.

Progressives in Congress, for their part, had lost the battle to slow the war mobilization. Now they would work "tirelessly," as historian Nancy Unger notes, to prevent America's plutocrats from tightening "their stranglehold on the economy."[9] Progressives would rise up in the preparedness financing debate and push for special tax levies on war contractors and stiff new taxes on excess corporate profits.

And they would call for an estate tax, a direct and permanent federal levy on the grand accumulations of private wealth America's rich left behind at death.

An estate tax, declared Representative Meyer London, the Socialist Party congressman from New York City, would deliver both desperately needed revenue and a powerful body blow against plutocratic power. In the United States, London argued, we do not allow lawmakers to pass their legislative power on to their sons. Why should we as a free people allow the "inheritance of a financial power" that transfers from fathers to sons the power "to shape the life of the country"?[10]

Most Democrats in Congress took a narrower view. They kept their emphasis on revenue alone, on the dollars the federal government needed and rich people had. The Democratic Party, went one typical comment from Representative Charles Crisp from Georgia, had "no fight to make on wealth honestly acquired." But the party believes, Crisp told his colleagues on the Ways and Means Committee, "that a man should contribute to the support and maintenance of the government according to his ability to pay." We can raise, Crisp continued, "the entire amount necessary to pay the expenses of this preparedness from the wealth of the country."[11]

The Capitol Hill mastermind behind the preparedness financial package that would eventually emerge, Representative Cordell Hull from Tennessee, had successfully guided the landmark 1913 federal income tax bill through Congress three years earlier. His new tax legislation would extend that bill's progressive tax principles on a number of fronts. The Revenue Act of 1916 would more than double tax rates for affluent Americans. Income over $2 million would face a 15 percent tax rate, up from 7 percent. Only Americans making over $4,000 would pay any income tax at all, a threshold high enough to keep the income tax a levy on only Americans of substantial means. The new Revenue Act also imposed a tax on the estates the wealthy left behind at death. This new federal estate tax featured graduated rates running from 1 to 10 percent and kicked in on estates valued at over $50,000, a fortune far above the savings most Americans could ever hope to accumulate.[12] For businesses, the Revenue Act had a new tax on war mobilization–related "excess profits." The legislation overall, noted Edwin Seligman, then the nation's premiere academic advocate for progressive taxation, amounted to a victory for "fiscal justice."[13]

Conservatives demurred in that assessment. Republican Representative Richard Wayne Parker from New Jersey complained that Cordell Hull's legislation aimed "to enable 99 people to tax the hundredth man and to put the bulk of the taxation upon the thousandth man."[14]

Congressional Democratic leaders, on the other hand, would be pleased with their handiwork. They had prudently addressed the fiscal emergency. They had raised the tax rate on America's wealthy to what they considered the fullest extent conceivable. None of them could imagine a tax burden on the rich any heavier than the tax rates in the 1916 Revenue Act. Income tax rates, announced Henry Rainey from Illinois, a future House Speaker, had reached their "very highest notch."[15]

Rainey would end up, just a year later, glaringly wrong. What upset his normally astute internal political calculus? War. Real shooting war would finally arrive, and warriors against plutocracy like Amos Pinchot would make the most of it.

Woodrow Wilson won reelection in 1916 campaigning as a peace candidate. His unambiguously simple slogan: "He kept us out of war." But Germans made staying out difficult. In February 1917, their unrestricted submarine warfare began targeting the ships of neutral nations, not just the allied powers. That move, the German high command undoubtedly understood, would almost surely bring the United States into the conflict. The German gamble: Their newly enhanced U-boat fleet would be able to choke off Britain's supply lanes and end the war before any Americans would ever be able to meaningfully engage.

The German choice to make this gamble would confront American progressives with a dreaded choice of their own. Most of the progressive community, respectable reformers and radicals alike, had been opposing the Wall Street war clamor. But war, despite their best efforts, now seemed imminent. Should they swallow hard and give that war their patriotic support or continue their opposition?

The Socialist Party opted for opposition. The European war, Socialists stressed, had always been a rich man's fight. Why should workingmen agree to die in a struggle that would only enrich the already wealthy—at worker expense? Most respectable reformers went the other way. On April 2, 1917, President Wilson had asked

Congress to declare war to make the world "safe for democracy." A war for democracy abroad, reformers argued, would open up new opportunities for enhancing democracy at home.

Resigned-to-war reformers moved with dispatch to seize these opportunities. On March 31, even before Wilson's war message, the national progressive organization that had led the push for peace, the American Union Against Militarism, declared a war of its own, a war on plutocracy. American Union Against Militarism activists would refashion their organization into a new American Committee on War Finance. Its basic goal: to place the war's financial burden on America's most affluent.

"The strongest pacifist influence in America today," the *Chicago Daily News* would report, has "suddenly turned from efforts to prevent war to means of financing it."[16]

"We do not believe," American Committee on War Finance chair Amos Pinchot would tell reporters at the group's launching, "that any real patriot wants the poor people of the nation to bear the burden of the cost of war in addition to the burden of fighting."

The new war's financial burden would be incredibly massive, far greater than Wilson's preparedness drive. And with that greater cost would come starker fiscal options than lawmakers had faced a year earlier in the preparedness debate. The nation could meet the prewar preparedness bill by doubling the highest tax on rich people's income from 7 to 15 percent, a tax hike that left the nation's wealthiest families only slightly inconvenienced. To meet the bill for waging actual war in Europe, such half measures would no longer suffice. Either the nation would have to tax the rich at significantly higher rates or borrow from the rich by selling war bonds, a policy choice that would likely leave the United States even more plutocratic.

This stark choice thrilled reformers in Amos Pinchot's circles, figures like E. W. Scripps, the maverick San Diego publisher who had built up a national newspaper chain and founded the news service that would become United Press International. Scripps and reformers of like mind figured that war would enable a thrust against plutocratic fortune that peace would never countenance.

"The country will be the gainer by tapping and reducing the great fortunes," Scripps wrote Amos Pinchot shortly after the American Committee on War Finance went public, "and once the people learn how easy it is, and how beneficial to all parties concerned it is to get several billions a year by an Income Tax, the country hereafter may be depended upon to raise most, if not all, of the revenues for the Nation, and the States, and the cities from this source."[17]

"I dread the killing of men. I dread the syphilization of vast numbers of our men," Scripps passionately continued, "but I gladly welcome the financial consequences of war."

Summed up the publishing giant: "From the source which none of us have yet even dreamed of—that of the infliction of a great war—we may draw the greatest reform and the greatest blessings to our people."

The American Committee on War Finance would be the vehicle progressives rode to realize these blessings, and Chairman Pinchot drove the committee at an unrelenting pace. Within weeks after the war's declaration, the committee had assembled a network of two thousand volunteers across the country, circulated tens of thousands of "pledge" flyers, and started publishing that pledge as an advertisement in major daily newspapers. Those who signed the pledge were committing themselves "to further the prompt enactment into law" of the boldest tax-the-rich proposal any American political group had ever advanced. They were demanding a cap on income, what the committee would call "a conscription of wealth." No American, the committee tax plan for the war proposed, ought to be able to retain after taxes "an annual net income in excess of $100,000"—and this income limit should remain in effect "until all bonds and other obligations issues for war purposes are paid."[18]

The detailed version of the committee's tax plan called for a 2 percent "normal" tax on income over $3,000 for couples, with a series of steeply graduated surtax charges above that, ending with a 98 percent levy on all income over $150,000. The bottom line: No one, after taxes, would have a residual income above $100,000, a bit over $1.75 million in today's dollars.

The committee's initial pledge leaflet carried endorsements from nineteen prominent progressive leaders and personalities. Among them: famed muckraker Will Irwin, publisher E. W. Scripps, and Sidney Hillman, the leader of the Amalgamated Clothing Workers of America, by some measure the nation's most innovative and successful trade union. Amos Pinchot himself would become a "conscription of wealth" whirlwind, writing, speaking, and reaching out in ever-wider circles.

"If the government has a right to confiscate one man's life for public purposes," he pronounced soon after the group's entry onto the national political stage, "it certainly ought to have the right to confiscate another man's wealth for the same purposes."

The basic committee pamphlet—entitled *Who Shall Pay for the War?*—provided a deepened tax-the-rich analysis. Americans of means, the pamphlet noted, "cannot bear the main burden of defending the nation in the field or on the sea because there are not enough of them." But these Americans of means "can and should bear the money burden." Declared the committee: "A large war tax, even to the point of taking all above an income of $100,000 a year, would not in any way cripple or discourage these more fortunate citizens." Indeed, the pamphlet went on, "reducing large incomes for the period of the war and until the war debt is paid" would have "a salutary effect on the country." Heavy taxes on the rich, "by reducing the demand for luxuries," would "lower the cost of necessaries to the general public" and help prevent the inflation that would otherwise ravage average families.

E. W. Scripps submitted a memorandum to the House Ways and Means Committee that expressed a similar idea:

> Some of us have very large incomes. We employ servants who produce nothing for the common good, and only minister to our vices. We purchase costly and showy clothing, houses, food, furniture, automobiles, jewelry, etc., etc., the production of which has taken the labor of many hundreds of thousands of men and women, who, if they were not so employed would be producing other commodities in such quantity as to cheapen them and make them more accessible to the poor.
>
> An enormously high rate of income tax would have the effect of diverting all this labor, what is given to practically useless things, into other channels where production would be useful to the whole people.[19]

The public reaction to the committee's income cap proposal would be encouraging. Signed pledges, many accompanied by contributions, poured into the committee's Manhattan office. The letters came from every corner of the country—from Osawatomie, Kansas, the site of Teddy Roosevelt's famed 1910 New Nationalism speech, to Terre Haute, Indiana, the hometown of Socialist hero Eugene Debs. From D. B. Byrns, the sales manager of the Detroit Piston Ring Co., and

G. J. DeMars, the proprietor of DeMars Drug Store in Fertile, Minnesota. From Pastor J. Sommerlatte of Baltimore's Zion Reformed Church and Henry Lehr, president emeritus of Ohio Northern University. Miss Sarah Dubow of 20 West 114th Street in New York sent in seventy-five signed pledges, and one Floyd Davis sent in a dozen from Dove Creek, Colorado.

In Ohio, John D. Fackler, a leading Republican progressive, joined with a Du Pont scion to form a Cleveland branch chapter of the national Committee on War Finance. Their organizing would convince the Cleveland City Council to forward Congress a resolution backing the $100,000 income limit. Further west, in Minnesota, the St. Paul Association of Public and Business Affairs, "composed of nearly five thousand business and professional men," adopted a similar resolution urging the "conscription of dollars as well as of men," with the goal of totally absorbing "all incomes in excess of $100,000 per year." Even a New York banker—George Foster Peabody, a former Democratic Party national treasurer—signed on to the "conscription of wealth" cause.

From labor came endorsements from the Brotherhood of Locomotive Engineers and the United Mine Workers. Agricultural leaders formed a Farmers' National Committee on War Finance, led by the secretary of the National Dairy Union and a past master of the Pennsylvania State Grange. From academia came a statement signed by 309 professors of economics from forty-seven colleges and universities including Cornell, Dartmouth, Harvard, the University of Chicago, and Wisconsin.[20] Every citizen, the economists resolved, has a duty "to share in war's burden to his utmost."

"For some the duty is to fight; for others to furnish money," the statement related. "For all the duty is without limit to amount. The citizen who contributes even his entire income, beyond what is necessary to subsistence itself, does less than the citizen who contributes himself to the nation."

Amos Pinchot would inform the press that his committee had also approached "the richest men of the country, including Messrs. Rockefeller, Morgan, Astor, Carnegie," for their support. Unfortunately, he quipped, "there has been no response from those who have added amazingly to their fortunes during the past three years through profits on war materials."

The nation's fabulously wealthy—and their most avid advocates—would respond to the "conscription of wealth" campaign with predictable hysterics. A New York *Evening Sun* editorial would claim that a tax rate of even 40 percent on high incomes would lead to the "destruction of purchasing power" and "economic collapse."[21]

American businessmen will take their capital to Canada, mega-millionaire Otto Kahn threatened in the *New York Times*, if taxed at confiscatory levels, "a development which cannot be without effect upon our own prosperity, resources, and economic power." Amos Pinchot quickly pounced on Kahn's crude threat, pointing out to reporters that Kahn had, since the war began, built himself "an enormous Fifth Avenue palace" and added to his holdings "perhaps the most magnificent country place in America." With the wartime cost of living soaring and thousands of schoolchildren in New York "unable to maintain their grades on account of malnutrition," Pinchot continued, a man of means must have a "certain degree of detachment" from reality "to fight war taxes on wealth."[22]

Kahn quickly realized he had blundered. He told the press that he did "greatly regret" if what he said gave the impression that he was suggesting "the evasion by wealthy men of taxation during the war." He only meant his comments, Kahn insisted, to apply to the *post*war scene. No men of enterprise would ever abandon their nation in wartime, he explained. But after the war young entrepreneurs might be "apt to seek" their fortunes elsewhere "if the reward for enterprise is too greatly diminished in America."[23]

By mid-May 1917, some serious diminishing seemed to have become politically viable. The "conscription of wealth" campaign had redefined the nation's perspective on taxing the rich. Less than a year earlier, after the passage of the 1916 Revenue Act, a tax rate at 15 percent on the nation's highest income bracket appeared impressive. Now Americans were buzzing about the prospect of a 100 percent top-bracket tax rate.

Pinchot would bring that buzz to the nation's capital. On May 15, he testified before the Senate Finance Committee. He explained the American Committee on War Finance proposal and noted the breadth of support the proposal was generating from groups and individuals as diverse as the Congregational Church Conference of Kansas to a governor of a Federal Reserve Board bank. In six weeks' time, Pinchot observed, organizations representing "several million people" had passed "resolutions endorsing our plan and offering co-operation and support."[24] Pinchot linked that support to public disgust at America's staggeringly unequal distribution of wealth. With 2 percent of Americans owning 65 percent of America's wealth, he told Congress, we had been "rather extravagant here in America." We had maintained, "apparently for social or ornamental purposes, a very large number of multi-millionaires." The "conscription of wealth" movement aimed to help the nation put these "ornamental" fortunes to good use.

Pinchot's movement would find in Congress a number of spirited advocates.

"So long as there is an income to be found in the country so large that it yields to its possessor a surplus over and above what he needs for the comfort or even luxuries of life for himself and his family," Robert La Follette told his Senate colleagues, "I am in favor of taking such portion of that surplus income by taxation as the Government needs for war purposes, and if it needs it all, I am in favor of taking it all before we take one penny from the slender income of the man who receives only enough to provide himself and family with the bare necessaries of life."[25]

In the House, Representative Edward Little from Kansas wondered "why a man with over $100,000 income should want to retain a cent of it, above that, when his country needs it." Critics of taxing the nation's surplus income at 100 percent tax, Little noted, were charging that the proposal would be "a tax on success." Retorted Little: "Well, what are you going to lay your taxation on—failure?"[26]

But support for the 100 percent tax-cap proposal would not go beyond Capitol Hill's progressive core. Out of the House Ways and Means Committee came a revenue bill loaded with new consumption taxes on gas, electric lights, telephone and telegraph service, postage stamps, and imports. The income tax rates in the Ways and Means legislation, Amos Pinchot charged, left the nation's super rich in a "privileged position."[27] The Senate Finance Committee bill appeared even worse. Pinchot called it a "disloyal proposal." In September, he sent the House-Senate conference committee working on the revenue legislation a long missive that laid out the pending bill's inadequacies. At that point, Pinchot and his fellow progressives realized that the first round of the war finance battle had not gone their way. Pinchot's powerfully written communication to the conference committee, republished as a pamphlet, would serve as their first salvo in that battle's round two. National labor union and reform journals would run the pamphlet text, often in full, throughout the fall.

"Mr. Pinchot," noted one of those national publications, the *Machinists' Monthly Journal*, in October 1917, "deserves the greatest credit for the fearless manner in which he presents this matter to Congress and the public."[28]

Fearless indeed. Declared Pinchot to the House-Senate conference committee: "It is up to every real American citizen to see to it that the war is conducted honorably, and not degraded into a golden business opportunity for a small minority of unpatriotic persons. Neither the United States nor any other country can carry on a war which will make the world safe for democracy and the plutocracy at the same time. If the war is to serve God, it cannot serve Mammon."[29]

The war revenue bill finally enacted in October 1917 would be a deep disappointment to progressives. Congressman Fiorello LaGuardia, the outspoken radical Republican from New York City, dubbed the legislation "a piece of soak-the-poor legislation." His amendments to exempt America's poorest from consumption taxes on cheap candy and gas bills had all failed. LaGuardia did, notes one biographer, enjoy one brief moment of legislative satisfaction. His colleagues— "less observant than he as to how the rich used their leisure"—had overlooked and let into the final law a LaGuardia amendment that taxed box seats in opera houses.[30]

Progressives saw only faltering half steps toward effective progressive taxation in the new war revenue bill. Instead of taxing the rich, they charged, lawmakers were relying much too heavily on borrowing from them. One leading reform journal, the *Public*, saw "no excuse" for a revenue policy that raises less than a quarter of the war's first-year costs through a "conscription of wealth" and more than three-quarters through borrowing.

"War profits aside," the journal continued, "our vast accumulations of wealth in the hands of a few men controlling our natural resources and the basic industries dependent on them are a national scandal."[31]

Tax historians have generally not shared the harsh contemporary progressive judgment on the 1917 Revenue Act. The legislation, they note, more than quadrupled the tax rate on income over $2 million, from 15 to 67 percent. The Revenue Act also, writes W. Elliot Brownlee, more firmly "embraced" the concept of taxing excess corporate profits. The 1916 tax on the excess profits of munitions makers became in the 1917 Revenue Act "a graduated tax on all business profits above a 'normal' rate of return." The new excess profit tax would rise to 60 percent on profits above a 33 percent rate of return. This taxation, observes Brownlee, "outraged business leaders." Top corporate executives "believed their financial autonomy to be in jeopardy."[32]

"Much like the 1916 act," sum up historians Steven Bank, Kirk Stark, and Joseph Thorndike, the 1917 act had a clear focus on "soaking the rich."[33]

So why did so many World War I–era progressives consider this "soaking" no more painful for the rich than a nice hot bath? They certainly could see that plutocrats—and the corporations that generated their fortunes—now faced substantially higher taxes. In 1916 a wealthy American who reported $300,000 in income, the equivalent of over $5 million today, paid less than $30,000 of that income in federal income tax. That wealthy American's tax bill, after the tax increase in the 1917 Revenue Act, would be almost $93,000 on the same income.

A significant hike, to be sure. But that wealthy taxpayer would have faced a $200,000 tax bill under the "conscription of wealth" proposal. Amos Pinchot and his fellow progressives expected lawmakers in Congress to come much closer to that $200,000 "conscription of wealth" target than $93,000. Their campaign, after all, had won widespread public support. The American people, as Pinchot testified to the Senate Finance Committee in May, "are solidly behind the movement." Yet six months into the war, that movement had fallen short. The egalitarian surge that had been hammering plutocracy ever since the early 1900s—and had been registering steady progress for most of those years—had not been able to push its prized "conscription of wealth" proposal into law.

Why did Pinchot and other reformers fall short? Their movement in 1917 needed more than a widely popular specific tax proposal. The movement needed unity. To have any hope of enacting a proposal as threatening to plutocracy as Amos Pinchot's "conscription of wealth," the egalitarian movement needed the entire progressive community, reformers and radicals alike, pushing together. But a key sector of that community, America's Socialists, would be missing in action. Socialist Party activists did precious little pushing during the war for a "conscription of wealth." They would be too occupied just struggling to survive.

The socialist press had been the radical movement's proudest institutional achievement. Hundreds of newspapers and magazines published in nearly every major language gave millions of Americans—an audience far beyond the dues-paying membership of the

Socialist Party—a monthly, weekly, and even daily alternative to the plutocratic press. Year after year, these periodicals had informed, inspired, and expanded America's progressive rank-and-file.

The war to make the world "safe for democracy" would silence the vast bulk of this vibrant press. The silencer-in-chief would be Postmaster-General Albert Burleson. He would deftly turn the Espionage Act, legislation enacted two months after the United States entered the war, into a sledgehammer against dissident printing presses. The law banned "false reports or false statements with intent to interfere with the operation or success of the military or naval forces of the United States." Burleson would evolve that ban into marching orders for local postmasters that denied mailing rights to any periodicals that would "embarrass or hamper the Government in conducting the war."[34] Under Burleson, local postal authorities could declare a specific issue of any publication "unmailable." Once censored in this manner, a publication could no longer claim to be "continuous" and qualify for subsidized second-class mailing rates. Once denied second-class mailing privileges, dissident publishers could no longer afford to circulate their publications.[35] Burleson went even further with socialist publications that could afford the extra freight. He illegally prevented the *Milwaukee Leader*, the most significant socialist paper in the Midwest, from sending or receiving first-class mail.[36]

Sometimes real sledgehammers, not postal regulations, would silence the socialist press. In Seattle, a mob smashed up the office of the radical *Daily Call*. A few months later, the paper went out of business.[37] To stay in business, the socialist movement's flagship publication, the *Appeal to Reason*, found itself forced to assume a pro-war stance. The paper would never again, after that abject surrender, exhibit the plutocracy-fighting spirit that had made it a global publishing giant. The once-mighty *Appeal* would fade away completely by the early 1920s.[38]

Federal, state, and local authorities—and allied vigilantes—had as little respect for the spoken word as the printed one. Federal agents arrested Eugene Debs for making an antiwar speech in Canton, Ohio. A trial in September 1918 found the words Debs spoke that day— "The master class has always declared the wars: the subject class has always fought the battles"—a violation of the Espionage Act. Debs would get a ten-year sentence.[39]

Other left antiwar groups suffered similar fates. In Minnesota, nineteen counties prohibited the Nonpartisan League from holding any public meetings.[40] In Chicago, federal officials raided the IWW headquarters, confiscated files, and destroyed office equipment and furniture.[41] In the Arizona copper boomtown of Miami, local trade unionists had declared the conflict in Europe a "purely commercial war brought about by the concentration of wealth." Union activists soon faced prowar zealots organized in paramilitary squads. One such vigilante group swept up thousands of strikers from Bisbee and Jerome, stuffed them in sealed railroad boxcars, and "deported" them into the desert. In August 1917, a Montana mob in Butte, another copper mining center, hung a noose around the neck of Wobbly organizer Frank Little, then "cut off his genitals," one historian notes, before flinging "his beaten and mutilated body off a railroad trestle to dangle until he died."[42]

In some parts of the country, mostly ethnic communities where the war remained deeply unpopular, Socialist candidates defying the wartime repression actually sustained or even increased their vote totals. The Wilson administration could censor the *Milwaukee Leader*, the newspaper Socialist congressman Victor Berger edited, but the administration couldn't stop Milwaukee voters from reelecting Berger to Congress. His colleagues in Congress would not be amused. They refused to seat Berger after his 1918 reelection. Voters promptly reelected Berger in a special election. Again Congress refused to seat him. Berger would not get to occupy his rightful place in the House of Representatives until 1922.[43]

Long before then, the Socialist Party had ceased to function as an important national political force. In Oklahoma, site of the party's strongest statewide organization, Socialist electoral support dropped from 21 percent statewide in 1914 to 15 percent in 1916 to 4 percent in 1918.[44] The war to make the world "safe for democracy" had made America a distinctly unsafe place for plutocracy's fiercest foes.

The intense and often rabid wartime suppression of America's Socialist Party overshadowed an equally cruel irony: The Wilson administration, to win the war, was relying on measures that smacked of socialism.

During the war years, observes historian Robert McElvaine, the federal government would manage the US economy "in a completely unprecedented fashion." Some industries—the nation's railroad lines and telegraph operations—would come totally under federal control.

Others remained under private management, but followed directives from the federal government's new War Industries Board. A separate National War Labor Board would keep the "labor peace" by actively encouraging collective bargaining. At every turn, a "planned economy," with workers an acknowledged if junior partner, seemed to be emerging. Some progressive reformers figured this national economic planning would continue to evolve and even blossom in postwar America. The conflict, mused philosopher John Dewey in 1918, had definite "social possibilities."[45]

The Wilson administration's assistant secretary of labor, a veteran progressive stalwart with roots in the Henry George "single tax" movement, would enthusiastically hail the social justice potential of what he called "war patriotism."

"Since this war began, humanity has made long strides," Assistant Secretary Louis Post would write in the *Public*. "Many an erstwhile plutocrat to whom 'labor,' except for an individual workingman acquaintance here and there, had meant nothing more human than 'labor-cost' in corporation ledgers, is beginning to realize that 'labor' in the mass is as human as any individual worker they happen to know and like."[46]

The war's "forward drift," Post forecasted, would lead to "higher labor standards after the war." Plutocrats were losing ground.

"The influence of the barons of industry," Post crowed, "is weakening."

Walter Lippmann, a young journalist who had worked for Schenectady's Socialist Party mayor before cofounding the *New Republic* and becoming a confidant of President Wilson, shared that enthusiasm. He saw a nation "committed as never before to the realization of democracy." In the war's wake, Lippmann gushed, a victorious America would be turning "with fresh interest to our own tyrannies—to our Colorado mines, our autocratic steel industries, our sweatshops, and our slums."[47]

That optimism seemed realistic by the war's end, at least within those sectors of the progressive movement that had accepted the war and dodged the repression and terror targeted against those progressives who had not. Progressive supporters of the war had indeed regained, on a variety of battlefronts, some serious momentum.

On the war-financing front, the federal government's ravenous need for new revenue had driven lawmakers back to the drawing board after the passage of the disappointing 1917 War Revenue Act.

Federal expenditures for 1917 had soared to $19 billion, triple the cost of the entire Civil War.[48] In the face of these rising costs, the 1917 revenue legislation had quickly become inadequate. Meanwhile, from the grassroots, local groups were still pressing for wealth conscription.

"We believe that as we have conscripted men, so should wealth be conscripted by means of a heavy graduated income tax," resolved the North Carolina division of the Farmers' Educational and Co-operative Union of America midway through March 1918. "The dollar should not be more sacred than man."

The Revenue Act of 1918 brought the nation closer to this con-scripting spirit. The legislation lowered the threshold for the top federal income tax bracket in the 1918 tax year from $2 million to $1 million and raised the top-bracket tax rate from 67 to 77 percent. For 1919 and 1920, the act set the top rate at 73 percent, still over ten times the top rate in 1915. This top rate would only apply to a relative handful of taxpayers, those super rich making over what today, after inflation, would equal about $15 million. For America's somewhat more pedestrian rich—those taxpayers making between $100,000 and $150,000 in 1918, a take-home that would range between about $1.5 and $2.25 million today—the 1918 Act still constituted a sizeable "conscription of wealth" advance. The tax rate for this millionaire tax bracket jumped from the underwhelming 31 percent in the tepid 1917 Revenue Act to 64 percent in the much more progressively ambitious 1918 legislation.[49]

These new higher tax rates on America's richest took at least some of the regressive sting off the Wilson administration's heavy wartime borrowing. Administration officials and celebrities had spent two years barnstorming the nation on behalf of "liberty bonds," and these campaigns had convinced millions of Americans of means, large and small, to loan money for the war effort. Wilson Treasury Secretary William Gibbs McAdoo had always hoped, notes tax historian W. Elliot Brownlee, "that after the conclusion of the war, middle-class bondholders would be repaid by tax dollars raised from corporations and the wealthiest Americans."[50] The 1918 Revenue Act seemed to deliver on McAdoo's promise.

And a reinvigorated labor movement also seemed at war's end poised to keep that promise. Union membership doubled during the war, to over five million right after the armistice.[51] Unions entered the postwar world more entrenched, economically and politically, than they had ever been before.

The Catholic Church hierarchy would soon give America's rapidly growing labor movement still another positive jolt. On Lincoln's birthday, February 2, 1919, the church released a *Bishops' Program for Social Reconstruction*—a reform guidebook authored by Monsignor John Ryan, the long-time progressive champion—that endorsed labor's right to organize, called for a host of government programs ranging from public housing for workers to social insurance for health and old age, and envisioned a major worker role in managing America's enterprises.[52] The *Bishops' Program* blasted the "insufficient incomes for the great majority of wage-earners and unnecessarily large incomes for a small minority of privileged capitalists" and urged "heavy taxation of incomes, excess profits, and inheritances" to narrow that gap.[53]

This new statement, the boldest political statement America's Catholic Church hierarchy had ever released, jazzed an overall postwar atmosphere already "electric with radical ideas," as historian Alan Dawley puts it.[54] Average Americans now had both motive and opportunity, as never before, for committing significant social change.

Motive had grown out of the war. The conflict had raised worker expectations.

"The workers of the Allied world have been told that they were engaged in a war for democracy," explained Basil Manly, the staff director of the prewar Industrial Relations Commission and the last chairman of the War Labor Board. "They are asking now, 'Where is that democracy for which we fought?'"[55]

More motive came from worker anger at spiraling inflation. Few workers felt they had shared adequately in the wartime prosperity. Rising prices had been eating away their wages nearly ever since the war began in Europe back in 1914.

Opportunity, in the meantime, was coming from the nation's changing demographics. Right after the war, industrial workers would make up over 40 percent of the nation's workforce.[56] Blue-collar workers overall accounted for 59.7 percent. America, observes Alan Dawley, had "more miners, railway workers, and cotton textile workers than ever before or since."[57] Blue-collar "social weight" had never been heavier.

In early 1919, this social weight would begin to make itself felt in a broad worker economic and political offensive that extended from sea to shining sea. Some leadership for this offensive came from America's most established unions. The railroad brotherhoods launched a campaign to nationalize the railroad industry, plutocracy's most important power base over the previous fifty years. Railroad executives were demanding the exact opposite, an immediate post-war return of all railroad lines to their "rightful" owners. The railroad union alternative—what became known as the "Plumb Plan" after Glenn Plumb, the Chicago labor lawyer who designed it—envisioned a federal takeover that would place America's railroads under the "democratic control" of tripartite boards representing workers, the public, and management.

To run the campaign for this Plumb Plan, the railroad unions hired Edward Keating, the former Colorado congressman who had actively advocated for a "conscription of wealth" income limit. Keating started a weekly newspaper to promote the Plumb Plan, and the paper would soon evolve into *Labor*, a national trade union paper with eight hundred thousand paid subscribers.[58]

Five times that many workers, an incredible four million in all, would walk out on strike in 1919, nearly one in five industrial workers nationwide.[59] But these huge numbers only tell part of this nation-shaking story. The United States had never before seen a strike wave so broad. A national steel strike united workers from a range of ethnic groups. A walkout by Chicago packinghouse workers linked white and black workers. In Boston, police officers struck. And in Seattle workers staged the nation's first-ever citywide general strike.

Seattle shipyard workers, thirty-five thousand strong, had walked out in January 1919, demanding the right to bargain. Employers quickly vowed to replace them permanently if they didn't return to work. In response, the rest of the Seattle labor movement rushed in to offer support and solidarity. On February 6, Seattle unions shut the city down. Business as usual came to a total standstill. No public transportation, no schools, no shopping in the city's great emporiums. Workers, relates labor journalist Dick Meister, kept essential services going. They delivered milk and cooked meals in dozens of locations around the city. For six days, hardly anything else moved.[60]

Seattle Mayor Ole Hanson considered the all-encompassing walkout the first stage of an American Bolshevik revolution, and the American Federation of Labor's conservative national leaders appeared as spooked as the mayor. The AFL national hierarchy pressured local AFL leaders to end the walkout, and the local leaders did. But the spirit behind the general strike survived. In those heady days, among progressives all across the country, anything seemed possible, even a Bolshevik-like revolution. In Seattle, Butte, and Portland, Oregon, activists even organized Soviet-style soldier, sailor, and worker councils.[61]

The already wobbling—from wartime repression—Socialist Party would fracture amid the heightened hopes these massive strikes were fanning. The party foreign-language federations that enrolled members from Russia and Eastern Europe considered Victor Berger and other national party leaders entirely too cautious. They demanded more aggressive mass revolutionary action and reorganized themselves into a new American Communist Party pledged to support Russia's fledgling Bolshevik government. Another group of radicals formed a like-minded Communist Labor Party.[62]

The splintered Socialist Party now stood almost totally unable to provide much leadership to the grassroots fires burning across the nation. The party's principled decision to oppose entry into the war had generated only an organizational disaster. But events had confirmed one major aspect of the case Socialists had leveled against those progressives who had entered into the war camp. US entry into Europe's war, Socialists had argued, would leave America's plutocracy as flush as ever. That prediction would prove correct.

Midway through 1918, a Federal Trade Commission report on wartime profiteering revealed that the net income of US Steel had ballooned from just under $100 million in 1915 to $478 million in 1917. Even after taxes, the steel giant was still pocketing earnings that ran well over double the prewar level.[63] In the same period, the nation's four largest meatpackers saw their profits leap sevenfold.[64] DuPont ended the war with coffers overflowing enough to buy control over General Motors, a takeover later overturned.[65] Even the temporarily expropriated prewar owners of America's railroads had no cause for angst. The government guaranteed them, straight through the war, hundreds of millions in fees.[66]

This corporate cash tide would translate into huge wartime earnings for the wealthy Americans who held the corporate reins. "Conservative estimates," one Wall Street tax lawyer would later write, put the number of Americans with at least $1 million in 1919 net worth at forty-two thousand.[67] That same year, sixty-five Americans reported *incomes* over $1 million.[68]

All these wealthy Americans had no intention of rolling over before the 1919 worker offensive. They had motive and opportunity too. Their motive—to resist the worker surge by whatever means necessary—came from sources both traditional and strikingly new. Postwar plutocrats had ample personal privilege to defend, just like their prewar predecessors. But the postwar rich had an additional motive for striking back at striking workers, an additional reason to resist concessions. These postwar plutocrats now lived in a world with an actual workers' state, a socialist republic. The specter haunting Europe had now become reality in the new Russia. If they gave an inch, America's plutocrats feared, the United States could well sink into Soviet status.

America's rich also had a political opportunity they did not enjoy before the war. In prewar America, plutocrats had confronted a political opposition united in fury against grand accumulations of private wealth and power. Respectable reformers and radicals of all stripes could and did work together to expose and challenge plutocratic power. The war changed everything. The war severed, almost completely, the links between respectable reformers and radicals by infecting the American body politic with a virulent virus that attacked anything that could be branded "socialistic." The prewar Socialist Party had operated as the left flank of a broad progressive movement. Within that movement, activists were constantly exchanging ideas and inspiration. The resulting interplay left reformers and radicals both more politically effective and more committed to common action against wealth's grandest concentrations.

The war's repression ended this interplay and left socialists and more radical-left activists marginalized, blocked off from the broader progressive movement. In any age, the more marginalized political activists become, the more frustrated they feel. Frustration, given marginalization acute enough, can erupt in flights of violent fancy that, in turn, serve as the pretext for wider repression, more thorough marginalization, and ever greater frustration.

This politically debilitating cycle would start playing out during the war years. In Oklahoma, once the proudest Socialist Party state stronghold, hundreds of renegade Socialists actually took up arms in August 1917. Their fantasy? These tenant farmers and sharecroppers, note historians John Womack Jr. and Roxanne Dunbar-Ortiz, "believed that millions of armed working people across the country would march with them to take Washington."[69] Authorities would eventually arrest 458 of these Oklahoma reds for their "Green Corn Rebellion."

Only a few months later the Russian Revolution would deepen the demonization of America's socialist left. The nation's press painted the October Revolution in overwhelmingly lurid tones, and, by war's end, socialism had become a "red menace," a political hobgoblin that defenders of privilege could and would employ with relish and demagogic abandon.

The 1919 national steel strike demonstrated how devastatingly effective this "red menace" hobgoblin could be. With steelworkers increasingly enraged over sixty-nine-hour workweeks and inflation-shriveled paychecks, US Steel would refuse to sit down and bargain with union representatives.[70] Steel industry flacks then quickly portrayed the subsequent September 1919 strike as a dangerous step toward "Bolshevizing industry." Newspaper headlines would repeat that theme over and over. "Stand by America," read one. "Beware The Agitator Who Makes Labor a Catspaw For Bolshevism," read another.[71] US Secretary of War Newton Baker would add to the hysteria as US troops were rushed into the steel town of Gary, Indiana. He denounced "violent agitation by so-called Bolsheviki and radicals counseling violence and urging action on behalf of what they call social revolution."[72] In the end, federal troops, state police, company guards, small armies of strikebreakers, arrests, picket-line clubbings, and race-baiting—combined with a national AFL leadership more obsessed with squashing potential radical rivals than defending harassed strikers—would doom the national walkout to inglorious and total defeat.

The pattern set by the great steel strike would repeat across the nation throughout 1919. America's employers joined in "open shop" campaigns to cleanse away the union stain. Employer associations devoted to fiercely free-market "open shop" ideology urged corporations to take off the gloves and battle unions by any means necessary. Employers the nation over brought in thugs and gunmen to keep their workers in line. Ensuring an "open shop," notes historian Alan Dawley, would require "the country to pay for the maldistribution of wealth and power with the coin of violence."[73] Nearly everywhere, the 1919 strike wave came up against "red menace" hysteria and employer intransigence, and then shattered. All strikes had come to seem, notes historian Robert Murray, as "conspiracies against the government" and "plots to establish communism."[74] Of the year's estimated thirty-six hundred walkouts, adds Murray, in only a few cases did strikers come away with anything resembling a victory.[75] Labor ranks, at an all-time high just months after World War I ended, began to rapidly dwindle.

Labor's political efforts would fall short as well. Lawmakers dismissed the labor-backed Plumb Plan to permanently nationalize the nation's railroads without any serious consideration. The Esch-Cummins Act that lawmakers passed instead, Plumb Plan organizer Edward Keating would later observe, added considerable insult to injury. Effective in March 1920, the legislation didn't just restore the nation's railroads to private control. The restoration continued the massive federal fees America's railroad corporations had received during the war—at a $920 million annual rate—for six months after the railroads went back to their original private owners.[76]

By 1920, the red-menace hysteria had claimed as victims both the Socialist Party and militant trade unionism. But the damage would extend far beyond socialist and trade union circles. The hysteria placed the entire reform ethic under suspicion. Employer and superpatriot groups, notes historian John Graham, would carry the battle against progressive thought "into every area of life their ample funds afforded."[77] The red-baiters had pamphlets stuffed into worker paycheck envelopes and circulated lists of subversive periodicals to boycott. By mid-1920, adds red-scare historian Robert Murray, countless "college professors, public school teachers, clerics, and social reformers had abandoned what seemed to be a hopeless fight, canceled their subscriptions to liberal magazines and newspapers, and either maintained a stony silence or leaned over backwards to appear as conservative" as their tormentors.[78]

The loss of progressive church advocacy would be a particularly damaging blow to the reform cause. Attacks on agencies like the Methodist Church Federation for Social Services—for "leaning toward Bolshevism" by opposing open-shop drives to destroy trade unions—would silence the moral outcry against obscene concentrations of private wealth. America, notes Robert Murray, now "had to be content with having the money-changers in the temple; no one dared drive them out."[79]

Reformers did mount a counterattack of sorts, but the thrust of that counter would be telling. The basic content of prewar progressivism—its energetic assault on plutocratic power—had become too suspect to defend. The counterattack against the red-menace hysteria, as historian John Graham points out, would focus "exclusively on civil liberties."[80]

Economists Irving Fisher and Scott Nearing did not share much political ground either during World War I or in the immediate aftermath. Fisher, a Yale academic, had become a pillar of establishment economics. By the war's end, Nearing had lost teaching jobs at Swarthmore College and Toledo University for refusing to rein in his socialist views. But both academics shared a sense that the long years of prewar struggle over concentrated wealth had to end, sooner rather than later, with outright victory for one side.

"Our society will always remain an unstable and explosive compound as long as political power is vested in the masses and economic power in the classes," Fisher would note in 1919. "In the end one of these powers will rule. Either the plutocracy will buy up the democracy or the democracy will vote away the plutocracy."[81]

"Democracy aims at equal opportunity; plutocracy aims at special privilege," Nearing would write the next year. "Like oil and water, the two ideas cannot mix."[82]

In 1920, the identity of the victor finally seemed clear. Norman Hapgood certainly thought so. Hapgood, the *Harper's Weekly* editor behind the influential Louis Brandeis best seller *Other People's Money*, had been appointed ambassador to Denmark early in 1919, before the red scare began to sweep the nation. He returned to the United States that December, near the height of the hysteria. He would be struck by "the silence of such liberal leaders as remain."[83] Respectable reformers, Hapgood believed, had a responsibility to keep politics centered on the only goals that mattered to economic progress. First, "to produce primarily things that are needed." Second, "to produce them uninterruptedly." Third, "to distribute them equitably."[84] Respectable reformers, just a year after the Great War, were failing in that responsibility. On the American political scene, equity no longer seemed to matter.

The plutocrats had survived to thrive another day—and another decade.

Chapter Four

THE RICH MUCK UP MODERNITY

In the America that entered the 1920s, the rich ruled. The best evidence for that rule just might have been Calvin Coolidge, the exceptionally dull lawyer from Massachusetts who became vice president of the United States in 1920. Three years later he would be president. In a nation with a legitimate claim to democratic status no character the likes of Calvin Coolidge could ever rise to a position of political preeminence.

Successful politicians in democracies almost always display at least some aptitude for charming the people they encounter. Coolidge displayed next to none. He never engaged in small talk, or much of any talk at all. "Silent Cal," they called him. "Sour Cal" might have made a better fit. Quipped Alice Roosevelt Longworth, Teddy Roosevelt's oldest daughter: Calvin Coolidge must have been "weaned on a pickle."[1]

Other luminaries of the day found Cal much less a laughing matter. In 1927, US Supreme Court Justice Louis Brandeis would attend a Coolidge presidential address on the occasion of Washington's birthday. He would try to describe for a friend how painful he found the experience.

"When I tried to recall the next most depressing and distressful experience of a lifetime," Brandeis wrote, "I had to go back to 1894, when in preparing for the Public Institutions Hearings, I went to Long Island (Boston Harbor) Poor-House hospital and passed through the syphilitic ward. I had a like sense of uncleanness."[2]

Dwight Morrow didn't share this Brandeis perspective. Morrow and Coolidge had become fast friends as undergrads at Amherst College. Years later, Morrow would emerge as a Wall Street power broker, a senior partner in the J. P. Morgan banking empire. In 1918, after stints as a state senator and lieutenant governor, his buddy Cal found himself narrowly elected governor of Massachusetts. The nation took no notice. But over the next year all eyes would turn to Massachusetts when overworked and underpaid Boston policemen went out on strike, a job action that would soon rank among the most notorious walkouts in US history. After some hesitation, Coolidge issued a defiant declaration—"There is no right to strike against the public safety by anyone, anywhere, anytime"—that charmed defenders of public propriety more than Silent Cal's sour demeanor ever could.

Dwight Morrow now saw an opportunity. His buddy had gained the national stage. Now he could become a star. More to the point: Now Morrow, the ultimate Wall Street insider, could make him a star.[3] By June 1920, Morrow had convinced delegates to the Republican National Convention in Chicago that they had an up-and-coming political celebrity in their midst. Coolidge cruised into the vice-presidential nomination, victory in November, and then, after President Warren Harding's 1923 death, the White House itself. As president, he would return the favor to Morrow. House of Morgan bankers would dominate the new Coolidge administration.

"I have never seen," J. P. Morgan Jr. later exulted, "any president who gives me just the feeling of confidence in the country and its institutions, and the working out of our problems, that Mr. Coolidge does."[4]

Few progressives in the early 1920s knew the backstory behind Calvin Coolidge's swift ascent to America's political summit. But they understood, at a deeper visceral level, the political reality that Calvin Coolidge represented. The rich had regained the upper hand after the turmoil of world war and postwar red scare. A generation of intense progressive political activity—picket lines and petitions, mass marches and ballot-box majorities—seemed to have come to naught. The plutocracy stood.

The new president elected in 1920, Senator Warren Harding from Ohio, called this plutocratic restoration "normalcy" and scoffed at the notion that plutocrats had returned to power—or had ever even held it. Progressives like Bob La Follette, as Harding charged during World War I, had attempted to "instill in the hearts of men envy, jealousy, and suspicion of all who succeed." They had irresponsibly spread "the impression that wealth and graft are in control of our government."[5]

Once inaugurated, Harding felt absolutely no need to do anything that might counter this "impression." His choice for secretary of the treasury would be Andrew Mellon, the Pittsburgh banker and industrialist who ranked as one of the world's richest men and never tired of flaunting his enormous fortune. Mellon, notes historian Arthur Mann, "dressed expensively, dined expensively, drank expensively."[6] And contributed extensively, Mann could have added, to the massive GOP war chest that helped smooth Harding's ride into the White House. In 1920, Mellon's overall contribution to the Republican cause, in donations and loans, totaled almost $7 million in today's dollars.[7]

Progressive institutions, meanwhile, lay in shambles. The proud and vibrant Socialist Party no longer offered much in the way of an antidote to plutocracy. The party could claim only eleven thousand dues-paying members in 1921, a tenth of the party's already depleted 1919 total.[8] Over nine hundred thousand Americans did vote for the still-imprisoned Eugene Debs in the 1920 presidential election. But the vote for Debs would be a last gasp, a salute to a beloved leader and a futile protest against two major-party candidates, the Republican Warren Harding and the Democrat James Cox, who spent the campaign avoiding the great issues of wealth and power that had resounded so powerfully only a few years before.

Those progressive reformers who had supported the war effort—and avoided the repression rained down upon the antiwar Socialists—would stagger into the 1920s almost equally dispirited. The great reforms in political process they had championed as a check on plutocratic power, everything from primaries to recall elections, did not seem to be providing much of a check. The rich and powerful had figured out rather quickly that their ample cash reserves could turn these reforms against reformers.

The Non-Partisan League's most successful candidate in North Dakota would be the first reformer to learn that lesson. That candidate, Lynn Frazier, had been reelected governor in 1920, after defying his state's banking and commercial interests in his first term. Frazier's signature first-term legislative victory—the 1919 creation of a state-owned bank— had inspired progressives all across the nation. But that same victory had infuriated state and national financial movers and shakers. In 1921, these deep pockets would mount a "recall" campaign against Frazier and two other elected Non-Partisan League statewide officeholders, the first such recall under the progressive constitutional reforms North Dakota voters had approved just the year before.[9] Frazier soon became the first governor ever recalled from office in American history.

Progressives nationwide had celebrated the progressive electoral reforms in North Dakota and other western states. Their celebration, the most thoughtful among them now realized, had been premature.

"Let us not deceive ourselves. Lack of proper political machinery is not the trouble," as Amos Pinchot would write. "Our difficulty is that public opinion is normally controlled by the railroads, trust, and banking interests through the surplus funds which are accumulated by the process of monopoly. As long as these interests dominate, as long as they hold the bulk of power, they will use against us any improvements in political machinery that we may devise.[10]

The next year, 1922, the seventy-four-year-old Richard Pettigrew, the former US senator from South Dakota, would pen a memoir that surveyed the American political landscape. He shared Pinchot's despair. Pettigrew's memoir noted that he had "known personally the last ten presidents of the United States" as well as "the leading business men who backed the political parties and who made and unmade the presidents."[11] This proximity to power had left Pettigrew deeply pessimistic. The "accumulated wealth of the United States," he believed, had taken control over every lever of political and civic power that mattered.[12] The wealthy didn't just run the government. They controlled "all of the channels of public opinion—the press, the schools, the church." They even controlled "the labor unions through the control of their leaders."[13]

Progressives, of course, had not totally disappeared from American political life. But they seemed cowed, and their timidity only compounded the frustration that Amos Pinchot and like-minded activists would feel, a frustration that rubbed raw at a December 1922 national gathering of beleaguered progressives in Washington, DC. The railroad union brotherhoods had earlier in the year launched a "Conference for Progressive Political Action" and hoped to unite the nation's various reform strands into an ongoing nonpartisan organization that could support progressive candidates. Pinchot attended the December gathering, joining an assemblage of "outstanding American progressives" who included "Republicans, Democrats, independents in good standing, senators, congressmen, editors, and publicists."[14]

"A number of admirable speeches were made, denouncing the role of plutocracy and demanding its immediate destruction," Pinchot later recalled.

The conference resolutions committee inhaled this fervor and drafted a program for progressive action that featured "a strong railroad plank directly assaulting one of the principal sources of plutocracy's power," its tight control over the nation's transportation. But that program plank alarmed the timid conference leaders. They sent the resolutions committee the word to discard the railroad plank and report, related Pinchot, "nothing more radical" than a declaration "favoring the extension of the presidential primary law to all states in the Union."

Pinchot saw the dispiriting episode as "typical of what the progressives have been doing." They gather together and at length and eloquently depict the capture of government by America's industrial and financial powers that be.

"They do this well. Through much practice, they are good at it," Pinchot would write. "Then they put their heads together to legislate out of existence this duress of dominant men, and they solemnly select some perfectly ridiculous and inadequate thing like direct presidential primary."[15]

Pinchot's fellow progressive, Senator George Norris from Nebraska, would feel the same anguish and irritation. All hope of appreciable progressive progress seemed lost.

"Under the present conditions in Washington and conditions which have existed ever since I came to Congress, it is almost impossible to obtain effective legislation in the interest of the people," the Republican Norris would announce halfway through the Harding administration. "I have been bucking this game for twenty years and there is no way of beating it. I've done all I could. Now I'm through."[16]

George Norris would regain his political composure and soldier on. New progressive initiatives might be off the table, after all, but the progressive surge that ended in 1919 had accomplished a great deal before the plutocratic pushback, on fronts as varied as progressive taxation and child labor. Could progressives in 1920s America defend the changes they had wrought? Or would the reempowered rich rise up and roll back—wipe away—a generation's worth of progressive change?

The politically sophisticated rich knew better than to attempt a total rollback. The nation, they understood, had fundamentally changed over the previous two decades. Years of progressive organizing against plutocracy had changed it. The rewards from America's economic growth, Americans in large numbers still believed in the early 1920s, had not gone to the fit and deserving. They had gone to the ruthless and well connected. Given this deep-seated popular consensus, America's awesomely affluent could no longer just take. To retain wealth and power, they had to give. They had to give those without wealth and power a sense of hope. They had to convince average Americans that the nation didn't need unions or government regulations or, God forbid, socialism to see a better tomorrow. They had to coax and cajole average Americans into accepting business leadership. If government would just get out of the way, they needed to help these average Americans understand, this business leadership would usher them into the middle class they so wanted to enter.

This new corporate charm offensive caught progressives somewhat off guard. Labor activists and their allies knew how to do battle against union-busting goons. But now employers were unveiling new weapons. They were battling unions with sociologists and initiatives designed to enhance worker well being. Some top corporations put pension and health care plans into effect. Others spruced up factory washrooms and lunchrooms, or sponsored lectures to help "little mothers" care for their infants.[17] Still others, notes historian Paul Buhle, bankrolled sports leagues for their workers and "even held human relations classes to improve foremen's factory demeanor."[18]

Corporate leaders hoped these velvet touches would help workers see unions as totally unnecessary in the modern 1920s workplace. But corporate fists still bulged behind that velvet. You don't need unions, Corporate America's new "welfare capitalism" made plain to workers, but we won't tolerate them either.

By the fall of 1920, businesses across the nation had organized themselves into employer associations expressly devoted to driving unions out of America's workplaces. New York State alone, notes Irving Bernstein's classic labor history of the era, boasted fifty of these associations, Illinois forty-six. These employer groups typically assembled and circulated blacklists of union sympathizers. Employers would refuse to hire listed workers—and fire any they might discover they already had on their payrolls. Workers who did get hired often had to agree, by signed contract, that they would never join a union or try to organize one.[19]

All this strong-arming went by the name of the "American Plan," a label that nearly two dozen state employer groups agreed upon at a January 1921 meeting in Chicago. The assembled employers proclaimed themselves the guardians of the "open shop," the workplace "with equal opportunity for all and special privileges for none."

In practice, "open shop" meant no rights for anyone. Free speech? Workers learned quickly to watch what they said, on the job and off.

Management had spies everywhere. Labor espionage, in fact, became a major business in the 1920s. In Chicago, the local telephone directory carried two pages of private detective agencies eager to provide employers antiunion spy service. These agencies didn't just feed the names of "agitators" into blacklists. Their spies also acted as agents provocateurs. They baited workers into hopeless strikes and even violence.

Employers had the armaments necessary to prevail in any eventuality. They stockpiled, relates historian Irving Bernstein, "tear and sickening gas, shells and guns to discharge them, and, to a lesser extent, machine guns."[20] And the private detective agencies employers hired had a special incentive to egg on this arms buildup. They typically took commissions from munitions companies for the firepower corporations requisitioned. But employers didn't always have to pay for antiunion muscle and munitions. In some communities, local American Legion chapters helped break up picket lines and manhandle strikers for no charge.[21] In others, a resurgent Ku Klux Klan did the brutalizing.[22]

Judges at all levels, meanwhile, saw little evil in any of this and did their best to safeguard employer interests. Supreme Court decisions shielded employers from picketing and boycotts. Lower court injunctions routinely crippled labor's capacity to conduct effective strikes.

This "American Plan" antiunion offensive began to pay dividends almost immediately. Trade union membership nationwide dropped by nearly a third in the three years after 1920, and the union unraveling would spin on throughout the decade.[23] The United Mine Workers entered the 1920s as the nation's largest union, nearly a half-million members strong. By 1928, the union's ranks had shrunk to only fifty thousand.[24]

Uninspired union leadership certainly contributed to this decade-long slide. Established union officialdom often did battle against internal union rivals—especially from the left—with far more energy than they exerted against employers. By decade's end, unions in the United States had virtually no pulse outside a few isolated strongholds. Pronounced visiting Australian journalist H. G. Adam in 1928: "America is an employer's paradise."[25]

American business now faced few checks and balances in the nation's workplaces. Business leaders would soon gain that same "freedom" in the marketplace. They had beaten back unions. Next on the corporate agenda: beating back federal and state attempts at seriously regulating business behavior.

By 1920, decades of progressive reform had dotted America's economic landscape with an assortment of state and federal regulatory agencies and statutes. In industry after industry, corporate leaders had watchdogs looking over their shoulders. Corporate executives deeply resented this scrutiny, particularly in those rapidly growing industries that promised grand fortune to the nation's most enterprising—and ruthless—entrepreneurs and investors.

No industry in the early twentieth century promised greater returns than electric power, and that reality had kept power utilities on the nation's political center stage throughout the century's first two decades. Progressive reformers demanded public ownership of these "natural monopolies." At the local level, their efforts helped establish a network of municipally owned power plants. At the state level, victories would be more limited. Progressives won only the right to limit private utility rate-gouging through utility commissions that essentially guaranteed companies a limited profit based on how much they had invested in their power-generating operations.

Utility giants soon figured out how to game the new state regulatory arrangements. The more they could claim they had "invested," the more they could charge consumers. The key would be how the utility commissions defined investment. The utility companies would cite "book value"—their net worth in the marketplace—as the appropriate definition, for obvious reason. The difference between this book value and the dollars companies had actually invested to provide power to customers could be enormous. The Carolina Light and Power Company, for instance, had a "book value" five times greater than its actual investment in providing customers electricity.[26]

The new state regulatory agencies could have and should have called the private utility giants to account on this bogus bookkeeping. But in state after state these agencies had fallen under power company domination. Where state regulators did stick to their guns, the utilities simply went to the courts and had friendly judges overrule state regulatory determinations. State regulation, angry progressives groused, amounted to no regulation at all. Industry insiders, among themselves, agreed.

"I know of no other manufacturing industry," Frederick Sackett, a former power utility president and a future US senator from Kentucky, gloated to a power industry conference, "where the sale price of the product is fifteen times the actual cost of production of the article sold."[27]

In 1920, Woodrow Wilson's last year in office, progressives would slip through a victory they hoped would undercut the utility industry's plutocratic power. The legislation they managed to enact created a Federal Power Commission and gave the new commission the authority to determine how much power utilities were actually investing in their operations. Federal regulators suddenly had the ability to pop inflated rate bases—and deflate utility superprofits. But the new federal power agency would do no popping in the early presidential years of Woodrow Wilson's successor, the exceedingly business-friendly Warren Harding. On the Harding administration's much-less-than-vigilant watch, the power industry conducted rate-gouging business as usual. Then, all of a sudden, catastrophe struck. A series of Harding administration corruption scandals around public lands and energy policy outraged the public and reenergized reformers. They began once again demanding public ownership of America's energy resources.[28] Amid the tumult, the utilities feared, the new Federal Power Commission might actually wake to its responsibility to the public interest.

The utilities responded with a massive public relations campaign to vilify federal regulation as an "unsound experiment," a threat to the "self-government" that Americans so prized. Their most prominent campaigner would be Herbert Hoover, the US secretary of commerce. Hoover would "author" articles and speeches that the power industry reprinted and widely circulated—five hundred thousand copies of Hoover's October 1924 tract on the dangers of "Government Ownership," seventy-five thousand copies more of his October 1925 offering on "Why the Public Interest Requires State Rather than Federal Regulation of Electric Public Utilities."[29] Hoover's Commerce Department and the power industry would work ever closer as the 1920s unfolded. In 1927, the top two federal power "regulators" in Commerce would even shift over to the chief power industry lobby group. One would become the group's top executive, the other would run the group's public relations apparatus. Hoover himself would carry his crusade against government "interference" into his 1928 presidential campaign.

"I do not favor," candidate Hoover reflected at an early October campaign rally in Tennessee, "any general extension of the federal government into the operation of business in competition with its citizens."[30]

Hoover's election a month later sent the share price of power utility stocks skyrocketing. That stock market surge, the trade journal

Electrical World understated, reflected "a sentiment prevailing among utility executives as well as in banking circles that Mr. Hoover's triumph in the national election augurs well for the electric public utility companies."[31]

Hoover's election augured well for all of Corporate America. The business campaign against government "interference" in the marketplace had succeeded. Assorted regulations from the Progressive Era did remain formally on the books, but few regulators felt in the regulating mood. Business could once again do business as business pleased.

Top corporate executives now faced no serious threat from labor in the workplace or regulators in the marketplace. They had flattened the labor movement. They had rolled back the fledgling regulatory state. They had won the freedom to monumentally multiply their income and wealth.

America's rich would royally enjoy that multiplication. In the 1920s they didn't just pummel labor and tame federal regulators. They slashed the taxes on their winnings.

Over the first two decades of the twentieth century, American progressives had scored their most resounding victories on the tax front. America had entered the new century with a totally plutocratic tax code. The nation's wealthy faced no taxes whatsoever on their incomes in 1900. By the end of World War I, these wealthy faced a 77 percent tax on income over $1 million. The 1918 tax act that established this stunning 77 percent rate still remained on the books when Warren Harding took office in March 1921. Under the act's provisions, the top federal tax rate had dipped slightly, to 73 percent. Businesses, for their part, still faced an excess profits tax, and the heirs of the wealthy faced an estate tax that subjected bequests over $10 million to a 25 percent federal levy.

America's men of property considered all these rates abjectly outrageous. They demanded relief. But the politicians who did their bidding had a problem. The Eighteenth Amendment to the Constitution ratified in early 1919 had outlawed the consumption of "intoxicating liquors" and, in the process, turned off the spigot on a prime source of federal revenue, the federal excise tax on alcohol. Federal revenue had to come from somewhere. The nation couldn't afford to slash federal income and estate taxes, most lawmakers agreed, unless Congress came up with a new revenue source.

Conservatives had a new source in mind: a national sales tax. They urged Congress to replace "confiscatory" tax rates on income with a levy that would essentially shift the nation's tax burden off the shoulders of the affluent onto average Americans. Business groups ranging from the US Chamber of Commerce to the New York Board of Trade quickly rallied around the sales tax proposal. They saw the measure, notes tax historian Joseph Thorndike, as a "replacement for the profits tax."

Conservative lawmakers saw the sales tax as something considerably nobler. A national retail sales tax, opined Republican senator George Higgins Moses of New Hampshire, would "strike down the vicious principle of graduated taxation" that amounted to "a modern legislative adaptation of the Communistic doctrine of Karl Marx."[32]

But Secretary of the Treasury Andrew Mellon refused to jump on the sales tax bandwagon. The income tax, he argued, had become "firmly embedded in our system of taxation."[33] Any attempt to gut it, Mellon left unspoken, might provoke a public pushback and jeopardize the GOP legislative majority. His alternative: Keep the income tax, but reduce the rates. Eliminate the excess profits tax, but put in place a stiffer tax rate on corporate income.

This stance demanded enormous personal political discipline from Mellon. He yearned to do much more to help his fellow rich, particularly on the estate tax. The 1919 death of long-time Mellon family friend and business associate Henry Clay Frick had deeply troubled the megamillionaire treasury secretary. Frick had been at the aggressive cutting edge of plutocracy's drive to tame the US worker. Back in 1892, as the executive in charge of Andrew Carnegie's steelworks, Frick had broken the steelworkers union in the bloody Homestead Strike. At his death twenty-seven years later, he left behind a fortune the *New York Times* estimated at $150 million, the equivalent of about $2 billion today. State and local estate taxes would eventually take nearly $10 million out of the Frick fortune, after the final assessed value of Frick's estate fell by a striking half to $77 million. Mellon would blame the estate tax for the drastic drop-off in the Frick estate's value. In reality, other factors—most notably the bursting of the World War I asset bubble—contributed far more to the nosedive.[34]

Mellon, of course, had ample personal reason for wanting to blame the estate tax. At the time, he held an estate far greater in size than Frick's. Repealing the tax would save his heirs millions. But Mellon would not let his personal distaste for the estate tax cloud his political judgment. The estate tax had wide public support. The tax proposal he put forward in 1921—a package that would become known as the "Mellon plan"—would ignore the estate tax and focus instead on ditching the excess profits tax and slicing the top income tax rate from 73 down to first 40 and then 25 percent.[35]

This Mellon plan reflected a bipartisan consensus. Top Democrats fully shared Mellon's hostility toward high tax rates on high incomes. Woodrow Wilson's last treasury secretary, David Houston, had declared in 1920 that "such rates cannot be successfully collected."[36] And Houston's predecessor, Carter Glass, had denounced the excess profits tax as "a penalty on brains, energy, and enterprise."[37]

But not all Democrats in Congress felt that way, and tax-the-rich Democrats had enough progressive GOP support to complicate legislative life for Mellon and the tax-cutters. Mellon's crew had to appease both these progressives and beg for votes from the promoters of the national sales tax notion. In the end, Mellon would walk away with a compromise victory. The Revenue Act of 1921 would drop the top tax rate from 73 percent on income over $1 million to 58 percent on income over $200,000.[38] The legislation also repealed the excess profits levy.[39] Advocates for America's wealthy did pick up some other little-noticed victories in the compromise legislation, like preferential treatment for capital gains income from the sale of stocks and other assets.[40] They also kept out of the final law a Senate-passed provision that would have opened to public inspection the total income tax that affluent Americans were actually paying.[41]

Not a bad start for Mellon. He took his half-plus loaf and came back for the rest in 1924. This time, he came out swinging at the estate tax as well. The federal tax on the estates that affluent Americans leave behind, the treasury secretary would write in a book published that spring, ought to be abolished outright.

"The social necessity for breaking up large fortunes in this country," Mellon's new book pronounced, "does not exist."[42]

Most of the country disagreed. *Collier's* magazine, then one of the nation's largest mass-circulation periodicals, had run a series of articles the previous fall that made a vivid case for strengthening estate taxation. In the early nineteenth century, the series pointed out, Britain's super rich had banished the Highland Scots from their moors and mountains to make way for private hunting preserves. In 1910, *Collier's* observed, America's two wealthiest families held enough wealth to buy up all the farmland in New England and create their

own preserve![43] Even the *Saturday Evening Post*, America's top-circu-
lation magazine and a vocal advocate for cutting the nation's top tax
rates on income, declined to back Mellon on the estate tax.

Mellon, ever the political realist, would not push for total estate tax
repeal in his April 1924 testimony before the Senate Finance Committee. He called for an estate tax rate cutback instead and asked
Congress to drop the top tax rate on income all the way down to 25
percent. Once again Mellon and the White House would have to
compromise to get an income tax reduction. But this time progressive Republicans and Democrats had more legislative clout than they
held back in the 1921 tax debate. The ranks of progressives had swelled
slightly in the 1922 congressional elections, and congressional investi-
gations into various Harding administration scandals had the White
House somewhat back on its heels.

Mellon would eventually get another cut in the top income tax
rate, down to 46 percent, but he would pay a price to get it. The 1924
Revenue Act actually raised, not lowered, the top estate tax rate, from
25 to 40 percent. And lawmakers didn't stop there. They enacted a "gift
tax"—a levy on large transfers of wealth from the wealthy to their
favored inner circle—to prevent the wealthy from sidestepping the
estate tax by "giving" their money away to family and friends.

Lawmakers also revisited tax disclosure. To discourage tax cheating
by the wealthy, they passed a provision that opened taxpayer names
and addresses—and the amount of tax paid—to public inspection.[44]
A displeased President Calvin Coolidge signed the final tax bill into
law in June 1924. Andrew Mellon would be even more displeased. He
would start plotting still another assault on the nation's progressive
tax rates. Who would stand up against him this next time around?
Who would give tax progressivity a stouthearted defense? Not the
Democratic Party.

In July 1924 the Democrats gave their presidential nomination to
John W. Davis, a Wall Street lawyer tied to the J. P. Morgan empire.
The choice outraged America's besieged grassroots progressives. They
considered Davis and Coolidge equally abominable on taxes and
nearly every other issue. So did Wisconsin senator Bob La Follette.
The Republican insurgent announced his own bid for the White
House after the Davis nomination, and activists would soon line up
behind his independent Progressive Party candidacy.

La Follette's campaign began with great hope and expectations and fiery rhetorical blasts at America's reinvigorated 1920s plutocracy.

"The equality of opportunity proclaimed by the Declaration of Independence and asserted and defended by Jefferson and Lincoln as the heritage of every American citizen," La Follette's new Progressive Party platform proclaimed, "has been displaced by special privilege for the few, wrested from the government of the many."

The platform would go on to "denounce the Mellon tax plan as a device to relieve multi-millionaires at the expense of other tax payers." Other planks would call for a "surtax on swollen incomes" and "progressive taxes on large estates and inheritances."[45]

Activists close to La Follette knew he had no chance to win a majority, or even a plurality, in the November general election. He did, on the other hand, seem to have a possible shot at carrying enough states to deny an Electoral College majority to either Coolidge or Davis. If that happened, state delegations in the House of Representatives would decide the election. In that process, progressive lawmakers would hold the swing votes. The major party that wanted those votes would have to back off any move to trim taxes on the rich and respect labor rights.[46]

Or so went the fantasy. In reality, the ragtag Progressive Party effort had no hope of prevailing in the seven or eight states needed to deny Coolidge or Davis a majority. The nation's various progressive strands simply remained too feeble—and divided—to mount the electoral effort required.

One division among progressives revolved around the nation's various Communist Party splinter groups and their offshoots. Most reformers would have nothing to do with any progressive who had any relations at all with Communists. The red scare remained too recent and raw a fact of American political life to risk any Bolshevik taint.

Progressive lawmakers in Congress worried about a different sort of taint. A number of those lawmakers would be up for reelection in 1924 on one of the major-party lines. These progressive legislators feared that any campaigning they might do on behalf of La Follette's independent candidacy would cost them votes from straight-party-line voters who had backed them in the past.

Those progressives eager to form a full-fledged new party and break cleanly with Democrats and Republicans had their own divisions. Veteran activists yearned to rebuild a facsimile of the prewar Socialist Party. Younger union activists frustrated by the ever-cautious leadership of American Federation of Labor president Samuel Gompers wanted to form an explicit new "Labor Party."

Other progressives considered all talk about a full-fledged new party premature and an unwelcome distraction from La Follette's presidential candidacy. La Follette agreed, and his Progressive Party effort would focus only on the White House. That decision suited the AFL leadership just fine. AFL chief Samuel Gompers wanted no part of any long-term challenge to the two major parties. In truth, he didn't really want any part of La Follette's candidacy either. But Gompers had no choice. Between the antilabor Coolidge, the Republican incumbent, and the antilabor Davis, the Wall Streeter the Democrats had nominated, he could find no "lesser evil" to support. The AFL would endorse La Follette.

Endorse, but not support—in any meaningful way. La Follette had expected millions of dollars in campaign aid from Gompers and the AFL, but he seems to have received no more than $50,000. In all, the entire La Follette campaign only raised a quarter-million dollars for the entire 1924 election effort.[47] La Follette would enter the fall campaign with virtually no campaign war chest—and no clue how to campaign in a new-fangled America filled with radios, admen, and movie theater newsreels. The aging sixty-nine-year-old would never gain any political momentum. Or mainstream media support. Only one newspaper group, the Scripps-Howard chain, backed La Follette editorially.[48] The rest of daily press largely echoed the GOP attack mantra. La Follette, the Republicans charged, was promoting "Bolshevism." Employers reinforced the Republican assault. In some cities, factory owners even threatened to shut down their plants if La Follette were elected, the same tactic that had helped defeat the Populist Party–backed candidacy of William Jennings Bryan in 1896.

La Follette ended up carrying only one state, his own Wisconsin. He did capture almost five million votes, 16.6 percent of the vote, and came in second to Coolidge in most of the West. The Democrat Davis took only the segregated South. Coolidge would walk away with an overwhelming Electoral College majority and a larger GOP majority in both the Senate and the House.

The GOP victory at the November 1924 ballot box cleared away the last obstacle to plutocracy's restoration. The ringleader of insurgent Republicans opposed to tax cuts for the rich had been decisively defeated. In less than a year, La Follette would be dead, finally falling to overwork and ill health.

Treasury Secretary Andrew Mellon would now move to undo America's last remaining pillars of progressive taxation. His new iteration of the Mellon plan proposed to chop the top tax rate—46 percent on income over $500,000 in 1924—down to 20 percent, as well as eliminate the gift and estate tax. Republican leaders enthusiastically welcomed the new Mellon proposal. Taxes on the wealthy, Republican National Committee Chairman William Wood from Indiana would declare in one 1925 address, unleash economic dynamics that work "directly to the injury of the wage earner, the agricultural producer, and the small business man."[49]

Conservative political operatives worked hard to mobilize those small businessmen. They fashioned networks of "tax clubs" that barraged Congress with petitions that labeled high tax rates on the nation's top income brackets a "national emergency."[50] Small-town bankers—in Texas and throughout the South—flocked to the tax clubs. These local bankers didn't earn enough to benefit from the cuts in top tax rates Mellon was proposing, but they worried that rich bank depositors facing high tax rates would yank out their deposits and put their money in tax-exempt government bonds instead. Democrats like John Nance Garner, the influential Texas congressman who led the charge against the Mellon plan in 1924, would feel the pressure from these local bankers. They switched sides. The House would pass a friendly version of the new Mellon plan by a 390–25 margin. The fiery New York GOP progressive, Fiorello LaGuardia, found himself in that lonely twenty-five. With the Mellon plan in effect, LaGuardia argued in vain, the income tax would no longer have the capacity "to prevent the accumulation of enormous fortunes, and the control of industry and commerce that goes with such large fortunes."[51]

The final legislation that Congress deposited on President Coolidge's desk in 1926 gave Mellon most of what he wanted: a big cut in the top income tax rate, from 46 to 25 percent, the repeal of the gift tax, and a halving of the estate tax rate. Congress even killed the tax payment disclosure measure that had been enacted in 1924.[52] For the ultrarich, Mellon's legislative triumph meant the biggest tax break in American history. The federal tax bill on $1 million in income dropped by two-thirds.[53] For Mellon personally, as the nation's third biggest taxpayer after John D. Rockefeller and Henry Ford, the savings would be in the millions.

"Mr. Mellon himself," Republican insurgent Senator George Norris would note, "gets a larger personal reduction than the aggregate of practically all the taxpayers in the state of Nebraska."[54]

Mellon was becoming so rich, notes biographer David Cannadine, "that he had no idea precisely how wealthy he was."[55] His net worth, just over $80 million in 1923, would be estimated as high as $600 million, about $8 billion today, six years later. The convenient 1926 repeal of the federal gift tax would enable Mellon to start shifting this fortune to his heirs and end-run the still extant estate tax.

Mellon, ever the class warrior, would share his good fortune with his fellow plutocrats. Treasury Department officials quietly spread the word that the department would gladly review any requests for refunds on taxes paid since 1917. The requests—from tax lawyers and accountants for America's superwealthy—flooded in. The list of refunds granted would eventually fill twenty thousand pages and total $1.27 billion. Mellon personally would pocket $7 million in refunds, with another $14 million in refunds for his corporate holdings.[56]

To the victor belong the spoils. The plutocrats had won the tax battle. Rebates on past taxes paid would be their spoils.

The 1926 tax triumph complete, the 1920s could now roar. America's corporate movers and shakers had everything they claimed they needed to make America prosper. No powerful union presence. No "regimentation" by regulation. No "confiscatory" taxes. No government spending of any significance that might generate budget deficits. Business leaders had been warning Americans for years not to take any action that could undermine "business confidence." Government had now done everything that business claimed necessary to restore that confidence.

A grateful business class exulted. America, its celebrants gushed, had truly entered a "New Era." A future of unparalleled progress and comfort now seemed near. Business would lead the way. Average Americans would only need follow.

The reward for following the business lead would be enormous, almost unimaginable. Or so fervent business boosters pledged. Commerce Secretary Herbert Hoover pronounced in 1928 that the new Republican policy initiatives would soon have America "in sight of the day when poverty will be banished from this nation."[57] America's "people's capitalism," economist Thomas Nixon Carver would add, had left socialism, sovietism, and other radicalisms completely irrelevant.

"It is just as possible to realize equality under capitalism," Carver would assure, "as under any other system."[58]

These corporate claims had credibility. Signs of the New Era, a wondrous modern age, seemed to be popping up everywhere. American kitchens of the 1920s had electric refrigerators and shelves stacked with safe and healthy canned fruits and vegetables. Living rooms had radios. Newly paved streets abounded with cars, and motorists could take those cars for drives on newly invented—and beautifully manicured—parkways. The essential character of American daily life seemed to be changing right before America's eyes.

The nation's standard of living, the *Troy Record* enthused in 1926, had risen "so high that the average family enjoys today luxuries and necessities that were formerly regarded as luxuries."[59] In 1922, only the affluent had radios. By 1929, radio sales had soared fifteenfold. Automobile sales over the decade had tripled.[60] Similar patterns held for electric irons and vacuum cleaners and washing machines. Americans, newspaper editorialists opined, owed these magnificent new wonders to the wise rule of America's wealthy.

"When the making of millionaires is accompanied by such an increase of general prosperity," gushed the *Pittsburgh Gazette Times*, "the country may well pray for more of them."[61]

Workplaces were changing too. The same electricity and engineering know-how that were transforming how Americans spent their hours at home were also transforming how they spent their hours on the job. The nation was experiencing a productivity revolution. By 1929, the share of manufacturing horsepower that came from electricity had multiplied six times over the 1909 total.[62] By decade's end, one worker could produce four thousand bricks a day. The total just before the World War: four hundred.[63] Overall, in the six years between 1923 and 1929, manufacturing output per worker hour of labor jumped by a third.[64]

All these dizzying changes were even wowing Americans who had challenged the nation's corporate elite in years gone by.

"What the socialists dreamed of," noted an astonished Edward Filene, the maverick retailer, "the new capitalism has made a reality."[65]

But this "New Era" that so thrilled Filene and the rest of America's comfortable would prove a mirage. The vast majority of Americans went the entire 1920s without ever turning on their own radio or taking a Sunday drive down a new parkway. In 1929, the nation had just one car for every five people, one radio for every three homes.[66] And many Americans who did gain car keys and radio boxes during the decade had to go deep into debt to get them.

In the pre–credit card days of the 1920s, debt meant paying for cars and appliances via the installment plan. "Enjoy while you pay," went the advertising slogans. And Americans did pay—in monthly outlays for principal and interest. Between 1925 and 1929, the volume of this installment credit more than doubled.[67]

Without installment-plan credit, Americans simply could not afford the goods they were producing. And they could not afford these goods because they were not sharing in the rewards the newly bountiful American economy was creating. Rising worker productivity could have easily translated into rising worker wages. But where wages did increase, they nudged up at a snail's pace. Output per worker hour in the cutting-edge electric light and power industry rose 39 percent between 1923 and 1929. Average worker hourly earnings over those six years increased only 6 percent.[68]

The rest of the economy followed the same pattern. With unions mostly nonexistent, employers faced little pressure to raise wages as productivity increased. So they didn't. The new wealth created funneled instead into corporate profits and dividends. Executives prospered. Shareholders—still a small fraction of the population— prospered with them. In 1928, analysts at Wall Street's Guaranty Trust estimated that America's millionaire total had soared sixfold since 1923.[69] Midway through 1929, at least thirty thousand Americans held personal fortunes worth $1 million, the equivalent of about $13 million today.[70] In that same year, 513 taxpayers reported *incomes* over $1 million. These high-flyers averaged $2.36 million before taxes and $1.99 million after.[71]

Just over a fifth of America's families that same year earned less than $1,000, according to a Brookings Institution study.[72] Four in ten families were making less than $1,500, seven in ten less than $2,500. In the cities, an income that size in 1929 essentially meant "a cold-water apartment and subsistence diet."[73] The nation's most affluent 1 percent in 1929, calculates University of California economist Emmanuel Saez, took home on average thirty-eight times more income than the average of America's bottom 90 percent of income earners. The nation's top tenth of 1 percent outpaced this bottom 90 percent average by 184 times.[74]

The residences of these ultrawealthy lined Manhattan's Park Avenue. A three-mile stretch of that byway early in 1929 hosted five thousand families worth a combined $3 billion. The world had never seen such a geographic concentration of wealth. Park Avenue hosted four times more millionaires than Britain, "more millionaires per square block," marvels wealth historian Larry Samuel, "than per square mile anywhere else."[75]

Amos Pinchot, the affluent New York attorney turned warrior against plutocracy, walked those Park Avenue blocks in the 1920s. Years earlier, he had delighted in that stroll. But his amblings on the avenue now thoroughly depressed him, politically and physically. Park Avenue and America's rich had gone through "a metamorphosis," Pinchot would write. The Park Avenue rich had come to "constitute in a very real sense a privileged or governing class comparable to the prewar aristocracies of England, France or Italy." Their wealth towered over the rest of America, as did their residences. New York's wealthy, Pinchot sadly recorded, "have permitted this Avenue to be built up almost solidly with skyscrapers so that, in spite of its width, Park Avenue has become, except for a few brief hours each day, a great sunless gulch of high winds and shadows."[76]

The typical Park Avenue family, the Park Avenue Association reported, spent $70,000 a year on furnishings, over $900,000 in today's dollars. The Park Avenue rich imported fireplaces and wood paneling from English manor homes. They winked at Prohibition and outfitted their duplexes and triplexes with brass-railed private barrooms.[77]

The rich spent and spent. But in the end they could not spend enough, could not personally consume enough, to keep America's economic engine humming. America's highly productive factories needed customers with cash—many millions of them—to thrive and expand. If America's wealth had been shared, at even modest levels, these millions would have materialized. That sharing never took place. Some men of wealth would come to understand the resulting danger. "Mass production," as the millionaire Utah banker Marriner Eccles would write, "has to be accompanied by mass consumption," and mass consumption, in turn, requires a relatively equal distribution of wealth.[78] The United States didn't have that distribution in the 1920s. We had instead, Eccles noted, "a giant suction pump" drawing more and more wealth to the already rich and "taking purchasing power out of the hands of mass consumers."

"In consequence, as in a poker game where the chips were concentrated in fewer and fewer hands, the other fellows could stay in the game only by borrowing," the Utah banker explained. "When their credit ran out, the game stopped."

Until that stopping moment, the concentration of America's income and wealth would have the nation's economy on a wild roller coaster ride. The problem at the root of that wild ride: The rich simply had too much money sloshing in their pockets. The nation's richest 0.1 percent—just twenty-four thousand families—held over a third of the nation's wealth.[79] They could and did consume some of that. They could and did invest in productive enterprises with some more. But that still left the wealthy with huge stashes of cash looking for profit-making opportunities. These wealthy did what the wealthy always do when the cash in their pockets runneth over. They speculated.

First in real estate. The surge in automobile manufacturing created a booming market for suburban and vacation homes. Developers, notes economic historian Polly Cleveland, rushed to cash in.[80] They bought up and subdivided huge chunks of acreage. Banks greased the way with "shoestring mortgages" that enabled purchasers to pick up property without putting much of their own money down. Property and home prices, amid this growing speculative mania, shot up spectacularly. Around Chicago, land values rose over four times faster than population growth from the end of World War I to 1926. Between 1920 and 1926, San Diego would see an 80 percent leap in the value of building permits.[81] In Florida, the land boom's epicenter, an elderly man from Pinellas County found himself committed to a sanitarium—by his sons—after he put his $1,700 life savings into a local land deal. In 1925, the value of that Pinellas parcel hit $350,000. The committed elderly gentleman then won his release and sued his sons.[82]

The land bubble popped in 1926. In Florida, a wave of bankruptcies then hit banks and developers with hurricane force. Creditors settled for tiny fractions of a penny on the dollar. In Boca Raton, one typical bankruptcy settlement left an engineering firm owed $30,764 with just $30.76.[83] But the real estate bust in no way dampened the nation's speculative spirit. The action merely shifted to Wall Street and the stock market. Americans had, of course, been trading stocks for generations. But nineteenth-century stock traders, as financial historian Lawrence Mitchell notes, mostly "saw corporate securities as a way to get a steady return while protecting their principal." By the 1920s, most traders had become speculators, ever ready to pounce and profit off "the fluctuations of an increasingly volatile market."[84]

Wall Street bankers fed this growing speculative frenzy. They assembled armies of sales agents who descended on Americans of middle-class means—professionals, shopkeepers, and other small businesspeople—with dreamy promises of substantial and worry-free reward. Few Americans could afford to take the stock market plunge, no more than two million out of a 125 million population.[85] But "margin accounts" would help these two million create an enormous demand for financial product. At the start of 1928, an investor buying "on margin" could pick up an eighty-five dollar share of RCA stock with just ten dollars. By year's end, that share was selling at $420. The investor could sell, pay off the original seventy-five-dollar margin loan, and walk away with a $330 profit off a ten dollar initial investment.[86]

Everyone with a modicum of money seemed to want in on this game, and Wall Street bankers graciously obliged. They gobbled up real-life brick-and-mortar enterprises from their private owners and turned the enterprises into stock certificates suitable for public consumption. But America only had so many real companies. Wall Street bankers would invent new ones. They created "investment trusts" that would have no other purpose than to own shares of stocks in other companies. Each investment trust would then issue its own shares of stock.

"Holding companies" would operate on a similar principle. Their principals would use other people's money, raised through the stock market, to collect real companies within particular industries, most notably railroads and utilities. They would proceed to loot the companies—and consumers—in these broad holding company empires.[87]

Investment trusts sold $400 million worth of stock in 1927, notes one history of the era by journalist Linda McQuaig and tax law academic Neil Brooks, and $3 billion worth just two years later. One immense railway holding company organized by movers and shakers at J. P. Morgan would all by itself amass a $3 billion value.[88]

By decade's end, the corporate pillars of America's real economy—General Motors, Chrysler, General Foods, Standard Oil—had tossed their chips into the Wall Street frenzy too. These corporate giants could make more money supplying money for margin loans than they could investing in their own operations. Speculators would pay dearly and willingly for that money. Interest rates on margin loans would rise up to 10 and 12, then even 20 percent.[89] No matter. If investments continued to rise at RCA-like rates, the speculators could still make a killing.

Not as much, naturally, as the Wall Street insiders who were nurturing the speculation. These fabulously rich insiders chafed at the income taxes the federal government still expected them to pay. At 25 percent on income over $100,000, the top federal rate was still running more than triple the 7 percent top rate in effect as recently as 1915.

The savviest of Wall Street's rich saw the Republican Party at this point as something of a dead-end. Republicans in Congress had tried and failed—with their national sales tax proposal—to come up with an alternative source of revenue to the income tax. But an easier alternative beckoned: the repeal of Prohibition. But Republicans could never push that repeal. They remained too culturally beholden to Midwest Protestant temperance values and voters. The big-city Democrats, on the other hand, could go after Prohibition. The obvious strategy for Wall Street's savviest: take control of the Democratic Party and make repealing Prohibition the party's top platform plank. With repeal, alcohol would be legal and taxable once again. The revenues from resuming federal excise taxes on alcohol would be enough to offset halving the income tax. The rich, notes historian Robert McElvaine, would give America's workers beer. America's workers would give the rich a tax cut.[90]

The scheme almost worked. Deep pockets around Pierre du Pont, president of the DuPont empire, lined up behind New York governor Al Smith, a Wall Street pal with the common touch, and Smith, once he had the 1928 Democratic nomination in hand, named Wall Street financier Jakob Raskob chairman of the Democratic National Committee. Smith would campaign as a "wet"—and fiscally to the right of Republican Herbert Hoover.

But Hoover had the momentum of the Roaring Twenties behind him and romped to an easy victory. The DuPont backroom maneuvering may have even reawakened Hoover's inner Populist. Newly inaugurated, in March 1929 Hoover would pronounce that "excessive fortunes are a menace to true liberty by the accumulation and inheritance of economic power."[91] He then retired from service the presidential yacht.

That symbolic gesture may have momentarily raised some worried eyebrows on Wall Street and Park Avenue. Still, the nation's rich had no real reason to fear Hoover, or anyone for that matter. The nation's two major parties had now both become cheerleaders for a national economic order that championed the pursuit of grand fortune. "Everybody Ought to be Rich," as the headline over a 1929

Ladies Home Journal article by Democratic National Party Chairman Jakob Raskob put it.[92]

The rich, to be sure, still had worries. Yacht owners had a devil of a time convincing their fellow rich to join them on yachting excursions. No one wanted to be stuck on board a two-hundred-foot yacht, trapped with boring company, for days on end. "The problem of getting a yacht full of congenial guests for a cruise of any length" had become such a headache, Samuel Blythe, an upstate New York editor and Rochester Yacht Club member, would write, "that most yacht owners give up in despair after a few tries." Their yachts would sit forlornly, unused, for years at a time.[93]

Not all vessels of the wealthy would suffer this fate. First National Bank of New York president George F. Baker Jr. used his lovely boat nearly every day. He commuted via speed cruiser to Wall Street from his home on Long Island, shaving and dressing on board.[94] In the fall of 1929, Baker's sun-drenched commutes would suddenly darken. The Wall Street house of cards, the endless pyramiding of investment trusts, had begun to topple. Baker and a half-dozen fellow Wall Street bankers would raise a quarter-billion dollars to calm the markets, but the markets would have no calming. America's greatest speculative bubble had now burst. Americans with money ran scared. They began yanking savings out of their bank accounts. Banks failed, businesses went bankrupt, workers lost jobs. America no longer roared. American plutocracy had failed.

Chester Bowles, a young Yale grad and a successful Madison Avenue advertising executive when the crash hit, would later mull over that failure. The decade of the 1920s had demonstrated, he would write, "that prosperity cannot continue unless enough income is being distributed to all of us—farmers and workers as well as businessmen."[95]

The plutocrats had had their opportunity, and they had blown it. America had given them everything they desired. The freedom to do whatever they wanted. The power to bend others to their will. And ever-grander fortunes as both incentive and reward. America choked on those fortunes. A maldistribution of income and wealth that severe the American economy simply could not swallow.

"Even with the most business-minded administration in our history, even with falling taxes and a government surplus, even with everything that businessmen thought they needed to insure continued prosperity," Bowles reflected, "we could not duck that basic issue for more than a few tinsel-decorated years."

Chapter Five

GREAT DEPRESSION AND GRAND CONFUSION

Over five hundred taxpayers reported incomes over $1 million in 1929. Three years later, the IRS would count only twenty million-dollar returns.[1] The widening economic collapse that began in 1929 left almost all Americans, the rich included, financially poorer and psychologically shaken.

"The present depression," the former *Vanity Fair* editor Edmund Wilson wrote in 1931, "may be one of the turning-points in our history, our first real crisis since the Civil War."[2]

Year by year, the economy sank ever deeper into distress. The "present depression" evolved into the "Great Depression." And no corner of America could escape the squeeze. On the farm, cows that sold for eighty-three dollars in 1929 would fetch twenty-eight dollars in the early 1930s. In the nation's great manufacturing hubs, factories went silent. Steel production plummeted by 59 percent. Unemployment soared to over 25 percent.[3] Detroit had 302,000 auto workers on the job in 1929. By 1931, the city's auto workers totaled just 185,000.[4] Those workers who kept their jobs kept most all of their wages—at first. Large employers loudly pledged a no-wage-cut policy in the Depression's early months. They would keep their pledge, by and large, until US Steel broke ranks in September 1931. In quick order, the nation's other economic giants matched US Steel and sliced wages 10 percent.[5]

Perceptive reporters would soon be describing a nation that no American had ever experienced. Gerald Johnson, a veteran journalist with newspapers from New York to his native North Carolina, had a particularly pungent take on how the new hard times were hitting the "ordinary American."

"If that ordinary American was a workman, he had no job; if a farmer, he had no market; if a small merchant or manufacturer, he had no customers," Johnson wrote.[6]

And families would have no homes. Banks repossessed. Landlords evicted. Reeling households, writes labor historian Paul Buhle, would have "their worldly goods moved onto the street unless 'reds' halted the police and 'renegotiated' with the authorities."[7]

Average Americans had never before experienced such economic suffering, mainly because average Americans in every previous national economic meltdown had lived on the farm. They had the land to fall back on. They could raise much of what they ate. They could get by with little cash income. By the early 1930s, that rural America had largely disappeared. Only a fifth of Great Depression–era working Americans made their living off agriculture.[8] America's vast majority lived urban existences. They had no land. Without cash, they didn't eat.

Private charity helped. A little. In New York, a "businessmen's committee" provided twelve thousand jobless half-time "made work" at fifty-four dollars per month. The City Welfare Bureau, a public agency, chipped in with home relief checks that rose up to $6.60 per week for families with children. All combined, private and public relief in New York reached a grand total of ninety thousand families with a jobless head of household. In the summer of 1932, New York had 391,000 such households.[9]

The hard times extended deep into America's modest middle class. In the New York borough of Queens, developers had constructed the model suburban community of Sunnyside Gardens in the 1920s. The families of about five hundred professionals—writers, architects, small businesspeople—called Sunnyside Gardens home when the hard times first hit in 1929. Three years later, a survey found family income in Sunnyside Gardens down by half. Family bank savings account balances had fallen 76 percent, unpaid dentist and doctor bills had risen 150 percent. Half the development's families had been forced to cancel their life insurance policies.[10]

At the upper-class level, most wealthy families suffered financial setbacks of some sort. In 1932, Bethlehem Steel chief Charles M. Schwab would even famously declare that "there are no rich men in America today."[11] Schwab was exaggerating, in a material sense. Most rich remained financially secure. They kept to their normal routines and enjoyed their normal comforts. But Schwab's declaration rested on much firmer psychological ground. The rich no longer felt rich. More to the point, they didn't feel in control. They had lost their plutocratic grip on the future.

Matthew Josephson, a New York writer of modest means, had an artist friend who had married into a wealthy family. Josephson would from time to time attend dinner parties at the couple's "charmingly decorated house in the East Fifties." At one, the wealthy hostess stood to offer an unexpected "formal little speech of farewell." The couple's income from stocks and bonds, the hostess announced, had fallen by 25 percent. The couple would be leaving Manhattan "to live in a simple country house" and, she added with dignity and seriousness, "to wait there for The Revolution!"

Years later, Josephson would still remember the scene vividly: "Everyone laughed nervously. But in 1932 and 1933 rich people sometimes sounded like Marie Antoinette being driven from the Palace of Versailles."[12]

This fear of social upheaval oozed throughout comfortable circles. "Revolution, not prosperity," seemed just "around the corner," Randolph Paul, then a Wall Street tax lawyer, would recall nearly two decades later.

The rich felt themselves dead-center in an angry America's crosshairs. Everywhere they looked, someone seemed to be taking aim at their wealth and power and the "New Era" they had so proudly proclaimed back in the 1920s. That New Era, their values, now stood revealed as a fraud of monumental proportions. The blame for the calamity that had befallen America rested squarely on their shoulders.

"No earthquakes, or tidal waves, or volcanoes had damaged the land," as journalist Gerald Johnson put it. "No pestilence like the Black Death had swept away the workers. No invading army had burned down the factories and torn up the railroads and highways. No convulsion of nature of any kind had smitten the United States. Nothing had failed, except the economic system, that is, business."[13]

"We have permitted business and financial autocracy to reach such a point that its logical political counterpart is a Mussolini," echoed the widely respected philosopher John Dewey in 1932, "unless a violent revolution brings forth a Lenin."[14]

And a Lenin didn't appear out of the question to America's rattled elite. New York's Union Square saw so many Communist Party demonstrations that people were only half jokingly referring to the dilapidated park as "Red Square." At one protest, on May Day, 1932, sixty thousand people showed up. The nervous police had machine guns at the ready on rooftops overlooking the square.[15]

Out in the country, conservatives shared an equal sense of dread. One fearful leader of the agricultural establishment, Edward O'Neal of the American Farm Bureau Federation, brought Congress a warning in testimony delivered early in 1933: "Unless something is done for the American farmer, we will have revolution in the countryside in less than twelve months."[16]

Angry farmers from upstate New York to Oregon, some armed, were resisting foreclosures, overturning milk trucks, and refusing to make payments to banks. Similar raucous behavior was breaking out on city streets. Groups of thirty or forty unemployed men, relates historian Robert McElvaine, would regularly march into large chain stores and demand food. Most of the incidents went unreported. Newspaper editors "feared publicity might precipitate other such actions."[17]

Much larger groups of protestors—World War I veterans—began marching on Washington to demand early payment of the bonuses Congress in 1924 had promised to pay out in 1945. By the summer of 1932, a "Bonus Army" encampment in the nation's capital would hold over twenty thousand veterans and their families. The US House of Representatives felt the veterans' pain—and public pressure—and endorsed the early bonus payout. The Senate rejected it. The Hoover administration then had the veterans forcibly—and bloodily—evicted when they refused to call off their protest.[18]

Back in the early 1920s, the nation's men of property had been able to count on veterans from the American Legion to bust up picket lines and help them keep the labor "peace." Now veterans were challenging their plutocratic betters. And other former New Era allies of property had become restive as well, even the Catholic Church hierarchy. A new 1931 encyclical from Pius XI informed the faithful that government had an obligation "to adjust ownership to meet the needs of the public good." *America*, a conservative Catholic magazine, chose to take the pope's words seriously. The editors called for more government control over the economy and deemed capitalism as Americans have known it "a stupid and malicious giant."[19]

America's besieged plutocrats could, on the other hand, still count on the full faith and support of the nation's elected leaders. The nation's top politicos continued to genuflect before men of means.

The policy prescriptions elected officials advanced would essentially boil down to appeals that the wealthy do the right thing. The wrong thing, President Hoover and congressional leaders of both parties agreed, would be any step that jeopardized "business confidence."

President Hoover initially approached the crisis with the same can-do engineering zeal that had won him fame as the world's top emergency food relief coordinator during World War I. The Hoover White House quickly forged grand partnerships with business to get the economy moving again, with a "no wage cut" pledge a key element of that effort. Hoover even boosted spending somewhat for public works. But nothing Hoover did seemed to be enough to restart America's economic engine. And the more the economy lurched backward, the more Hoover accepted the basic plutocratic perspective on the hard times. The Depression, the plutocrats held, amounted to an economic natural disaster. Such disasters could not be predicted or prevented. The American people simply had to have patience and faith in their betters. If they did, all would eventually be well.

"All the really important millionaires," as the widely syndicated conservative columnist Arthur Brisbane assured America, "are planning to continue prosperity."[20]

The veteran progressives still in Congress had no patience. They seethed. The leaders of both major parties, New York congressman Fiorello LaGuardia confided in a 1931 letter to fellow GOP insurgent George Norris from Nebraska, were still legislating "on fundamentals laid down in the age of the stage coach, the spinning wheel, and tallow candles." That tendency, LaGuardia added, had concentrated "great wealth under the control of a few families in this country" and left "large masses of workers entirely at their mercy for their very existence."[21]

Democratic and Republican leaders alike seemed equally committed to keeping those few families in control of that great wealth, no matter how brutal the crisis might become. And by late 1931 the fiscal brutality of the crisis had become too blatant to ignore. The federal government was collecting far too little revenue from a Depression-ravaged economy to function. The government, the White House and congressional leadership both understood, had to raise more revenue. But the new revenue the government so desperately needed, top Democrats and Republicans also agreed, must not come from the rich.

In November 1931, just before Thanksgiving, Democratic Senate floor leader Joseph Robinson from Arkansas arrived back in Washington to drive that point home with comments the *Washington Post* called "so conservative as to sound like a statement from Secretary of the Treasury Andrew Mellon." Robinson warned against any move that might subject the nation's wealthy to significant new taxation. Serious people understood, the Democratic Party Senate leader would explain, that the government could only tax the rich so much "without discouraging investment and production."[22]

The new House Speaker, the Democrat John Nance Garner from Texas, stressed the same theme the next month. He delivered what the *Los Angeles Times* Washington correspondent would dub a "mild spanking" to his Democratic Party colleagues who had had the nerve to suggest boosting tax rates on high incomes back to wartime levels.[23] A few weeks later, another leading Democrat, acting House Ways and Means Committee Chairman Charles Crisp of Georgia, continued the spanking. The nation could never meet its fiscal emergency by "soaking the rich," Crisp informed his colleagues. Average Americans will have to "gird" themselves for "tremendous sacrifices." A national sales tax, or some other tax that demanded "stamina" and "backbone" from all Americans, was going to have to be levied.[24]

The Hoover administration agreed, in part. The Treasury Department would ask Congress to enact new or higher federal excise taxes on many everyday purchases and services, everything from tobacco to telephone calls. But the Republican Hoover administration would not go along with a national sales tax. Undersecretary of the Treasury Ogden Mills, soon to become treasury secretary after Andrew Mellon resigned to become ambassador to Great Britain, asked Congress instead to up the nation's top income bracket tax rate from 25 to 40 percent and lower the income threshold that determines who has to face federal income taxation. All married couples making over $2,500—about $41,000 today—should be paying income tax, urged Mills. If Congress adopted the Treasury plan, he noted, the number of Americans with federal income tax liability would rise from 1.9 million out of a nation of 120 million to 3.6 million. Mills, himself an heir to a megamillion banking and mining fortune, would even ask Congress to raise the federal estate tax rate.

What explains the White House's sudden willingness to contemplate slightly higher tax levies on America's comfortable? Hoover administration officials may have considered a little political discretion here the better part of valor. Better to modestly increase taxes on the wealthy than to risk the popular wrath that a national sales tax might unleash.

Republican and Democratic leaders in Congress had no such fears. The pressure they felt came from newspaper publisher William Randolph Hearst, the powerful media magnate who had emerged as the national sales tax notion's most fervent advocate. Hearst even bankrolled an all-expenses-paid congressional junket to Canada to see a national sales tax in action. The flamboyant publisher had no particular philosophical fondness for taxing sales. Neither did any of his fellow wealthy Americans. They simply wanted Congress to put in place an alternative to taxing income. Their income. Americans, as Hearst wrote in a nationally circulated editorial in March 1932, must "carry on a sustained crusade Morning, Evening, and Sunday against the present Bolshevist system of income taxation."[25]

The Democratic Party majority on the House Ways and Means Committee obediently obliged. Lawmakers on the panel repudiated the Hoover administration and nixed any income tax hike. They passed instead an almost all-encompassing national sales tax, a 2.25 percent manufacturer's excise levy on everything but food.[26]

What happened next would floor top Democrats and their calculated bid to position the party as a reliable partner for America's rich and powerful. Wall Street financier Jakob Raskob and his deep-pocketed pals in the party hierarchy had gone too far. Americans pushed back. They mounted the first national political surge against plutocracy since the Great Depression began.

The surge broke out almost as a matter of spontaneous political combustion. From across the nation, average Americans began bombarding congressional offices with angry complaints about the pending new national sales tax. In the face of this surprise bombardment, rank-and-file Democrats in Congress joined with LaGuardia and other progressive House Republicans and killed the national sales tax proposal by a stunning 223–153 margin. Amid House floor shouts of "soak the rich!" and "conscript wealth!"—the battle cry of the World War I income limit campaign—they then raised the top income tax rate from 25 percent over $100,000 to 63 percent over $1 million.[27] The new higher tax rates, notes tax historian Elliot Brownlee, would double the effective tax burden on America's richest 1 percent.[28] The final tax bill this rank-and-file lawmaker revolt generated also raised the top estate tax rate—from 20 to 45 percent on bequest value over $10 million—and, in a move designed to counter estate tax avoidance, restored the gift tax as well.

House Democratic Majority Leader Henry Rainey would not

be happy about any of this. "We have made a longer step in the direction of communism," he told his House colleagues, "than any country in the world ever made except Russia."[29] But Rainey remained above all else a savvy politician. He saw clearly that Americans overwhelmingly supported higher taxes on the wealthy, and now he would make the best of a bad situation. The evening after the crushing defeat of the sales tax proposition, Rainey spoke live on a national CBS radio hookup and positioned the new taxes on the rich as a fiscally prudent step toward balancing the federal budget. He would also do his best to convince Americans that the rich had now sacrificed quite enough.

Lawmakers in the House, Rainey told the nation, had raised income taxes on the wealthy "to the very breaking point" and taken "the major parts of big estates." Even "the most violent advocate of 'soaking the rich' ought to be satisfied," the Democratic majority leader pronounced. "We have 'soaked the rich,' I assure you," Rainey would repeat for emphasis at the close of his radio address.[30]

In fact, the soaking had been more of a quick rinse. Even after the increases, taxes on the nation's wealthy remained substantially lower than top rates in effect during World War I. The bulk of the tax dollars the new revenue legislation raised would come from new and increased excise taxes, some on luxury items like furs but most on everyday items like chewing gum and lubricating oil.[31] Even so, the 1932 tax fight did mark a turning point. The rich and their political enablers had reached for the brass ring, a national sales tax, and the American people had slapped them down.

In Albany, the state capital of New York, an ambitious governor took notice. Just two weeks after the tax brouhaha in Washington, Franklin D. Roosevelt, a leading candidate for the 1932 Democratic Party nomination, would begin a remarkable series of addresses that aligned his candidacy four-square with America's grassroots push against plutocracy.

The first of these addresses, broadcast April 7 in NBC's *Lucky Strike Hour*, would champion the "forgotten man at the bottom of the economic pyramid" and blast away at a national administration that "can think in terms only of the top of the social and economic structure."[32] Hoover, Roosevelt charged, had "sought temporary relief from the top down rather than permanent relief from the bottom up." He had placed billions "at the disposal of the big banks, the railroads, and the corporations of the Nation."

Less than two weeks later, at a Jefferson Day speech in St. Paul, Minnesota, Roosevelt elaborated on the danger of favoring one class over another, the few over the many: "In much of our present plans, there is too much disposition to mistake the part for the whole, the head for the body, the captain for the company, the general for the army."[33] The next month, at a commencement address at Georgia's Oglethorpe University, still more on the same theme. Roosevelt delivered a stirring call for "bold, persistent experimentation" to aid the "millions who are in want."

"Do what we may have to do to inject life into our ailing economic order," the presidential hopeful would explain, "we cannot make it endure for long unless we can bring about a wiser, more equitable distribution of the national income."[34]

The New Deal had begun.

Franklin Roosevelt made for an unlikely standard-bearer against plutocracy. Franklin and his wife Eleanor both came from genteel families of privilege. They lived lives far more elegant than all but a small sliver of Americans. The couple, notes one FDR biographer, "lived in three different houses at various seasons of the year, always employed at least five servants, maintained a large yacht and numerous smaller boats, automobiles, and carriages, dressed in fashion, belonged to expensive clubs, traveled extensively, and gave generously to political and charitable causes."[35]

Franklin entered politics as a Democrat, unlike his distant cousin and Eleanor's uncle Theodore. Also unlike Theodore, Franklin would early on show no particular reforming zeal. In 1911, as a freshman New York State legislator in Albany, Franklin Roosevelt played no role in the legislative battles over industrial safety reform that followed the tragic Triangle factory fire.[36] FDR would be content to promote a vague "good government" agenda and duck under the class war swirling all around him.

Roosevelt far more resembled his distant cousin Teddy on the campaign trail. FDR showed a natural affinity for political stumping. People liked this jaunty young man. And the celebrated "Roosevelt" brand certainly didn't hurt FDR's political prospects. Theodore had campaigned all the way into the White House. Young Franklin saw no reason why he couldn't end up at the same destination. Rung by rung, Franklin followed Teddy's route up the political ladder. Teddy had been an assistant secretary of the navy. Franklin would be, too, during World War I. Teddy had been the Republican vice-presidential nominee in 1900. In 1920, Franklin ran for vice president on the Democratic ticket as the understudy for James Cox, a conservative and colorless former Ohio governor. The Cox-Roosevelt slate would be swamped. But no one blamed FDR. His political future still seemed as bright as ever.

Election over, Roosevelt settled in with a Wall Street law firm. The titans of Corporate America—Owen Young of General Electric, Edward Stettinius of US Steel, Daniel Willard of the Pennsylvania Railroad—would give him welcome, at a lavish black-tie dinner FDR's new law firm hosted to bring him into the business fold.[37] But the young Roosevelt, still not forty years old, would never fit in fully on Wall Street. He had too much of "old money" about him to be impressed by, or even particularly interested in, the "new money" Corporate America's "New Era" could offer. And naked business power grabs had always offended FDR's "good government" sensibilities. He had welcomed Woodrow Wilson's 1916 election as "the debacle of plutocracy."[38]

In the 1920s, other young men on the make quickly tossed aside any remnants of Wilsonian "idealism" they may have once held dear. They would rub shoulders, scratch backs, and share inside information as they sashayed down Wall Street's power alleys. Franklin Roosevelt would do no sashaying. In August 1921, a sudden illness diagnosed as polio left FDR paralyzed below the waist. He would spend the 1920s struggling to walk again. The convalescing would take Roosevelt to rural Georgia for weeks at a time. He would pass his free hours driving the Georgia country roads in a specially outfitted car, meeting and befriending families struggling to get by. The encounters would have a deep impact on the aristocratic New Yorker. FDR, says biographer Jean Edward Smith, would be "thrilled at his exposure to the life of ordinary people."[39] He would never forget.

Nor would FDR lose his passion for politics. Roosevelt and his inner circle refused to let his disability taint him as damaged goods. They all conspired to hide Roosevelt's paralysis from public view. They succeeded. In 1928, FDR would be elected governor of New York. The road to the White House now seemed clear once again, and Roosevelt would charge down that road as a man of the people. On July 4, 1929, at the dedication for the new local headquarters of New York City's Tammany Hall Democratic Party machine, Roosevelt would have the party faithful cheering as he called for resistance against grand accumulations of economic power. Without that resistance, he warned, "all property would be concentrated in the hands of a few, and the overwhelming majority would become serfs."[40]

America's "overwhelming majority" would shortly feel that impending serfdom. The stock market crashed that October. In short order, the hard times that Roosevelt had witnessed all throughout the 1920s on the dusty back roads of Georgia began spreading over the paved byways of New York. Roosevelt would take this widening distress far more seriously than his fellow elected leaders, either in Washington or other state capitals. In March 1930 FDR created the first state commission to target joblessness and soon after became the first governor to endorse the push for unemployment insurance.[41] A year later, New York established a Temporary Emergency Relief Administration, the nation's first, to speed assistance to Depression-devastated families. Roosevelt had lawmakers foot the bill for the assistance with a 50 percent hike in state personal income taxes, an increase that would place the relief-funding burden squarely on the state's most affluent.[42]

"It is clear to me," Roosevelt maintained, "that it is the duty of those who have benefited by our industrial and economic system to come to the front in such a grave emergency and assist in relieving those who under the same industrial and economic order are the losers and sufferers."[43]

Revenue from this 1931 income tax increase would not be enough to foot the rising bill for relief. In 1932, Governor Roosevelt came back to lawmakers for more. He secured a doubling of state taxes on income, gasoline, and Wall Street financial transactions. The new gas tax would hit average New Yorkers, but the package as a whole still kept the bulk of the burden on the state's deepest pockets.[44]

In Washington, a leading Senate critic of America's rich and powerful would be impressed. This Democrat from the Deep South liked what he saw Roosevelt doing in New York. He appreciated FDR's advocacy for the "forgotten man." He shared Roosevelt's commitment to a "more equitable distribution of the national income." At the 1932 Democratic convention in Chicago, with Roosevelt's bid for the nomination hanging by the slimmest of threads, this Southern senator would go behind the scenes and twist all the arms he could grab to keep Southern delegates in line for FDR.

The Southern delegates did stay in line. Roosevelt took the nomination on the convention's fourth ballot, outlasting both House Speaker John Nance Garner from Texas, the congressional leader who had "spanked" fellow Democrats for expressing tax-the-rich sentiments at the start of the 1932 session, and Al Smith, the 1928 Democratic presidential nominee who had schemed with party boss Jakob Raskob on the failed attempt to turn repeal of Prohibition into a huge tax break for America's wealthy. Roosevelt's political guardian angel at the 1932 Democratic convention, the eccentric and blustery Senator Huey Long from Louisiana, would gain no public plaudits for his pivotal role. But FDR insiders knew what had transpired.

"There is no question in my mind," Roosevelt political operative Ed Flynn would later write, "but that without Long's work Roosevelt might not have been nominated."[45]

FDR had defeated his rivals John Nance Garner and Al Smith for the nomination. But he needed their support to carry the general election in November. In Roosevelt's entire adult lifetime, no Democrat had ever entered the White House without a split in Republican ranks, and, in 1932, Republicans entered the fall campaign united. No progressive Republican had broken ranks to challenge Hoover with an independent candidacy. Roosevelt could only hope to win if he could keep all the Democratic Party factions united behind him, and that would mean throwing bones to conservative Democrats. John Nance Garner would get the vice-presidential nomination, and the 1932 party platform would sound conservative notes. The platform pledged that Democrats would reduce federal spending and balance the federal budget.

FDR campaigned on that same pledge. He would give conservatives what they wanted to hear, and he would give progressives the same consideration. They would be able to find in FDR's campaigning what they wanted to hear as well.

In September, at San Francisco's Commonwealth Club, FDR proudly situated his campaign in the ongoing, centuries-long struggle against government "conducted for the benefit of a few who thrived unduly at the expense of all." He committed himself to the work "of distributing wealth and products more equitably, of adapting existing economic organizations to the service of the people."[46] The next month, in Detroit, Roosevelt attacked the notion "that if we make the rich richer, somehow they will let a part of their prosperity trickle down to the rest of us." He went on to quote approvingly from a sermon distributed earlier in the year by the Council of Churches.

"The concentration of wealth carries with it a dangerous concentration of power," Roosevelt read from the sermon. "It leads to conflict and violence. To suppress the symptoms of this inherent conflict while leaving the fundamental causes of it untouched is neither sound statesmanship nor Christian good-will."[47]

This Council of Churches warning against violence would prove somewhat prophetic. Four months later, a would-be assassin's bullets would miss FDR at an appearance in Miami and fatally wound the mayor of Chicago standing beside him.

"I have always hated the rich and powerful," Giuseppe Zangara, the unemployed Italian immigrant bricklayer who fired the shots, later told police. "I do not hate Mr. Roosevelt personally."[48]

By that time, Mr. Roosevelt had become President-Elect Roosevelt, after overwhelming the incumbent Hoover in the November election, sweeping all but six states and collecting over 57 percent of the votes cast. But this sweep would be as much a vote for change as a personal triumph for FDR. Americans were voting for relief from a political system that seemed to answer only to the rich. They would give their votes to any candidate who promised to deliver that relief.

Even a candidate as improbable as Hattie Caraway.

Until 1931, former schoolteacher Hattie Caraway had been the unassuming life partner of Thaddeus Caraway, an obscure US senator from Arkansas. But the senator's death that year would thrust his widow onto the public stage. In December 1931, the Arkansas governor appointed Hattie Caraway to the Senate, a common practice at the time. A pro forma election the next month cemented her temporary Senate status for the one year left in her husband's term.

Top Arkansas politicians, meanwhile, jockeyed for position in the upcoming 1932 summer primary that would determine the occupant of the Thaddeus Caraway Senate seat for the next full six-year term. No one paid any attention to Hattie. Why would they? No woman in the history of the United States had ever won a Senate election for a full six-year term. Hattie Caraway hardly appeared the woman who would shatter that political glass ceiling. In Washington, she uttered not one public word in the Senate chamber for four months. Then in May 1932 Hattie Caraway suddenly did speak. She announced her candidacy for a full Senate term, an announcement that must have been the source of no small merriment in Little Rock political circles. Six men had already announced bids for the Democratic Party nomination. They all had constituencies and political credibility. Hattie Caraway had nothing.

Except Huey Long. Caraway had caught Long's attention in the Senate chamber when she bucked the Senate leadership and backed a proposal he had advanced to limit the personal fortunes of America's richest. Now Long would back Caraway.

Two weeks after the Democratic national convention, where Long played the pivotal backstage role that put FDR over the top, Long's campaign aides from Louisiana began blanketing Arkansas with literature that hailed Hattie Caraway as the people's choice in the battle against plutocracy. In August, Long himself joined the campaign, making "four, five, six speeches a day," writes historian Alan Brinkley, driving "at breakneck speed along bumpy country roads" to reach audiences that swelled into the thousands. Long drew five thousand in Hot Springs, over twenty thousand in Pine Bluff, almost thirty thousand in Little Rock, "the largest political gathering in the history of the state."[49] At every stop, Long talked up his proposal to limit grand fortune and Hattie Caraway's support for it.

"Think of it, my friends! In 1930 there were 540 men in Wall Street who made $100,000,000 more than all the wheat farmers and all the cotton farmers and the corn farmers of this country put together," Long told his attentive Arkansas listeners. "And you people wonder why your belly's flat up against your backbone."[50]

On the August 9 Arkansas primary—the only Election Day that counted in a state where Democrats had no serious competition from Republicans—voters showed their backbones. They gave Hattie Caraway an astonishing upset victory. She more than doubled the vote of the primary's second-place finisher. For the first time ever, the United States Senate now had a woman elected to a six-year term—and Huey Long had a reliable Senate ally.

In the fall, Long would turn his attention to putting an ally in the White House. On behalf of the Roosevelt campaign, Long barnstormed across the Great Plains, drawing amazingly large crowds in Kansas, Nebraska, and the Dakotas. FDR wouldn't really need the help Long provided. Americans had already made up their minds, and Herbert Hoover never had a chance. The popular rage against him went strikingly deep. One hitchhiker, newspapers reported, made his way from California to New York in just five days carrying a sign that read, *Give me a lift or I'll vote for Hoover.*[51] Americans saw the incumbent president and his crowd as apologists for the awesomely affluent, and they wanted those apologists out.

Unfortunately, the constitutional calendar would keep the lame-duck Hoover in office long after the November 1932 election—until the following March 4, then the day new presidents took office. The months after November, months spent waiting for FDR, seemed to last forever. The nation's economy continued to deteriorate. The White House diddled while "lines of destitute men and women," the influential economic analyst Stuart Chase would later remember, "shuffled around whole city blocks, awaiting bowls of soup."[52] A quarter of the nation's adults had no jobs.

An even greater share of Americans had no respect for the nation's rich and powerful. The wealthy and their friends in high places had demonstrated they had no solutions. Indeed, the folly and futility of what had become the core Hoover administration approach—appealing to the public spiritedness of the rich—had never seemed clearer. In Michigan, the automobile tycoon Henry Ford was shoving Detroit into a major financial crisis. A major Detroit bank needed Ford, its biggest depositor, to "subordinate" his claims, so the bank could cover withdrawals from other smaller depositors and avert a bank-run panic that could spread across the country. The Hoover administration sent Department of the Treasury Undersecretary Arthur Ballantine, a New York corporation lawyer, to Detroit. He urged Ford to cooperate. Ford refused.

"If the crash has to come," he told Ballantine, "let it come."

Ford would be ready. He had a thousand-man private army, he said, "to guard his grandchildren" against the rioting unemployed.[53]

Any real solution to the distress of those unemployed, Stuart Chase and other thoughtful observers understood, would have to tackle inequality, the staggering gap between America's rich and everyone else. That gap had both created the crisis and stalled the recovery from it. America's "inefficient distribution of wealth," as Wall Street tax lawyer Randolph Paul noted, "diverts too much income to groups that tend to save a large part of their income and leaves too little to those who must spend all of their income on consumption goods."[54]

Paul's perspective had deep roots in America's pre–World War

I progressive past, and that past remained a presence as the nation awaited Roosevelt. The 1914 classic by Louis Brandeis, *Other People's Money and How the Bankers Use It*, had been reissued in an affordable edition.[55] Brandeis himself remained a sitting Supreme Court justice. Just days after FDR's inauguration, in March 1933, a Brandeis high court opinion would echo the Randolph Paul diagnosis.

"There is widespread belief," Brandeis would write, "that the existing unemployment is the result, in large part, of the gross inequality in the distribution of wealth and income which great corporations have fostered; that by the control which the few have exerted through great corporations individual initiative and effort are being paralyzed, creative power impaired and human happiness lessened."[56]

So what to do? In February 1933, the Senate Finance Committee would conduct hearings on how to extract the United States from the deepening economic calamity. A steady stream of business leaders paraded before the senators. Most simply regurgitated corporate orthodoxy. Balance the federal budget. Reduce the federal debt. Utah banker Marriner Eccles would dissent. "When it came my turn," Eccles would later write, "I challenged all that had been said up to that point and was practically alone in doing so."[57]

Eccles shared that day on Capitol Hill the perspectives he had honed in a brilliantly successful business career. His bank holding company had twenty-six banks, and the millionaire Mormon also presided over an assortment of other business concerns in industries as varied as construction and milk. Eccles believed that men of ample means had rigged the economic game. Only government could undo the consequences of that rigging. America would only be able to exit the Depression, Eccles would tell anyone who would listen, "through government action in placing purchasing power in the hands of people who were in need of it."[58]

The day after his testimony in Washington, Eccles met in New York with FDR adviser Rexford Tugwell, in a meeting that Stuart Chase had brokered.[59] Tugwell warmed immediately to what Eccles had to say. The Columbia University economist had studied years earlier with Scott Nearing, the socialist economist who had warned against plutocracy's threat to American democracy. Other key players in the FDR inner policy circle, what would soon be known as Roosevelt's "brain trust," shared that dread of plutocratic power. Raymond Moley, a Columbia political scientist, had been raised on the philosophy of Henry George, the late nineteenth-century "single tax" critic of wealth concentration. In May 1932, Moley had pushed Roosevelt to break decisively with Democratic Party conservatives and campaign aggressively against the basic economic orientation that "sees to it that a favored few are helped" in hopes "that some of their prosperity will leak through to labor, to the farmer, and to the small businessman."[60]

That advice had served Roosevelt well in the campaign for the Democratic Party nomination. But candidate Roosevelt had labored with great success throughout the general election campaign to keep conservative Democratic leaders in line behind him. He had mixed in orthodoxy with his more egalitarian campaign pitches. What would FDR now do as president? Move boldly against the inequality that had crashed the economy? Follow the basic spread-the-wealth prescription coming from thoughtful analysts and maverick business leaders like Eccles? Or govern as he had run his general election campaign and try to move forward without unduly alarming the conservative power brokers FDR felt he needed politically to keep by his side? If FDR chose to make a bold strike against wealth and power, he would lose these conservatives. But he would certainly have the American public. Disgust at the wealthy would only mount in the weeks right after FDR took up White House residency.

On inauguration day in 1933, the Senate Banking Committee opened an enormously high-profile set of hearings into banker malfeasance before and after the 1929 crash. The lead committee inquisitor, former New York Assistant Attorney General Ferdinand Pecora, pounded witnesses relentlessly and generated one bombshell revelation after another. The nation's top bankers, his probing revealed, had actively engaged in bribery to manipulate share prices. They had conducted phony stock sales to sidestep taxes. They had raided the savings of depositors and handed themselves and their cronies massive interest-free loans.[61]

Public outrage at these greed grabs soon turned into ridicule—for wealthy Wall Streeters—after one exasperated Senate champion of beleaguered bankers complained that Pecora was creating a "circus" atmosphere with his hearings. That complaint would instantly inspire an enterprising Barnum & Bailey publicist. The next day, this publicist walked into the hearing room and dropped a circus performer just a few inches over two feet tall onto the lap of J. P. Morgan Jr., the son of America's most celebrated plutocrat and the chief of the Morgan banking empire. Outrageously comical photos of the encounter would grace front pages all across the country.[62]

America's bankers as a group, the rich as a class, had perhaps never before enjoyed so little public esteem—or stood as politically vulnerable. President Roosevelt had an enormous personal mandate, a huge majority in both House and Senate, and an American people ready to follow any leader who dared challenge the orthodoxy the rich had so obstinately defended. But Roosevelt would not dare. In the early days of his presidency, he did not lay siege on the reigning economic orthodoxy. The problem? He still subscribed to much of it himself. His general election campaign pitches for fiscal prudence had not all been sheer political calculation. An old-timer like Louis Brandeis could see boldly into the future. Roosevelt—in the spring of 1933—could not.

Brandeis had a coherent program for ending the Depression. Tax the rich to raise funds for a job-creating public works program. Go after grand personal fortunes by taxing away all inheritances over $1 million. Subject giant corporations to federal excise taxes that would fall far heavier on large companies than small. Create an unemployment insurance system that would force corporations to bear responsibility for maintaining worker purchasing power. Prohibit financial institutions from playing speculative games with depositor cash. To give banks competition, expand the postal savings bank system, the operation—in effect since 1911—that paid average Americans 2 percent interest for maintaining modest savings accounts with the post office.[63]

Roosevelt had no coherent plan. Like Brandeis, FDR certainly did want to alleviate the economic distress average Americans were suffering. Unlike Brandeis and other progressive political leaders, FDR would not advance any solution that might unduly inflame men of means to do battle against him.

On banking, for instance, Roosevelt rushed to stabilize a collapsed private system, not replace it or give it public competition. FDR declared a bank holiday hours after his inauguration, then had Congress rubberstamp an Emergency Banking Act five days later that essentially guaranteed anxious depositors their deposits would be safe. Four days after that move, banks reopened and depositors returned with the bulk of the cash they had pulled out in panic. The bank panic over, FDR seemed content to let bankers restore the system that had collapsed. The White House put on the table no reforms that went appreciably beyond anything that the Hoover administration had proposed. The only significant ideas for real reform would come from members of Congress. Lawmakers added to the White House banking legislation limits on the branch empires big banks could create and required banks to pay premiums that would finance a new system of federal insurance for bank deposits.[64] To prevent banks from taking investment gambles with these newly insured deposits, lawmakers also wrote into the legislation provisions that prohibited any one bank from conducting both investment banking and commercial banking operations.[65] In June 1933 Roosevelt would unenthusiastically sign the Banking Act of 1933—Glass-Steagall, as the legislation would become known—into law.

The same pattern would follow on other major initiatives that emerged out of FDR's famed "First Hundred Days." White House proposals would shore up the most powerful institutions of the crumbled old order. Proposals for "bold, persistent experimentation" that might aid the "millions who are in want" would come not from Roosevelt, but from the ranks of progressive lawmakers.

Senator Hugo Black from Alabama would advance one of those experiments, an act to create jobs by limiting the workweek to thirty hours. American workers who did have jobs were then averaging about forty-nine hours a week. Limiting the regular hours any one worker could work would force employers to create new jobs, the American Federation of Labor argued, and the AFL pitch had support from a who's who of veteran progressives, everyone from Monsignor John Ryan and Fiorello LaGuardia to businessman Edward Filene. The hours bill that Senator Black would introduce, drafted by the AFL, prohibited from interstate commerce any product manufactured in an establishment where workers labored for more than five days a week and six hours a day. AFL president William Green would advocate for the legislation with a rhetorical militance he seldom ever manifested. Labor, Green declared in Senate testimony, would not even shy from "class war" to get the legislation through.

The Senate passed the Black bill on April 6, 1933, and that vote, notes historian Benjamin Hunnicutt, would prompt "Roosevelt and his advisers, who had been engrossed in the banking crisis, to take their first legislative steps toward economic recovery."[66] On behalf of the administration, Labor Secretary Frances Perkins drafted legislation for the House Labor Committee that incorporated the Black bill and added a variety of other provisions, including a federal minimum wage.

Corporate America would erupt in behind-the-scenes rage and pressed upon the White House an alternative plan from the US Chamber of Commerce. The Chamber plan, with various modifications, would emerge in May as the FDR administration's National Industrial Recovery Act. The legislation's basic goal: to stabilize prices and production, industry by industry. Within each industry, the legislation stipulated, business, labor, and government would together set codes of conduct on everything from how much businesses could charge to how many hours workers could labor.

Opponents of the NIRA—Huey Long among them—charged that business would end up dominating the industry-by-industry deliberations. The new National Recovery Administration, Long predicted, would help large corporations fix prices and marginalize competition from smaller businesses.[67] The legislation passed anyway, on the last day of the 1933 congressional session. The White House had slipped into the bill just enough sweeteners to neutralize the opposition, most notably a clause—Section 7(a)—that recognized the right of workers to organize into unions.

But the legislation carried no enforcement mechanisms. The NRA codes would only rebound to labor's advantage in industries where labor already had a historic presence. In the garment industry codes, Sidney Hillman of the Amalgamated Clothing Workers would be able to work out standards with industry leaders that established a thirty-five-hour week for the makers of women's garments and a thirty-six-hour week, coupled with 20 percent wage increases, for the men's garment trade.[68] Elsewhere, the industrial codes would mainly benefit large employers.

In agriculture, largely the same story. The 1933 Agricultural Adjustment Act sought to stabilize production and increase prices by paying farmers to reduce their acreage. That policy would quickly help large commercial farm operations at the expense of poor farmers. The large farm owners typically reduced their production by eliminating the acreage they rented out to tenant farmers and sharecroppers. Tenants and sharecroppers, robbed of income, ended up dispossessed and homeless. Reformers in the Agriculture Department saw what was happening. They would try—and largely fail—to get large farm owners to share their federal cash bounties with the poor who had rented from them.[69]

In all, the Roosevelt administration moved fifteen substantial pieces of legislation through Congress over its first hundred days. By and large, notes Great Depression historian Robert McElvaine, "Roosevelt tried to work within the existing power system, not to transform it." The Civilian Conservation Corps and other new federal relief efforts did provide needed help and jobs to millions of Americans, but none of these efforts "posed a serious threat to existing power relationships." The outdoor Civilian Conservation Corps jobs for young men, for instance, paid a dollar a day, not enough to put any pressure on local employers to raise wages.

Of the initiatives that emerged from FDR's fabled first hundred days, only the new Tennessee Valley Authority, the giant public utility that brought affordable electric power into states from Virginia to Mississippi, posed any potential challenge to "the established order." The TVA could demonstrate, notes McElvaine, "that a government-owned business could compete successfully with private enterprise."[70]

Other early New Deal legislation directly undercut the public sector. The Economy Act enacted soon after FDR took office slashed government worker salaries by 15 percent and also cut government benefits to veterans. Rank-and-file Democratic lawmakers refused to support the Economy Act legislation. Sixty-nine Republicans did support it, and only this conservative GOP support would push the bill to passage.[71] In early 1933, FDR was talking the fiscal language conservatives liked to hear: overpaid federal workers, federal spending cuts, balanced federal budget.

By year's end this language was no longer resonating in White House circles. In the heady spring of 1933, the economy had seemed poised to recover. Six months later, the "recovery" was going nowhere. Top New Dealers had set aside the advice new thinkers like Utah banker Marriner Eccles had to offer.[72] Now they began reconsidering. The first hundred days hadn't fixed the economy. Maybe more aggressively spreading the wealth—by upping federal spending to create jobs and accepting larger federal budget deficits along the way—would. In December, Treasury officials brought Marriner Eccles into Washington for talks. In February 1934 they made him a special Treasury adviser. The following summer, Roosevelt elevated Eccles to the top slot at the Federal Reserve, where the maverick Utah banker would start shifting control over the Fed out of Wall Street and into Washington.[73]

A second chapter of the New Deal was beginning. FDR the practical pol had edited chapter one. Now in this next chapter, the edits would come from the American people through a variety of popular movements. In this second phase, New Deal proposals would flow far bolder. They would much more directly threaten the rich that FDR had once thought he could appease.

Chapter Six

A TIDAL WAVE OF POPULAR PROTEST

In February 1934, Representative Ernest Lundeen from Minnesota placed before Congress an exceedingly bold idea. He would call for an adequate income for every jobless American. The legislation he introduced guaranteed all unemployed workers the average wage they had been making on their old jobs and bankrolled that guarantee with new taxes on the wealthy and their inheritances.[1]

Lundeen's legislation had emerged out of the nation's Unemployed Councils, militant local groups the Communist Party had organized to resist evictions. But support for the Lundeen bill went beyond Unemployed Council ranks. Union locals around the country backed the legislation, as did various ethnic and mutual aid societies. This energetic movement behind the bill would be an augury of things to come. The "gathering forces of popular discontent," as historian Alan Dawley notes, were forcing "redistributive ideas onto the political agenda."[2]

The redistributive ideas took various shapes. Some reformers pointed to the massive tax evasion and avoidance that the Pecora Commission had unearthed and emphasized the importance of ending the games rich people were playing at tax time. Their solution: public disclosure of income tax records. If wealthy taxpayers knew their returns would be open to public inspection, reformers argued, they would be far less audacious with their tax avoidance. Disclosure would also help members of Congress identify the tax code loopholes that needed to be plugged with new legislation.[3]

In 1934, Senator Robert La Follette Jr. from Wisconsin, the son of the old progressive warhorse, had enough support to add a disclosure mandate to the Senate version of the 1934 Revenue Act. The final Revenue Act legislation would include a watered-down version of La Follette's proposal. Every American subject to the income tax would have to file a new form—soon to be known as the "pink slip" for the paper's color—that revealed the taxpayer's name, address, gross income, deductions, taxable income, and tax liability.[4] The passage of this modest tax disclosure mandate appalled the richest of America's affluent. They quickly began lining up friendly lawmakers and the funding necessary for a full-blown national disclosure repeal campaign.

Few political observers gave the repeal effort any chance. The rich, after all, were not exactly cutting a sympathetic figure in Great Depression America. But the deep pockets behind the effort tied their "cause" to the sensational Lindbergh baby kidnapping trial then filling the nation's front pages. If taxpaying Americans had to disclose their incomes, the argument went, kidnappers would gain a wider pool of targets. This PR juggernaut carried the day. In less than three months, historian Marjorie Kornhauser relates, the campaign to repeal the Revenue Act's income tax publicity provision "went from hopeless to a complete success."[5] Lawmakers repealed the income tax disclosure mandate.

Another disclosure mandate on corporate executive pay would have far more staying power. Veteran reformers like Felix Frankfurter, a renowned Harvard law academic close to Louis Brandeis, had been attacking Great Depression executive paychecks as "absurdly disproportionate to service performed." In 1933, Senator Edward Costigan, a Democrat from Colorado, enlisted in Frankfurter's campaign against executive excess and worked into law legislation that required banks, public utilities, and major corporations involved in interstate commerce to compile and release data on top executive salaries.[6] In 1934, the first data required under the new executive pay disclosure mandate became public. In Great Depression America, the numbers created quite a stir. Between 1928 and 1933, a Federal Trade Commission report on the new pay data revealed, American Tobacco's G. W. Hill had collected salary and bonuses that totaled almost $4 million, the equivalent of over $66 million today.

"For the captains of industry to be drawing down large salaries is unconscionable and unpatriotic," Senator Burton Wheeler of Montana pronounced. "It is this kind of thing that does more to make for socialism and communism than all the propaganda from soap-boxes and Soviet Russia."[7]

Lawmakers in Congress responded by adding to the 1934 Revenue Act an even stiffer salary disclosure mandate. They required corporations to list the names of any executives making over $15,000, a bit over $250,000 today, in their corporate income tax returns.[8]

The congressional offensive against excessive executive paychecks would go beyond disclosure. Hugo Black, a Democratic lawmaker—and, like Felix Frankfurter, a future Supreme Court justice—took the lead. Black's great insight: Congress couldn't directly set limits on private corporate executive pay. But Congress could impose limits indirectly by leveraging the power of the public purse. Corporations in Depression-era America, Hugo Black understood, were routinely pocketing federal tax dollars through loans and government contracts. Why not deny these tax dollars to corporations that lavished rewards on their top executives? Why should taxpayers be subsidizing excessive executive pay?

In 1932, before FDR's election, Black had battled to get the Reconstruction Finance Corporation, the newly created federal agency that aimed to revive the economy with loans to cash-strapped businesses, to deny aid to corporations that paid their executives over $15,000. Congress would not go along, but Black kept at it. In 1933, an amendment he introduced went into law and denied federal air- and ocean-mail contracts to companies that paid their executives over $17,500. That same year, the Senate voted to impose a $17,500 limit on executive pay—nearly $300,000 in today's dollars—for any corporation in line to receive a new or extended Reconstruction Finance Corporation loan.[9]

The Reconstruction Finance Corporation chairman, the millionaire Houston banker Jesse Jones, would deftly derail the salary limitation drive, notes historian Mark Leff, "with a well-timed grandstand play on railroad salaries." Under pressure from the RFC, the Southern Pacific Railroad agreed to cut executive salaries up to 60 percent, a move that dropped the railroad's highest executive pay to $60,000, slightly over $1 million today. The RFC, Chairman Jones pledged, would apply comparable limits to any future corporation getting a loan from his agency. Lawmakers took Jones at his word and dropped the fixed $17,500 executive pay limit provision that the Senate had passed. Under the final legislation, RFC loans could only go to companies that had shaved executive pay down to levels the Reconstruction Finance Corporation deemed "reasonable." Jones, once outfitted with this new discretionary authority, would adopt a far more expansive definition of "reasonable" than he had applied to the Southern Pacific. His Reconstruction Finance Corporation would never again wage as aggressive a pay-reduction campaign against excessive executive compensation.[10]

Still, President Roosevelt did show signs that he took excessive executive compensation somewhat seriously, particularly after former Chase Manhattan Bank President Albert Wiggin told the Pecora Commission that he had awarded himself an astounding $100,000 pension. In October 1933, right after the Wiggin testimony, the White House told reporters the administration would be formulating legislation to curb executive excess. With that news, *Newsweek* reported, "shivers coursed up and down spines of highly paid executives."[11]

The Roosevelt administration went on to discuss—internally—the possibility of using the income tax to penalize exorbitant executive compensation. But the only action on that front would come from lawmakers. In 1932, progressives in Congress had unsuccessfully tried to deny corporations "business expense" tax deductions for any executive pay they paid out that ran over $75,000.[12] In 1934, these lawmakers made another unsuccessful stab at the same goal.

A bit of success would come, in that same congressional session, when progressives took a more general tax-the-rich approach. Congress would amend the 1934 Revenue Act to boost taxes between 1 and 3 percentage points on most tax brackets above $8,000, about $140,000 in today's dollars. Lawmakers also plugged a variety of tax loopholes that wealthy taxpayers were regularly exploiting.[13]

President Roosevelt would never publicly oppose any of these efforts to press down on the nation's highest incomes, but rarely would he endorse them either. FDR, notes historian Mark Leff, "still relied on business collaboration to secure recovery." Taxing the rich heavily, Roosevelt still feared, would depress business confidence and end hopes for an economic rebound. FDR would not go that way. Until pushed.

The push would come from seemingly everywhere. From newly energized unions. From cities and states where the old Socialist Party had made some of its deepest inroads. From the rural South. From urban Catholic neighborhoods. From old people, a demographic that had never mattered before politically.

The unions owed their new energy to FDR. Or, to put the matter more accurately, enterprising labor leaders would give Roosevelt the credit for the new union militancy that erupted in 1934. Just a year earlier, fewer than two million Americans had carried union cards, a deep dip from the five-million-strong union movement at the beginning of the 1920s.[14] The New Dealers of 1933 had not made reversing that slide any part of their initial agenda, but they had thrown a bone to labor in the final legislation of the first hundred days, the soon-to-be celebrated section 7(a) of the National Industrial Recovery Act.

America's workers, section 7(a) read, "shall have the right to organize and bargain collectively through representatives of their own choosing, and shall be free from the interference, restraint or coercion of employers of labor, or their agents, in the designation of such representatives or in self-organization or in other activities for the purpose of collective bargaining or other mutual aid or protection."

What did all that mean? John Lewis, the United Mine Workers president, had a translation: "President Roosevelt wants you to join your union."[15]

And miners by the tens of thousands did join. His union refreshed, Lewis won the first National Recovery Administration industry code that made significant concessions to workers. Mine owners agreed to an eight-hour day and five-day week. They even agreed to payroll "dues checkoff" and began regularly deducting union dues from employee paychecks, a move that immediately stabilized union finances. But Section 7(a) would only take Lewis and the mineworkers so far. The energy they could take from it could not overcome resistance to unions at the nation's "captive mines," those operations owned directly by steel companies. To take on the steel industry's mines, Lewis and the UMW would have to take on the steel industry—and the American Federation of Labor hierarchy.

The AFL's conservative leaders still held to the craft-union mindset. Unions, they believed, should organize by trade, plumbers and pipefitters over here, railroad firemen and oilers over there. But most factory workers had no "trade." A craft-based trade unionism could never successfully organize a US Steel. Only an industrial approach—building unions that represented all workers at a particular enterprise, whatever their daily task might be—could pull off that level of organizing.

Advocates for craft and industrial unionism had been doing battle within the US labor movement for generations. Advocates for industrial unionism had typically come from the left end of the political spectrum, and Lewis realized that advancing an industrial unionism agenda within labor wouldn't get anywhere without the support of the left activists he had worked so hard to crush back in the 1920s. Lewis made his peace with the left and moved to coalesce, within the AFL, all those unions open to mass industrial organizing.[16] His effort would soon take formal shape in a "Committee for Industrial Organization," and this new CIO would quickly start riding the new labor militancy breaking out all across the United States. In 1934, a million and half workers staged an estimated eighteen hundred walkouts.[17]

A walkout in Toledo would be one of the biggest. The initial conflict pitted the nation's largest auto-parts supplier, the Electric Auto-Lite company, against workers demanding union recognition, seniority rights, and a 10 percent wage hike. Electric Auto-Lite founder Clem Miniger had been one of the New Era's business superstars in the 1920s. He sailed his yacht on Lake Erie, boasted about the thirty-four-story Miniger Building he would construct in downtown Toledo, and held a fortune estimated at $84 million, over $1.1 billion today. Amid the devastation of the Great Depression, notes historian Irving Bernstein, Electric Auto-Lite had a simple business plan: keep wages low and make auto parts "more cheaply than the auto companies could make for themselves." Unions complicated that plan. Electric Auto-Lite would not tolerate them.

The union recognition struggle at Electric Auto-Lite began in February 1934 and stretched into June. Along the way would come pitched battles of bricks and bullets that left two strike supporters dead, court injunctions, tear-gas bombs, and mass picketing—organized by the American Workers Party, a small but feisty group led by a radical Dutch-born preacher—that circled the Auto-Lite plant with thousands of unemployed workers. Late in May, eighty-five local Toledo unions voted to support a citywide general strike, and in early June that threat would help workers settle on terms that prompted a massive labor victory parade.[18]

Observers sometimes called Toledo a "little Detroit." The Twin Cities in Minnesota could have passed for a "little Chicago." St. Paul had a powerful gangland presence, and Minneapolis hosted a vicious antiunion employers' group, the Citizens' Alliance, that did not shrink from violence to keep the city union-free. Violence would come in 1934 when a Minneapolis Teamsters local struck in May for shorter hours and a $27.50 weekly wage. Truck traffic in the city soon came to a virtual halt, and hand-to-hand battles between strikers and the Citizens' Alliance army filled the city streets.

A mediated agreement did bring some calm, but employers essentially ignored those mediated clauses they would rather not follow. New battles broke out. One confrontation between strikers and police left two workers dead and sixty-seven wounded. The subsequent funeral procession drew an estimated hundred thousand marchers. The eventual final agreement would be a union triumph, and the victory celebration lasted twelve hours.[19]

In Minneapolis, what had become a multiunion general strike would halt the city's transportation. In San Francisco, a far more sweeping walkout in 1934 shut down the entire city after a battle between striking longshoremen and police—rocks and bolts against bullets and tear gas—ended with two workers dead. No trolleys ran during the San Francisco general strike. Even bars and nightclubs shut down. The strike committee kept food markets and nineteen restaurants open. Little else functioned. An estimated 130,000 workers stayed away from work.

The pressure for the San Francisco walkout had come from below, from rank-and-file workers. Most local union leaders had gone along grudgingly, and these leaders jumped at a government arbitration plan. The general strike would last four days, ending on July 19, and the longshore union would eventually walk away with victory on the core striker demand, control over the waterfront hiring halls.[20]

Roosevelt administration officials could have torpedoed the workers' cause at several different junctures in the San Francisco struggle. They didn't. Secretary of Labor Frances Perkins considered the red-baiting ranting of local employer groups little more than hysteria. To one business charge that unionists out to "destroy our most sacred institutions and traditions" had seized power in San Francisco, Perkins coolly replied that "the only 'sacred institutions and traditions' which the strike leaders sought to destroy were low wages and graft-ridden hiring halls."[21]

The pressure that FDR felt came at the ballot box as well. Serious third-party movements were growing across the country. In Wisconsin, the two sons of "Fighting Bob" La Follette gave up on the fantasy of promoting progressive causes from within the Republican Party and organized a new Wisconsin Progressive Party in the spring of 1934. The new party swept the state that November, winning seven of ten congressional seats, a Senate seat for Robert Jr., and gubernatorial victory for brother Phil.[22] Both had originally been elected as Republicans. Both would speak out forcefully against the same plutocracy their father had so long opposed.

"I am not interested in trying to maintain the status quo in our economic life," young Bob declared. "Devices which seek to preserve the unequal distribution of wealth now produced will halt the progress of mankind and, in the end, will retard or prevent recovery."

"I am a radical," Governor Phil La Follette agreed. "There is no alternative to conscious distribution of income."[23]

Minnesota had a governor, Floyd Olson, who considered himself more radical than Phil La Follette. Olson had first won his state's top office in 1930, as the Farmer-Labor Party candidate in a three-way race with a Democratic and Republican challenger. His party united rural and urban progressives of all stripes, not just farmers and workers. In the early Depression years, the party's egalitarianism particularly appealed to clergymen like Theodore Mondale, a Republican who had cast his first vote for William McKinley in 1896. In a Depression-ravaged state, this father of the future vice president rallied behind Olson's challenge to the state's rich and powerful. Reverend Mondale would explain why in a local newspaper: "I believe the greatest danger confronting capitalism is the ever increasing concentration of wealth in the hands of a few."[24]

Governor Olson faced a hostile state legislature in his first term. In his second, he had more support and scored a string of legislative victories: passage of Minnesota's first income tax, a two-year moratorium on farm foreclosures, incentives to encourage the creation of business cooperatives, and a ban on injunctions in labor disputes.[25] In the 1934 Minneapolis general strike, Olson refused to give employers the backing they demanded. Olson supported the New Deal, but not uncritically. Roosevelt might face a third-party challenge in 1936, Olson warned, if the New Deal dragged its feet.[26]

In other states, insurgents essentially took over existing major parties from the inside. In North Dakota, candidates of a revived Nonpartisan League ran as Republicans and won every top state office—the governorship, a US Senate seat, and both congressional seats—up for grabs in 1932.[27] In Washington State, activists with the Commonwealth Builders elected US senators in 1932 and 1934 and then, as the Washington Commonwealth Federation, dominated the state Democratic Party.[28]

In California, the most famous writer of the Socialist Party's early

1900s heyday, novelist Upton Sinclair, would stun the political world when he won the August 1934 California Democratic Party gubernatorial primary. Sinclair's "End Poverty in California" platform had captured the imagination of a state where a quarter of the population needed public or private relief to get enough to eat. His 1933 book, *I, Governor of California, And How I Ended Poverty: A True Story*, had been a huge best seller, the biggest in California history, and his movement's weekly tabloid, *The EPIC News*, had built a regular readership over half a million Californians strong.[29]

By the fall of 1934, some two thousand local EPIC clubs were promoting the idea of "production for use," the movement's vision for an alternate California economy. Under this "production for use" program, the state government would take over idle factories and farms, turn them over to California's unemployed, and let these jobless produce goods that would change hands in a market network separate from the standard cash economy. The rich, in the meantime, would pay higher taxes. The EPIC program Sinclair championed called for an income tax to replace the state's existing sales tax. The new income tax would only impact Californians who made over $5,000 a year, about $85,000 today, and the rates for the new levy would rise progressively and top off at 30 percent on income over $50,000.[30] In an EPIC California, Sinclair would note, the "Big Business men" would begin "to realize that it was no longer an advantage to gain enormous incomes, because the State income tax took so large a share of them."[31]

The "Big Business men" of California had no intention of ever letting that tax hike come to pass. In the Democratic Party primary, the campaign of Sinclair's main competitor had circulated massive quantities of bogus leaflets that urged the "Exploited Masses" to follow the lead of a nonexistent "Young People's Communist League" and vote for Sinclair. This primary election red-baiting would have little impact. Sinclair won more primary votes than any candidate in the state Democratic primary had ever received.[32]

California's "Big Business men" would regroup for the general election and unleash upon Sinclair and EPIC the most media-savvy smear campaign US politics had ever seen. Hollywood movie magnates flooded theaters with fake newsreel footage that portrayed Sinclair supporters as bums and Communists. Studio executives dunned their employees for contributions to an anti-Sinclair war chest and loudly threatened to yank the film industry out of California if Sinclair triumphed. California's newspapers waged a similarly relentless campaign of distortions against Sinclair. One of the few papers that gave Sinclair a fair hearing, the *Beverly Hills Bulletin*, had its advertisers pressured to pull their ads. The paper's landlord, a local bank, ordered the *Bulletin*'s owner to vacate his offices, even after he offered to pay higher rent.[33]

The vicious attack on Sinclair shoved Roosevelt into a political corner. A celebrity socialist candidate had become the Democratic Party's official nominee and was campaigning as a New Deal supporter. Victory for his conservative Republican opponent would leave a key state in anti–New Deal hands. But California's rich and powerful—in both major parties—considered Sinclair nothing short of an existential menace. They would stop at virtually nothing to see him defeated. FDR let them. He kept his distance.

On Election Day in November, EPIC candidates for the California state legislature did well, winning thirty seats. Sinclair would be crushed. Voters weren't voting against "production for use," one historian has argued. They were voting against the "atheism, free love, and Stalinism" that the smear campaign had pinned on Sinclair.[34]

America's rich and powerful would try to mount a counterattack at the national level as well, and FDR himself would be the target. The rich had never trusted Roosevelt. The moderation of the early New Deal had not won them over.

In August 1934, shortly before Sinclair's primary victory in California, Wall Streeter Jakob Raskob resurfaced as the chairman of the Liberty League, a new group with a letterhead full of industrialists like General Motors president Alfred Sloan and conservative Democratic Party has-beens like former presidential candidates John Davis and Al Smith. With ample funding from the Du Pont family, the Liberty League set about building a network of local chapters dedicated to decrying the New Deal as "the end of democracy."[35]

In the somewhat rawer world of Texas oilmen, the rich didn't bother with such philosophical epithets. They damned the New Deal as the "Jew Deal." Their leader would be John Henry Kirby, a lawyer turned timber baron turned oilman who rated as the top businessman in Texas in the 1920s. Kirby fancied himself even more than that. He spent the New Era years popping up regularly on presidential commissions in Washington, DC. He would be a frequent guest and adviser in the White House and also served a stint as president of the National Manufacturers Association.

Kirby lived well. He owned a three-story brick mansion in Houston and kept a manse for getaways, called the "Dixie Pines," in New York's Adirondack Mountains. But the Depression would slam Kirby's business empire hard. Bitterness now inflamed his standard-issue conservative persona. His downtown Houston Kirby Building, notes Texas oil historian Bryan Burrough, would soon become "a warren of shadowy, interconnected ultraconservative groups, all devoted to promoting white supremacy, fighting labor unions and communism, and, above all, defeating Roosevelt's reelection in 1936."[36] Kirby would bring his groups together under a new group he labeled the Southern Committee to Uphold the Constitution, in effect a Deep South version of Raskob's Wall Street–heavy Liberty League.

The hired guns who ran the various pushbacks against America's cresting egalitarian tide would train most of their fire on taxes and reds. The American Taxpayers' League secured free national radio time for dozens of programs that promoted balanced budgets and a 25 percent cap on federal tax rates.[37] Media kings like William Randolph Hearst would try to hurry along another red scare. Hearst even deployed spies on college campuses to identify "red" professors.[38]

All these attempts to sway public opinion didn't do much swaying. Did some rich and powerful conspire to end run public opinion altogether? Retired Major General Smedley Butler, a maverick marine, charged just that in November 1934 testimony before Congress. Butler recounted how a Wall Street group and assorted army officers had approached him about staging a military coup and named General Hugh Johnson, the recently fired director of the National Recovery Administration, as a top plotter choice for military dictator. Rumors would soon swirl in New Deal cocktail party circles. Harvard's Felix Frankfurter related one to journalist Matthew Josephson. The staff who had cleaned out Johnson's desk after he left the NRA, the rumor went, found a military map of Washington, DC, with every public building marked.[39]

Could some of America's rich have actually plotted to bring down the republic? If they did, the effort never moved beyond the grumbling stage. The more significant political reality: Huge numbers of Americans in 1934 thought the rich capable of plotting to bring down the republic. The wealthy had wrecked the economy. Why wouldn't they destroy democracy too?

In a 1934 debate in New York City, before an audience of two thousand, the legendary attorney Clarence Darrow gave voice to this popular mood.

"Civilization has been destroyed by those who own it, by the people who have the vast wealth, the masters of the world who will not permit a fair distribution of its products," the seventy-seven-year-old lawyer despaired.[40]

In the November 1934 elections, Americans would vote in record numbers against those they saw as shilling for that wealth. For the first time in modern American history, the party of a sitting president gained seats in a midterm election. In the House of Representatives, the number of GOP seats fell from 117 to 103. Democrats saw their ranks grow from 313 to 322, and parties to the left of the Democrats—Progressives and Farmer-Laborites—picked up another ten. And party affiliation didn't tell the whole story. Republicans still had progressives within their ranks. The new GOP congressman from New York City elected in 1934, Vito Marcantonio, stood clearly to Roosevelt's left.[41]

And conservative Republicans who did win often didn't win running as conservatives. In California, the deeply conservative Republican who beat Upton Sinclair in the gubernatorial race did his best to position himself as no great friend of wealth and power. GOP gubernatorial candidate Frank Merriam called for a thirty-hour week in his campaign and endorsed the "Townsend Plan," an increasingly popular, California-based drive to end Depression misery by guaranteeing a decent income to every elderly American.

Dr. Francis Townsend, the Southern California physician behind this plan to jump-start the national economy, did not see himself as any particular threat to the wealthy and their fortunes. The doctor had just been minding his own business, his story went, until one morning in 1933 when he looked outside his window and saw three old women in the alley by his Long Beach home scavenging the garbage cans for food. Distressed, Townsend dashed off to the local Long Beach newspaper a letter that proposed a bold and simple plan to end the shame in his community's alleyways. Let the federal government send everyone over sixty years old $150 a month, a figure the doctor would later raise to $200. The catch: The seniors had to agree to spend each entire monthly check within thirty days.

Everyone, Townsend argued, would benefit from this arrangement, not just the elderly. Younger people would have fewer people competing for jobs in the marketplace, and that marketplace would quickly recover from the Great Depression doldrums as purchases by the elderly stimulated business activity that otherwise would never take place.

Townsend's idea took off almost instantly. Volunteers in Long Beach started collecting petition signatures. On New Year's Day 1934, Townsend opened up a one-room office and started mailing out literature to doctors and clergy and anyone else he thought might be interested. Local "Townsend Clubs" soon formed throughout Southern California and then spread beyond. Within a year Townsend Clubs were nearing a half-million dues-paying members. The movement would have a national weekly newspaper and a staff of one hundred.[42]

Most veteran progressives looked on Townsend and his movement with dismay. They had read the fine print on Townsend's plan. The good doctor proposed to pay for his monthly outlays to seniors with a sales tax. In effect, he would be shifting dollars from one set of Depression casualties, average American consumers, to another, the nation's elderly.[43] Progressives saw nothing "progressive" about that.

But Americans who flocked behind Townsend's banner saw things differently. They saw a plan all about sharing wealth with those in need, an "Old Age Revolving Pension Plan," as the Townsend plan's formal moniker put it. Americans in 1934 would consider sharing the wealth one mighty fine idea. And no one spoke to that idea more passionately, or persuasively, than the junior United States senator from Louisiana, the firebrand Huey P. Long.

America's plutocracy feared Huey Long. America's plutocracy—the Louisiana branch—created him.

In Louisiana they called plutocrats "Bourbons," a label Republican reformers had bestowed upon the state's traditional elite after the Civil War. The Bourbon kings of France had tried to reconstitute the old order after the French Revolution, and Louisiana's antebellum ruling planter class had the same aim in mind during the political wars of Reconstruction. The Louisiana planters welcomed the Bourbon tag. They *did* want to turn back the clock as far as they could. Reconstruction had put in place a public education system. The Bourbons, after Reconstruction collapsed, essentially dismantled it in the late 1870s. Only bad ideas—like a fair day's pay for a fair day's work—could come from educating the Louisiana poor. The Bourbons liked their rural labor cheap. Better yet, they liked their labor in chains. No state had a convict-lease system more notorious than Louisiana's in the late nineteenth century. The mortality rates for convicts leased out to the state's rich planters and businessmen ranged up to 20 percent, a higher death rate than Louisiana's laborers had known as slaves.

Convict labor fattened Bourbon fortunes, and Louisiana's rich would, in turn, pay as little of those fortunes in taxes as possible. State lawmakers spent next to nothing on roads and infrastructure or anything that might require taxing the Bourbon rich to fund.[44]

By the early 1890s, white farmers in Louisiana had begun reaching out to black farmers as they organized a Populist movement to end Bourbon rule. The Bourbons responded with massive vote fraud. They would not even bother to hide their fraudulent intent. Any Louisiana citizens unable to protect their ballots, as the Bourbon Baton Rouge *Daily Advocate* pronounced early in 1892, "are not worthy of the rights of citizenship."[45]

After the 1892 elections, the Bourbons would move to strip the unworthy of those rights. They concocted all sorts of constitutional amendment schemes to disenfranchise the state's poor, whatever their color, and set the stage for a showdown 1896 election between the Bourbon Democrats and a Populist-Republican alliance. The Bourbons, charged Louisiana Populist leader Hardy Brian, were moving "to perpetually place this government in the hands of the rich, depriving the poor of any rights except to eke out their lives in hovels."[46]

This time the state powers-that-be would not stop at vote fraud. Populists saw their activists shot, their printing presses wrecked, their black supporters whipped, and worse. In 1896, one-fifth of all the nation's lynchings took place in Louisiana. The Bourbons would romp to Election Day victory. In six parishes with an 1890 census count of 3,278 adult males, the Bourbon gubernatorial candidate tallied 15,976 votes—compared to 139 for his Populist challenger.[47]

Populism in Louisiana would sputter out of existence. In the last issue of the movement's last surviving newspaper, in March 1899, Populist stalwart Hardy Brian candidly explained his movement's failure.

"We refused to take up the gun [and] so we lost," wrote Brian. "The fight will be won some day, but by [unchristian] methods."[48]

Later that same year, a farmer from Brian's north central Louisiana parish would make one of the final state legislative bids on a Populist-sounding platform.[49] H. P. Long Sr. lost, of course, but his young son Huey would grow up listening to his father's stories. The father would still be telling them, as an old man, in 1935.

"I seen this domination of capital, seen it for seventy years," H. P. Long Sr. would tell the world. "What do these rich folks care for the poor man? They care nothing—not for his pain, his sickness, nor his death. Maybe you're surprised to hear me talk like that. Well, it was just such talk that my boy was raised under."[50]

By 1935, his boy Huey had been battling plutocracy for twenty years, and he never shied from employing "unchristian methods" along the way. His critics would call him the "dictator" of Louisiana. In 1934, the FBI and Justice Department officials even prepared memoranda on the case for sending federal troops into Louisiana to "restore republican government."[51]

As governor of Louisiana, Huey Long did not pay much attention to republican procedural niceties. He shoved his bills through state legislative committees and subjected state employee paychecks to automatic deductions that pumped up a huge cash slush fund that Long could use to buy and reward political support.[52] Elected in 1928, Long could not constitutionally run for reelection. He ran for the US Senate, won, and continued to rule Louisiana as a *de facto* governor.

But Long never bought votes or kept people from voting. He never had to. He had a political mission that his fellow Louisianans supported. Huey Long would free his neighbors from the rule of the rich. That would be Long's goal right from the start of his political career. Only 2 percent of the American people, as the twenty-four-year-old Long wrote in 1918, owned "about sixty-five or seventy percent of the entire wealth of the United States." With "wealth concentrating, classes become defined," he went on, and "there is not the opportunity for Christian uplift and education and cannot be until there is more economic reform."[53]

Long's first electoral victory made him a member of the state Railroad Commission, a do-nothing agency that held nominal regulatory authority over railroads and utility companies in Louisiana. The agency, with Long's prodding, would do plenty. The commission rolled back unjustifiable telephone rate hikes, broke up oil company pipeline monopolies, and improved utility services.[54] Long's principled advocacy for Louisiana's working people would soon earn him support statewide, not quite enough to win a 1924 bid for governor, but well more than enough to triumph in 1928, with the biggest victory margin in state primary history.

Just thirty-five years old, Long became governor of one of the most troubled states in the country, a plutocratic haven where over a quarter of adults could not read, incomes ran half the national average, and poll taxes kept half the state disenfranchised.[55] The Long reform whirlwind began almost immediately: night schools for illiterate adults, free textbooks and school buses for children, paved roads for motorists. The entire state had less than three hundred miles of highway when Long took power. Six years later, the state boasted 3,754 miles of real roads.[56] Funding for health care in Louisiana tripled. A new state medical school arose in six months.[57]

What Long didn't do sometimes cheered state residents as much as what he did do. He did not engage in race-baiting politics. The NAACP *Crisis* magazine would rate him "the only southern politician in recent decades to achieve the national spotlight without the use of racial and color hatred as campaign material."[58]

But Long would be no miracle worker. In a desperately undeveloped state, in the middle of the terrible national economic catastrophe, he could only do so much. Lasting relief for Louisiana's poor demanded change at the national level, and Long had no doubt he could deliver that change. He had originally come into office, notes historian Alan Brinkley, battling the corporations and problems that plagued Louisiana. In the early 1930s, he would expand his focus to the nation's staggering "concentration of wealth"—and bring that focus to the nation's capital.[59]

"I had come to the United States Senate with only one project in mind, which was that by every means of action and persuasion I might do something to spread the wealth of the land among all of the people," Long would later write in his autobiography. "The wealth of the land was being tied up in the hands of a very few men. The people were not buying because they had nothing with which to buy."[60]

Long came from a deeply religious household and would almost always express his egalitarian mission in biblical terms. "No, I never read a line of Marx or Henry George or any of them economists," he would note early in his Senate career. "It's all the law of God."[61]

"Now as long as the Government permits the pilin' up of huge individual fortunes, which is expressly forbidden in Leviticus," he told a

1932 interviewer in New York, "we are goin' to have crime and spoilin' and trouble."[62]

Long played the flamboyant showman in the Senate's regular 1932 session. But he would return to Washington after the November elections a much more serious lawmaker. FDR's victory, coming on the heels of Long's stunning success on behalf of Hattie Caraway in Arkansas, had the young senator hopeful that America's wealthy might soon see their comeuppance. Franklin Roosevelt, Long pronounced, "has assumed the leadership of this Nation in order that he might carry out the one great necessary decentralization of wealth in America."[63]

Roosevelt as president would quickly disappoint. Two weeks into FDR's inaugural year, Long introduced bills to limit income and wealth.[64] Roosevelt paid no attention. Long spent the first hundred days battling, only sometimes successfully, to give the New Deal's initial legislation a more Populist cast. FDR was not listening. But Americans were. FDR had his "fireside chats," a national radio dialogue with the American people. Long had his own national radio dialogue. He gave his first broadcast on NBC five days after Roosevelt's first fireside chat. Many more Long broadcasts would follow over the next three years.[65] Long's theme would almost always wind back to the importance of redistributing the nation's treasure.

"To cure all of our woes," he told his radio audience in February 1934, "it is necessary to scale down the big fortunes, that we may scatter the wealth to be shared by all the people."[66]

Long didn't depend on radio to spread the share-the-wealth word. He turned his own state newspaper, the *Louisiana Progress*, into a nationally circulated *American Progress* and mailed out free as many as 1.5 million copies of every issue.[67] Long also boasted the largest staff in Congress. Sixty stenographers kept Long's letters and printed matter flowing all across the country.[68] The basic political message of all this material: outrage at the inadequacies of Roosevelt's New Deal. "Not a single thin dime of concentrated, bloated, pompous wealth, massed in the hands of a few people, has been raked down to relieve the masses," Long complained early in 1934.[69]

His response: the creation of a national network of local activists dedicated to breaking the grip of great fortunes. Long called his new organization the Share Our Wealth Society. He announced the group in an early 1934 radio address and welcomed into its ranks anyone committed to redistributing the nation's wealth. One year later,

Long boasted an astonishing twenty-seven thousand local Share Our Wealth clubs. He had over eight million names on file, and his staff opened sixty thousand letters a week.[70]

The actual Share Our Wealth plan Long's local clubs promoted would go through evolving iterations. Share Our Wealth, at its core, limited both individual wealth and income. If the Share Our Wealth platform became the law of the land, anyone would be able to keep tax-free a fortune worth $1 million. Above that, an annual graduated tax would kick in. Over $8 million, the rate would be 100 percent. Annual income over $1 million—and inheritances over $1 million as well—would face this same 100 percent tax rate. The revenue from all these taxes on the rich would go toward bankrolling a nest egg of $5,000 for every family in need, "enough for a home, an automobile, a radio, and the ordinary conveniences." Families would be entitled to an adequate annual income, at least $2,000 a year. Share Our Wealth would also have the federal government provide old-age pensions and veteran benefits, aid to education, and a vast array of job-creating public works.[71]

The various dollar figures in the Long plan would change regularly, and critics charged that the numbers never added up. Long didn't fuss with the numbers. Why bother? No one knew how much wealth the wealthy held. The government kept no reliable statistics. Long would be content to hammer home what he considered an incontrovertible truth: The rich could easily afford to sacrifice huge portions of their wealth, enough to materially improve the well being of every American family in need.

Most activists in established left groups considered Long's share-the-wealth prescription simplistic, even demagogic. Anyone who claims they can "do away with concentration of wealth without doing away with capitalism," a Communist Party analyst in New York charged, was engaging in sheer "humbug."[72] Norman Thomas, the former Presbyterian minister who led the 1930s remnants of the Socialist Party, considered Share Our Wealth "positively dangerous because it fools the people."[73]

Carleton Beals, a widely read progressive journalist, would be a bit more forgiving. Long, he acknowledged, "dared put his fingers into the real ulcer of social evil in American life."[74] But Long's approach, Beals continued, could never bring adequate relief to working people in a modern industrial society.

"We need more wealth, not its dissipation or even its redistribution," Beals argued. "We need distribution of economic power. We need the socialization of the basic means of production."[75]

Other progressive groups—the state Farmer-Labor and Progressive parties in the Midwest, among them—would begin to moderate their misgivings about Long as 1934 moved along. Something fundamental, they sensed, was stirring in their rank-and-file supporters and the American people as a whole. Long had hit a nerve. He was speaking to a deep yearning for economic justice that resonated with millions upon millions of Americans. Progressives serious about social change could not afford to dismiss him. Long had to be engaged. And not just Long.

Out of Michigan had come another advocate for economic justice, a fantastically popular radio priest who didn't fall neatly into any traditional right-left typology. Father Charles Coughlin had built a massive listening audience, initially with biblical parables and blasts at Communists and the anti-Catholic Ku Klux Klan and later with sermons that sought "to inject Christianity into the fabric of an economic system woven upon the loom of the greedy."[76] The more the Depression deepened, the more Coughlin began to sound like Huey Long. If lawmakers in Washington "refuse to legislate against the concentration of wealth," the radio priest intoned late in 1934, "then we are perfectly justified in accusing them of playing politics with misery."

Coughlin by then had a weekly audience that averaged ten million. No regular radio show in the world had more listeners. The mail flow to his office complex would sometimes peak at over one million pieces per week.[77]

Like Huey Long, Coughlin would soon move to translate his massive following into a political movement. In November 1934, the priest unveiled a new "National Union for Social Justice." Wealth comes from our natural resources and labor, the preamble to the new group's creed declared. This wealth would belong to us all "except for the harsh, cruel and grasping ways of wicked men who first concentrated wealth into the hands of a few."[78]

Long and Coughlin circled warily around each other. They had no personal relationship, and the remedies they offered up would differ. Long, as Alan Brinkley notes, called "for a frontal assault upon great fortunes." Coughlin emphasized "the somewhat less direct remedies of currency manipulation and banking reform."[79] But what Long and Coughlin both shared ideologically far exceeded what had them divided. They were both raising, points out Brinkley, "issues that only a few years before had seemed all but dead: issues of privilege, wealth, and centralized power, and of the failure of political institutions to deal with them."[80]

In Washington, the New Dealers who ran the nation's most important political institutions were beginning to feel more than a bit uneasy about the grassroots ferment that Long and Coughlin had so successfully tapped into. Political observers had begun to speculate about a potential grand alliance of the "lunatic fringe"—a political movement that united Huey Long and his Southern base, Father Coughlin with his Northeast and Midwest urban ethnics, and California's Francis Townsend, who had of late been inching toward the Long and Coughlin perspective.

Could Long and his fellow "lunatics" turn their vast activist armies into actual votes? In the spring of 1935 the Democratic National Committee would secretly seek to find out. The DNC commissioned what amounted to the first-ever "scientific" public opinion poll for a presidential race. Straw ballots and a cover letter—under the letterhead of a nonexistent *National Inquirer* newspaper—would go out to one hundred and fifty thousand potential voters. The ballot cards gave the survey recipients a choice between FDR, a generic Republican, and "Huey P. Long or another candidate." Long had not at that point declared any candidacy for the White House. Nor had Coughlin. Even so, the "Long or another candidate" choice still drew 11 percent of the thirty-one thousand voters who completed the poll. Long and the lunatics clearly had enough potential support to swing any election from FDR to the Republicans.[81] If Long did declare, if he did link up with Coughlin and Townsend, if he did draw sympathetic nods from various progressive state third-party groups, who knew how high Long's vote tally could go?

FDR would not wait to see. In the spring of 1935 the president launched a second "hundred days," a restart of the New Deal, only this time with the goal of gaining—regaining—the confidence of an American people that had lost all patience with plutocracy. FDR had hinted at what would come in his January 1935 State of the Union address. "We find our population suffering from old inequalities, little changed by past sporadic remedies," FDR had candidly admitted. "In spite of our efforts and in spite of our talk we have not weeded out the overprivileged and we have not effectively lifted up the under-privileged. Both of these manifestations of injustice have retarded happiness."

Out of the White House would now come a series of measures to attack those "old inequalities." Collectively, they would make for a brilliant preemptive strike against the growing sense that Roosevelt's New Deal had tread too timidly. These new initiatives would speak more directly to average Americans. The new Social Security Act that FDR proposed would address the economic insecurity that had driven millions of elderly Americans to the Townsend Plan. For the millions of unemployed and their families, the new New Deal would offer a Public Works Administration with a $5 billion budget, a far more ambitious jobs effort than FDR had previously embraced. For workers demanding union representation, FDR would sign into law the National Labor Relations Act, a measure that created an appara-tus for protecting workers' right to organize and bargain collectively over the wealth that American industry was creating. Roosevelt did not propose the NLRA. New York senator Robert Wagner did, and the White House actually objected to what Wagner was proposing. But FDR would sign the final bill—and wisely claim credit for it.[82]

Roosevelt's grandest antiplutocratic gesture would come last. In June 1935, FDR finally moved on taxes.

America remained at that time a land where tax burdens fell hard-est on those least able to pay. In 1934, state governments collected $230 million in regressive sales taxes and only $140 million in more progressive income taxes.[83] At the federal level, excise taxes on con-sumption—levies, notes historian Joseph Thorndike, that "fell squarely on the shoulders of Roosevelt's famous Forgotten Man"—brought in up to half of federal revenue.[84] The president, over his first two years in the White House, had taken no steps to remedy this situation.

Huey Long would not be the only notable to notice. One good government group of illustrious Americans, the People's Lobby, had been pressing Roosevelt to overhaul the tax system ever since his inauguration. The group's highly respected leaders—the philosopher John Dewey, the theologian Reinhold Niebuhr, the economist Stuart Chase—had been petitioning and testifying for a tax system to help "achieve an adequate, equitable distribution of consuming and pur-chasing power." They called for stiff taxes on corporate cash stashes, higher estate and gift taxes, and higher income tax rates on Ameri-cans with comfortable incomes.[85]

In the Senate, meanwhile, insurgent Republican George Norris of Nebraska was demanding a stiff progressive tax on large estates, and a variety of other senators, progressive Democrats and insurgent Republicans alike, had floated their own plans to hike tax levies on the wealthy and their corporations. In late April 1935, Robert La Follette from Wisconsin gave this legislative advocacy for taxing the rich much wider public visibility.

"The administration of President Roosevelt has thus far failed to meet the issue of taxation," La Follette charged in a national radio address. "Progressives in Congress will make the best fight of which they are capable to meet the emergency by drastic increases in taxes levied upon wealth and income."[86]

Many of FDR's top officials saw higher taxes on the rich as every bit as necessary as La Follette did. The Utah banker Marriner Eccles, now the chairman of the Federal Reserve, had told Congress in March that "our problem now is one of distribution of income." The ordinary Americans whose consumption could be sparking an economic recovery didn't have enough income to consume. The nation's dollars were stagnating instead in the overstuffed pockets of the rich. "The most effective way of achieving a better balance," Eccles told Congress, "is through income taxes."[87]

New Dealers in the Treasury Department felt the same way. In February 1935, they passed to the White House a plan for a significant tax overhaul. FDR refused to push it. But the growing support for "Share Our Wealth" soon had Roosevelt reconsidering. FDR would tell his aide Raymond Moley that something had to be done "to steal Long's thunder." Roosevelt would tell a William Randolph Hearst representative in May that he just might have to "throw to the wolves the forty-six men who are reported to have incomes in excess of one million dollars a year."[88]

On June 16, the same day his Social Security bill passed the Senate, Roosevelt threw them. The president delivered his first "Message to Congress on Tax Revision." The address would be historic. No sitting president had ever so plainly made the case for taxing the wealthy and their works. FDR began by openly admitting the inadequacies of the nation's current tax code.

"Our revenue laws have operated in many ways to the unfair advantage of the few," the FDR message acknowledged, "and they have done little to prevent an unjust concentration of wealth and economic power."[89]

That concentrated wealth and power, the president's message continued, endangered the democratic essence of America.

"The transmission from generation to generation of vast fortunes by will, inheritance, or gift is not consistent with the ideals and sentiments of the American people," the president contended. "Such inherited economic power is as inconsistent with the ideals of this generation as inherited political power was inconsistent with the ideals of the generation which established our Government."

FDR would go on to attack the case against taxing the rich. All the nation's people, through their government, had created a society that enabled some to prosper. The most prosperous, the president argued, needed to recognize that contribution.

"People know that vast personal incomes come not only through the effort or ability or luck of those who receive them, but also because of the opportunities for advantage which Government itself contributes," the president explained. "Therefore, the duty rests upon the Government to restrict such incomes by very high taxes."

Conservative Republicans quickly charged that Roosevelt was playing politics. His message, GOP members on the House Ways and Means Committee claimed in a statement, aimed at "undermining the increasing political strength of the two chief exponents of the 'share-the-wealth' and 'soak-the-rich' philosophy by making a bid for the support of their large army of followers."[90] The GOP conservatives would be absolutely right. FDR's tax message had precious few specifics and came accompanied by no draft legislation. The White House seemed in no hurry to actually accomplish anything on tax reform. FDR seemed to be content with headlines that trumpeted his willingness to tax and soak the rich.

But progressives in the Senate moved to keep FDR's feet to the tax fire. Nearly two dozen senators demanded action before the end of the 1935 session. If he wanted to maintain his tax-the-rich political momentum, FDR had little choice. He would have to seriously engage in the legislative process, and he did. But Roosevelt's hasty interventions would help move to passage a bill more symbol than substance. Under the new tax eventually enacted in 1935, only relative handfuls of America's wealthy would pay appreciably more in taxes. The top federal income tax rate, then 63 percent on income over $1 million, would rise to 79 percent, but only on income over $5 million. The top tax rate on estates would rise, too, from 60 to 70 percent, but only on bequest value over $50 million.[91]

Progressives did not hide their disappointment. The radical New York Republican Vito Marcantonio deemed the final legislation "a creampuff, milk-and-toast, innocuous, and meaningless gesture."[92] The *New Republic* magazine lamented that FDR had taken "only a tiny step toward redistributing wealth."[93]

But business leaders went berserk. Their well-publicized fury at Roosevelt's tax-the-rich rhetoric would make the 1935 tax legislation FDR signed into law seem far tougher on the rich and powerful than the facts on the ground warranted. The FDR-backed tax bill, complained House Ways and Means Republicans in their minority report, only made sense for a nation about "to adopt the communistic system."[94] One conservative Southern paper, the *Charleston News and Courier*, called the tax bill a "soak-the-brains program" that targeted "energy, thrift, and the will to deny self and to achieve."[95] The tax provisions of the new Revenue Act, harrumphed upstate New York GOP congressman Bertrand Hollis Snell, had been "designed not to produce revenue but to confiscate property for the use of a vast federal bureaucracy."[96]

If the plutocrats hated FDR's tax bill, many Americans understandably concluded, the tax bill must indeed effectively share the wealth. The one man who might have set America straight on that score, Huey P. Long, would not be around to argue the point. On September 8, 1935, barely a week after the FDR tax bill became law, Long was shot at the Louisiana capitol in Baton Rouge. He died two days later.

The 1935 tax bill would not be FDR's last word on taxing the rich and sharing the wealth. Roosevelt was just getting started. He campaigned for reelection in 1936 as he had not campaigned the first time around in 1932. This time, FDR did no fence-straddling. He would throw no bones to keep corporate leaders content. He campaigned, as he pledged in early 1936, against "the forces of privilege and greed."[97] We must, he told Congress in his annual January message, "wage unceasing warfare" against "our resplendent economic autocracy."[98]

Members of Congress would wage only a little of this warfare in their 1936 session. The president asked lawmakers for a new tax on undistributed corporate profits, the piles of cash that many corporations chose to park in income-generating financial assets instead of investments in new production. Taxing these stashes, reformers held, would discourage tax avoidance by wealthy shareholders. Lawmakers delivered a "watered-down version" of what Roosevelt sought as they rushed to end the congressional session and get back home and start campaigning for what promised to be an enormously pivotal election.[99]

FDR would have two rivals in his 1936 reelection campaign, the Republican governor of Kansas Alf Landon and a Populist-spirited congressman from the Northern Plains, William Lemke of North Dakota. Lemke ran as a candidate of the Union Party, a marriage of political convenience between Father Coughlin, Francis Townsend, and Huey Long's rather mean-spirited successor, Rev. Gerald L. K. Smith, a shady Midwest minister who had hooked up with Long in Louisiana and grabbed the reins of the Share Our Wealth movement after Long's death.

The Union Party never mounted a serious campaign. The nation's progressive movements would quickly shun it. Roosevelt would give them no other political choice. In the 1936 campaign FDR made himself the presidential candidate progressives had been dreaming about their entire lives. He came out swinging against the plutocrats, the "economic royalists" as the president dubbed them, and never let up.[100] "We shall continue to use the powers of government to end the activities of the malefactors of great wealth who defraud and exploit the people," declared the very first plank of Roosevelt's 1936 Democratic Party platform.[101]

At Franklin Field in Philadelphia, before an audience of one hundred thousand, Roosevelt welcomed his party's nomination and eloquently outlined a magnificently egalitarian narrative of American history.[102] In 1776, Roosevelt began, Americans had sought and won freedom "from the tyranny of a political autocracy—from the eighteenth-century royalists who held special privileges from the crown." But the onset on the industrial age had brought forth a new civilization and "a new problem for those who sought to remain free."

"Economic royalists," FDR explained, had "carved new dynasties" and built new kingdoms upon their "concentration of control over material things." The "privileged princes of these new economic dynasties" had "created a new despotism," a new "industrial dictatorship." Private enterprise had become "privileged enterprise." "In the face of economic inequality," the president continued, the "political equality we once had won" had become "meaningless."

"To some generations much is given," FDR would conclude. "Of other generations much is expected. This generation of Americans has a rendezvous with destiny."

FDR's rhetorical fusillade against plutocracy would continue straight through the entire campaign. The "forces of selfishness and of lust for power," Roosevelt would tell his final campaign rally in New York's Madison Square Garden, had never before "been so united against one candidate as they stand today." Added Roosevelt: "They are unanimous in their hate for me—and I welcome their hatred."[103]

The president didn't just offer fiery rhetoric to progressives in his 1936 campaign. He offered leadership. He campaigned less as the nominee of the Democratic Party and more as the leader of a national progressive coalition that would stretch from veteran crusaders against grand fortune like Fiorello LaGuardia, now the mayor of New York City, and the La Follettes of Wisconsin to the millions of Americans who thrilled to the biblical share-the-wealth cadences of Huey P. Long.

The Republican progressives in Congress would ride with Roosevelt and desert their party's nominee. In Minnesota, the Farmer-Labor Party endorsed Roosevelt, and the Democrats in the state ran no opposition to the Farmer-Labor candidate for governor. In Nebraska, Roosevelt endorsed veteran Senate progressive George Norris, not his Democratic Party challenger.[104] In New York, a new American Labor Party ballot line let lifelong socialists vote for Roosevelt without having to pull down the Democratic Party lever.[105]

In 1936, FDR no longer needed the institutional base of the old Democratic Party. A new institutional partner had arrived on the scene, the newly organized mass industrial unions, the CIO of John Lewis and Sidney Hillman. With labor's help, Roosevelt was ushering onto the American scene a new political lineup, notes historian Jean Edward Smith, "a unique alliance of big-city bosses, the white South, farmers and workers, Jews and Irish Catholics, ethnic minorities, and African Americans that would dominate American politics for the next generation."[106]

Plutocrats had no clue how to respond. The Liberty League gathered twelve Du Ponts and two thousand other deep pockets in Washington's Mayflower Hotel—"the greatest collection of millionaires ever gathered under one roof," the *New York Times* quipped—for speechifying by Al Smith that blasted FDR and New Dealers for disguising themselves as Karl Marx and Lenin.[107] Employers would stick attacks on Social Security in their pay envelopes. Republican nominee Alf Landon would become steadily shriller as the campaign wore on. The New Deal, he warned, would lead America down to the guillotine.[108]

Landon did manage to raise a hefty war chest. His campaign spent $14 million to Roosevelt's $9 million, but Republicans would get little for their outlay. Roosevelt would take 60.8 percent of the popular vote and all but eight electoral votes of the 531 cast. America's premiere family of "economic royalists," the Du Ponts, couldn't even carry their hometown of Wilmington, Delaware, a traditional Republican bastion.[109] Norman Thomas, the Socialist Party candidate, had won almost nine hundred thousand votes in 1932. In 1936, he tallied less than two hundred thousand. Against the rich, Roosevelt had assembled a remarkably broad coalition.

FDR began his second term with even larger congressional majorities than in his first. His first term had blunted the Great Depression. His second, Americans hoped, would end it. That would be a tall order. Unemployment had shrunk significantly over FDR's first four years, from 25 to just under 10 percent. But two-thirds of America's families were still making less than $1,500 a year.[110] Inequality remained staggering. The nation's bottom two-thirds had no savings, the top one-third $7 billion.[111]

The newly reelected Roosevelt seemed eager to take on that inequality.

"The test of our progress is not whether we add more to the abundance of those who have much," he pronounced at his cold and rainy inauguration in January 1937. "It is whether we provide enough for those who have too little."[112]

In Franklin Roosevelt's second term, the New Deal largely failed that test. The great victories of November 1936 would be squandered. The president would give America's shaky plutocracy a huge break. FDR, the consummate political pro, would commit two colossal political blunders, the first a product of pride and petulance, the second a failure to break from ideological convention.

Conservatives called no shots as Congress convened in 1937. They had just one stronghold: the Supreme Court. On the day of FDR's second inaugural, Warren Harding had been dead for over thirteen years, but three of the four justices that Harding had appointed to the Supreme Court still served. Of the remaining justices, none had been nominated for the high court by FDR.[113] No president before FDR had ever gone through a four-year term without an opportunity to nominate a single Supreme Court justice.

FDR could have lived with that. He could not live with the threat that the high court posed to the New Deal. In 1935 and 1936, the Supreme Court ruled six New Deal legislative initiatives unconstitutional. The most significant casualty: the National Industrial Recovery Act, the legislation that included the celebrated section 7(a), the clause that gave workers a federal blessing to organize.

Shortly after that May 1935 ruling against the NIRA, Congress had passed the National Labor Relations Act, legislation that created what the NIRA had not, a regulatory apparatus for guaranteeing workers a free and fair opportunity to vote for union representation. But America's most virulently antiunion employers refused to cooperate with the new labor relations framework that the NLRA established. They filed lawsuit after lawsuit to delay the act's on-the-ground implementation. Legal experts predicted that employers would prevail. The Supreme Court, almost everyone in the know expected, would strike the NLRA down.

Roosevelt could not stand to see that happen. In early February 1937, he announced a court reform plan that would give him, if Congress agreed to it, the capacity to pack the Supreme Court with his own nominees. The president's proposal generated an almost immediate political firestorm. Even some notable friends of the New Deal considered FDR's thrust a dangerous executive power grab.

Meanwhile, American workers were going about defending their right to collectively bargain for a fair share of the nation's economic bounty in a far more dramatic manner. They would "sit down" on the job. They would, as labor historian Jim Pope puts it, "self-enforce" the new Labor Relations Act.[114] Workers would stage over five hundred sit-down strikes after the NLRA's passage. The first came early in 1936 against the Firestone Tire & Rubber Company in Akron. Workers stopped their factory's conveyor belt, kept at their places, and prevented any new product from moving until fifty-five hours later, when management agreed to reinstate a fired union worker.

The sit-down movement burst more fully into the national consciousness later that year, after auto workers inspired by FDR's November reelection began occupying entire plants and demanding union recognition. The auto-industry sit-down battles spilled into early 1937. At various points armed police stormed the occupied plants, only to be driven back by the workers inside and the automobile door hinges they let fly upon their attackers. Workers would be shot and wounded. Their supporters would mass picket and rally by the tens of thousands.

Recalcitrant employers, CIO leaders made plain, had only themselves to blame for these rank-and-file worker revolts. Accept the National Labor Relations Act bargaining framework, John Lewis and other CIO union presidents advised Corporate America, and the sit-down wave would most certainly subside.

General Motors finally settled with workers in mid-February 1937, and in March the Supreme Court started reversing course. A majority surprisingly upheld a minimum wage law from Washington State. In April, an even more stunning development: Amid an unrelenting sit-down surge, the high court upheld the National Labor Relations Act. In May, a conservative justice announced his retirement, finally allowing FDR to pick one of his own.[115] The Supreme Court would no longer hang like a dagger over the neck of New Deal legislation.

At that point, FDR could have quietly folded up his controversial court-packing plan and gone about his New Deal business. But the president stubbornly kept pushing, alienating would-be New Deal allies and giving conservative Democrats and Republicans common cause. In July, a battered Roosevelt threw in the towel. He hadn't just lost on his now totally unnecessary Supreme Court reform plan. He had lost all legislative momentum. Conservatives no longer saw the president as invincible. They would now more boldly oppose his legislative agenda, plant roadblocks, and unite to kill the New Deal experiments they found the most distasteful, like the 1936 New Deal tax on undistributed corporate profits.[116]

Roosevelt's second blunder of 1937 would be an ironic twist on the first. In the Supreme Court fight, FDR turned a victory into a defeat. On the economy, he declared victory far too prematurely.

Victory on the economy did seem imminent early on in 1937. The massive public works spending and aid programs put in place in 1935 had begun to revive the nation's marketplaces. Production lines were coming back to life. Maybe coming back too fast, more conventional Roosevelt administration officials feared. Inflation might be around the corner if the government continued to aggressively stimulate the economy. The federal government, the traditionalists believed, should cut back on federal spending and move back toward a balanced budget. Late in April 1937, Roosevelt agreed and accepted substantial cutbacks in the federal programs that were putting dollars into the pockets of millions of Americans—at the same time new Social Security taxes were kicking in and taking dollars out.[117]

Within months of these developments, the economy would do an about-face. Unemployment skyrocketed back toward 20 percent. The stock market sank. By April 1938, FDR would understand the error of his budget-cutting ways. The president pushed through Congress a new spending program to pump back up the New Deal public works and basic aid efforts. But the new dollars would be too little, too late to get the economy moving before the fall 1938 elections.

Roosevelt had not kept his promise. The New Deal had not provided "enough for those who have too little," and Election Day would find the New Deal base dispirited. Democrats lost seventy seats in the House, seven more in the Senate.[118] For the rest of his term, FDR would now face ever-tougher legislative sledding.

With the opening of the new 1939 congressional session, the Great Depression had now outlasted the great New Deal victory of 1936. The rich had outlasted the New Deal as well.

In the early stages of Roosevelt's second term, that survival had seemed an iffy proposition to the nation's most exalted pundit, Walter Lippmann. In May 1938, the syndicated columnist took the occasion of the death of America's richest man, John D. Rockefeller, to pronounce that the colossal private fortune had become obsolete in modern America. Old John D., wrote Lippmann, had lived long enough—ninety-seven years—"to see the methods by which such a fortune can be accumulated outlawed by public opinion, forbidden by statute, and prevented by the tax laws."[119]

The rich had indeed taken something of a hit during the New Deal. The effective tax rate on the nation's top 1 percent—the share of their income the rich actually paid in taxes, after loopholes—had more than doubled, from 6.8 percent in 1932 to 15.7 percent in 1937.[120] The nastiest of America's super rich wheeler-dealers even went to jail. In 1938, former New York Stock Exchange President Richard Whitney, a Harvard-educated blue blood with the Mayflower in his family tree and a J. P. Morgan senior partner for a brother, would be sent upriver to Sing Sing for fraud and embezzlement.[121] Six thousand people gathered at New York's Grand Central Station to watch armed guards shuffle Whitney onto the prison-bound train.

But the rich had by no means departed the American scene. In 1939, *Town & Country* magazine conducted what one historian calls "the first real quantitative study of wealthy Americans."[122] The magazine surveyed the two thousand butlers and other highly paid servants who subscribed to a trade journal for elite domestics. The wealthy families that employed these butlers, the survey found, kept an average of eleven servants each. By 1939, other chronicles reported, private planes had replaced private railroad cars in wealthy households.[123] Debutante balls—for introducing young women of wealth to suitably wealthy potential suitors—remained a standard rite of passage in superrich circles.[124] In 1938, about a thousand debutantes made their debuts at an average cost of $8,000 each, at a time when three-quarters of America's families were making less than $2,000 per year.[125]

Walter Lippmann had been right in one respect: The nation's political culture had changed fundamentally, to the detriment of the ultrawealthy. By over a two-to-one margin, Gallup pollsters found, Americans felt "there is too much power in the hands of a few rich men and large corporations in the United States."[126]

The nation's workplaces had changed as well. The rich now faced a rival claimant to the wealth America's factories were generating. Union membership had nearly tripled over the Depression years, from under three million in 1933 to 8.5 million in 1940.[127] And rich tax dodgers faced far more scrutiny than ever before. Congressional panels, prodded by FDR, were naming names and shaming even the most illustrious of the nation's wealthy households. New laws were catching up to wealthy tax dodgers almost as quickly as their lawyers could devise new dodges. The wealthy who did pay their taxes would become public heroes and heroines. Actress Carole Lombard told the nation in 1938 that she "gave the federal government 65 per cent of my wages last year, and I was glad to do it too." The tax dollars she paid, Lombard added, all go into the "improvement and protection of the country."[128]

"Probably no other news item," the *New Yorker* magazine would later note, "ever did so much to increase the popularity of a star."

Americans clearly wanted a more equal nation. They would soon get it.

Chapter Seven

FIGHTING FASCISTS, CAPPING INCOMES

Franklin Roosevelt's New Deal saved America from social collapse—and the fascism that rolled across Europe. The New Deal also saved for America's rich their privileged perch in American life. The rich would not be grateful. That ingratitude would irritate FDR throughout the 1930s. How could the rich not realize, FDR fretted to aides and advisers, how close the nation had come to catastrophic revolution—or Fascist reaction?

By decade's end, the irritation Roosevelt felt had turned to anger. The rich weren't just failing to understand how explosive social reality had become. In FDR's eyes, they seemed to be deliberately subverting the New Deal's efforts to defuse the nation's explosive social tension. The Supreme Court, for instance, had ruled the National Labor Relations Act constitutional, but business leaders refused to take the high court's cue. Most continued to resist collective bargaining by any means necessary. On Memorial Day 1937, outside the gates of Republic Steel in Chicago, ten union supporters would be shot dead—all from behind.[1]

New Dealers, FDR included, blamed the nation's corporate elite for the "second depression," the sudden and unexpected downturn that knocked the recovering economy backward late in 1937. America's corporate giants, they charged, were manipulating their monopoly power to keep prices high and wages low. Business, FDR noted in his 1938 annual message to Congress, had given the nation "food for grave thought about the future." Corporate "concentration of economic control" was working "to the detriment of the body politic."[2]

Secretary of the Interior Harold Ickes would be considerably more blunt. The "irreconcilable conflict" between the money power and the American people, he charged, "has come into the open as never before, has taken on a form and an intensity which makes it clear that it must be fought through to a finish—until plutocracy or democracy—until America's sixty families or America's 120 million people win."[3]

But by decade's end, FDR's attention had begun to turn to another "irreconcilable conflict"—the impending showdown in Europe between democracy and fascism. War appeared increasingly likely. Two decades earlier, as assistant secretary of the navy, a much younger Franklin Roosevelt had been right at the center of the US war mobilization effort. FDR knew as well as anyone in Washington how much sacrifice a new mobilization would demand. He would expect all Americans to unselfishly do their part. But business leaders in the days before Pearl Harbor did not cooperate. Roosevelt would never forget. He devoted the rest of his life to defeating fascism. If that meant delivering a body blow or two to plutocracy along the way, FDR would be happy to oblige.

World War I had required an unprecedented increase in federal spending. The cost of World War II would run unprecedentedly higher, eight times the bill for World War I.[4] In 1940, of course, no one in Washington could know exactly what the new global conflict that had already begun in Europe might end up costing the United States. But analysts did know that the costs would be immense if the United States entered the war—and painfully difficult to bear for a nation still not free from Great Depression.

Average Americans would only bear new sacrifices, FDR believed, if all Americans shared in the sacrificing, rich as well as poor. That reality would make taxing the rich—and the corporations that made them ever richer—more than just a matter of fiscal prudence. The nation surely needed the many millions that higher tax rates on the rich could generate. The nation needed even more to see the rich feeling a real squeeze at tax time, not just a slight nuisance.

Five years earlier, in 1935, Roosevelt had spoken dramatically about the importance of taxing the rich. But FDR's rhetoric had been political grandstanding, a maneuver to suck the political momentum out of Huey Long's Share Our Wealth campaign. Things had changed since then. Taxing the rich for Roosevelt had now become both profoundly personal and politically necessary. The ungrateful rich had done their best to sabotage his New Deal. Now the president would make them pay. But he would make them pay to save democracy at its darkest hour. In the spring of 1940, FDR began the fiscal drive to mobilize a mighty nation. He left no doubt about his egalitarian intentions.

"Not a single war millionaire," FDR told the nation, "will be created in this country as a result of the war disaster."[5]

Business leaders had other ideas. They felt little sense of urgency and saw no reason to place their profits, current or future, in jeopardy. If the president wanted the nation's corporations to start producing war matériel, fine. But FDR shouldn't expect companies to divert resources from peacetime products that were making them money. Nor should FDR expect companies to build permanent new manufacturing capacity that might turn into a drag on future earnings once the demand for war hardware had passed. Let the federal government pay business enterprises to build new factories for tanks and airplanes. Or give them massive tax breaks to do the building.[6] Above all, don't start talking about taxing the "excess profits" that ramping up for war might start generating.

Business had faced an excess profits tax back during World War I. Business leaders didn't like excess profit taxes then. They didn't like them in 1940 either. If business accepted the concept of profit "excess," business would be conceding that government could set a "normal" level of profit. And if business allowed government to set a standard for "normal" profits, how could business prevent government from taxing profits above that standard once a war emergency had passed? Any "excess profits" tax imposed at a time of emergency had the potential to become a permanent tax.[7]

Corporate America would win the first round of the 1940 excess profits tax battle. FDR's Treasury Department had wanted a new Revenue Act that defined excess in relation to return on invested capital. If business invested capital, Treasury felt, business certainly had a right to a certain percentage of that investment as profit. But any profit over that percentage should be considered excess and eminently taxable.

Conservative Democrats blocked this initial New Deal wartime excess profits push, and the Revenue Act that passed Congress in late June 1940 raised new tax dollars primarily from individuals making under $100,000 a year. Regular corporate tax rates rose in the new legislation, but only slightly.[8] Senator Robert La Follette from Wisconsin would label the revenue measure "the most inequitable tax bill enacted by Congress in the last decade."⁹ The Revenue Act's passage came just as France was surrendering to the Nazis. On July 1, a week later, FDR would ask Congress to try again.

"We are asking even our humblest citizens to contribute their mite," Roosevelt told Congress. "It is our duty to see that the burden is equitably distributed according to ability to pay so that a few do not gain from the sacrifices of the many."¹⁰

The devil would now be in the details. Congressional conservatives hadn't ruled out forever an excess profits tax in June. They had instead argued they needed more time to figure out what would be considered excess, return on investment or simply higher profits than a company had been making right before the defense emergency began. Corporate executives would end up with best of both worlds. The second Revenue Act of 1940, passed in October, allowed corporations to choose their excess profits yardstick. Those companies that had made huge profits right before the emergency could choose to key their tax returns to their average earnings before the emergency had started. Those companies with small pre-emergency profits could go the invested capital route—and in the process shelter the increased profits the war emergency had brought. Conservatives made this generous choice still more business-friendly in March 1941 when Congress retroactively amended the October 1940 legislation. Thousands of businesses then quickly rushed out to claim hundreds of millions in tax refunds. Corporations, complained Treasury Department Assistant Secretary for Tax Policy John Sullivan, were completely shredding the intent of the excess profits tax levy. They were reaping enormous earnings and paying no tax.¹¹

Trench warfare over taxes would continue in the corridors of Congress throughout 1941. In September, with the war in Europe looking ever more dire, New Dealers would finally make some progress on FDR's aim to see that "a few do not gain from the sacrifices of the many." Treasury Secretary Henry Morgenthau had wanted a 100 percent tax on all corporate profits above a 6 percent return on investment.¹² That proposal wouldn't fly. But the new Revenue Act of 1941 would hike the regular tax rate on corporate earnings from 24 to 31 percent and impose a new surtax of 7 percent on profits over $25,000. The top individual tax rate, in the meantime, would rise to 81 percent on income over $5 million, a top rate higher than the top rate in effect during World War I.

Taxes on corporations and the wealthy, conservatives in Congress once again believed, could not possibly go any higher. On December 5, 1941, Senate Finance Committee chairman Walter George declared that federal taxes had reached "near-maximum" levels in the new Revenue Act and couldn't be increased appreciably without endangering the entire economy.[13]

Two days later the Imperial Japanese Navy bombed Pearl Harbor.

By the attack on Pearl Harbor, FDR had spent nearly two frustrating years struggling and failing to get corporate leaders to treat the war in Europe as something decidedly more than an unexpected business opportunity. He had created one new advisory commission after another, turned on his charm at various points, twisted arms at others. Nothing seemed to work. At one point, FDR had installed a top General Motors executive, William Knudsen, at the head of the federal government's preparedness bureaucracy. Late in August 1941, just a few months before the attack on the US Pacific fleet, FDR had to reorganize Knudsen out of the preparedness picture. The GM honcho had simply not been able to instill in his fellow industrialists the necessary sense of urgency.[14]

The shock of Pearl Harbor did at first seem enough to impart that needed urgency and a little patriotism, to boot. One of the nation's two top business lobby groups, the National Association of Manufacturers, soon after Pearl Harbor urged that "all income over and above that needed to keep our business structure alive should be taxed to the limit—leaving only enough for survival." Not to be outdone, the nation's other corporate lobbying giant, the United States Chamber of Commerce, made a pitch for "maximum rates on excess profits, going to 100 percent if possible." This "first blush of enthusiasm for the strict limitation of war profits," the Treasury Department's Randolph Paul would later note, almost totally evaporated when "enemy bombers failed to arrive" at America's doorstep.[15]

Paul, an experienced Wall Street tax lawyer, had become FDR's top adviser on tax matters. He would watch in horror that first spring after Pearl Harbor as corporate leaders and conservatives in Congress started pitching for a national sales tax and other assorted levies that would shield the comfortable from the war's enormous tax burden. The Chamber of Commerce called for a 10 percent national sales tax. The president of the New York Stock Exchange urged a lower tax on capital gains, the profits from buying and selling stocks, bonds, and other assets.[16]

Labor attacked the new charge for a national sales tax. So did officialdom in the Roosevelt administration. Treasury Secretary Morgenthau told the House Ways and Means Committee that such a tax "bears disproportionately on poor people whose meager incomes go almost wholly for consumer goods."[17] FDR himself told reporters that a national sales tax would amount to a "'spare-the-rich' tax."[18]

Late in April, FDR took an alternative to the American people. He unveiled a seven-point program to fund the war and prevent a devastating inflationary spiral that might crash the peace. The first of his seven points: heavier taxes, especially on the rich.

In 1935, in FDR's first-ever address that tackled taxes, the president had offered up no specifics on how much more he intended the rich to pay, a dead giveaway to political insiders that Roosevelt had no serious intention in soaking anybody at tax time. This time around, over four months after Pearl Harbor, the president did have specifics.

FDR first addressed corporate profits. All business profits—"not only in making munitions" but profits derived from any business at all—"must be taxed to the utmost limit." Then came the details on individual income taxation. The president told America that "discrepancies between low personal income and very high personal incomes should be lessened." In a time of "grave national danger, when all excess income should go to win the war," he continued, "no American citizen ought to have a net income, after he has paid his taxes, of more than $25,000 a year."[19]

This $25,000 bombshell, Randolph Paul later acknowledged, didn't come from Roosevelt's Treasury Department experts.[20] The figure came from the president himself. Where did FDR get the idea? The *New York Times* front-page story on the president's tax-cap proposal credited the notion to the United Auto Workers, the CIO's fastest-growing affiliate.[21] Other press reports would simply label the cap a CIO proposal. That connection had some logic behind it. Roosevelt's top labor adviser since early on in his administration had been Sidney Hillman, the president of the Amalgamated Clothing Workers and the initial number two to John Lewis in the CIO leadership ranks. Years before, in 1917, a much younger Sidney Hillman had been a leading trade union presence in the Committee on War Finance campaign for a 100 percent tax on all income over $100,000.

Had Hillman suggested an income ceiling to FDR in their many private conversations? Perhaps. But the same advice was also coming from other sources. Marriner Eccles, the New Deal Federal Reserve Board chairman, had been part of a team of economic advisers that FDR had tapped before his April 27 income-cap address. The advisers, Eccles would later write, had recommended that "a ceiling of fifty thousand dollars after taxes should be placed on individual incomes, thereby dramatizing the equality of sacrifice implicit in the proposed over-all program."[22]

How did the notion of an income limit get to Eccles? The idea of capping income in wartime had actually been floating around reputable public policy circles for some time, at least since 1936 when the *Annals of the American Academy of Political and Social Science* had published an article by John Flynn, the former managing editor of the old *New York Globe* and a frequent commentator in top national magazines like *Harper's* and the *New Republic*. Flynn proposed a wartime income tax calibrated "not to permit even the topmost tax-free incomes to exceed $10,000," an income slightly more than $160,000 in today's dollars.[23] Flynn actively promoted his wartime income limit before Congress and would proudly note in a later article that his proposal had won "unanimous approval" from the members of the Senate Munitions Committee and Committee on Military Affairs.[24]

Stiff limits on income—realized through a tax rate that either hit or closely approached 100 percent—would have one appeal not immediately obvious in progressive public policy circles. Such stiff limits could help the nation do war against wartime inflation while at the same time advancing an equity-minded agenda. In wartime, as Randolph Paul would explain, increases in income typically "had no place to go," since most consumer goods would be in short supply. If left in the pockets of well-off consumers, these new income dollars would spark a "wild competition" for scarce goods that would make skyrocketing prices, black markets, and illegitimate profits "the order of the day."[25] The biggest losers would be people with low incomes, the biggest winners those "persons with high incomes, who can maintain their standards of living despite higher prices."[26] Extremely high taxes on the affluent could keep this unfair inflation from ever taking off.

All of these lines of thought may have encouraged FDR's decision to call for a $25,000 limit on individual income. But none of them explain the enormous political capital that FDR went on to invest in the income cap fight. What does? Only the fury Roosevelt felt at the nation's deepest pockets. America's most vocal rich considered FDR a traitor to his class. FDR had come to consider America's most vocal rich traitors to democracy.

Americans of means initially reacted guardedly to the president's April 27 call for a $25,000 individual taxpayer income limit. Chamber of Commerce President Albert Hawkes would tell reporters he remained confident that "most of the men in the higher brackets are willing to make their full contribution" to winning the war. But he would need, Hawkes added, "careful consideration to make any definite comment upon what a $25,000 limitation of income would do in the wrong direction."[27]

"No one can have any legitimate objection to a wartime limitation on individual incomes of $25,000," Monsanto President Edgar Queeny echoed, "provided this limitation ends with the cessation of hostilities when the Nation will again need the stimulus of individual initiative and willingness to take capital risks."[28]

Other business leaders would be more openly supportive. The $25,000 income cap, expressed W. N. Banks, the president of the American Cotton Manufacturers Association, "will help to prevent the inflationary spiral."[29] Gushed William Jack, the president of a Cleveland aircraft parts plant who had personally come under fire for his $145,000 salary the year before: "Anything the President says will be backed up by every man in this place."[30]

Additional enthusiastic support came from leading national celebrities. Hollywood star Sonja Henie enthused that "no sacrifice is too great to win this war."[31] Her fellow Hollywood favorite Ann Sheridan regretted that she had "only one salary to give to my country."[32]

Newspaper editorial reactions varied, but few major newspapers came out blasting against FDR's income cap proposal. The critique of FDR's remarks from the arch-conservative *Chicago Tribune* would be decidedly oblique.

"The people will deprive themselves of much to win the war and prevent inflation," the first *Tribune* editorial on FDR's plan read, "but they will hope that any decisions taken will be inspired by a genuine desire to minimize the damage rather than by political considerations or the desire to reform our society."[33]

In Congress, those most leery of any tax changes that might "reform our society" would react to FDR's $25,000 limit with predictable hostility. Senator Robert Taft from Ohio, a ringleader in conservative Republican ranks, sarcastically wondered why the president hadn't set his income limit at $10,000 or even $2,500. Among rank-and-file Democratic Party lawmakers, the *New York Times* would report "quite a sizable degree of support" a few days after Roosevelt's address. But Democratic Party congressional leadership would be considerably less friendly. House Ways and Means Committee Chairman Robert Lee Doughton from North Carolina told reporters he could not see "any feverish demand" for FDR's income cap among his committee's members. The Treasury Department's Randolph Paul would soon inform those members in a closed executive session that Treasury was preparing an implementation plan for the president's income cap proposal. A committee member told Paul not to waste his time, since committee members "were going to vote down the proposal immediately for good and all."[34]

Paul and the Treasury Department proceeded anyway with an implementation plan and presented a "supertax" proposal to the Ways and Means panel on June 15. Under the Treasury proposal, taxpayers would first calculate their regular income tax. Any net individual income after that tax above $25,000 would be subject to the 100 percent supertax. For couples, the supertax would be applied to net after-tax income over $50,000. In practice, Paul noted, the supertax would only kick in on couples with before-tax incomes of $185,000, around $2.5 million today. After taxes—the regular federal income tax and the supertax—these couples would retain $50,000 in income, or about $700,000 today. Paul's congressional testimony would defend FDR's cap as a key step toward building and maintaining public support for the war effort.

"The great masses of our people will more cheerfully bear substantial reduction in standard of living," he testified, "if they know that no group is being favored, that rich and poor alike are giving up the comforts of peacetime in order that we may more effectively prosecute the war."[35]

The House Ways and Means Committee thanked Paul and promptly ignored his counsel. The panel shelved the FDR income cap the very next day.[36] In the months ahead, Ways and Means would continue working on new war-funding legislation. Roosevelt would continue working for his income cap. At the summer's end, he reiterated his call for a $25,000 cap in a Labor Day radio talk that drew more listeners than any episode of any commercial radio program that had ever aired.[37] His tax plan, the president told the American people, would be "the only practical way of preventing the incomes and profits of individuals and corporations from getting too high."[38] Congress needed to act on his tax proposals, said Roosevelt, by October.

FDR almost certainly knew by then that his administration was not going to be able to get a $25,000 cap over the obstacle course congressional leaders had waiting for it. He had, in fact, already begun making his own end run around Congress—through administrative action. In June, after the income cap plan's drubbing in House Ways and Means, FDR's war procurement agencies had sent a hundred thousand war contractors a pamphlet that warned against excessive executive compensation. Salary packages over $25,000, the federal contracting pamphlet indicated, could be "open to question and subject to limitation."[39]

The limitation would come on October 3, after Congress ignored the deadline FDR had announced in his Labor Day message. The White House unveiled a presidential proclamation that created a new federal Office of Economic Stabilization. The proclamation directed this new agency to issue regulations that would limit salaries after taxes to $25,000 per year. Under FDR's new marching orders, the Treasury Department would also begin denying corporations tax deductions for any salaries over $25,000. On top of all that, the wartime Office of Price Administration would not consider salary over $25,000 a legitimate business expense that corporations could claim as a reason to raise prices. And corporations would not be able to claim salaries over $25,000 for reimbursement under cost-plus government contracts.[40]

FDR's bold move caught conservatives off guard.

"The only logical stopping place for this movement is a completely communistic equalization of incomes on a straight per capita basis," fumed Princeton economist Harley Lutz. "We are being taken rapidly toward communism, not by acts of Congress, but by executive edict."[41]

This sort of fulmination reflected a deeper conservative frustration. FDR was successfully redefining the terms of the war finance debate. The congressional wrangling no longer involved a national sales tax. The new post–Pearl Harbor revenue bill lawmakers were debating would most definitely "soak the rich." The only question would be by how much, something close to Roosevelt's 100 percent tax on income over $25,000, or simply a top-bracket marginal rate higher than any

America's rich had ever before experienced. Lawmakers would end up with the latter.

The Revenue Act of 1942 enacted on October 21 would represent a truly massive change in federal tax policy. For the first time, the federal income tax would become a mass tax. In 1939, only one out of every thirty-two Americans paid a federal income tax. In 1943, under the new Revenue Act, a third of the American people, essentially everyone with a steady job, would become an income tax payer.[42] All income over $624 a year, just under $9,000 today, would now face income taxation.

What did the change mean for average working families? A married couple making $2,700 a year, about $37,500 today, would pay $254.60 in federal taxation under the new Revenue Act, the equivalent of just over $3,500 today. That family would also receive a postwar tax credit equal to about a fifth of that.[43] All corporate and individual income at America's economic summit would face significantly higher tax rates. Up to 80 percent of total corporate profit, excess and otherwise, could now go to Uncle Sam.[44] The top individual tax rate—81 percent under the second 1941 Revenue Act—would jump to 88 percent.

But these numbers understate the enormity of the new legislation's bite on plutocratic income. Under the 1941 Revenue Act, the top 81 percent federal income tax rate only applied to income over $5 million, or nearly $70 million today. The new 88 percent top rate would apply to all income over $200,000. High incomes below the $200,000 threshold would face stiff tax rates as well. On income between $60,000 and $70,000—the equivalent of between about $835,000 and $970,000 today—a 75 percent tax rate would kick in.

The end result: Under the new Revenue Act, a single taxpayer making exactly $1 million in 1943 would see a tax hike from $655,139 to $809,995.[45]

Conservatives could barely believe the scene they saw unfolding in Congress. The new tax legislation, the publisher of the *New Bedford Standard-Times* would rage in a full-page *Washington Post* ad, amounted to a call for "class warfare and not war revenue." Indeed, publisher Basil Brewer continued, the legislation "will dry up future revenue—by destroying incentive."[46] The legislation, Brewer thundered, might even "lose the war"!

New Dealers scoffed at that warning. But they would soon face some serious losses of their own—at the ballot box. The November 1942 midterm elections saw the Democrats lose fifty seats in the House and another eight in the Senate. The New Deal's spectacular 1936 Election Day triumph now stood nearly totally erased. The Democratic majority in the House had shrunk from 242 to 10, in the Senate from 60 to 21.[47] On paper, Roosevelt still held a majority in both chambers. In reality, Democratic and Republican conservatives now held the upper hand.

Roosevelt would not sulk after the 1942 election. He did not for a moment consider the election results a repudiation of his policies, and for good reason, since the American people hadn't repudiated his policies. Only the voters who made it to the polls in November did, and those voters didn't include millions of average working Americans. In 1942, government policy and bureaucratic happenstance effectively disenfranchised the American working class.

The War Department simply could not ensure the right to vote to servicemen and -women far from home. Some eighteen states had regulations on the books requiring voters to register in person and gave soldiers no exemption. Other states did not allow absentee voting. Still others had absentee voting deadlines that made voting almost impossible for men and women in uniform. Most Southern states also had a racist poll tax on the books, and only two Southern states exempted soldiers from having to pay it. In the end, notes historian Don Inbody, only a half of 1 percent of the nation's five million active-duty service personnel voted in the 1942 election.[48]

Service personnel wouldn't be the only ones disenfranchised. Huge numbers of un- and underemployed Americans had left their hometowns to find work in new war industry plants. They faced the same bureaucratic roadblocks that military men and women faced. The overall electoral picture: About fifty million Americans had voted in the 1940 election. In 1942, only twenty-eight million did.[49]

How would FDR react politically to the new postelection balance of power in Washington? Would Roosevelt back off his equity-in-sacrifice agenda? He would not. FDR still believed he had the American people with him, and he would soon have independent evidence. A month after the November elections, pollsters at Gallup found Americans supporting, by a 47 to 38 percent margin, a limit on the income "that each person should be allowed to keep per year in wartime after paying all taxes." The most preferred cap threshold: $25,000.

FDR had a second reason for not backing off: The landmark 1942

Revenue Act legislation had not accomplished nearly as much as Roosevelt and the Treasury Department wanted, either from a revenue or an equity perspective. The legislation did raise $7 billion in new revenue, more than the federal government had collected in any single year before 1941.[50] But the war effort was demanding far more revenue than the new tax legislation promised to provide. The 1942 legislation simply left too many excess dollars in the pockets of America's wealthy and the businesses that kept them wealthy. Depletion tax breaks alone for the nation's big oil companies were denying the federal government over $200 million in revenue annually.[51]

The rich, Roosevelt believed, were still not sacrificing. The president would not change course. He no longer had a majority in Congress inclined to vote his way. But FDR still had cards he could play, most notably his control over the federal agencies working to mobilize the American people and the American economy for war and victory. Roosevelt had played the first of these cards before the election, in early October, after Congress had refused to move forward on his $25,000 income cap proposal. He had ordered his new Office of Economic Stabilization to put the squeeze on excessive corporate executive paychecks in the burgeoning war industries.

In late October, Economic Stabilization Office director James Byrnes, who had stepped down from the US Supreme Court to lead the new agency, issued regulations to implement FDR's directive. Byrnes put the gross, before-tax corporate executive salary limit at $67,200, a figure that would leave top executives with no more than $25,000 after paying their taxes, life insurance premiums, and other fixed obligations.[52] Byrnes also established a maximum fine of $1,000 and up to a year in jail for any cap rule violation and denied corporations tax deductions on the entire salary paid out to cap rule violators, not just "the amount in excess of $25,000."[53]

After the November election, reinvigorated conservatives would go after Roosevelt's corporate salary cap directive. The *Chicago Daily News* charged before Thanksgiving that "President Roosevelt's recent action in limiting salaries to $25,000" followed "the trend of government by dictatorial decree" and represented "further adoption of the Communist party platform." The Communist Party of the United States, the *Daily News* helpfully pointed out, had gone on record in 1928 calling for a "graduated income tax, starting with incomes above $5,000 and increasing gradually, so that all incomes over $25,000 per year are confiscated."[54]

Two weeks later, a *New York Times* dispatch found "a storm of controversy throughout the country" around the $25,000 salary cap. Opponents, the *Times* reported, were labeling the cap "a social reform borrowed from the Communists and imposed under the shield of war." FDR's defenders were countering that top executives "should be willing to get along on more than $2,000 a month while marines endure tortures on Guadalcanal Island for $60 a month and room and board."[55]

In January, the conservatives elected the previous November took up their seats in Congress. The sparring began immediately. In his January budget message to Congress, Roosevelt dropped a not-so-subtle hint that his administration might move to extend his $25,000 cap on corporate executive salaries to *all* income over $25,000. The nation needed to raise more revenue to win the war, the president explained, and average Americans were going to have to make more sacrifices.

"I cannot ask the Congress to impose the necessarily heavy financial burden on the lower and middle incomes unless the taxes on higher and very large incomes are made fully effective," the president's message continued. "At a time when wages and salaries are stabilized, the receipt of very large net incomes from any source constitutes a gross inequity undermining national unity."[56]

For conservative politicians, FDR had now become an existential threat, as astute reporters had begun to notice.[57] If Roosevelt succeeded in his move to cap incomes at anything close to $25,000, how would lawmakers carrying plutocracy's water ever be able to raise the campaign cash they counted on the nation's deepest pockets to provide? FDR had to be stopped. For starters, his $25,000 salary cap directive had to be eliminated. That cap, California GOP congressman Bertrand Gearhart told reporters, amounted to "pure communism."[58]

More moderate Democrats now ran for cover. They pushed a compromise plan that would freeze corporate executive salaries at their level the day the United States entered the war. Roosevelt responded to House Ways and Means Chairman Robert Doughton with a compromise offer of his own. FDR pledged to "immediately rescind" his executive order capping executive salaries if Congress passed his supertax proposal limiting singles and married couples to $25,000 and $50,000, respectively, after taxes.[59]

The Ways and Means Committee leadership didn't bite at Roosevelt's offer. The pay freeze proposal would go instead to the House floor, as an amendment to legislation that would raise the federal debt ceiling. The debate that followed lasted a raucous four hours.[60] New Deal policies, one news account related, had never before "received the rough handling they got in the House today."[61]

The rough handling translated into a stinging defeat for FDR, by a 268-to-129 vote margin. The House raised the debt ceiling, as the president wanted, but attached to the debt-ceiling bill provisions that revoked his $25,000 pay cap order and substituted the executive pay freeze proposal instead. The Senate then undid the Pearl Harbor executive salary freeze. Senate Finance Committee chairman Walter George, a Democrat from Georgia, stuck in the bill instead a new provision that prevented the president from doing anything that might lower executive salaries below their levels between January 1 and September 15, 1942.[62] The president's $25,000 pay-cap order, Senator George told his colleagues, "accomplished no good and had no purpose except a fanciful purpose of producing a state of equality."[63]

"Equality of income," George continued, "has no place except in a communistic state."

New Deal–oriented Democrats in the Senate reluctantly went along with George's debt ceiling package, and the George plan passed by a 74-to-3 vote. Senate New Dealers felt they had no choice. The debt ceiling had to be raised for the sake of the war effort. The House would feel the same way, and the Senate bill, with the House signed on, moved to Roosevelt's desk late in March 1943. FDR refused to sign, choosing instead to let the debt ceiling bill become law without his signature, since he didn't have the votes to override a veto. But Roosevelt refused to give up his income cap advocacy. He blasted the repeal of his executive order. The move, he angrily charged, would mean windfalls for about seven hundred and fifty corporate executives making over $100,000 a year.[64] Congress, FDR added, had authorized a military draft that required average Americans to risk their lives for just $600 a year in pay, regardless of what they had earned previously in civilian life. Now Congress was refusing to reduce the salary of undrafted executives no matter how high their income might be.

Congress, the president advised, could make amends for this basic injustice. FDR once again urged lawmakers to move "at the earliest possible moment" to impose a "special war supertax on net income, from whatever source derived, which after the payment of all taxes exceeds $25,000."

"I still believe," as he put it, "that the nation has a common purpose—equality of sacrifice in wartime."[65]

Conservatives in Congress did not share that purpose. Just one month after the April repeal of the salary cap executive order, they shoved before Roosevelt an incredibly arrogant proposal to cancel the taxes America's affluent owed on their 1942 incomes.

This new battle had its roots in a widely supported Treasury Department move to shift federal income tax collections to a "pay-as-you-go" basis. Up until 1943, the small proportion of Americans with federal income tax liability paid their taxes the year after they made their income, since no system for withholding taxes from income then existed. The nation now desperately needed that system. The enactment of the Revenue Act of 1942 meant that many more Americans than ever before would owe federal income tax. With the nation at war, the federal treasury needed their new tax dollars as quickly as possible.

Virtually no one in American political life challenged that assessment. But any switch to pay-as-you-go withholding would create a transition problem. If tax withholding were put in place in 1943, the affluent who owed taxes for 1942 would have to pay in 1943 both the taxes they hadn't yet paid for 1942 and the taxes they were incurring for 1943.[66] Treasury Department officials brought Congress a common-sense solution for this transition problem. They would allow taxpayers to defer part of their 1942 tax bill and pay if off over several years.

Beardsley Ruml, a power broker in New York business circles, had a different idea. Ruml proposed a blanket forgiveness on the federal income taxes Americans owed for 1942. Even with that forgiveness, tax revenues—from the new withholding—would continue to flow into the IRS, and taxpayers would be spared the injustice of paying double on their taxes in 1943.

Ruml had the stature to secure a hearing. He served as both the treasurer of America's most famous department store, R. H. Macy, and the chairman of the New York Federal Reserve Bank. Ruml also had the support of America's wealthy. Their savings from his scheme would be enormous, particularly for those making money hand over fist from the war effort. The Ruml proposal did carry a so-called "anti-windfall" provision, but the provision had no real teeth. Under the "Ruml plan," Charles Marcus of the Bendix Corporation would pay only $177 in taxes on his 1942 income of $77,000.[67]

In May 1943, Roosevelt denounced Ruml's scheme in a message to the House Ways and Means Committee. The cancellation of taxes due for 1942, FDR pointed out, "would result in a highly inequitable distribution of the cost of the war and in an unjust and discriminatory enrichment of thousands of taxpayers in the upper income groups." If Ruml had his way, average Americans "including those now on the battle fronts" would end up "obliged to shoulder the burden from which our most fortunate taxpayers have been relieved."[68]

Roosevelt's firm stance would slow but not derail the Ruml forgiveness campaign. The House and Senate agreed on a modified transition to withholding that offered forgiveness for 75 percent of taxes paid in either 1942 or 1943 and gave taxpayers until March 1945 to pay their unforgiven tax liability.[69] FDR signed the bill in June 1943. Treasury desperately needed a withholding system in place to collect the new revenue the 1942 tax law promised to raise. Roosevelt could not responsibly delay that withholding with a veto unlikely to prevail in the end.

Instead of going all-out against the Ruml scheme, the president chose to seek another boost in tax rates. His goal: reducing the share of war costs the federal government had to borrow from two-thirds of the war bill to one-half. Reducing borrowing would make the war's burden more equitable. The biggest lenders to the government, after all, would always be those who had the means to buy government bonds. By reducing the amount of borrowing necessary, the administration would be reducing the amount of bond interest paid out to these affluent Americans. Instead of borrowing from the rich, in effect, the Roosevelt administration wanted to tax them.

In October 1943, Treasury Department officials presented a program that asked Congress for $10.6 billion in new taxes.[70] The new proposal, Treasury's Randolph Paul would later write, would not call outright for FDR's $25,000 income cap. But the proposal's increased surtaxes on personal income, Paul noted, had been designed to "achieve substantially the same effect."[71] Under the new Treasury plan, the effective tax rate on a couple making $100,000 would rise from 68.6 to 82 percent. The top tax rate on income over $5 million would rise to 95.7 percent, with income between $1 million and the top bracket facing a 94.6 percent tax rate.[72]

Republican lawmakers gave the administration proposals an intensely hostile reception. Any additional tax increases on Americans, their argument went, threatened "the future solvency of business" and "the liquidation of the middle class."[73] Many Democrats would also be none too welcoming—and none too eager to move quickly on any new tax measure. The House and the Senate wouldn't deliver a new Revenue Act onto FDR's desk until February 1944.

This new Revenue Act Congress sent the president only raised a fifth of the new dollars that the Treasury Department had requested and actually widened business tax loopholes by extending the infamous depletion allowance from the oil industry to mining, timber, and steel. FDR vetoed the bill. He attacked the legislation as "not a tax bill but a tax relief bill, providing relief not for the needy but for the greedy."[74]

Interior Secretary Harold Ickes, tax historian W. Elliot Brownlee relates, urged FDR to go "to the people with his case against the Congress" for disgracing the nation with "a vicious bill designed to protect the rich at the expense of the poor."[75] Roosevelt saw no point. He simply no longer had the votes in Congress to move a tax agenda as ambitious as the New Deal was pushing. Lawmakers quickly overturned FDR's veto. No president had ever before had a revenue act veto overturned.

FDR's top tax adviser at the Treasury Department, Randolph Paul, saw the writing on the wall. He stepped down as Treasury general counsel a month after the overturned veto.[76] The nation had apparently gone as far down the tax equity road as FDR and his fellow New Dealers could take it.

But the setbacks the Roosevelt administration had suffered on the $25,000 salary cap executive order, on pay-as-you-go tax forgiveness, and the Revenue Act veto were obscuring a much more fundamental reality. The New Deal had visited upon plutocracy a level of taxation that could scarcely have been imagined. In general terms, points out tax historian W. Elliot Brownlee, the rich in 1944 would pay about four times more of their income in taxes than the rich paid at any point during World War I.[77]

Even the Revenue Act enacted over FDR's veto left many of the rich owing more in taxes. In 1939, the year the war in Europe began, the first dollar of income over $200,000—about $3.3 million today—faced a 66 percent federal income tax rate. In 1944 and 1945, that first dollar over $200,000 faced a 94 percent tax rate.

The contrast over a longer time span would be significantly more stunning. In 1929, a year of near-total plutocratic domination, the nation's richest 0.1 percent paid just 10.9 percent of their total incomes in federal income tax. The 121,767 taxpayers at this lofty summit averaged $938,000, in today's dollars.[78]

In 1939, after a half-dozen years of the New Deal, the 130,880 taxpayers in the nation's most affluent 0.1 percent averaged just $467,662 in today's dollars, a half million less than the incomes they averaged in 1929. But these 1939 rich paid taxes at nearly twice the 1929 rate. Uncle Sam would collect 18.1 percent of their total income.

The real haircut for America's richest wouldn't come until the war years. In 1943, the booming war economy would have top 0.1 percent incomes averaging $612,837 in today's dollars. But IRS records show that federal income taxes in 1943 took 55.3 percent of that income. After federal taxes, the 135,105 taxpayers in the nation's richest 0.1 percent of 1943 had just $273,886 in income, as measured in today's dollars. After taxes, the richest 0.1 percent of 1929 averaged $835,728, over three times as much. The loopholes conservatives in Congress opened up in the 1944 Revenue Act would reduce the effective hit on high incomes, but only slightly. In 1944 and 1945, the top 0.1 percent of Americans would pay 50.4 and 49.7 percent of their incomes in federal income tax, respectively, about five times the tax rate they had paid in 1929.

Average tax rates on the richest of the rich—the top 0.01 percent—would reach 71.7 percent in 1943. The 13,511 Americans who made up that tiny top fraction of the US population would be left with $520,882 in after-tax 1943 income, in today's dollars. The top 0.01 percent in 1929 cleared after taxes $3,773,300, over seven times as much.

By war's end, in short, America's rich had never had less of the means necessary to domineer.

Roosevelt's relentless drive to make sure the war created "not a single war millionaire" had made an incredible difference. His refusal to take "no" for an answer on his $25,000 income cap proposal had kept the entire war finance debate revolving around the rich and how much they ought to be paying in taxes. Conservatives didn't want that debate. They wanted a national sales tax that would shunt the war's heavy burden onto average Americans, but FDR's aggressive advocacy for equity never allowed a sales tax to gain traction. Roosevelt would not get all he wanted on the tax equity front. But he did get plenty, enough to deliver against plutocracy a staggering knockdown.

The knockdown FDR delivered would be no purely personal triumph. He had help. Organized labor was marching with him every step of the way. Unions, particularly the new CIO industrial unions, beat their drums for FDR's $25,000 income cap all through the war years. In January 1943, for instance, CIO Secretary-Treasurer James Carey would tag team with National Farmers Union president James Patterson for a national radio debate on FDR's $25,000 salary cap order. The pair went up against the chairman of Universal Pictures and Senator John Danaher, a Republican from Connecticut.[79]

That August, after the repeal of FDR's $25,000 salary cap order, CIO President Philip Murray launched what the *Los Angeles Times* would call a union offensive for a "$25,000 ceiling on individual income to offset what he termed 'selfish minority' Congressional demands for a sales tax."[80] Two months later, the CIO rallied an assortment of national groups to call for a $25,000 limit, and the next month an even broader coalition—including the NAACP and six other national groups—attacked the House Ways and Means Committee for failing to adequately tax "high personal incomes" and "unparalleled corporate profits," then went to restate support for capping income at $25,000.[81]

The CIO's support for Roosevelt's tax agenda would be more than rhetorical. The incredibly low turnout in the 1942 midterm elections—and the resulting huge gains for the New Deal's most fervent opponents—had shoved the CIO deep into electoral politics. CIO leaders had watched fiercely antilabor politicos like Martin Dies from Texas get elected to Congress in 1942 with the votes of no more than 5 percent of their constituents. They vowed to organize politically as never before and "stem the reactionary tide."[82]

In July 1943, the CIO leadership unveiled the vehicle for this organizing, the new CIO Political Action Committee. Observers didn't quite know what to make of "the PAC." The new formation made no claims to be a political party. But the new PAC did all the things political parties did—raise funds, circulate political literature, get out the vote—and more as well. The PAC launched intensive political education efforts that aimed to win union member hearts, not just their votes.

Labor had done political action before, but never on so comprehensive a scale. The PAC established national offices in New York and Washington and fourteen additional regional offices that covered all forty-eight states.[83] The new PAC, CIO leaders pledged, would be "a permanent organization, a mighty force devoted to keeping the great majority of Americans vigilant and alert in guarding their proper political interests."[84] Labor political action had traditionally been about rewarding friends and punishing enemies. The new PAC, by contrast, actively promoted a vision for a new society, and this vision drew from the many different strands that wove through America's progressive past and New Deal present.

From the anti-"bigness" activism that Louis Brandeis had inspired would come a focus on restraining monopoly power. The 1930s had ended with a New Deal fixated on rooting out economic concentration. The intense concentration of the war years would revive that interest. In 1944, the nation's two hundred and fifty biggest corporations held 78 percent of all major war contracts and ran 79 percent of the new factories built with federal dollars.[85]

From the old Socialist Party and the left parties that had spun out of the Socialist Party orbit would come the conviction that America's working stiffs, once organized in a spirit of social solidarity, could and should help lead the nation.

From progressive businessmen like Edward Filene would come the understanding that no nation can have vibrant mass markets without mass purchasing power. The last landmark New Deal social legislation enacted, the Fair Labor Standards Act of 1938, had inaugurated a federal minimum wage at a rock-bottom twenty-five cents an hour. New Dealers considered this first federal minimum just a foot in the door. The new CIO PAC would seek to knock that door wide open.

From the bitter battles against private corporate control over "natural monopolies"—in everything from electric power to telephone lines—would come calls for TVAs all over America. New Dealers like Tennessee Valley Authority Director David Lilienthal believed that TVA-like programs in America's great river valleys had the potential to "awaken in the whole people" a forgotten "sense of common purpose." Democratically accountable TVAs, Lilienthal preached, would be able to nurture and protect America's natural resources.[86]

From the New Deal disciples of the British economist John Maynard Keynes and homegrown Keynesians like Marriner Eccles would come the understanding that private markets could never be counted on to self-correct. Government needed to intervene, and those interventions needed to be carefully and democratically planned to ensure all Americans jobs and preclude future depressions.

And the glue that would hold all these progressive strands

together? That would be the ongoing struggle to shear America's rich down to democratic size. Neither lasting prosperity nor enduring peace would ever be attained, as New Deal Senator Robert Wagner from New York put it in a 1944 speech, "upon the narrow foundation of a privileged few."[87] The nation would never be able to realize mass purchasing power if the nation's wealth kept siphoning off into a handful of bank accounts. Monopoly power, New Dealers believed, only sped that siphoning. By clamping down on monopoly behaviors with TVAs that prevented private control over natural monopolies and antitrust regulations that curbed monopolistic practices in the rest of the private sector, a postwar America could keep new wealth from amassing unconscionably at the top. By progressively taxing whatever new income and wealth did manage to amass, the federal government would raise the revenue needed to enrich the lives of average Americans and keep the economy humming.

The clearest academic expression of this antiplutocratic imperative would come from Charles Merriam, a founder of modern American political science and a reformer with a personal history that went back to Teddy Roosevelt's Republican progressivism. In 1941, Merriam published a lecture that asked whether American politics had become little more than "a cloak for old-fashioned and unbending capitalism, for pluto-democracy."

"Are we struggling for the glory, fame, profit, position, and prestige of a few?" Merriam would wonder. "Or are we parts of a great movement for the emancipation of mankind, for new life bursting through the old-time shells?"[88]

We had to be, he concluded, shell-bursters.

"The root problem of democracy in our day," Merriam would contend, "is to see that the gains of our civilization are fairly distributed and translated into terms of the common good without undue delay."[89]

CIO publicists would spell out that same notion in a more down-to-home wording.

"Democracy can work," Joseph Gaer would write in a celebratory 1945 book on the new CIO PAC. "Our present economic system can be made to work—provided it is made to work for the benefit of all. Free Enterprise must therefore be understood as freedom of opportunity, and not freedom to waste the nation's resources and manpower to satisfy the avarice of a few."[90]

Taxes, FDR's wartime Vice President Henry Wallace also stressed, would play a pivotal role in the struggle against this plutocratic avarice. Wallace told a Seattle audience in 1944 that to ensure "profits for the many instead of the few, it will be necessary after the war to use our taxation system for economic objectives much more skillfully than we have in the past." That would mean, above all else, continuing "heavy, steeply graduated taxes on personal incomes after the war."[91] Americans needed to learn from the horror of Nazi Germany, Wallace had written soon after the United States entered the war. We needed to tax away grand concentrations of private wealth because demagogues like Adolf Hitler could only come to power with plutocratic financial support.

"The demagogue is the curse of the modern world," Wallace explained, "and of all the demagogues, the worst are those financed by well-meaning wealthy men who sincerely believe that their wealth is likely to be safer if they can hire men with political 'it' to change the signposts and lure the people back into slavery of the most degraded kind."[92]

A nation that took all these lessons to heart could work wonders. Men and women hovering in and around the CIO PAC didn't just believe that. They knew it. They were witnessing these wonders with their own eyes all throughout the World War II years of struggle and sacrifice. The United States of the war years was doing almost everything progressives envisioned that a nation ought to be doing: taxing the rich and corporate profits at steeply progressive rates, regulating business as never before, respecting labor rights, running major economic enterprises. Conservatives had always claimed that no free modern economy could ever survive a set of public policies as "antibusiness" or "socialist" as these. But America's World War II economy wasn't just surviving. America's economy was thriving. Industrial production had soared. The Great Depression had finally exited, stage left.

Progressives, everywhere they looked, saw their fondest dreams turning into social and economic realities. Corporate titans were grumbling about their personal tax bills and bargaining collectively with their workers for the first time ever. The titans had little choice. Worker walkouts in 1940 and 1941 had left FDR convinced that war production would be constantly interrupted if corporations continued to deny workers their basic rights. FDR moved to end that denial. He placed the CIO's Sidney Hillman in charge of war mobilization labor policy, and the savvy Hillman would in turn do battle against military procurement officers who routinely passed out contracts to nonunion corporations that regularly violated the National Relations Act.

In 1941, Hillman had a lucrative army truck contract shifted from the intensely antiunion Ford Motor Company to the already union-organized Chrysler. Hillman's pressure from Washington, coupled with worker pressure from the factory floor, eventually brought the mighty Henry Ford to heel. In May, the legendary industrialist finally agreed to negotiate with the CIO United Auto Workers. That same spring, a similar set of pressures brought Bethlehem Steel and its lavishly paid CEO, Eugene Grace, to the bargaining table. In quick order, two of the nation's most important union-resisting industrial corporations had seen the error of their ways.[93] Other antiunion employers followed suit. The overall number of American workers with union cards would rise from 8.5 million in 1940 to 13.5 million in 1943.[94]

Elsewhere in the economy, progressives saw Uncle Sam actively involved in the economy as never before, not just planning but owning. By the middle of the war the federal government held 10 percent of the nation's steelmaking facilities, 50 percent of machine tool, 70 percent of aluminum, and 90 percent of aircraft manufacturing operations.[95]

For average Americans, the war's new economic relationships were paying off in every paycheck. Hourly earnings in manufacturing plants rose 60 percent between January 1941 and January 1945. Weekly earnings rose even more, by 80 percent, since workers were laboring plenty of overtime hours. Prices only rose 30 percent over those same four years, observes labor historian David Brody, making for "a very substantial increase in real income."[96] And more workers had real income. Unemployment plummeted from about nine million in July 1940 to under eight hundred thousand in September 1943. The newly employed had benefits that had never before existed on a mass scale. Companies and unions were bargaining into effect new pension systems, health insurance plans, paid holidays, and other fringe benefits that didn't count against federal wartime ceilings on wage increases. The federal government gave employers an additional incentive to provide these new fringes: Employers could treat their new outlays for medical and insurance benefits as tax-deductible business expenses.[97]

Federal taxation of excess corporate profits during the war created another incentive for improving worker well being. If you were a wartime CEO, why waste time devising new strategies for squeezing your workers? Higher profits wouldn't do your company much good. They stood likely to be taxed away as excess profit. And higher profits wouldn't do you much good personally either, not when income in the top individual tax brackets faced tax rates as high as 94 percent.

Higher taxes on Americans sitting at the top of the economy. Jobs, better wages, and fringe benefits for Americans at the bottom. The nation during World War II was following the ultimate progressive egalitarian game plan, leveling up from the bottom, leveling down from the top. The Great Depression had given way to what historians Claudia Goldin and Robert Margo would later dub the "Great Compression."[98]

Progressives during the World War II years didn't yet have a clever label for the new society that was emerging all around them. But progressives—and enlightened business leaders—most certainly did sense the emergence of a distinctly new, consciously planned society. That "a planned economy can make people happier than a system of free enterprise," progressive economist Stuart Chase wrote early on in the war, may be "open to debate." But no serious person, Chase contended, can possibly debate that "planned economies are coming so fast you can hear the wind whistle around their edges."[99]

The chairman of the board for General Electric, Philip Reed, agreed. "Our political, social, and economic scheme of things after the war will resemble neither the 1920s nor the 1930s," he noted in *BusinessWeek*. "The war will advance by several decades the trends away from laissez-faire and toward economic planning under government supervision."[100]

Sweeping predictions like these had a fairly intoxicating impact on New Deal progressives. American society, if not all humanity, appeared on the cusp of enormously hopeful change. The war was upending America, in one welcome way after another. Why couldn't that upending continue in peacetime? As economist Stuart Chase pointed out, "It does not take a very high IQ to ask why we cannot keep prosperous making plowshares if it has been proved that we can keep prosperous making swords."[101] Early in 1943 President Roosevelt reinforced this sense that the progressive moment had finally arrived. Declared the president: "Freedom from want for everybody, everywhere, is no longer a Utopian dream."[102]

No one in the New Deal would express this notion of a "people's revolution" any more powerfully and consistently than Henry Wallace, the progressive Republican from Iowa who had served eight years as FDR's secretary of agriculture before becoming his vice-presidential running mate in 1940. Wallace, notes historian Norman Markowitz, essentially redefined the World War "in radical democratic as against conservative balance-of-power terms," and nowhere more so than in a widely reprinted May 1942 address that promised a "century of the common man."[103]

The "people's revolution," Wallace reminded Americans, had been unfolding all across the world ever since the American Revolution. We had won freedom of religion, freedom of expression, and freedom from the fear of secret police. But we had not yet won "freedom from want for the average man." Wallace envisioned an America where the middle class, up to then a narrow swatch of the population that sat between the rich and America's vast and poor majority, would become a mass class.

"What most of us visualize for the America of the future," Wallace reflected early in 1943, "is not a nation of propertyless workers but rather an America where all can become members of what has been called the 'middle class,' where all can share in the benefits which that class has enjoyed in the past."[104]

Wallace described this new mass middle class in vivid detail. Average Americans, he forecast, would enjoy the quality of life currently available only to small businesspeople and lawyers, doctors, and other professionals. In Wallace's new mass middle-class America, the typical American would have "a car neither old nor ramshackle, decent clothes, and books." He would have his choice of "movies or theatre, trips, vacations, high school and college for his children"—in other words, a quality of life that "only a minor portion of our people has enjoyed in the past." The American people could have this future, Wallace advised, but only if we triumphed over plutocracy once and for all.

"The issue is very simple," Wallace told a Seattle audience in February 1944. "The question is whether the people, keeping themselves fully informed, can operate through democratic government to keep the national interest above the interest of Wall Street. Or will the old-line politicians, financed from Wall Street, again succeed in making Washington the servant of Wall Street?"[105]

Millions of Americans thrilled to the vision Henry Wallace presented, but skeptics certainly abounded. Many of these skeptics wanted for the nation just what Wallace wanted. They just couldn't get the numbers to add up. At a 1944 meeting of the American Economic Association, Dr. Julius Hirsch of the New School for Social Research gave these numbers a depressingly close reading and gave new meaning to economics as the "dismal science." The United States, Hirsch noted, currently had nine or ten million more people with jobs than the nation had employed in 1939. After the war, with no more insatiable demand for war matériel, how could the nation possibly keep the nine or ten million newly employed Americans employed— plus find work for the nation's eleven million discharged service men and women? America, Hirsch predicted, would find it "impossible to create full productive employment."[106]

Nonsense, progressive economists responded. Postwar America would have more than enough valuable work that desperately needs doing, enough valuable work to keep all Americans productively employed once peace came.

"We need to rebuild America—urban redevelopment projects, rural rehabilitation, low-cost housing, express highways, terminal facilities, electrification, flood control, reforestation," Harvard economist Alvin Hansen reassured Americans. "We need a public health program including expansion of hospital facilities. We need a nutrition program. We need more adequate provision for old age. We need higher educational standards in large sections of our country. We need a program to improve and extend our cultural and recreational facilities."[107]

"We have seen how it is possible to mobilize the productive capacities of the country for war," Hansen concluded. "We can also mobilize them for peace."

But progressives had no illusions. They knew they faced a daunting task. The war had, to be sure, energized millions of Americans with a deeply ennobling vision of the future. But the war had also strengthened conservative forces in Congress. The war's disenfranchisement of millions of dependable New Deal voters had left Congress with a majority hostile to the New Deal. The Republicans and Democrats in this new conservative majority considered planning little more than economic despotism. Starting in 1943, they would either eliminate or harass to the point of distraction all the major New Deal agencies working to build the postwar future. They abolished the New Deal's National Resources Planning Board. By 1944, they had also eliminated most of the New Deal's most iconic programs—the Civilian

Conservation Corps and the Works Progress Administration, among them—and passed legislation that restricted labor's right to strike and make political contributions.[108]

These conservatives played to public frustrations. The war years were demanding sacrifice on a daily basis. Wartime rationing had millions of Americans going without sugar and gasoline, ketchup and tires. After the 1942 Revenue Act, millions of Americans were also paying federal income tax for the first time. Amid all the sacrifice, many yearned for a little "normalcy," just as many had after the upheavals of World War I.

Conservatives had an appealing message for frustrated voters. Enough with the sacrificing. Cut those taxes. Cut them overall by 50 percent, demanded the Republican Post-War Tax Study Committee, the panel responsible for shaping the 1944 GOP platform tax plank.[109] Repeal the excess profits tax, demanded Midwest businessmen in what would become known as the Twin Cities Tax Plan.[110] Other conservatives would push a constitutional amendment to limit the top federal income tax rate—94 percent in 1944—to 25 percent.[111]

These conservative initiatives would ensure America two radically distinct visions in the November 1944 elections. One vision would make a national celebrity out of Vivien Kellems, a Connecticut manufacturer who had declared in December 1943 that she would not withhold income tax from her employee paychecks. "Our forefathers did not intend that a little group of Communists in the White House should pick our pockets and throw everything we've got into the bottomless pit of relief and support the whole world," Kellems told a Philadelphia women's club in April 1944.[112]

The other vision would directly challenge the emptiness of conservative "free enterprise" sloganeering. "'Free enterprise' ought to mean freedom from unemployment, monopoly, and gross inequality in the distribution of income," as economist Donald Bailey Marsh pointed out.[113]

President Roosevelt spelled out the building blocks of this broader freedom in his January 1944 state of the union address. FDR outlined an eight-point agenda designed to guarantee Americans adequate employment, food, shelter, education, and health care and ensure the American people the freedom to do enterprise without unfair monopoly competition. Roosevelt called his agenda a "second Bill of Rights." The CIO would soon dub the FDR list an "Economic Bill of Rights" and make it the centerpiece of the federation's entire political program.

Which vision would prevail? The CIO PAC would move mountains—of paper—to undo the disastrous results from the 1942 congressional elections. The PAC distributed an amazing eighty-five million pieces of campaign literature in 1944. CIO election broadsides would be reprinted widely in the labor and foreign-language press and even read out loud on sympathetic radio stations.[114] CIO activists supplemented the paper blitz with face-to-face contacts. Their goal throughout: doubling the voter turnout, from the one in three eligible voters who had cast ballots in 1942 to two of every three in 1944. That proved difficult. Millions of men and women in uniform still faced a voting obstacle course. Many more service personnel would vote in 1944 than voted in 1942, but only 2.6 million of the 9.2 million voting-age men and women in the armed forces ended up returning ballots, just a 29.1 percent turnout. The turnout among eligible civilians: about 60 percent.[115]

With so few votes from New Deal–leaning soldiers, the CIO had no chance of reaching the two-thirds turnout goal. The CIO also had no chance of matching the enormous amounts of cash conservatives put into the 1944 campaign. Overall, a labor analyst would note after the election, the CIO's PAC spent "considerably less than the 1940 contributions to the Republican Party by five wealthy families alone."[116]

For labor, the election results would be disappointing. They would not undo the damage from the 1942 elections. The Republicans had gained fifty House seats in 1942. Democrats gained back only twenty-two in 1944 and lost a Senate seat.[117] The Democrats did retain their majorities in both the House and Senate. But the difference between a "Democratic majority" and a "New Deal" majority would soon once again be clear.

After the election, Roosevelt wanted Democratic leaders in Congress to eliminate the House Un-American Activities Committee, a temporary panel whose fulminating against Communists in the New Deal had helped fuel Republican red-baiting against Democrats in the 1944 campaign. This red-baiting had proved invaluable for the Republicans. Hysterical charges about Communist influence, as historian Norman Markowitz notes, gave them "a way to attack the New Deal's supposed collectivist tendencies without indulging in suicidal assaults" against Social Security and other popular New Deal social legislation.[118] In January 1945, House Democratic leaders Sam Rayburn and John McCormack ignored FDR's push to dissolve HUAC and let Mississippi Democrat John Rankin, a notorious racist and anti-Semite, maneuver to make the committee an ongoing congressional fixture.

Would the slight electoral gains of 1944 clear the way for any progress at all on a more ambitious postwar agenda? Progressives in Congress did have some reason to feel slightly optimistic. Before the elections, they had witnessed a major legislative triumph that demonstrated just how powerful a force grassroots mobilizing could be.

Early in 1944, FDR had proposed legislation to ease the transition of returning service personnel into the peacetime economy. The Roosevelt bill did not have much meat to it. The president apparently didn't feel he had the votes to get a more meaningful package through Congress. A meaningful package would be expensive, and the conservative majority had already demonstrated an unwillingness to make any expenditures that might be used to justify continuing high taxes on high incomes.

But this particular spending battle would be different. Veterans had become an enormous constituency. Eighty percent of Americans born in the 1920s would eventually have a military connection.[119] And the main organization that represented veterans, the American Legion, would not be pleased with the tepid transition support that Roosevelt's initial bill offered. The Legion had about three million members at the time and posts in every congressional district. In quick order, these posts mobilized a firestorm of pressure on Congress to strengthen the FDR legislation. The Legion wanted for veterans what progressives wanted for all Americans: help with higher education and finding jobs and low-cost loans for buying homes and businesses.[120] Progressives in Congress rallied to the Legion cause. Eventually, so would enough conservatives to get a Legion-backed legislative package narrowly passed in June 1944.

The new Servicemen's Readjustment Act—the "GI Bill"—gave returning veterans up to $500 per academic year for college tuition and the right to a monthly living allowance while they were pursuing their education. The bill also gave vets access to up to a year of unemployment benefits, plus federal loan guarantees to lower the cost of mortgage and business loans.

The eventual impact of the GI Bill on American society would be huge. College suddenly became a real option for millions of average

American families. By 1947, veterans would make up just under half the nation's total college enrollment.[121] Low-cost GI Bill mortgages had a similar impact on the housing market. Millions of working families, thanks to the legislation, would become homeowners for the first time.

The foundation for a new, mass middle class was now taking shape. Early in 1945, progressives moved to build upon that foundation by guaranteeing all Americans the right to a job, a key plank of FDR's 1944 Economic Bill of Rights. The "Full Employment Bill" that Montana's James Murray introduced in January called on the federal government to finance whatever loan programs and public investments might be necessary to ensure that the economy was operating at full-employment levels. Murray's ambitious bill would soon die a death of a thousand cuts. Republicans and conservative Democrats slashed out of the legislation all mention of full employment. World War II would end with no guarantee of a job for every American.[122]

The war would also end without Franklin Roosevelt in the White House and Henry Wallace a heartbeat away. Roosevelt had let the 1944 Democratic convention dump Wallace from the Democratic ticket. But Wallace campaigned brilliantly for FDR in the 1944 presidential race anyway and ended up, in the fourth New Deal term, as Roosevelt's secretary of commerce, a pivotal position for the transition to a peacetime economy.

Roosevelt would never see that transition begin. He died suddenly on April 12, 1945. His death left Harry Truman, the former senior senator from Missouri, in the White House. Truman had never been aligned with New Deal progressives. Even so, thoughtful progressives had reason to feel somewhat sanguine as the war was drawing to a close. True, they no longer had a champion in the White House, and progressive New Dealers were certainly playing defense in Congress. But they had great victories to celebrate and defend. The high tax rates on the wealthy they had put in place remained in effect. The federal government now had the financial wherewithal to help America's poor majority become a mass middle class.

Few returning GIs had any sense of these new federal fiscal realities. But many knew that something fundamental about their country was changing. Private Charles Pinkas, a liberated and wounded prisoner of war, could testify to that. Private Pinkas found himself in a

Miami Beach luxury hotel as the war was closing down, along with thousands of his wounded fellow soldiers. Rooms at these hotels before the war had gone for up to ninety dollars a night, over $1,100 in today's currency. Now those same rooms housed recuperating vets. The soldiers passed their days and nights enjoying the pastimes— deep-sea fishing and midnight cruises on Biscayne Bay—that used to belong only to vacationing millionaires.

"This isn't the army," Private Pinkas told reporters, "it's paradise."[123]

Chapter Eight

RED SCARE, RED RIVAL

Americans didn't know quite what to expect in the years right after World War II ended. Would the economy sink back into Great Depression? Or would America's economic engine roar ahead? The answer, educator William Van Til told the nation's young people in a remarkable social studies textbook written soon after the war, would depend on the economic policies Americans chose to adopt.[1] And those choices would change the course of the lives those young people would lead.

If Americans made wise choices that staved off another Depression, the educator assured his young readers, "you'll be freer to choose whether to marry early" and "have more say about what jobs you take." You'll even be able to live "free from drudgery," he continued, thanks to the wonders of electric irons, vacuum cleaners, and washing machines. The "world of tomorrow" could be ours. We as a nation and as a free people just had to make the right choices.

"Under the goad of war, we built a system of production that dwarfed 1929," Van Til concluded. "If anything like the same level can be made permanent for peacetime, the result will be standards of living for you and others beyond your dreams."[2]

Van Til's textbook laid out with admirable balance the economic policy options Americans had before them. We could turn private enterprise loose, or we could place on the economy rules and regulations designed to keep business operating in the public interest. We could together plan where we wanted private enterprise to be headed, or we could give public enterprise a much more prominent place in our everyday economy. Thoughtful progressives like Van Til knew their history. After World War I, the American people had never had the opportunity to conduct a reasoned debate on our economic future. Hysteria had choked off reason. America's wealthy and powerful had grabbed back the "freedom" they had lost, undoing in the process the wartime policies that had ever so slightly leveled down America's top and leveled up the bottom. Would that disastrous history repeat after World War II?

At first, that didn't appear to be the case. The new president, Harry Truman, seemed intent on recognizing that America's working people, through their unions, needed to have a place at the economic table, as did the general public through its elected leaders in government. In November 1945, Truman convened a high-powered, three-week National Labor-Management Conference that brought to Washington three dozen business, labor, and public officials. They all made nice. They didn't reach many specific agreements. But they were talking. Business leaders seemed not just resigned to labor's place at the table, but comfortable with it.

"Labor unions are woven into our economic pattern of American life, and collective bargaining is a part of the democratic process," Eric Johnston, the president of the US Chamber of Commerce, openly pronounced. "I say recognize this fact not only with our lips but with our hearts."[3]

This era of good feeling would be short-lived. Major employers soon did not even pay lip service to labor's role as an equal partner. For the next three years, Corporate America would struggle to reclaim the outright supremacy business interests had lost by the war's end. Workers would struggle, too, for the "promised world of tomorrow." World War I had failed to "make the world safe for democracy." This new clash would make America safe for the world's first mass middle class.

The economic turmoil after the war began almost immediately. On September 2, 1945, Japanese authorities signed the surrender papers that ended World War II. Within a month, the Pentagon was canceling wartime contracts. Over a million war-industry workers would soon be out of work, often with virtually no advance notice.[4]

Workers who didn't lose jobs typically lost hours. The overtime that war production demanded evaporated. Fewer hours meant smaller paychecks, and workers began pressing for higher wages to regain their lost income. Employers resisted. In many economic sectors, federal price controls remained in effect, and businesses claimed they couldn't grant wage increases without raising prices. Labor and federal officials didn't buy that contention. They both argued, notes historian Joshua Freeman, "that most employers could raise wages without raising prices and still take a healthy profit."[5]

Federal officials would keep price controls in effect straight through most of 1946, and unions would strike in the greatest wave of walkouts the nation had ever seen. The first of the strikes to gain national attention broke out in New York City just three weeks after the Japanese surrender. Some fifteen thousand elevator operators, doormen, and other commercial building support workers took to the picket lines after building owners refused to accept new contract terms that a War Labor Board mediation panel had recommended.[6]

The strike paralyzed the city's economy, and not just because New York's skyscrapers at the time had few automatic elevators. New York's other unions respected the picket lines the strikers had up all around the city. They refused to cross. New York's garment industry shut down completely. Overall, 1.5 million workers would be idle. After a week, New York Governor Thomas Dewey—the losing GOP presidential candidate in 1944—convinced the commercial building strikers and employers to accept an arbitrator. The subsequent settlement favored the strikers.

The New York walkout may have lent a sense of urgency to the Truman labor-management conference that began early in November 1945. But the conference would in no way put a damper on the spreading strike wave. That same month, the United Auto Workers began a 113-day walkout against General Motors, America's biggest and most powerful corporation. The striking auto workers saw their walkout in terms far broader than a simple contract dispute in a single industry. They seemed intent, notes labor historian Paul Buhle, on speaking to the public at large and that public's deep desire for a new America. The strike slogan: "We fight today for a better tomorrow." Notables like Eleanor Roosevelt, Franklin's widow, rushed to the UAW side, and the business magazine *Fortune*, observes Buhle's account of the walkout, painted UAW strike leader Walter Reuther "as a coming representative of the consumer in a triumvirate of national leadership with capital and government."[7]

By year's end, 3.5 million American workers had walked out on strike. The striker total the next year, in 1946, hit 4.6 million, over 10 percent of the nation's workforce.[8] The ferment spread almost everywhere. In over half a dozen cities—from Rochester in New York to Oakland in California—disputes that involved single employers turned into general strikes. In Rochester the strife started when the city abolished the jobs of hundreds of public employees newly organized into a local affiliate of the fledgling Federation of State, County and Municipal Workers. The May 1946 citywide walkout shut down everything from taxi service and movie theaters to Rochester's two daily papers and ended in a clear-cut union victory.[9]

In Oakland a general strike erupted almost spontaneously in early December 1946 after police tried to escort downtown delivery trucks slated to refill the stock of two struck department stores. Retail clerks, mostly women who were making less than sixteen dollars a week, had walked out on strike over a month earlier.[10] At the general strike's height, an estimated thirty thousand local workers festively shut down and occupied Oakland's downtown. Two days later, city officials agreed not to use police as strikebreakers, and the general strike ended. The retail clerks would stay out on strike for over another six months and finally win a decent contract in May 1947.[11]

The local unions that drove the Oakland general strike belonged to the Teamsters and other national unions affiliated with the American Federation of Labor. The AFL had by then dropped its historic hostility to industrial unionism and regularly organized beyond craft lines to compete with CIO unions. At the local level, by the mid-1940s, AFL and CIO union leaders had often become indistinguishable. The AFL local activists could be as militant and imaginative as their CIO counterparts. Only politics separated them. AFL unions had been obsessively anti-Communist since the red scare after World War I. The CIO unions that emerged in the mid-1930s applied no political litmus tests to their activists.

Republicans tried to make the CIO and Roosevelt pay for that political tolerance during World War II. They painted Sidney Hillman, the CIO leader closest to FDR, as a dangerous red sympathizer, a charge that no doubt amazed and maybe amused labor insiders who knew that Hillman and Communist Party activists within the Amalgamated Clothing Workers had been battling for years.

The wartime red-baiting against the CIO peaked in the fall 1944 election campaign. "Mrs. Luce Assails Red Putsch in Labor Unions," read one typical *New York Daily Mirror* headline that October. Luce, a Republican member of Congress from Connecticut and the wife of the *Time* media empire chieftain Henry Luce, attacked the CIO

Political Action Committee as a "newly-laid egg out of the Hillman hen by the red roosters."[12] Hillman deftly deflected the red-baiting. Those who branded him a "Communist Jew," he responded, were doing Hitler's dirty work. The right-wing media moguls, Hillman told the convention of the United Electrical, Radio, and Machine Workers Union, never miss "an opportunity to drag in the fact that I am a Jew and that I was born in Lithuania—I don't apologize to anyone for it!"[13]

After the war, the right-wing red-baiting became more difficult to defuse. The Soviet Union, a wartime ally, had now become a postwar rival, and CIO leaders had come to see the Communist activist presence in their ranks as an albatross they could no longer abide. AFL leaders, even the progressives among them, shied even further away from any union activity that might impart them a Communist tinge. In the Oakland general strike, the city's top AFL leader, a respected progressive, turned down CIO support because he feared headlines screaming "Reds Cause Anarchy Downtown."[14]

Midway through 1946, the purge in CIO ranks would be well underway. Unions rewrote their constitutions to bar Communist Party members or sympathizers from holding elected union office. Top union officials who had worked side by side with Communist Party members for years would now do everything possible to drive activists with CP backgrounds out of influential positions.[15] Each union concession to the growing red-baiting frenzy only emboldened conservatives and their campaign to demonize anything that smacked of New Deal progressivism. The postwar world of the 1940s was now beginning to resemble the aftermath of World War I: a massive strike wave, followed by a massive red scare.

The resemblance would go further still. After World War I, conservatives in Congress launched a direct offensive against the conflict's high taxes on America's most fortunate. After World War II, conservatives would rail against New Deal taxes on the rich as heartily as they went after New Deal Communists. For America's right wing, the two went hand in glove. "Soak the rich" amounted to ominous Communist code.

"For years," the top Republican on the House Ways and Means Committee thundered in 1946, "we Republicans have been warning that the short-haired women and long-haired men of alien minds in the administrative branch of government were trying to wreck the American way of life and install a hybrid oligarchy at Washington through confiscatory taxation."[16]

The year before, two months after the war ended, conservatives had pushed through a Revenue Act that cut tax receipts for 1946 by nearly $6 billion, about 13 percent of the federal government's revenue total. The tax cut eliminated the excess profits tax and gave all taxpayers—the nation's wealthiest included—individual rate cuts.[17] The legislation dropped the tax rate on income from $2,000 to $4,000, about $25,000 to $50,000 today, from 23 to 19 percent and the rate on income over $200,000, about $2.5 million today, from 94 to 86.5 percent.

The tax cuts for average Americans in the new Revenue Act, progressives charged, amounted to flimsy political cover for giveaways to America's richest. Asked Representative Herman Andersen, a progressive Republican from Minnesota: "Why must we in order to help Bill Smith, a $2,000 a year man, save $45, which he has been proud to pay toward our nation's upkeep, give our million-dollar-income friend $90,000?"[18]

President Truman signed the new Revenue Act on November 8, 1945. Progressives winced. They winced even more the next year when the president did nothing to help advance the Full Employment Bill, the legislation launched with such great progressive hope in early 1945. The final jobs bill that did pass, the Employment Act of 1946, would do nothing concrete to stimulate employment.[19]

Few higher-ups within the Truman administration lamented the full employment legislation's fate, mainly because few of them had any New Deal bona fides. By the summer of 1946, Secretary of Commerce Henry Wallace had become the last New Deal holdover in the Truman cabinet.[20] Truman's appointees would prove a bumbling bunch, and the Truman administration staggered from one domestic debacle to another. On price controls, indecisive and contradictory administration policy turned what had been an effective anti-inflation program over the war's last two years into a recipe for rapidly rising prices that left consumers fuming and conservatives gloating about government incompetence.[21]

The Truman White House response to the postwar strike wave would leave labor as alienated as consumers. The president urged striking General Motors workers to go back to work and trust fact-finding boards to resolve the strike issues. In May 1946, Truman told striking railway workers to pay no attention to their leaders and then asked Congress to give him the power to draft strikers into the army.[22]

Truman's ham-fisted approach to the strike wave soon united labor's combative factions. The nation's most prominent railway brotherhood leader pledged to go all-out to defeat Truman in 1948. AFL president William Green equated Truman's draft proposal with "slave labor under Fascism," and CIO president Philip Murray charged that Truman was seeking "the destruction of the labor movement."[23]

Progressives could only shake their heads in disappointment and disgust as the Truman White House stumbled along. "To err is Truman," they regularly muttered to each other.[24] The Republicans would have an even pithier catchphrase for the 1946 midterm election campaigns: "Had enough?"

The electorate certainly had. In the 1946 elections Democrats lost 111 seats in the House and, more importantly, the House majority. In the Senate, an equally dispiriting outcome for Democrats: They lost twenty-four seats and the Senate majority as well. Republicans now had control of both houses of Congress for the first time since 1930.[25]

Sidney Hillman, the architect of the progressive political rebound in the 1944 elections, would not be around for this 1946 electoral debacle. Never fit and hearty in his later years, Hillman suffered his fourth heart attack and passed away in July at age fifty-nine, nearly five months before the elections. Two months before his death, in Atlantic City, a strikingly pale and weak Hillman had chaired the biennial convention of the needle-trades union he had led for most of his adult life. Most of the Amalgamated Clothing Workers delegates on hand had known Hillman for years. They sensed this might be his last convention. A sympathetic reporter at the convention's adjourning session sent up to the stage a note that asked if Chairman Hillman could make some remarks that might sum up his philosophy. Hillman smiled and took the lectern. His had been a battle against plutocracy that stretched back four decades. He would share why he fought.

"This earth can be made a place where men and women can walk together in peace and friendship and enjoy all that this world can provide for," Hillman told his fellow activists, "but we must see to it that the power of government is placed at the service of the people instead of in the control of the privileged few, selfish, greedy people who do not accept the right of the common man and do not understand what democracy means."[26]

On the day after Election Day 1946, the "privileged few" seemed to be back in control. They would move with dispatch to try to consolidate their comeback.

Every plutocracy shares the same backstory. The privileged and powerful few expropriate a disproportionate share of the wealth that the many create. These few then hoard that wealth and make themselves more powerful still.

In the World War II years, the struggles of America's workingmen and women would finally upset that sequence. Unions had become a workplace presence strong enough to contest in whose pockets new wealth was going to flow. And tax rates on high incomes had risen so high that ever grander accumulations of private wealth had for the most part ceased accumulating.

No plutocracy could survive such a turn of events. In 1947, the new conservative majority in Congress would make turning the clock back its most fervent priority.

Conservatives set out to tame both the tax code and labor. The tax fight began as soon as the first session of the new Congress opened in 1947. Republican Harold Knutson from Minnesota, now the chairman of the House Ways and Means Committee, introduced a bill to cut all income tax rates by 20 percent. President Truman did not go along. The GOP's proposed tax cuts, Truman the fiscal conservative argued, would make it impossible to balance the federal budget. The president indicated he would support a modest cut in individual tax rates, but only if the Republicans agreed to higher corporate tax rates.

The new Republican majority ignored Truman and pushed ahead on its original plan. Truman responded with a veto. The Republicans then tried again. Another veto. The third time around, the GOP majority finally gathered enough votes to override the White House and get a tax cut through. But the final bill bore only passing resemblance to the original 20 percent cutback proposal. The legislation that finally became law early in April 1948 only cut the top income-bracket rate back from 86.5 to 82.1 percent. The new top rate would also be a far cry from the tax rate reduction America's top corporate executives had in mind. General Motors chairman Alfred Sloan had asked Congress to shear the top rate down to 50 percent.

"Excessive or confiscatory taxes as levied on the individual," the seventy-three-year-old GM executive had testified, "reduce savings for investment and discourage the sacrifice necessary to induce savings."[27]

The "confiscating" survived the new Republican majority. Conservatives would have much more to show for their efforts on the labor front. Labor's biggest gains over the previous decade had come through industrial organizing that gave unions the heft to challenge corporate giants. The sweeping labor legislation conservatives introduced in 1947—soon to be known as the Taft-Hartley bill after its sponsors, Robert Taft from Ohio and Fred Hartley Jr. from New Jersey—aimed to complicate that organizing. Under the legislation, employers could legally maneuver to divide skilled and unskilled workers.

Labor had also advanced through solidarity across *union* lines. In one citywide general strike after another, before and right after World War II, unions from many different industries and trades had come to the aid of striking workers. The incredible enthusiasm these solidarity actions almost always engendered quite often inspired previously apolitical working people into becoming lifelong progressive activists. Taft-Hartley aimed to break labor's solidarity spirit. The legislation outlawed secondary boycotts. Unions under the bill could no longer boycott companies that do business with struck companies. And Taft-Hartley also gave states the option of outlawing union-shop agreements, collectively bargained contracts that require newly hired workers to join their new workplace's union or pay a fee for the union's representational services.

Provisions like these made gaining a union foothold in previously unorganized industries or locales much more difficult. Other Taft-Hartley provisions sought to undermine unions at already organized workplaces. One provision allowed employers to petition for union decertification elections. Another forced union officers to file affidavits swearing they didn't belong to the Communist Party.

Conservatives billed Taft-Hartley as a "workers' bill of rights" that would shield individual working Americans from the tyranny of labor racketeers and Soviet sympathizers. They portrayed the bill as a necessary "reform" of the nation's labor law, in no way an attack on the right of Americans to join unions. Unions labored mightily to expose that portrayal. They stood united in opposition, if not together at anti-Taft-Hartley rallies. In New York, an AFL protest against Taft-Hartley filled Madison Square Garden. The next week, the CIO filled the Garden with an equally engaged protest.[28]

Unions considered Taft-Hartley a direct assault on their right—and ability—to exist. The bill's sweeping provisions gave managements a menu of union-busting options, they charged, and union literature would emphatically spell out the implications. One union protest pamphlet offered a chilling sequence that dramatized "one of the many ways" that Taft-Hartley could work to crush a local labor presence:[29]

1. Taft-Hartley law holds company not responsible for acts of its supervisory help.
2. Supervisory provokes union members who . . .
3. walk off the job.
4. The union is held liable.
5. The workers are fired.
6. Scabs are hired.
7. Scabs hold an election.
8. "Goodbye union!"
9. Employer can sue the union for damages.
10. The law protects the employer *all the way*!

President Truman also saw Taft-Hartley as an existential threat—to any hope that he might remain in the White House after the 1948 elections. The president could not possibly gain labor support in 1948 if he went along with Taft-Hartley. He didn't. Truman vetoed the legislation on June 20, 1947. Both houses of Congress overrode the veto only days later. The dreaded Taft-Hartley had now become law.

The full damage to labor from Taft-Hartley would not become evident for decades. But some repercussions from the legislation would be felt almost immediately. A number of unions had already purged activists with Communist Party connections before Taft-Hartley became law. With Taft-Hartley on the books, the vise quickly tightened on the CIO unions where union stalwarts with Communist Party connections still played key leadership roles. These unions counted among the labor movement's most dynamic. They were organizing constituencies that trade unionism had barely begun to reach. The United Electrical Workers, as labor historian Paul Buhle notes, "had pioneered the wage offensive for greater parity of women's wages to men's, an idea unthinkable in the AFL and most of the CIO." The Food and Tobacco Workers had aggressively organized African Americans in the South, as had the Mine, Mill, and Smelter Workers, also the leading organizing force among Chicanos in the Southwest. The International Longshoremen and Warehousemen's Association had mobilized native Hawaiians and Japanese workers on the islands and Filipinos in Alaskan fish-packing factories. The United Office and Professional Workers of America worked with white-collar women, the United Public Workers with government employees. The Marine Cooks and Stewards, notes Buhle, "had a certain notoriety as the gayest union in the nation."[30]

These unions were speaking to labor's future. In Taft-Hartley' wake, they would be raided, split apart, or expelled outright from the CIO. Some of the targeted unions managed to carry on, a shell of their former selves, as labor movement pariahs. Others disappeared. Only left activists in the West Coast Longshoremen, the union forged out of the great 1934 San Francisco general strike, would prove too tough to crack. They beat back repeated efforts to deport their outspoken leader, the Australian-born Harry Bridges, and remained a significant independent labor force throughout the postwar years.

Opportunists within labor routinely used Taft-Hartley as a club to hammer committed progressive rivals. More principled CIO leaders anguished over the anti-Communist pressure. To resist Taft-Hartley might jeopardize all they had created. Most went along.

The anguish over how to respond to the new red scare wouldn't be confined to the labor movement. Within the New Deal Progressive movement as a whole—the "Popular Front" as many called it—activists struggled throughout 1946 and 1947 to put together new political formations that could keep the movement from splintering. Henry Wallace did his best to rally these efforts. Be on guard against the "plutocrats and monopolists who will try to brand us as Reds," he told the most prominent of the new groups, the Progressive Citizens of America.

"We are more American than the neo-Fascists who attack us," said Wallace, who by then had been shoved out of the Truman cabinet. "The more we are attacked, the more likely we are to succeed. I say on with the fight."[31]

But the fight would increasingly pit "progressives," those New Dealers who resisted the pressures to turn postwar politics into a single-minded crusade against the Soviet Union, against "liberals," those New Dealers who felt that only by embracing the emerging Cold War could they free the New Deal from the "fellow traveler" taint and continue an economic and social reform agenda. In the aftermath of Taft-Hartley, the lines between two factions hardened. The Popular Front—the united struggle against "plutocrats and monopolists"—crumbled.

World War I had split the Progressive movement. Now the aftermath of World War II was having that same impact. But this time, a difference: The plutocrats and monopolists would split too.

The red scare after World War I almost completely snuffed out America's social reform spirit and gave plutocracy an opportunity to dismantle the two institutions that had the potential to significantly decrease inequality. The plutocrats seized that opportunity. They erased the steeply graduated World War I tax rates that threatened to level down America's economic summit. They reduced to irrelevancy—and in some places smashed—the labor movement that threatened to level up America's economic base. In the 1920s, the nation's workers kept precious little of the wealth they created.

The aftermath to World War II also smothered the social reform spirit. New Dealers would continue to press for social reform legislation—for full employment, for an expansion of public housing, for national health care. None of these efforts advanced legislatively. But this time around plutocracy would not be able to turn back the clock. The immediate postwar years ended with steeply graduated income taxes still on the books and labor unions bruised but breathing.

What explains the contrasting outcomes after World War I and World War II? Why did the nation's two most pivotal equalizing institutions—progressive taxation and a vital labor movement—survive the one and not the other? We can credit that survival, in significant part, to the behavior of rich people. After World War II, unlike after World War I, a critical mass of America's rich and powerful accepted and even welcomed high taxes on high incomes and a serious union presence.

What sold these rich and powerful on accepting progressive taxation and strong unions? The more appropriate question: What *scared* these rich and powerful into accepting progressive taxation and strong unions? World War II scared them. Humanity had never seen such carnage and devastation. The Soviet Union scared them. The United States now faced a rival for global hearts and minds. The future scared them. With atomic bombs now unleashed upon the world, the next war might be humanity's last.

The old economic order had nothing to offer that could calm any of these fears. The old economic order—a capitalism that concentrated wealth, that left workers without the wherewithal to consume the modern world's bounty—had created the global economic instability of the Great Depression years. The old order had made the cataclysm of World War II almost inevitable. The old order, if restored, would only turn the world's peoples toward the Soviet alternative. If America failed to create a more stable and just postwar world, the most reflective of America's power brokers most sincerely believed, horrific global conflict would surely reappear.

US Treasury Secretary Henry Morgenthau articulated this emerging perspective at the opening of the 1944 conference designed to reorder the world's financial system.

"All of us have seen the great economic tragedy of our time," Morgenthau told the global notables assembled at a mountain resort hotel in Bretton Woods, New Hampshire. "We saw the worldwide depression of the 1930s." That depression had brought the world "unemployment and wretchedness"—and worse. The victims of economic catastrophe fell prey "to demagogues and dictators."

"We saw bewilderment and bitterness," the treasury secretary concluded, "become the breeders of fascism, and finally, of war."[32]

Men of property could not afford to risk this sequence ever again. They needed a more stable world, and the most reflective among them agreed that private enterprise could not guarantee that stability. Only government intervention in the economy could ensure the steady employment so necessary to keep dangerous demagogues at bay. But stability required a measure of justice as well, a more equal distribution of income. Societies where wealth concentrated at the top simply could not generate the mass purchasing power that economies needed to grow and prosper.

"The outstanding faults of the economic society in which we live," as the eminent and influential British economist John Maynard Keynes had explained in his 1936 masterwork, "are its failure to provide for full employment and its arbitrary and inequitable distribution of wealth and incomes."[33]

By the end of World War II, elites in both Britain and the United States had come to accept this Keynesian analysis. These elites, notes historian Ethan Kapstein, "drew a firm connection among economic deprivation, social conflict, revolution, and war, and they were determined to derail that causal train."[34]

Corporate leaders in the United States who gravitated to this perspective hovered in the orbit of the Committee for Economic Development, a business group launched in 1942. The CED, notes historian James Allen Smith, constituted "a new kind of policy research organization," an enterprise "run by businessmen and funded directly by business, rather than by endowed foundations."[35] In October 1944, the CED's William Benton, an eminent business leader who had cofounded the illustrious Benton and Bowles advertising agency, published a twelve-point summary of the new committee's creed in *Fortune*, America's most prominent business magazine.

"Prolonged and severe depressions, as the result of which millions lose their savings and their jobs," contended Benton, "cannot be accepted as natural and irremediable phenomena." The "people's elected representatives and the agencies of government," his *Fortune* article continued, needed to promulgate "constructive" policies on taxes and public expenditure that would even out "excessive swings in the business cycle." These policies, in turn, needed to conform to community "standards of justice."[36] And what did these community standards demand? "An economic system based on private enterprise, Americans believe, can better serve the common good, not because it enables some men to enrich themselves, but because it develops a high and rapidly rising level of living," Benton's declaration explained.[37]

And where did unions fit into all this?

"To compensate for the weakness of their individual bargaining position," Benton acknowledged directly, "wage earners need the right to combine into organizations for collective bargaining."[38]

Business leaders like Benton recognized unions as legitimate economic players. They believed that government could and should intervene in the economy to prevent economic misery. And they felt deeply that decency demands far more from an economic system than great wealth for a few. All these attitudes would amount to an outright and influential rejection of the plutocratic orthodoxy that had so long reigned in America's highest corporate and financial circles. The work of the Committee for Economic Development, observes historian James Allen Smith, helped start "moving many businessmen away from free-market fundamentalism."[39]

The business skeptics on this fundamentalism would include some corporate superstars. Charles Wilson, the president of General Electric who took a stint at running the War Production Board for FDR, raised eyebrows in 1944 when he endorsed postwar full employment. "If only more business leaders would take this viewpoint," Chester Bowles, another business leader who had gone into wartime government service, would note to FDR, "there would be very little question of our ability to come through the next few difficult years with a vigorous economy and a unified people."[40]

Bowles had made his fortune on Madison Avenue as William Benton's partner in Benton and Bowles. He joined the Roosevelt administration to help in the war effort and ended up managing the price control apparatus. In 1946, Bowles endeavored to prevent a third world war with a widely accessible book, *Tomorrow Without Fear*, a pitch-perfect plea for greater equality and lasting peace that generously tapped the former advertising executive's considerable talents.

"Let us suppose that 1 percent of the population were to receive 95 percent of our entire national income, with the remaining 5 percent spread among the rest of us," Bowles invited his readers to imagine. "Could our system—could any system—work on that basis? One percent of the people couldn't possibly consume 95 percent of all the goods and services which the rest of us could produce." And if the top 1 percent affluent couldn't consume that output, Bowles went on, "they would have no reason to use their savings to build more and more plants and facilities to produce more and more goods which they couldn't consume, either." In this unequal, unbalanced economy, Bowles reasoned in *Tomorrow Without Fear*, we would never see enough production to create all the jobs we need, a reality that "demonstrates the nonsense of the contention that the way our national income is divided among us has nothing to do with how much we produce or how many of us have jobs."

"I don't know how far toward greater equality of income we need to go in order to keep our economy running at high speed, and no one knows," he would add. "I do know that we must make some moves in this direction if we are to avoid another collapse."[41]

And compete with the Russians. Only a capitalist America that valued equality, Bowles contended, would be able to triumph in global competition with the Soviet Union. He ended with a warning for his fellow men of property: "If our present system fails to keep our people fully employed and our production running near or close to capacity levels, our people will insist that our system be modified."[42]

The next year, 1947, would see another powerful plea for greater equality from a familiar figure in elite New York economic circles. Attorney Randolph Paul had spent the 1930s defending some of America's biggest companies before the US Board of Tax Appeals. His clients had ranged from both General Motors and Ford to Standard Oil of California.[43] No one knew the federal tax code—and all its loopholes—better than Randolph Paul. That knowledge had made Paul, who also served as a director at the New York Federal Reserve Bank, invaluable to the New Deal. In the summer of 1940 Paul helped the Treasury Department write the excess profits bill that Congress eventually rejected. Six months later, after Pearl Harbor, Paul formally joined the Treasury Department staff and labored to help FDR ensure that America's wealthiest carried their full share of America's tax burden.[44]

Two years after the war, back in private practice, Paul published his public policy opus. His new book, entitled *Taxation for Prosperity*, presented a carefully argued case for continuing high wartime tax rates on peacetime high incomes. *Taxation for Prosperity* drew a distinction between "a mature economy" and a "mature approach to economic problems."[45] The immature in a mature economy, Paul noted, preach "the gospel that taxes are for revenue only." In fact, taxes in a mature economy offer us "one of the most powerful instruments for influencing the social and economic life of the nation."[46] Taxes can help "express public policy on the distribution of wealth and income." They can "subsidize or penalize particular industries or interest groups." They can "offset the ebbs and flows of business cycles."[47]

"Well-planned taxes," Paul went on, could help us avert that next depression.[48] By "well-planned" taxes, Paul meant steeply graduated progressive taxes. Such levies kept as much money as possible in the pockets of "people in the lower brackets," and that made sense as public policy since lower-income people "have a higher propensity to spend." Their spending keeps "the wheels of industry turning."

For people in higher income brackets, by contrast, a "well-planned" tax system meant high tax rates, also sensible public policy.

"The people with high incomes can best afford to contribute to the support of the government," as Paul explained in *Taxation for Prosperity*, "and the failure to impose substantial taxes in the upper brackets would seriously injure the morale of the rest of the taxpaying public."[49] And high taxes on people of high income offer still another bonus. They "perform the valuable service of preventing more saving than our economy can absorb," soaking up the excess that would otherwise wind up in destabilizing speculation.

Can taxes on the rich ever go too high? That danger, Paul acknowledged, does certainly exist in an economy that "depends upon the profit motive." So taxes on the rich ought always be kept at a level that "enables some accumulation of protection for wives and dependent members of families and fosters economic activity on the part of the producing members." But the "need for this incentive probably stops when we reach the highest brackets," Paul quickly added. At that point, rates ought to rise "very sharply."[50] We need, at the end of the day, "to counteract undue concentration of wealth."

"If the nation's wealth flows into the hands of too few rather than into the hands of the many," Paul emphasized, "the resulting amount of saving will be greater than can be absorbed. Our economy can take only so much of this sort of thing before it has a violent convulsion."[51]

Defenders of economic orthodoxy accepted none of this reasoning. In 1947, amid the Republican push for a significant cutback on federal tax rates, Senator Robert Taft of Ohio gave his retort to the likes of Randolph Paul. Enough with all this chatter about economic stability and excess savings, Taft sputtered. The advocates of continuing high taxes have "obviously" only one "real reason" for wanting to keep tax rates on high incomes high: They want government "to have more money to spend."

"The best reason to reduce taxes is to reduce our ideas of the number of dollars the government can properly spend in a year," Taft insisted, "and thereby reduce inflated ideas of the proper scope of bureaucratic authority."[52]

Taft and his fellow conservatives would not get their way on taxes in the eightieth Congress that opened in 1947. The legislation they passed over Truman's veto still left the nation's top tax rate over triple the top rate that ushered in the 1930s. But conservatives had another chance to restore orthodoxy in the upcoming 1948 election. They felt confident that voters would at long last place one of their own in the White House—and reverse the New Deal.

Harry Truman, midway through 1947, looked like a sure loser in the 1948 elections. Henry Wallace appeared likely to make a third-party bid for the White House, and a substantial chunk of voters appeared willing to back him. June polling put support for an independent Wallace candidacy at 13 percent.[53] Truman could not possibly beat back any Republican challenger if he lost so much of the New Deal's core vote.

Truman had an obvious task ahead. He had to somehow rally those in that lost core back to his side—and he did. A new Harry Truman emerged, a Truman that bore virtually no resemblance to the president who so angered progressives in 1946. This new Truman positioned himself as a champion of economic and social justice. He ran "as a cross between a Populist and a New Dealer," notes historian Norman Markowitz, "clearly further to the left in his public statements than any other major-party candidate in the twentieth century."[54]

"The Republican Party favors the privileged few, not the many," Truman orated in his 1948 convention acceptance speech. "For fifty years it has been under the control of the friends of special privilege."[55] Those Republicans, Truman reminded Americans, "gave tax relief to the rich, although I forced them to improve the bill some before they were able to pass it over my veto." Concluded the president's acceptance address:

> In 1932 we were attacking the citadel of special privilege and greed—we were fighting to drive the money-changers from the Temple. Today, in 1948, we are now the defenders of the stronghold of democracy and of equal opportunity—the haven of the ordinary people of this land and not of the favored classes or of the powerful few.

Truman would pound that theme again and again during his relentless "whistle-stop" 1948 campaign. At Toledo, in September, he called Taft-Hartley "just the opening gun in the Republican plan to go back to the days when Big Business held the upper hand and forced the working men to take only what they wanted to give them."[56]

In October, Truman defined the "basic difference between the two parties in economic matters" at an Indianapolis campaign stop. "The Republican Party, as it operates in Washington, favors the interests of a few small powerful business groups at the expense of the rest of the people," Truman charged. "This is the course that leads to depression."[57]

"We boast about our initiative, our inventiveness, our enterprise," he would go on to add. "All these things are important, but unless each group of our people gets a fair share of our national income, our prosperity will crash. This is a lesson we learned the hard way. We learned it under the Republican Administrations of the Twenties."

Truman's attacks on America's plutocratic past did not in the end totally erase Henry Wallace's support. Wallace's Progressive Party took almost 3 percent of the 1948 vote, enough ballots to deny Truman New York, Maryland, and Michigan, three states that a Democratic candidate could normally expect to win.[58] And segregationist senator Strom Thurmond from South Carolina, running against Truman's historic executive orders on racial discrimination, denied Truman four more states in the South that Democrats had routinely captured in the past. Truman won anyway. He took 50 percent of the vote in a four-candidate field, and his name didn't even appear on the ballot in Alabama.

Truman's upset victory stunned Republicans. The practical among them would now accept the New Deal. The rich, they acknowledged, would continue to face high tax rates. Labor unions would continue to bargain over the distribution of wealth in America's most important economic sectors.

This peacetime would be a different time.

Chapter Nine

LABOR AND THE TREATY OF DETROIT

In June 1947, an estimated sixty thousand CIO workers marched through the streets of New York City. They were angrily protesting the antilabor Taft-Hartley bill then pending before Congress. They were worrying about losing the union foothold that workers had struggled so hard to gain.

A dozen years later, on Labor Day 1959, trade unionists would be marching again through the streets of New York. This time they were celebrating.

This proud 1959 Labor Day march started up Fifth Avenue at just after ten in the morning, and the last of the 144,699 marchers—a union count that police officials accepted as accurate—wouldn't pass the reviewing stand in front of the New York Public Library until eight and a half hours later. The police estimated that four hundred thousand people watched the parade, the first Labor Day march in New York since 1920. The onlookers saw unionized stagehands and actors—in full costume—from *My Fair Lady* and over twenty other Broadway and Off-Broadway shows. They saw, the *New York Times* reported, "a tidal wave of massed electricians in white shirts."[1] They saw bakers and firefighters. They saw two hundred bands and fifty-seven floats and workers carrying signs and banners from over five hundred union locals. They even saw two baby elephants.

A good time would be had by all. And why not? Labor in New York had plenty to celebrate in 1959. In one sense, working people in New York had been marching for a dozen years—marching straight into the middle class. Over one million New York City workers carried

229

union cards by the late 1950s. Their union power, notes Josh Freeman's magisterial history of postwar labor in New York, "contributed to a remarkable rise in the working-class standard of living." Thanks to unions, "a way of life once largely restricted to the middle class—car and home ownership, vacations and travel, routine health care and college education—became accessible to workers and their families."[2]

And not just in New York. Workers were marching into the middle class all across the United States. Fourteen years after World War I, American working people had virtually no unions by their side and no dollars in their pockets. Millions lived in squalor. In 1959, fourteen years after World War II, over a third of Americans working in the private sector belonged to unions, and workers were moving, by the millions, into green new suburbs.

In this new America, unions had become political power players. Politicians in both parties respected their presence, their clout, and their achievement. The president for most of the 1950s, the Republican Dwight D. Eisenhower, assured Americans that "unions have a secure place in our industrial life."

"Only a handful of reactionaries," the immensely popular Eisenhower added, "harbor the ugly thought of breaking unions and depriving working men and women of the right to join the union of their choice."[3]

In the decades right after World War II, those workingmen and women would change America's economic rules and its distribution of income and wealth. And no one person would personify the rule-changing struggle better than Walter Reuther, the auto worker who would become America's most vibrant postwar union leader.

Val Reuther, the German immigrant father of Walter Reuther, had arrived in South Wheeling, West Virginia, in 1899, on the eve of a new, plutocratic century. He found a job at a nearby iron works and put in twelve-hour shifts, six days a week, for $1.50 a shift.[4]

Nearly three decades later, in 1927, Val's son Walter found a job at a company just outside Detroit that made auto bodies for Ford Motor. Not much had changed for workers in the intervening years. Young Walter worked the night shift, from five-thirty in the evening to seven in the morning. Each shift had just one half-hour break. At one point, young Walter worked twenty-one consecutive nights.[5]

Auto workers in Detroit had tried to organize a better deal for themselves. In 1913, the Industrial Workers of the World were actively rallying workers to the fight for an eight-hour day, but Ford Motor stole the IWW thunder. Right at the start of 1914, Henry Ford announced a new five-dollar daily wage for just eight hours of work. Within a matter of days, fifteen thousand hungry and cold job seekers were waiting outside the Ford gates. Those lucky enough to get a job soon found that the new five-dollar-a-day wage rate came with a catch. Newly hired workers had to spend six months in "probationary" status, at $2.55 a day. After six months, many of these probationary workers found themselves replaced by a new round of probationary hires. The five-dollar-a-day rate also didn't apply to women workers or unmarried men under twenty-two—or older men involved in a divorce action.[6] The five-dollar-a-day plan, on the other hand, did help ensure Henry Ford the best of both worlds. He enjoyed both a global reputation as a humanitarian employer and a pliant nonunion workforce.

Walter Reuther may not have known the details of Ford Motor history when he started work at a Ford supplier in 1927. But the young Reuther certainly knew the ways of America's industrial world. His father Val had been a dedicated socialist. Books by Eugene Debs and the like abounded in the Reuther household.[7] The Debsian vision of a fundamentally more equal America would remain with Walter Reuther for the rest of his life.

In 1945, Walter Reuther found himself in a position to advance that vision, as the United Auto Workers point man in the union's first postwar negotiations with General Motors. Workers at GM, Walter's brother Victor would write years later, had ended the war in an ugly mood. They felt instinctively "that their employers had feathered their nests exceedingly well during the crisis."[8] They wanted a much fairer share of the wealth their labor was creating. Walter Reuther brought a fresh labor perspective to the union struggle for that fairer share. Unions, he believed, needed consumers on their side, and his entire bargaining strategy with General Motors would revolve around gaining that consumer support. Midway through 1945, the Reuther led UAW demanded a 30 percent wage increase for GM workers, coupled with an agreement that GM would not raise prices.

Six weeks later, General Motors contemptuously rejected the entire UAW proposal. The contempt continued throughout the subsequent negotiations. GM personnel chief Harry Coen—an anti-Semite who would regularly spell out his name so people wouldn't get the idea that he might be a "Cohen"—at one point blew up after Reuther orated at the bargaining table on the importance of protecting consumers.

"Why don't you get down to your size and talk about the money you'd like to have for your people," Coen blurted out, "and let labor statesmanship go to hell for a while?"[9]

Reuther would not drop the "labor statesmanship." Until we get "a more realistic distribution of America's wealth," he would retort to Coen, workers wouldn't have enough consuming power to keep America's "machinery going."

"There it is again," Coen disdainfully spit out. "You can't talk about this thing without exposing your socialistic desires."

"If fighting for equitable distribution of the wealth is socialistic," Reuther replied, "I stand guilty of being a socialist."

"I think you are convicted," Coen then triumphantly pronounced.

"I plead guilty," said Reuther.

General Motors eventually came back with a proposal for a 10 percent wage hike—and no contract proviso on prices. Reuther countered with an imaginative offer: The UAW would agree to arbitration on the amount of wage increase if GM would agree to open its financial books and let an arbitrator determine how much of a wage increase GM could afford without raising prices. General Motors declined. The company called the UAW proposal "not an offer of arbitration but a demand for abdication." In response, GM workers struck. In all, 175,000 workers in ninety-five GM plants across the United States walked out.[10]

The workers had broad public support. But Reuther had less luck getting other unions to adopt his pro-consumer bargaining stance. The Steelworkers union settled its first postwar walkout—while the auto workers were still striking—for a modest wage hike, and federal price control officials quickly okayed an increase in steel prices. In that settlement's wake, the UAW, by then on strike for 113 days, had little leverage. The union would settle in 1946 for the same modest pay hike as the Steelworkers. And General Motors would subsequently win official federal price control approval for three price hikes.[11]

Two years later, General Motors and the UAW returned to the bargaining table. By that time, Taft-Hartley had become the law of the land. But the legislation would have little immediate impact on an already entrenched union, and the UAW had become entrenched in the auto industry. At General Motors, the union had won dues checkoff, a time-saving procedure that enables the automatic deduction of union dues from worker paychecks. Reuther by 1948 would also have wide and solid support among the auto-worker rank-and-file, particularly after he survived an assassination attempt that April, which the union blamed on antiunion auto-industry diehards working hand in glove with the Detroit mob.[12]

Top General Motors executives came to the 1948 negotiations less entrenched in their resistance to the UAW approach that Reuther had advanced in 1945. Reuther had argued that workers had a right to share in the new wealth that new technology and higher productivity were making possible. He had also argued that workers shouldn't be expected to let inflation eat away their wages. The UAW remained committed to these principles in 1948, and General Motors president Charles Wilson knew it. If GM insisted on corporate business as usual, the company would surely be in for another bruising labor-relations battle, exactly what General Motors didn't want. The company needed the uninterrupted production that only labor peace could guarantee.[13] The demand for automobiles was rising, and GM had already begun a massive $3.5 billion expansion program to meet that demand.[14] Another multimonth strike might ruin everything.

GM's Charles Wilson would not take that risk. He brought to the bargaining table a proposal that spoke to Reuther's UAW principles. On top of an hourly wage hike of eleven cents, General Motors would offer to lock into place additional wage increases that took both productivity gains and inflation into account. A 2 percent "annual improvement factor" would tie rising productivity to wages, and a new "cost-of-living adjustment"—or COLA—would link wages to the Consumer Price Index on a quarterly basis.[15]

Reuther, still recovering from wounds sustained in the assassination attempt, could not be at the bargaining table to hear the offer. But UAW bargainers brought the proposal to his bedside, and Reuther agreed to go along without much initial enthusiasm. The UAW accepted the 1948 agreement as a "holding operation," acceptable "only because most of those in control of government and industry show no signs of acting in the public interest." That public interest demanded that the federal government help force industry to accept wage hikes without price hikes. The federal government was not cooperating.

The new two-year 1948 agreement between GM and the UAW would work out spectacularly well from the General Motors perspective. In 1949, GM registered a larger annual profit than any corporation in US history.[16] Continued success, GM executives realized, would require continued labor peace. General Motors would be ready to deal in 1950. So would the UAW. The union arrived at the table with an even more ambitious bargaining agenda. The auto workers and all the other major CIO unions had been pushing since the war's end for federal legislation to extend the social safety net for all working families. But these efforts showed no promise of going anywhere. The big industrial unions had now recognized that reality and shifted their focus. They would battle to win safety nets—pensions and health care insurance—from individual corporations. In 1949, the US Supreme Court helped this new push along, ruling in the *Inland Steel* case that a management unwilling to bargain over fringe benefits would be committing an unfair labor practice.[17]

Labor now had the undisputed right to bargain on fringes, and Reuther and the UAW had figured out a bargaining strategy to make the most of that right. Up until then, John Lewis and the coal miners had set the strategic lead in industrial-level bargaining. Lewis had taken on his industry, the coal industry, as an undivided whole. Reuther thought that foolish. The UAW would take on the auto giants one at a time. An industry-wide strike, Reuther reasoned, might provoke a hostile federal government response. If workers at only one auto maker walked out, by contrast, most workers in the auto industry would still be working during the strike. Dues from auto workers still on the job could help support the strikers.

Targeting one giant at a time would also help the UAW establish industry-wide patterns. The union could establish a new benefit "principle" with one employer, then bargain with another employer that had more resources to turn this new principle into a benefit that would significantly enhance auto-worker-family standard of living.[18]

The pattern-bargaining approach worked just perfectly with pensions. In October 1949, a UAW strike threat convinced Ford Motor to agree to set aside enough money from profits to ensure every worker at sixty-five a hundred dollar monthly pension, counting the thirty-two dollars then available from Social Security. The union then struck Chrysler for 104 days to win the same benefit.[19] The principle in place, the UAW would now go after a $125 monthly pension guarantee from cash-rich General Motors in 1950.

Here, no strike would be necessary. GM wanted extended labor peace—a five-year contract—and the UAW agreed, in return for progress on pensions and other issues. The new GM-UAW pact signed in May 1950 guaranteed a $125 monthly pension, sweetened the auto worker cost-of-living raise formula, and increased the annual productivity wage adjustment. The agreement also had General Motors pick up half the bill for a new health insurance benefit. In effect, as historian Nelson Lichtenstein notes, the pact guaranteed GM workers "a 20 percent increase in their standard of living over the next half-decade." The pact would represent "the greatest economic gain won by any of the big unions since before the war."[20]

Fortune magazine hailed the new auto agreement as the "Treaty of Detroit," and that label stuck. This particular treaty, Corporate America clearly hoped, would put the class war on hold. General Motors was agreeing to share the wealth that workers were creating. In exchange, the UAW was ceding to management the exclusive right to make production decisions and stepping back from any attempt to bargain on behalf of consumers.

The basics of this Treaty of Detroit—productivity-based wage hikes above and beyond inflation, significant pension and other fringe benefits—soon spread throughout America's unionized heavy industries. The UAW itself, meanwhile, continued working to build a better package of basics. In 1955, the UAW's bargaining focus turned to the notion of a guaranteed annual wage as a desperately needed antidote to auto-industry production decisions that had factories feverishly hire to rush out new models, only to then slash hours and jobs when the frenzy ended. This endlessly repeating cycle meant constant economic insecurity for tens of thousands of auto-worker families and put heavy safety-net burdens on state and local governments.[21]

The first guaranteed annual wage the UAW negotiated in 1955—a provision for "supplemental unemployment benefits"—would not be particularly generous. But succeeding agreements had the "supplemental unemployment benefits," or SUB, offset a substantial share of the dollars workers lost when the auto companies either cut their hours below the standard forty or laid them off entirely. In the mid-1970s recession, the SUB plan would distribute over $400 million from GM earnings to eighty-eight thousand laid-off workers, an outlay significant enough to keep the downturn from turning into a far more desperate situation.[22]

The overall impact of the Treaty of Detroit on auto workers would be substantial. Average automobile worker wages almost doubled between 1947 and 1960 to $6,000 a year. That annual compensation totaled almost enough to allow the average auto worker to buy a five-room house and afford a four-year-old Chevy, the key elements that defined the federal Bureau of Labor Statistics yardstick for a "moderate" standard of living. Large numbers of auto workers measured up by that yardstick. The chief auto-industry cities—Detroit, Flint, Toledo—had more of their homes owner-occupied than almost any other cities in the nation.[23]

And the class war? Class skirmishes would continue despite the Treaty of Detroit, mainly because the big auto companies, explains historian Nelson Lichtenstein, "interpreted their detente with the UAW as an occasion to mount a workplace offensive to rewin from their employees" control over production standards and work schedules.[24] Auto workers on the shop floor would not accept that management take on their negotiated treaty. At Chrysler, workers used sit-downs and slowdowns straight through the 1950s, notes historian Jim Pope, "to achieve a substantial degree of control over shop floor conditions." In the Chrysler Dodge Main plant, workers "established their own 'fair' pace of work, which left them about fifteen minutes out of every hour."[25]

Similar situations existed in other industries that signed on to the Treaty of Detroit. The workers at America's giant manufacturing enterprises might be marching into the middle class, but they would be sitting down and slowing up along the way.

Detroit and other Midwest industrial centers would come to symbolize American manufacturing in the postwar years. But the East had its manufacturing centers as well, with New York City the biggest. Over one of every twelve Americans lived in the New York metropolitan area in 1950, and over a quarter of the city's workers labored in manufacturing.[26]

New York would be a different sort of manufacturing giant. The city had no single manufacturing industry comparable to steel or auto, and New York unions bargained with hundreds of manufacturing corporations, not a small handful. In this more decentralized economic environment, the labor movement in New York built its own unique entry ramp into the middle class. New York unions certainly endeavored to bargain better wages, hours, and working conditions for their members, just like their Midwest counterparts. But unions in New York also fashioned a web of institutions outside the traditional union framework—from housing developments to health clinics—that helped workers gain security and access to the amenities of middle-class life.

The New York City–centered International Ladies Garment Workers Union, for instance, ran a resort in the nearby Poconos Mountains and also operated sixteen medical clinics. The crown jewel of the ILGWU medical system: a six-story health center in the middle of Manhattan's garment district that had 148 doctors on staff and registered almost a half-million annual patient visits. By 1952, after ILGWU gains at the bargaining table, employer dollars were bankrolling the center, replacing dues money and user fees. The Amalgamated Clothing Workers had a similar center, with funding from both the union and employers.[27]

New York unions also helped develop another alternative to America's traditional fee-for-service medical care. The union-backed prepaid, group-practice health plan known as HIP operated local centers where union members could get everything from prenatal care to eyeglasses. HIP's first subscribers in the 1940s would be the 2,643 members of Chefs, Cooks, Pastry Cooks, and Assistants Local 89. By the mid-1950s, the HIP prepaid group practice would boast a half-million members.[28]

New York union leaders also worked closely with Blue Cross, the health insurance plan the city's nonprofit hospitals had set up, notes Josh Freeman, "to ensure themselves a steady income stream from insured patients while providing subscribers cost-protection in case of hospitalization." Local union leaders didn't just bargain Blue Cross insurance for their members. They sat on the Blue Cross board.

Union health care centers and clinics would help keep New York union members healthy. Collectively bargained health insurance paid their bills for major hospital treatment. But security from catastrophic income loss after sickness or accident hit would require union action on the political front. New York State had had a "workmen's compensation" program on the books ever since 1914, and this program funneled assistance to workers injured on the job. In 1949, the New York labor movement took another step forward and won a state law that required employers to provide thirteen weeks of income support for workers left disabled by accidents off the job.[29] By the late 1960s, observes Josh Freeman's history of postwar New York labor, "sickness and accidents no longer meant financial catastrophe for working-class New Yorkers."

"Disability payments provided partial income replacement," he explains, "while through union clinics, collectively-bargained health benefits, benefits offered by nonunion companies in part to forestall unionization, and government-sponsored programs passed with labor backing, most New Yorkers had ready access to modern medicine."[30]

New York's unions had an equally potent institutional impact on the housing market. At the state capital in Albany, unions backed legislation that helped non- and limited-profit redevelopment projects gain financing for cooperative housing projects. The huge New York electricians union, Local 3 of the International Brotherhood of Electrical Workers, would be a particularly active housing player. Working through a labor-management joint board for the electrical industry, the union fashioned a 103-acre complex that featured thirty-eight buildings with over 2,400 affordable apartments, a shopping center, offices for the union—plus "a public library, a union-sponsored savings bank, a coffee shop, a cocktail lounge, a bowling alley, and a large auditorium used for union, industry, and community functions."[31] All these building efforts helped workers in postwar New York start their baby-boom families in comfortable and affordable brand-new housing.

Unions worked just as effectively to keep the cost of existing housing stock affordable. World War II price controls had placed a fairly effective lid on the wartime rents working families faced. But in Washington, soon after the war, the conservative-dominated Congress exploited the Truman administration's bungling and eventually shut down the entire federal price control operation. In New York, unions had the political clout needed to keep rent controls in effect. By 1950, almost all the rental units in New York City—96 percent— had price limits of some sort. Rent control would become a fact of life in New York that meant both extra cash every month and greater life security for working New Yorkers. A sudden rent increase that they couldn't afford could no longer drive New Yorkers from their homes.[32]

Unions played the same role with New York's mass transit. Union lobbying helped keep transit rates low, and the low rates in turn kept ridership high. Some unions took the struggle against high prices up still another notch. They organized consumer boycotts against price excesses and sometimes even stepped beyond boycotts. One postwar New York City United Electrical workers local went out to Long Island and bought eggs straight from farmers for resale to members at prices under what those members could find in city stores.[33]

This egg maneuver would be part of labor's political effort to save effective federal price controls after World War II. That effort—and most other labor initiatives at the national level—struggled in Congress. But in New York and countless other locales where organized labor had a significant workplace presence, unions helped nurture a strikingly different political tone. Their weekly and monthly newspapers kept members informed and involved in political campaigns. And unions reached out beyond their memberships. Union voter registration drives, house-to-house neighborhood canvasses, and radio ad campaigns kept politicos on their toes. The more than one million women who joined union "ladies' auxiliaries" in the 1950s, adds historian Nelson Lichtenstein, would spend far more time "organizing their precincts than playing Mahjong."[34]

Labor had become in these 1950s an institutional presence in American life, a powerful and effective local and state advocate for programs that tended to share America's wealth and keep that wealth from concentrating. Most politicians came to accept—or resigned themselves—to this still relatively new turn of events. Some did not. In 1958, these recalcitrant politicians would mount a counterattack.

In August 1957, the United States slid into an economic downturn mild by Great Depression standards, but more severe than any recession since the end of World War II. America's auto makers and other giant industrial concerns were beginning to feel, for the first time since the war, some serious global competition. The giants could weather this squall, but their suppliers and many other firms could not. These smaller firms felt themselves under intense pressure to limit their labor costs. Unions stood in the way.[35] Conservative strategists saw an opportunity in this tension. The recession gave them a growing business constituency for a pushback against labor. And push they did.

In California and Ohio, two prime industrial states with strong union movements, right-wingers launched "right-to-work" campaigns under Taft-Hartley.[36] Until then, no state with a significant union presence had opted to exploit the Taft-Hartley provision that lets individual states prohibit collectively bargained agreements from requiring workers to either become dues-paying union members or pay a fee for the union's representational services. Conservatives in California and Ohio placed this "right-to-work" proposition on their November 1958 ballots.

The political stakes in these ballot battles would be huge, and not just for the labor movement. The clash would likely chart the Republican Party's future orientation as well. President Dwight Eisenhower and his wing of the party accepted labor's presence in America's workplaces and saw that presence as essential to economic and political stability. In California, similarly minded moderate Republicans had long held the upper hand within the state GOP, and Republican Governor Earl Warren had widespread public support after the war, as did Goodwin Knight, his successor.

But conservatives led by William Knowland, the son of a wealthy Oakland newspaper publisher, challenged Knight and squeezed him out of the 1958 gubernatorial race. Knowland, then a US senator, apparently felt a gubernatorial victory would give him a springboard to the 1960 Republican presidential nomination. He would campaign for governor in 1958 as a full-throated supporter of the California right-to-work ballot measure.

The battle over that ballot measure pit labor against corporate and conservative leaders who refused to accept the Treaty of Detroit and the implicit recognition of labor's right to prosper that the treaty represented. Labor raised an unprecedented $2 million for the campaign against right-to-work in California and also put before voters a ballot measure of its own, a soak-the-rich plan that would sharply jump taxes on large incomes and drop them on Californians in the state's lowest income brackets. Unions put no significant cash resources behind the campaign for the tax measure. They were using the tax measure instead, as one of the nation's top labor-beat reporters would note, "to divert part of the energy of business organizations" away from the right-to-work fight.[37]

That strategy and the overall labor mobilization against Knowland and "right-to-work" worked beautifully. On Election Day, voters crushed the right-to-work proposition and ended Knowland's political career. And California's Republican Party lost more than the governor's mansion. Democrats gained control of the California Senate for the first time since 1890 and the state assembly for the first time since 1942. Voters also rejected the right-to-work proposal on the Ohio state ballot. Labor had won a smashing victory. The conservative push to undo the postwar economic consensus had failed miserably. One 1958 Gallup poll showed 64 percent of Americans in favor of labor unions, only 21 percent disapproving.[38] Against such broad public support for unions, the conservative pushback had no chance.

What accounted for labor's mass public support? Unions were making an incredibly positive difference in the lives of average Americans, and most of them knew it. The vast majority of American adults in the 1950s still remembered what life had been like before World War II. In 1940, "one of every four Americans lived in slums," as pro–New Deal businessman Chester Bowles pointed out, and "fewer than half our children finished high school." Factory workers, mostly male, averaged $25.50 a week; women in clerical jobs did even worse, taking home just ninety dollars per month.[39] After the war, a totally different story. By 1948, a union roller operator at US Steel was making $2.31 an hour, or $92.40 a week. By 1958, union roller operators were making $3.57 an hour, $142.80 a week, over $570 a month, enough on one income to support an entire family in modest middle-class comfort.[40]

In 1961, a UAW rank-and-filer by the name of Frank Tuttle would write Walter Reuther a tribute on the twenty-fifth anniversary of Reuther's labor movement leadership. Tuttle had a special distinction. He had been the first Chrysler worker to start collecting a UAW-negotiated pension.

"On my 65th birthday in January 1950 I had three important messages before me," Tuttle wrote, one from Social Security "telling me that I had an assured life income of exactly $38.69 a month," one from Chrysler Corporation "declaring it would never grant the 'preposterous' pension demands of our union," and "one from you saying that those demands would be won, either at the bargaining table or at the picket line." Chrysler workers went to that picket line, Tuttle noted, and today "I am looking at pension checks of $157.46 a month."

"Without the protection of our union it is highly improbable that I would have lived to be 65 at all and without the union who would want to?" Tuttle asked. "Before our union, the best a worker could hope for was to die on the payroll—before he became old enough to be replaced by a younger worker."[41]

In postwar America, you didn't need to be a proud union member like Frank Tuttle to enjoy a modicum of middle-class security. The massive union presence in America's private-sector economy helped all workers. The best evidence of this powerful union impact? That would come from Sears, Roebuck and Company.

In the mid-1950s, Sears towered over American retail. In 1954, the company collected over $3 billion in sales.[42] No other retailer came close. The chief executive most business observers credited for this success, General Robert E. Wood, retired in that same 1954, after twenty-six years at the company's helm. The West Point–educated Wood had understood early on that the automobile had changed the retail landscape. Average Americans had shopped by mail-order catalog early in the twentieth century. With cars of their own, they could now drive to general merchandise department stores, and Sears under Wood would open up such stores all across America, by the hundreds.

Wood also understood that union success had profoundly altered America's overall economic landscape. Wood didn't like unions and liked them even less as he grew older. By the mid-1950s he figured prominently in far-right political circles. But Wood never bought into the old-line business response to unions. He would not hire labor spies and contract with union-busting goons. He endeavored instead to create in Sears a workplace attractive enough to employees that they would see no need to carry union cards.

Unions did repeatedly try to organize Sears, starting in the late 1930s. They made little headway. In 1957, unions represented less than 8 percent of the Sears domestic workforce.[43] Wood and Sears kept unions away with life and health insurance, sick pay, vacations, and separation allowances, notes historian James Worthy, "long before" these benefits became common practice in American industry.[44] Most of all, Wood and Sears kept unions away with extensive profit-sharing. The Sears profit-sharing plan applied to the half of Sears workers who stuck with the company more than a year. Those who lasted fifteen years would see the company put into the "Savings and Profit Sharing Pension Fund of Sears, Roebuck and Co." a sum that equaled five times the employee contribution. These dollars would be invested in various assets, mostly Sears stock, and the assets would pay dividends to profit-sharing participants. Veteran employees would routinely receive more from profit-sharing payouts than their wages.[45] Janitors making forty dollars a week could waltz into retirement with $2,500 in savings.[46]

If unions ever came to Sears, the company employee newspaper would regularly warn, the wonders of the Sears profit-sharing plan just might disappear.[47]

Sears management had this in-house newspaper carefully edited to maximize its credibility to Sears workers. In many ways, notes Sanford Jacoby in his history of the Sears approach to employee relations, the paper came across as a union tabloid. The editors even regularly and irreverently teased top Sears executives. And these same Sears executives also received no special perks. Seniority at Sears, not corporate rank, determined benefits like vacation and sick days. General Wood also kept management salaries below their level at other retailers. Wood wanted Sears to be seen as the "workingman's friend." He succeeded, at least enough to keep Sears overwhelmingly nonunion throughout American labor's mid-twentieth-century heyday.[48]

Sears would be an outlier in the nonunion private sector. Few nonunion concerns would work as hard as Sears to match the level of wages and benefits that unions were bargaining in organized companies and industries. But most all major nonunion companies outside the overwhelmingly nonunion South made some effort to ratchet up the pay and benefits packages they offered workers. They had little choice. With unions representing such a significant share of the private-sector workforce, nonunion concerns had to try to approximate union-level wages and fringes or go without workers.

Overall, the income of the median, or typical, American family would about double in the postwar years.[49] The bottom 90 percent of American families saw their incomes, in 2008 dollars, rise even more, from a $9,249 average in 1940 to $17,627 in 1950 to $23,458 in 1960 to $31,073 in 1970.[50] Most of this increase came from the higher wages that unions bargained—and nonunion companies had to try to match.

Unions impacted family incomes in other ways as well. The federal minimum wage rose steadily throughout the postwar years, from $3.40 an hour in 2009 dollars in 1947 to $8.71 in 1968.[51] Union political pressure drove the increases. Amid the festivities at the historic 1959 Labor Day parade in New York, union marchers carried signs that demanded a $1.25 *Minimum Wage for All Workers*, about nine dollars an hour today.

Union pressure also put more dollars in the pockets of the nation's elderly. In 1954, President Eisenhower ignored "fierce attacks" on Social Security from conservatives and business groups and signed a major expansion of the program.[52] Labor lobbying would play the key role. The legislation Ike signed to labor's cheers brought Social Security coverage to over ten million additional Americans. Social Security, Eisenhower declared, had to be extended "to reduce both the fear and the incidence of destitution to the minimum."[53] The labor movement was leveling up America's most powerless.

The labor movement was also leveling down those who counted among America's most powerful, the suits who sat in the nation's corporate executive suites.

Executive pay levels would never be an explicit subject of negotiation between labor and management. Companies retained the right to pay their executives whatever they wanted. But union leaders paid close attention to executive salaries and regularly pounded excess corporate profits in the press and in public appearances. The pounding, in turn, helped shape the political and economic environment. Companies that lavished pay on their executives stood to pay a steep price in the court of public opinion. Few companies dared to pay that price. Analysts from the MIT and Stanford business schools have gone back through the required pay filings of major US corporations since the late 1930s. The real value of typical top executive pay at major American corporations, they find, dropped from $1.1 million in 1940 through 1945—expressed in year 2000 dollars—to $900,000 in 1946 through 1949, then rose slightly to a $1 million average in the 1950s and 1960s.[54]

The top executives that the MIT and Stanford researchers tracked during these postwar years all rated in the most affluent and powerful 0.1 percent of Americans. Yet their inflation-adjusted earnings remained "remarkably flat" in the decades right after World War II, even as the size of the corporations they managed was growing substantially.[55] In fact, top executives wouldn't regain their pre–World War II pay levels until the 1970s.

Top executives in those "remarkably flat" years loudly bewailed their fates. The *Ladies Home Journal* interviewed one of America's "most successful executives" in 1959 and gave him anonymity to maximize his candor. "I'm president of one of the larger companies in the US," the executive told the magazine, "yet chances are I will never become a millionaire."[56]

His complaint gibes with the broader executive pay picture. The $1 million—in year 2000 dollars—that typical executives averaged in the 1950s took home would have been less than $170,000 a year in 1950s dollars.

We do know a great deal about the pay that went to one particular celebrated postwar CEO, the top executive at American Motors, George Romney, the father of 2012 GOP presidential candidate Mitt Romney. George Romney released his tax returns to *Look* magazine while he was getting ready to run for the GOP presidential nomination himself in 1968. Romney had become the CEO at American Motors in 1954. Over the next decade, his tax returns showed an average annual total income—his CEO compensation plus all his income from investments—of only $275,000, less than $2 million a year in today's dollars. A generation later, his son Mitt would accumulate from his executive business career a fortune worth over a quarter-billion dollars.[57]

George Romney would certainly count as an extremely wealthy American in the 1960s. But the gap between worker pay and Romney's income—and the income of top corporate executives like him—had narrowed considerably in the twenty years after World War II ended. Workers were entering America's middle class and the rich were sinking much closer down to it. Unions would push that equalizing dynamic forward in the postwar decades.

So would taxes.

Chapter Ten

A NATION SOAKS THE RICH

In 1950, Charles E. Wilson sat on top of the global business world. He ran General Motors, the most powerful corporation in the world. For 1950, Wilson reported to the IRS an income from General Motors and his personal investments that totaled $586,100. He paid $430,350 of that income in taxes.[1]

Charlie Wilson's tax bill wouldn't be unusual in the decades right after World War II. In the first five years after the war, the federal tax rate on income over $400,000 never dipped below 82 percent. In 1950, the top rate stood a fraction over 84 percent. That top rate would jump to 91 percent the next year and did not dip below that figure until 1964. America's wealthy had never seen tax rates that high for so long. Neither had the wealthy anywhere else in the world. In the middle years of the twentieth century, the United States took a bigger bite out of high incomes than any of the nations—like Sweden—that now rate as the world's most "egalitarian outposts."[2]

Ironically enough, this historic soaking of America's rich peaked under a Republican president, Dwight David Eisenhower. The enormously popular Ike, the architect of the Allied victory over Nazi Germany, entered the White House in 1953, and his entry at first gave America's stiffly taxed rich some reason to be optimistic. Ike had filled his new administration with men of substantial means. The first Eisenhower cabinet, commentators would chuckle, featured "nine millionaires and a plumber," the latter the new secretary of labor, a union leader Ike plucked from the plumbers union.[3] But Ike would soon disappoint those wealthy taxpayers eagerly awaiting tax relief from the new Republican president. His first state of the union address promised only "clarification and simplification" of the

247

tax code, nothing about rate reduction.[4] Eisenhower went on to give top-bracket tax cuts the cold shoulder throughout his eight years as president.

Any cuts in the tax rates on high incomes, Ike believed, would be fiscally irresponsible. The United States had an expensive Cold War to wage. The former five-star general would not countenance cutting taxes while "defense and other essential government costs" were still running at formidable levels.[5] Ike no doubt also had politics on his mind. Harry Truman had won reelection in 1948 railing against the rich and the Republican lawmakers who cut their taxes. Why cut taxes on high incomes and give Democrats another opportunity to make political hay?

But much more than fiscal prudence and political calculation lay behind Ike's determination to keep tax rates on America's wealthiest at New Deal levels. Eisenhower had lived through the social horror of the Great Depression. In 1932, he had watched as jobless veterans massed in Washington. He had been part of the military operation that evicted those veterans, burned their camp, and ended their Bonus March protest. The general who directed that operation, Douglas MacArthur, saw the eviction as a triumph over the red hordes. Eisenhower saw only a pitiful spectacle that his country must never let repeat. How to avoid that sort of social disruption? Ike subscribed to the same basic egalitarian worldview that so many other thoughtful movers and shakers took from their experience of depression and war. Americans must never again let wealth concentrate and destabilize the nation.

In 1960, at an address before an auto-industry dinner in Detroit, Ike gave his take on this worldview its clearest expression. We have evolved in the United States, the president would tell his business audience, a "socially conscious type of private enterprise" that "strives to benefit all the people."[6] We Americans also now recognize, Ike continued, the contribution "public enterprise" can make. In an ever more complex world, we had come to understand that government needs to help the people do "what the people cannot do for themselves."

With that understanding, Ike pronounced, has come the historic rise of the great American middle class.

"Other peoples find it hard to believe that an American working man can own his own comfortable home and a car and send his children to well-equipped elementary and high schools and to colleges as well," Eisenhower told the assembled auto-industry magnates. "They fail to realize that he is not the downtrodden, impoverished vassal of whom Karl Marx wrote. He is a self-sustaining, thriving individual, living in dignity and in freedom."

Unfortunately, Ike added, other nations have not yet learned the lessons that Americans had so wisely taken to heart.

"In many countries of the free world private enterprise is greatly different from what we know here," he explained. "In some, a few families are fabulously wealthy, contribute far less than they should in taxes, and are indifferent to the poverty of the great masses of the people."

"A country in this situation is fraught with continual instability," Eisenhower warned. "It is ripe for revolution." Any society that tolerates a "fabulously wealthy" class is asking for trouble. "Since time began," Ike reminded his comfortable corporate listeners, "opulence has too often paved for a nation the way to depravity and ultimate destruction." That depravity could also destroy us if we foolishly chose to let the rich "contribute far less than they should in taxes." That would not happen on Ike's watch. He would not lift a finger to lower the steeply graduated tax rates on high incomes that the New Deal had bequeathed to him. Let the rich grumble. Ike would not be moved.

The rich did grumble at postwar tax rates. Many did more. They raged.

Cameron Hawley raged. Hawley wrote best-selling novels that tapped his decades of executive experience in Corporate America. In a 1956 speech before the Pennsylvania Bar Association, Hawley deemed the federal income tax "responsible for a progressively more and more serious deterioration of the moral and ethical standards of a substantial segment of our citizenry."[7]

P. J. Redford raged. Redford managed the tax office for the Walgreen Co. in Chicago. The federal income tax, he wrote in 1957, "is just what Karl Marx advocated in his *Communist Manifesto*, written over a hundred years ago, as one of the ways to destroy our free society."[8]

And Richard Lounsbery raged too. Lounsbery had the good fortune to be born the grandson of the founder of the lucrative Homestake Mine in South Dakota. He also came into the world as an heir to the Kern County Land Company fortune in California. The *New York Times* dubbed him "the country's most successful personal manager of an inherited estate."[9] His stash of insurance stocks alone, the *Times* marveled, made him "a millionaire several times over." But taxes were eating far deeper into the dividend income from these stocks than Lounsbery felt appropriate.

"The United States government makes the old 'Robber Barons' look like children," Lounsbery told the *New York Times* in 1959. "I wouldn't anymore think of giving an old-fashioned ball in New York today than I would in Moscow. And there's no difference between the Republicans and the Democrats, either. The Republicans are socialists and the Democrats are communists—that's all."

The strangest tax ranter of them all would be T. Coleman Andrews, the eminent accounting company executive who served as Dwight Eisenhower's first chief of the Internal Revenue Service, the federal agency responsible for administering the income tax. Andrews hailed from Virginia, a normally Democratic state that Democratic senator Harry Byrd and his conservative "Byrd machine" had swung to Ike in the 1952 presidential election. The Richmond-based Andrews had been close to Byrd for years, but he didn't need his political connections to get the IRS top slot. Andrews had a distinguished record of accounting public service that went back to the 1930s. During the war, he had even served on Eisenhower's staff in North Africa.[10] Andrews had also served as the president of the American Institute of Accountants.

Eisenhower fully expected Andrews to do a bang-up job at the IRS. And he did. Andrews created an IRS telephone help line for ordinary citizens, spearheaded the simplification of tax forms, and aggressively went after well-heeled tax evaders. Six months into the Andrews era, his admirers at the National Civil Service League were observing that the new IRS commissioner seemed "determined to run the tax service along lines of honesty and genuine merit."[11]

Later that year, before an audience of six hundred accountants at the Waldorf-Astoria in New York, Andrews promised to crack down on illegitimate business tax deductions for entertainment expenses.[12] The next year, in 1954, he testified to Congress about IRS efforts to get tough on taxpayers "who deducted such items as yachts and honeymoons as business expenses." Businessmen should know better, Andrews told a House Ways and Means subcommittee.[13]

Andrews continued his outstanding work straight through his announcement, midway through October 1955, that he would be resigning at the end of the month "to re-enter business." Treasury Secretary George Humphrey hailed Andrews for the "wonderful job" he had done as IRS commissioner and noted that President Eisenhower "regrets very much indeed that Coleman Andrews is leaving."[14] Andrews did reenter business. He would become the president of the American Fidelity & Casualty Insurance Company. But he would not fade away. Six months after his resignation as the top federal tax-collection official, Andrews emerged on the cover of the *US News & World Report*, the nation's most business-friendly newsweekly, with a feverish denunciation of the federal income tax.[15]

"If we keep on at the present rate of taxation, we will come eventually to the point where no one will have anything to invest and the 'man on horseback' will be upon us," Andrews charged in a lengthy interview. "The government will own everything, and we'll be forced to do the bidding of commissars imbued with the idea that they know better how to spend our money than we, and vested with the authority to do it."[16]

Andrews went on in the interview to blast FDR's wartime call for a $25,000 income cap as "socialistic demagoguery" and then made clear that he objected to the basic notion of income taxation. Advocates of the income tax, he charged, have been "deliberately, avowedly, and unashamedly" aiming to "get at the rich" ever since 1894. The federal income tax, Andrews declared, "was conceived in vengeance."

"I cannot accept the proposition," he added, "that a revenue law ought to be used to penalize success."

The whole idea of taxing income, Andrews insisted, came directly from Karl Marx: "Maybe we ought to see that every person who gets a tax return receives a copy of the Communist Manifesto with it, so he can see what's happening to him."

Why this incredible turnaround, from respected enforcer of the nation's tax laws to frothing anti–income tax fanatic? Historians of modern Virginia politics haven't yet solved that mystery. We do know that while at the IRS Andrews had meetings with Joseph McCarthy, the Wisconsin senator who would become the symbol of red-baiting terror in the early 1950s. Andrews even called McCarthy "a great American."[17] Or perhaps fury over the Supreme Court's landmark 1954 *Brown v. Board of Education* ruling against school segregation started Andrews over the edge. We may never know the motives behind the Andrews about-face. But we do know that his turn against the income tax completely marginalized Andrews from America's mainstream political life. In the mid-twentieth century, anyone in public life who attacked the concept of steeply graduated progressive income taxation was essentially committing political suicide.

Andrews would soon descend deep into the world of ultra-right-wing conspiratorial politics. His first stop would be the States' Rights Party. He ran as the party's standard-bearer in the 1956 presidential election. Two years later, Andrews helped found the notorious John Birch Society, the extremist core of what would soon become known as the "radical right."[18]

In midcentury America, anyone or any group opposed to stiff tax rates on America's rich had to swim against a strong public tide. Some friends of the fortunate felt they could make progress anyway. They had a plan. To chop down steep tax rates on America's rich, they would swim below the surface, where the public wouldn't be able to see what they were doing until after they had done it. The plan came from the American Taxpayers Association, a group with close conservative business ties that had been pushing for tax cuts since the 1920s, and the Committee for Constitutional Government, a panel conservative Republican newspaper publisher Frank Gannett had organized in 1937 to battle the New Deal.[19]

In 1938, a Rhode Island industrialist with links to both groups drafted a constitutional amendment that would replace the 1913 constitutional amendment that enabled the federal income tax with new wording that limited the "maximum rate of tax" that Congress could enact to 25 percent, the top tax rate at the end of the 1920s. The new amendment's conservative boosters understood quite clearly that their proposal for a 25 percent income tax limit would be dead on arrival in Congress and deeply unpopular with the American public at large. But the tax-cappers had a strategy for end-running that public sentiment. Under the Constitution, two-thirds of the states could compel Congress to call a new constitutional convention. If they could gain support from anything close to the required two-thirds of the states, backers of tax rate cap believed, congressional leaders would panic at the prospect of a new constitutional convention and adopt the tax rate cap amendment to forestall that possibility.

Success would depend on stealth. The American Taxpayers Association purposefully began its new campaign, notes historian Isaac William Martin, "in states far outside of national media markets."[20] Inside those states, the campaign ringleaders would avoid legislative discussions open to the public. "No printed campaign literature survives from the earliest years of the campaign, and probably none existed," adds Martin. "The backers of the amendment lobbied state legislators in private." This stealth campaign made steady progress, then emerged on a larger stage in February 1944 when New Jersey signed on to the constitutional amendment resolution as the sixteenth state to take the plunge. But that success in New Jersey brought the tax-cap effort the publicity its advocates had worked so hard to avoid.

By that June, New Deal congressman Wright Patman from Texas was denouncing the pro–tax cap Committee for Constitutional Government as "the most sinister lobby in America." Shortly after that blast, Treasury Secretary Henry Morgenthau had his researchers release a report that documented how a 25 percent tax cap would shift the tax burden onto the backs of low-income Americans and cripple the federal government's capacity to respond effectively to national emergencies. The new publicity quickly stalled the secretive campaign. State lawmakers started defeating the resolution, and the tax-cappers had to regroup. They began adding various fudge clauses to their original amendment that would let Congress raise tax rates on the rich above the 25 percent cap if the nation faced an emergency.

The fudging brought a wider array of national groups behind the campaign in the early 1950s, the US Chamber of Commerce and the American Bar Association among them. But the concessions would also sap the enthusiasm of many of the tax-cap amendment's original advocates. The more conservative of the tax-cappers didn't want to give Congress an escape hatch that would allow tax rates on the rich above 25 percent. They simply wanted to end high taxes on high incomes once and for all. Without their militant antitax enthusiasm, the cap-the-tax-rate amendment campaign fizzled out in the mid-1950s.

Few noticed the campaign's demise. The effort enjoyed precious little public support. In June 1957, Gallup pollsters asked Americans if they favored changing the Constitution to place an income tax limit of 25 to 35 percent "on what any person would have to pay." Only 17 percent approved the proposition, with 68 percent objecting.[21] But public support for tax progressivity wouldn't be the only reason the tax rate limit campaign floundered. Political opportunism played a role too.

"High rates made loopholes valuable, and lawmakers in both parties tacitly embraced them," explains tax historian Joseph Thorndike. "As long as rates stayed high, members of Congress could do a brisk business selling tax preferences."[22]

These preferences brought the effective tax on high incomes down below the statutory rate in the postwar years, sometimes substantially so. "Liberals wanted to get rid of tax shelters, thereby making effective rates closer to statutory rates, but they were frustrated by conservative control of the Senate Finance and House Ways and Means committees," notes Bruce Bartlett, a one-time top policy aide to President Ronald Reagan. "Over the years, members of those committees had largely been responsible for creating the very loopholes that were the targets of reformers."[23]

The higher the statutory tax rate, the more valuable loopholes would be. The more valuable the loopholes, the more valuable would be lawmakers who could deliver them. How valuable? The guardian in chief of the biggest loophole of them all—the oil depletion allowance—would end up in the White House.

Back at the start of the twentieth century, oil didn't count for all that much in the US economy. Americans used oil for lighting and lubrication. Hardly anyone used oil for fuel. Railroad engines and steamships used coal instead. Oil remained relatively scarce, and John D. Rockefeller's Standard Oil monopoly exploited that scarcity to keep oil overpriced. But in 1901 everything changed. Oil prospectors hit a gusher at a marshy knoll known as Spindletop just outside Beaumont, Texas. Within a year, wells at Spindletop were producing more oil than the rest of the world combined.[24] That world now had a new cheap source of energy for anything mechanical that moved, especially those new-fangled automobiles.

Spindletop and the other new Texas wells were soon pumping up fortunes as furiously as black crude. Powerful corporate interests back East—the Mellon family of Pittsburgh, for one—would quickly dominate oil transporting, refining, and retailing. Locals in Texas concentrated on exploring and drilling.[25]

By World War I, the worldwide demand for oil seemed likely to outstrip production. Experts urged Congress to start giving prospectors and "wildcatters" some special incentives to start exploring in new territory. In 1919, lawmakers delivered the first of these incentives.[26] Seven years later, the special oil tax breaks of the war era became a permanent and enormously lucrative tax code fixture. Tax reformers would come to group all these tax breaks under the "oil depletion allowance" rubric. But the depletion allowance actually represented only one of the three tax breaks that made the oil business such a millionaire-maker.

Under the depletion allowance, an oilman could deduct 27.5 percent of his gross income off the top. An oilman with a million-dollar income, as the *New Yorker*'s John Bainbridge would explain to a rapt readership at midcentury, would consequently start with $275,000 in totally tax-free income. And that oilman could claim this 27.5 percent allowance year after year.[27] Over time, in other words, oilmen could receive a tax-free return on their investments that actually exceeded their original capital outlay. "In no other industry," marveled Bainbridge, "can a taxpayer enjoy this benefit."

A second tax rule allowed oilmen to deduct all the expenses for any hole that turned out to be dry. This rule made oil drilling irresistibly enticing for taxpayers wealthy enough to sit in the 91 percent tax bracket. A player at that lofty income level, Bainbridge explained, might invest $100,000 in a well. If the well turned up dry, no big deal. The gamble on that dry well would have cost the rich investor only $9,000, the difference between the $100,000 loss on the well and the $91,000 the investor would save on his federal income taxes after deducting the loss from the rest of his income. Our rich investor, Bainbridge summed up, "has had the fun of taking a hundred-thousand-dollar gamble at a sensationally low price."

The third tax rule loophole for oilmen gave them a special tax break for successful wells. Under this third lucrative loophole, they could immediately deduct all the "intangible expenses" of drilling a wet well, everything from geological studies to testing, instead of having to space the deductions out over the well's productive life.[28]

The tax savings from all these oil loopholes would be staggering. In 1942, a Treasury Department study documented that the oil depletion allowance cost the federal government three times more than the government would have shelled out if it had "paid the entire cost of all wildcat dry holes in 1941."[29] For oilmen, the tax breaks reduced the federal income tax to no more than a nuisance. Tax lawyer Jerome Hellerstein noted that one oilman he knew had collected $14 million in income over a five-year period and paid only $80,000 of that in federal tax. Oil kingpin John Mecom openly boasted that he paid just $5 million in taxes on $15 million in annual income—at a time when income over $400,000 was supposed to face a 91 percent tax rate.[30]

The oil depletion allowance would help oil become, as the *New Yorker* analysis put it, "by far the most important source of modern wealth in the United States."[31] That wealth amassed largely in Texas, virtually unknown to the rest of the nation. By the end of World War II, H. L. Hunt, Roy Cullen, Sid Richardson, and Clint Murchison counted among the richest individuals in America, notes Bryan Burrough's fascinating history of the Texas "Big Rich," and "no one knew it."[32]

That anonymity ended when *Life* and *Fortune* magazines started profiling the new Big Rich in 1948. The articles "had editors up and down the Eastern Seaboard scratching their heads," muses Burrough.[33] "America's richest man?" he imagines these editors thinking. "In Texas? And there were more?" Plenty more. In 1957, *Fortune* would name the seventy-six Americans who held fortunes worth at least $75 million. Over a third of the names on the list, twenty-six of the total, owed their wealth to oil.[34]

Oil wealth fueled a level of consumption that left the rest of America gaping and sometimes guffawing. In 1948, the spouse of Colonel Henry Russell of Dallas explained why her husband had just bought her a new Rolls-Royce. "It goes with my blue hat," she helpfully informed a curious observer.[35]

Clint Murchison's home—the largest residence in Texas, with thirty-four thousand square feet of space and nine servants—had a master suite with eight full-sized beds. This somewhat unusual setup, Murchison explained, would let whatever pals might be in the neighborhood "stay up all night talkin' oil" with him.[36]

In 1959, the oil-fueled Windfohr family staged the ultimate in debutante balls. The clan had the Olympic-sized swimming pool of Fort Worth's Ridglea Country Club covered with a custom-built parquet dance floor. The guests swayed to the music of three bands—one led by Louis Armstrong—and didn't stop partying until well past dawn. The morning sun wouldn't bother anyone. The hosts had thoughtfully handed out sunglasses.[37] This debutante ball set the Windfohrs back $100,000, upward of $800,000 today. But oilmen could afford outlays that lavish and still have more than enough leftover to defend their cherished oil depletion allowance from any attack.

The attacks came regularly. The US Treasury Department tried to eliminate oil's preferential tax treatment in 1933, 1937, and 1941.[38] In 1950, President Harry Truman called the oil depletion allowance the tax code's most "inequitable" loophole. In 1960, the Democratic Party platform pledged to "close the loopholes in the tax laws by which certain privileged groups legally escape their fair share of taxation" and then identified "depletion allowances" as "among the more conspicuous loopholes."[39]

The two most powerful lawmakers in Congress, House Speaker Sam Rayburn and Senate Majority Leader Lyndon Baines Johnson, both Texans, promptly ignored that identification. "The platform pertains only to loopholes, and I see none in oil," Johnson assured his most valuable constituents.

Johnson owed his Senate seat to the Texas Big Rich. In 1948, their vast fortunes allowed LBJ to run a Senate primary campaign the likes of which no candidate for public office in the United States had ever run. The Johnson campaign had a war chest huge enough to poll voters week after week, helicopter the candidate from one Texas town to the next, blanket the airwaves with slickly produced ad spots, and, in the end, buy enough votes to win the primary runoff by less than one-hundredth of 1 percent.[40] LBJ would go on to become majority leader and crush any fellow senator foolish enough to challenge oil's privileged tax position. In 1957, a Senate Republican from Delaware, John Williams, introduced a modest amendment that would have left the depletion allowance in effect, but reduced the rate from 27.5 to 15 percent. Only five senators, beyond the amendment's sponsors, had the courage to even support bringing the rate reduction up for a vote.[41]

Sam Rayburn played the same guardian angel role in the House of Representatives. The House Speaker only allowed Democrats committed to defending the depletion allowance to sit on the Ways and Means Committee, the panel that determined the tax bills that would reach the House floor.[42]

Johnson and Rayburn likely assumed that their noble record on behalf of the oil depletion allowance would be enough to get the Texas Big Rich to ignore the anti-loophole verbiage in the 1960 Democratic Party platform—and presidential candidate John Kennedy's 1958 Senate vote for an amendment that would have kept 27.5 percent depletion in effect, but only for oil producers making less than $1 million a year. They assumed wrong. The Big Rich came out blasting away at Kennedy's White House bid. John Mecom and friends took out full-page ads in the *Houston Post* urging oilmen to "stand united against the common and undivided forces which seek to destroy us and the system of competitive free enterprise our industry so clearly typifies."[43] And H. L. Hunt circulated two hundred thousand reprints of an anti-Catholic sermon after a Kennedy campaign appearance suggested that taking a look at reforming the depletion allowance might not be a bad idea.[44] Oil anger would almost cost the Democrats Texas in the 1960 race. In the end, they narrowly prevailed, but only because they had a Texan, Lyndon Johnson, on the ticket.

In mid-twentieth-century America, you didn't have to be an oilman to enjoy tax loopholes. The federal tax code offered deep pockets a variety of options for reducing their effective tax rate substantially below the marquee 91 percent top income-bracket rate. America's wealthiest could split their income up within their families, sociologist C. Wright Mills would note in his classic 1956 study of American wealth and power, and in the process shift significant sums of income from higher to lower tax brackets. They could donate a portion of their income to charity, take a tax deduction for the contribution, then receive annual income as long as they lived from the charitable fund they had created. At death they could limit the tax on their estates by setting up trusts for their grandchildren. And on and on.[45]

But no loophole outside oil depletion would be as wealth-enhancing as the special tax treatment for capital gains, the profits from wheeling and dealing stocks, bonds, real estate, and other assets. In 1959, Diners Club chairman Ralph Schneider reported an income of $600,000. If all of that $600,000 had come from "ordinary" income— that is, salary, bonus, dividends, interest, and the like—Schneider would have faced a federal tax bill amounting to just over 80 percent of his total income. That tax bill would have reflected the federal tax code's descending tax rates on income brackets, from a 91 percent tax on income over $400,000 and a 90 percent tax on income between $300,000 and $400,000 all the way down to a 20 percent tax on any income under $4,000 left over after standard deductions for dependents. But only $60,000 of Ralph Schneider's income came from salary, and most all of the rest came from capital gains subject to a maximum tax rate of 25 percent. Schneider's total tax came to just $175,000, or only 29 percent of his $600,000 income.[46]

This preferential treatment for capital gains made maneuvering to claim "ordinary" income as "capital gains" the nation's favorite tax-dodging game. The moguls and superstars of Hollywood would be this game's most avid players.

The film industry boasted some of America's highest incomes over the postwar years. In 1947, movie theater magnate Charles P. Skouras pocketed the highest corporate paycheck in the nation, the equivalent of over $8.2 million today. Hollywood's sizable incomes kept tax lawyers busy prospecting for loopholes. One favorite in the World War II years would be the "collapsible corporation." *Time* explained how such shelters worked late in 1945: A movie producer creates a corporation, makes a movie under the auspices of that corporation, holds the movie for six months, sells it, claims the profit on the sale as a capital gain, and dissolves the corporation that made the picture. Lester Cowan, the producer of the 1945 hit, *The Story of GI Joe*, collapsed his way to a $650,000 tax savings.[47]

Hollywood's tax shelter schemes set the corporate tax-dodging gold standard. The movie industry, as Duke University tax expert Charles L. B. Lowndes noted in 1953, "frequently takes the lead in tax fashions."[48] But public revulsion after World War II—and dedicated IRS professionals—would often shut down shelters not long after they appeared. Midway through 1946, as historian Eric Hoyt points out, the IRS would declare the "collapsible corporation" shelter illegal and go after film producers for unpaid taxes.[49]

Another prized loophole, the eighteen-months exemption, suffered a similar fate. In 1951, Congress exempted from US income taxes income earned abroad if the US taxpayer making that income had spent seventeen of the last eighteen months residing abroad. Lawmakers meant the exemption to help construction and oil workers laboring overseas. Hollywood's top talents suddenly felt the need to join these workers overseas and make movies abroad. US unions soon began attacking the loophole. Lawmakers took note. In 1953, they capped eighteen-month tax-free income abroad at $20,000.[50]

Eight years later, in April 1961, a newly elected president John F. Kennedy asked Congress to tighten the eighteen-month loophole and deny the $20,000 exemption to any Americans residing abroad in "economically advanced countries." That proposal represented part of a far broader tax reform package that Kennedy put before Congress "to keep our tax system up to date and to maintain its equity." Kennedy called for reforms to prevent corporations from deferring taxes on income they earned overseas. He recommended that companies no longer be able to claim yachts and hunting lodges as deductible business expenses. He proposed tax withholding on the checks that corporations and banks sent out for interest and dividends to keep affluent taxpayers from sidestepping taxes on the estimated $3 billion a year in interest and dividend income that was going unreported to the IRS.[51] Congress would adopt some of the Kennedy proposals in the Revenue Act of 1962.

The next year, 1963, would mark the hundredth anniversary of the IRS, and tax professionals had reason to celebrate. Loopholes did still dot the tax code, but the White House and lawmakers now seemed to be making good-faith efforts to shut those loopholes down. America's steeply graduated progressive income tax was working. The wealthy, at least those outside Big Oil, were paying a far greater share of their income in federal taxes than Americans of modest means. And the taxes they paid were significantly reducing grand concentrations of income and wealth.

By the 1950s, the incomes of America's super rich—the nation's top tenth of 1 percent—had dropped by half from their 1920s level.[52] The nation's richest tenth of 1 percent owned over 20 percent of America's wealth in 1929. A quarter century later, that share would be down to about 10 percent.[53]

In the America of the mid-twentieth century, corporations manufactured products, not megamillionaires. Steeply graduated tax rates on salary and bonus income had the same deflating impact on executive compensation as the nation's widespread union presence.

Michael Trotter graduated from Harvard Law School into this deflated corporate world in 1962. The nation's "high marginal income tax rates," he would remember years later, "largely kept executive compensation in check."[54] Too much of a check, leading corporate executives would regularly grouse. "Many of the top executives in some of our largest corporations have spent a lifetime in the field of industrial management without ever having been able to accumulate as much as a million dollars," Benjamin Fairless, chairman of the US Steel board, ruefully declared in the 1950s, "and I know that to be fact because I happen to be one of them myself."[55] In 1955, DuPont president Crawford Greenwalt testified to Congress that he was making half the compensation of his predecessor three decades earlier.[56]

Investment bankers and elite Wall Street law firms felt the same downward pressure on their compensation. Halfway through the 1950s, Goldman Sachs partner Sidney Weinberg, the most celebrated investment banker on Wall Street, spent two years orchestrating the initial public offering of the stock of the Ford Motor Company, the biggest sale of a privately held company's stock to the public in American financial history. A deal that colossal today would generate hundreds of millions of dollars in fees to bankers. For his two years of work, Weinberg collected $250,000.[57]

In those same years, adds journalist Malcolm Gladwell, principals in the nation's top law firms looked back wistfully at the days of opulence past. Roswell Magill, a partner at New York's eminent Cravath, Swaine & Moore, acknowledged in 1956 that law firms "can no longer honestly assure promising young men that if they become partners they can save money in substantial amounts, build country homes and gardens for themselves like their fathers and grandfathers did, and plan extensive European holidays."[58]

Those executives who dared to push the tax envelope—and carve out greater than ordinary rewards—would often find tax court judges ready and eager to push right back. Indiana executive Frederick Ernest certainly did. Ernest served as the top executive at a 1948 startup in the machine tool trade. The Korean War that began in 1950 had made that trade a hot one, and the revenues at Ernest's company had soared from $213,400 in 1949 to $3,237,000 in 1952. Executive pay at the company had soared too. The firm's four top officers saw their take-home jump over tenfold to $85,000, the equivalent of over $700,000 today. Accountants at Ernest's flourishing new company claimed this skyrocketed executive pay as a "reasonable" corporate outlay and an appropriate corporate tax deduction. But the IRS rejected that claim. A displeased Ernest took the IRS to court.

The legal dust wouldn't settle until 1961. A federal appeals court that year ruled that Ernest's machine tool firm could only deduct $35,000—about $300,000 today—of the $85,000 each of the company's top four executives received in compensation. These executives, the court concluded, owed their fabulous pay increases to the demand the Korean War had created for industrial retooling, not any individual business "sagacity and industry." Consequently, their company had no right to claim their huge paychecks as a reasonable and deductible corporate expense.[59]

Before the 1950s, emerging new industries had always created grand personal fortunes. Steel, automobiles, and oil had left the nation's economic landscape littered with dynastic wealth. The two greatest economic transformations of the 1950s—the advent of television and the suburbanization of America—created no lasting economic dynasties. The tax code of the 1950s wouldn't let them.

Business analysts from *American Heritage*, *Forbes*, *Fortune*, and the *New York Times* have over recent years assembled inflation-adjusted lists of the richest Americans of all-time. Most of the fortunes on these lists grew to king size before the federal income tax first became a permanent fixture in 1913. Other fortunes on these lists amassed after 1980, when tax rates on the rich began their steep downward descent. None of the lists of the all-time richest Americans include anyone who hit their economic peak in the mid-twentieth century.

Midcentury America, to be sure, still had rich people. But these would be rich people of a peculiar sort. In a 1969 book, *New Yorker* writer Kenneth Lamott gave the richest of his era a name. He called them the "Income Tax Rich."[60] That label made sense. You couldn't enjoy a great private fortune at midcentury unless you had a privileged relationship with the IRS. You either had to have inherited your fortune from a time before taxes in the United States became steeply progressive, or you had to have been doing your business in an industry—like oil—that shielded you from America's steeply graduated tax rates.

Fortune magazine's 1957 list of America's richest personalized this phenomenon. The *Fortune* list came divided into wealth tiers. In the top tier, between $700 million and $1 billion, the magazine found only one contemporary American fortune. That fortune belonged to oilman J. Paul Getty. In the second and third tiers, covering the range from $200 to $700 million, *Fortune* found fifteen grand accumulations of wealth, eight inherited, four more either directly or indirectly from oil. The fourth *Fortune* tier—between $100 and $200 million—had thirty wealthy Americans listed. Fifteen of these owed their good fortune to inheritance, another six from oil; and in the lowest tier, from $75 to $100 million, thirty-one more financially favored Americans, seventeen favored by inheritance and five by oil.[61]

Among America's grand inheritors, none lived as comfortably in the 1950s as Ailsa Mellon Bruce, the daughter of Treasury Secretary Andrew Mellon. Ailsa ranked as one of the eight richest Americans on the 1957 *Fortune* list, along with other three other Mellon progeny. Andrew Mellon had expired in 1937, but not before engineering as Treasury secretary what would prove to be a temporary repeal of the federal gift tax. With that tax on hiatus, Mellon had showered his daughter Ailsa and other dear ones with millions in tax-free gifts, a savvy end run around the estate tax that left Ailsa with a fortune grand enough at midcentury to support three residences in New York City, two in Greenwich, Connecticut, one in Palm Beach, and one more in Syosset, Long Island.

Ailsa only spent three weeks a year on Long Island, but maintained a year-round Syosset staff. Her complement of twelve domestics and twenty-two gardeners, notes historian David Cannadine, kept the cut-flowers in the Syosset manse's thirty-two rooms "changed daily, whether she was present or not."[62]

Ailsa could only afford to live this luxuriously because her father's insider manipulations of the temporary gift tax repeal had spared a huge portion of his prodigious wealth from the federal estate tax. Other scions of great wealth would not have that same good fortune. The wealth they inherited would go through the estate tax wringer. Between 1941 and 1976, the tax on estate value over $10 million sat at 77 percent.[63] The actual federal tax paid on *total* estate value would, of course, amount to much less than that 77 percent. Tax lawyers would see to that and make small fortunes of their own advising wealthy clients how to parlay gifts to charity and other loopholes into lower estate tax liabilities. But the estate tax, even after loopholes, had bite. And the money inherited after the estate tax did its biting would generate income that faced midcentury's 80 and 90 percent top marginal rates.

Those blessed with inherited wealth chafed at these rates. Anna Dodge, the widow of auto-maker Horace Dodge, simply could not bear the thought of having Uncle Sam levy a 91 percent tax on any dollar of her income. The wealthy widow invested her entire $56 million legacy from the Dodge auto fortune in tax-free municipal bonds. Dodge's bonds would yield only $1.7 million a year in tax-free interest, a royal sum in the 1950s but not enough to maintain the Palm Beach mansion Dodge had bought back in the 1920s. She eventually tore the mansion down and sold off the furnishings in 1957. But Dodge would go out in style, notes wealth historian Larry Samuel, with a grand just-like-the-old-days party.

"More than two hundred members of New York and Palm Beach society," chronicles Samuel, "danced to two orchestras, sipped from a champagne fountain, and snacked on Beluga caviar served from, of course, a carved-ice swan."[64]

Dodge also gave up her mansion in Grosse Pointe, Michigan, as well as her yacht and its seventy-eight-person crew. In an age of high taxes on high incomes, the grand baubles of America's plutocratic golden age had now become white elephants too expensive to maintain. "We super rich," one affluent essayist in *Time* magazine noted, "have unloaded our marble mansions on churches, embassies, labor unions, and institutions of learning that don't have to pay the taxes or cope with the servant shortage."[65] *Who Killed Society?* author Cleveland Amory would ruminate in a 1959 *New York Times* piece that the sons and daughters of grand fortune had little grandness in their future. The great manses of their parents would never be theirs to enjoy. Neither would the precious things in them. "Practically everything in sight in these houses is, because of the tax deductions involved, earmarked not for their children," Amory explained, "but for museums."[66]

Not all the rich would go the charitable deduction route. To spite the tax man, some would spend at various levels of wild abandon. A 1958 *Business Week* dispatch marveled that the rich "are coming out of their holes, and they're having a ball." What could account for this sudden splurging?

"The Draconian income and inheritance taxes levied on the rich," speculates historian Larry Samuel, "appeared to be instilling a use-it-or-lose-it philosophy."[67]

The squeeze on the midcentury rich wouldn't be just financial. The wealthy in the 1950s felt a growing middle class invading ever more of their physical and cultural space. The rich were losing their social preeminence. The nation no longer revolved around them. Average Americans increasingly saw the rich as deadweight, as obstacles in their way.

This new social reality had Eve Pell's to-the-manor-born mom seething in the postwar years. The Pells in the 1950s were still holding on to a grand fortune that traced back to colonial times. Eve would later title her moving memoir of growing up rich *We Used to Own the Bronx*. Back in the Gilded Age, Eve's great-grandmother had hosted "seated dinners of 125 people, one course after another, with a footman in livery standing behind each chair."[68]

Eve's mother would have been comfortable in that Gilded Age world. But she could never adapt to a new world where the rich had become curiosities from a past soon to be gone forever. "Mummy," Eve would write in her memoir of her 1950s childhood in what remained of Long Island's once-fabled Gold Coast, "especially hated the Sunday drivers who came out from New York City to look at the rich people's 'homes' and 'estates'—which we called 'houses' and 'places.'" Eve's mother also hated how the new suburban housing developments and the construction of the new Long Island Expressway were blocking off "the riding trails we used." Mummy "scoffed at the small, new houses with the flat, ugly roofs."

"All these lower-class people on their quarter-acres," writes Eve Pell, "were infringing on our territory, spoiling our rides, and cluttering up our roads with their cars."[69]

The fabulous mansions and estates of the "Gold Coast" had once stretched from Great Neck to Huntington on Long Island's North Shore. America's grandest families—Astors, Vanderbilts, Belmonts, Morgans—had almost all established lavish outposts along this thirty-mile belt of luxury. Midcentury would now see the estates of this past glory sliced and diced for middle-class consumption—or simply left to decay and disintegrate. The seventy-room Hillwood home of cereal heiress Marjorie Merriweather Post became the C. W. Post College administration building. Laurelton, the eight-level, eighty-four-room "private Eden" of Louis Comfort Tiffany, burned down in 1957.[70] Farther out on Long Island, the gaudiest palace of them all—financier Otto Kahn's 126-room "Oheka"—would become first a rest home for New York City sanitation workers, then a military academy, then a vandalized shell. The entrepreneur who bought the Oheka shell in 1984 ended up replacing four hundred windows and doors and filling three hundred trailer-trucks with decades of debris.[71]

With the markers of America's classic plutocracy literally crumbling all about, observers in the 1950s and 1960s found themselves speculating about a future without any super rich at all. "The massive fortunes of the 'Pittsburgh millionaires' of the nineteenth century and the 'Detroit millionaires' of the Twenties are a phenomenon not likely to be repeated," *New York Times* journalist Joseph Nolan, later an executive with Chase Manhattan Bank, speculated in 1955.[72] "The day of accumulating gargantuan new personal fortunes in the United States is just about ended," author Ferdinand Lundberg, a best-selling chronicler of America's wealthy, would add in 1968.[73]

Sociologist C. Wright Mills would argue that, in a sense, an America without a super rich had already arrived. We no longer had a plutocracy. We had a "corporate rich." Men of means, Mills explained, had come to "depend directly, as well as indirectly, for their money, their privileges, their securities, their advantages, their powers on the world of the big corporations."[74] Their prestige had become "a prestige of the office they command," their place atop the corporate hierarchy.[75]

"Instead of servants," as Mills wrote, a "row of private secretaries."[76]

To most Americans, the remnants of the old plutocracy that remained would appear increasingly pathetic.

Alfred Corning Clark, an heir to the original Singer sewing machine fortune, had left almost $50 million to his four sons at the end of the nineteenth century. The second-oldest of the four, Sterling, manically retreated into "cigars, Burgundy, paintings, silver, rare books, racehorses, and manor houses."[77] He stuffed his homes with thirty-nine Renoirs and, after one bout of paranoia, would refuse to speak to his brothers for thirty years. In the 1930s, hatred of the federal income tax turned poor Sterling into a political conspirator. He would be accused, notes one synopsis of Sterling's sad story, "of joining a cabal of Wall Street plutocrats plotting a coup to replace Franklin Roosevelt with a fascist dictator on the model of Mussolini."[78] After World War II, an elderly Sterling spited his brothers and federal tax collectors one last time. He hid his art collection away in the Massachusetts hinterland, "where he deemed it less likely to be destroyed in case of atomic attack."

Lucy Douglas "C. Z." Guest, the daughter of a Boston investment banker, married a national polo champion and hobnobbed with high society's midcentury finest. In a *Washington Post* interview, she explained why women of her station always had a governess raise their children: "Children need someone to discipline them. And after all, Winston didn't marry me to be a maid."[79]

J. P. Getty, the richest of America's midcentury rich, seemed to be a living, breathing cautionary tale for anyone who daydreamed about the glory that surely must come with fabulous fortune. The "human wreckage" of J. P.'s life, notes biographer John Pearson, "started piling up within the old man's lifetime." One son killed himself. Another "appeared intent on doing much the same through alcohol and heroin addiction."[80] Still another did fine—"at the cost of cutting himself off from anything to do" with his father's empire.[81]

America's midcentury politicians could read the zeitgeist of their age. They felt little awe for the men of fantastic means in their midst. To some, like Dwight Eisenhower, the super rich would be politically pitiful. In 1954, in a letter to his brother Edgar, Ike candidly shared his assessment of the super rich working to turn his Republican Party into a battering ram against the New Deal legacy:

> Should any political party attempt to abolish social security, unemployment insurance, and eliminate labor laws and farm programs, you would not hear of that party again in our political history. There is a tiny splinter group, of course, that believes you can do these things. Among them are H. L. Hunt (you possibly know his background),

a few other Texas oil millionaires, and an occasional politician or business man from other areas. Their number is
negligible and they are stupid.[82]

The steep progressive tax rates of the postwar years and the cultural
disdain for great wealth these taxes seemed to engender left Americans of means agitated and alarmed. Individuals of great talent would
never choose to soar, many would complain, in a society where tax
rates as high as 91 percent kept the rewards for success painfully puny.
In the 1957 Ayn Rand cult novel *Atlas Shrugged*, America's talented
few went on strike against oppressive government regulation and
taxation, convulsing the world and proving their indispensability.[83]

Other critics of the midcentury egalitarian order made more sober
cases. How could we expect Americans to take entrepreneurial risks,
their argument went, when rewards for risk-taking rated as so underwhelming? In 1951, the noted tax lawyer Godfrey Nelson despaired
that Americans simply did not appreciate "the vast toll that taxes are
now taking." Soak-the-rich policymakers "who predetermined that
high incomes must be leveled off by some process of liquidation for
the good of society," Nelson wrote in the *New York Times*, have failed
to consider the "possible devastating economic effects of draining our
people of their earnings." If current trends continue, he went on to
warn, "we shall reach the stage where individual incentives will disappear and private enterprise become 'a thing of the past.'"[84]

But private enterprise did just fine in the postwar decades. Entrepreneurs flourished. New industries emerged. The economy grew. No
one could "prove" that high taxes on high incomes actually helped
true entrepreneurs prosper. But some of these true entrepreneurs felt
the connection, one Berkley Bedell among them.

In the world as imagined by the Ayn Rands and Godfrey Nel-
sons, a Berkley Bedell could not possibly exist. The Iowa-born Bedell,
National Council of Churches General Secretary Bob Edgar would
later write in a preface to Bedell's life story, has "a resume that makes
Horatio Alger look like the manager in your local mini-market."[85]

Bedell seems to have had entrepreneurship in his DNA. He grew
up during the Great Depression in a northwest corner of Iowa known
as Spirit Lake. In 1937, paperboy Bedell won fifty dollars in a *Des
Moines Register* subscription contest and promptly invested his winnings in his own fishing fly business.[86] By his high school graduation,
Bedell had turned his bedroom into a warehouse and had hired two

classmates to help him manufacture his stock. In January 1941, he began his studies at Iowa State University and would return home nearly every weekend to run his business.[87]

Bedell spent the bulk of World War II as an army flight instructor, then picked his business up after the war right where he left off. By then, of course, tax rates on America's top-income brackets had risen to their all-time record high. Somehow, Bedell didn't seem to care. Between 1949 and 1957, his sales multiplied tenfold.[88] His enterprise, Berkley and Company, soon had the best-selling fishing line in the country.[89]

In the high-tax 1950s, Bedell constantly invested in his business, not in himself. His family would be one of the last in Spirit Lake to get a TV set. "Berkley thought it better," note biographers Larry Ramey and Daniel Haley, "to live life than watch it."[90] By 1960, his company would be worth $1.2 million, over $9 million in today's dollars. His oldest son Ken had no idea the company had reached that size until he read that net worth figure in a newspaper article. "Reading that newspaper," Ken later related, "made me realize for the first time that Dad was wealthy."[91]

By the mid-1960s, Berkley and Company sales had quadrupled from their late 1950s level, and the national business community was starting to take notice. In 1964, the federal Small Business Administration named Bedell its "small businessman of the year." The Iowa entrepreneur would accept his award plaque from President Lyndon Johnson in a Rose Garden ceremony outside the White House.[92]

That same year, Bedell voted for Barry Goldwater in the presidential race. He considered himself a conservative Republican. But the war in Vietnam soon started to crack his political persona. Bedell would run for Congress in 1972 as an antiwar Democrat and lose. He ran again in 1974 and won, eventually serving six successful terms before retiring for health reasons in 1986.

Once recovered, Bedell resumed a hectic schedule and entered the twenty-first century deeply concerned about America's growing inequality. He had done just fine for himself and his family during the soak-the-rich years. Why couldn't any entrepreneur? "When Eisenhower was president," he would tell his biographers early in the new century, "our income tax rates went up to over 90 percent. That did not seem to diminish people's drive to work hard."[93]

"The continued concentration of wealth in America," the 1964 national small businessman of the year would conclude in 2005, "will lead to problems in the future unless something is done."[94]

Chapter Eleven

A MIDDLE-CLASS GOLDEN AGE

Edward Keating committed his life to the struggle against plutocracy early on. At the age of seventeen in 1892, young Keating, a proofreader's assistant at a Denver newspaper, was already campaigning for Populist candidates. His youthful energy that year helped elect a Populist governor for Colorado.

Keating was just getting started on his plutocracy-busting career. He would become a crusading managing editor for the *Rocky Mountain News* and then win election to Congress in the great progressive upsurge of 1912. In Washington, he sponsored the first federal child labor law, the first pension bill for federal employees, and a model minimum-wage law for women and children.[1] Keating would never forget the floor debate on that minimum-wage legislation. A memoir penned a half century later described the scene: A fellow congressman who had inherited immense wealth "strolled into the chamber" and asked if Keating's bill covered domestic servants. Absolutely, Keating replied. The congressman then "moved an amendment excluding from the benefits of the act the women who had waited on him."

"It would be difficult for me to put into words," Keating wrote shortly before his death in 1965, "the contempt I felt for this pampered darling of Fortune."[2]

That contempt no doubt helped fuel Keating's avid support for a $100,000 income limit during World War I. Keating had not welcomed the war, and his vote against entering it would eventually cost him his congressional seat in the 1918 elections. The defeat did not sour Keating on politics. He simply shifted his lifelong battle against plutocracy to a new front. In 1919 he signed on with the railway unions and helped lead their drive to keep the nation's nationalized railroads in public hands. The prewar railroad owners eventually prevailed, but out of the struggle would come *Labor*, a railway union–sponsored newspaper that became, with Keating as editor, the nation's most important alternative source of information and inspiration for working people. Through the soul-crushing days of plutocratic resurgence in the 1920s and the hard times of the 1930s, Keating's *Labor* kept alive a vision of a better, more equal America.

Edward Keating edited *Labor* for over thirty years, long enough to see America realize far more of that vision than he probably ever dared hope. At his 1953 retirement banquet, the new US secretary of labor—a union man—would be on hand to pay his respects. So would the Speaker of the US House of Representatives and a host of leaders from the worlds of politics and labor.

Not one of these dignitaries had worked harder and longer than Edward Keating to create an America where average people mattered most. Not a one could feel any prouder of what average Americans had achieved over the first half of the twentieth century. Average men and women had made human history. They had created a nation where the majority of people no longer lived in poverty. In this new America, the United States that emerged after World War II, average people could buy their groceries, keep a roof over their heads, raise their families, and still have income—appreciable income—leftover. That had never happened before. Anywhere.

In this new America, the label "middle class" no longer evoked a narrow professional and small business stratum that rested uneasily between the rich above and the poor masses below. The middle class would now be tens of millions of Americans enjoying a security and a status that working people who grew up reading Edward Keating's *Labor* could scarcely have imagined.

Edward Keating was retiring into a different sort of sunset. He was retiring into a new middle-class golden age.

"Even in the smallest towns and most isolated areas," as *Time* magazine rhapsodized in 1953, "the U.S. is wearing a very prosperous, middle-class suit of clothes, and an attitude of relaxation and confidence. People are not growing wealthy, but more of them than ever before are getting along."[3]

"Luxury," *Fortune* magazine announced that same year, "has reached the masses in the U.S."[4]

An exaggeration, of course. But not by all that much.

In 1940, only 55 percent of homes in the United States boasted the complete complement of modern plumbing facilities: hot and cold running water, a flush toilet, a shower or bathtub.[5] By 1950, only one-third of homes lacked these basic amenities of daily existence. By 1960, only one-sixth.[6] Poverty numbers overall would tell a similar story. In 1936, essayist Dwight Macdonald noted in a widely circulated 1963 *New Yorker* analysis, over two-thirds of American families—68 percent—lived in poverty. The 1960 share of families in dire need: 23 percent.[7]

"We have abolished mass poverty," economist Stuart Chase, the coiner of the phrase "New Deal" a generation earlier, would declare in 1960.[8]

Chase and other contemporary observers saw more than just a fading away of what had been an impoverished American mass. They saw a new middle taking shape, a new age of democracy that jumbled together people who had previously shared precious little in common. "A truck driver now earns a larger income than many a college professor," Chase marveled, "and may send his boy to college."[9]

Or travel abroad, a luxury reserved almost exclusively for the well-to-do before the war. In 1960, a majority of the passports the State Department issued went to skilled workers, teachers, clerks, secretaries, housewives, and students, "a rather remarkable shift," notes wealth historian Larry Samuel, "in who was going where."[10] Average Americans could afford to travel. Back in 1940 US households held $27 billion in "discretionary" spending power. In 1953, researchers at the J. Walter Thompson advertising agency calculated, they had five times as much, $138 billion for spending on goods and services beyond the necessities of life.[11]

And these billions in disposable income grew even greater as the 1950s moved on. American personal income, President Dwight Eisenhower later noted in an autobiography, would jump 20 percent between 1952 and 1956 alone. In the middle 1950s, Ike related, "the bottom income groups were becoming richer, the rich were paying record taxes, and many from both groups were joining the 'middle class.'" America, Ike proudly declared, was both leveling up and leveling down.

"We still had our impoverished and our wealthy, but the new prosperity was reducing the relative size of both groups," Ike explained. "The middle class, as sociologists were pointing out, was becoming the widening band around the country."[12]

The families in this widening band wouldn't be swimming in plutocratic luxury. But they would be enjoying home swimming pools. In 1956, Anthony Brothers Pools, Inc. built two thousand pools in California's San Fernando Valley.[13] The entire nation had only 3,600 pools in 1951. In 1961 alone, builders put in seventy-seven thousand.[14] "Activities once exclusively reserved for the smart set," as historian Larry Samuel notes, "had become the stuff of weekend recreation for the average Joe."[15]

In the postwar decades, the lives of average Americans were changing at every stage of life, and fundamentally so. The changes would be particularly dramatic for the young. In 1950, only 8 percent of American young adults between twenty-five and thirty-four had completed four years of college. By 1980, the college-educated share of young adults had tripled, to 24 percent.[16] Federal dollars sped this increase along, first through the college aid the GI Bill offered, then through a Pell grant program that, unlike today's hollowed-out version, actually covered most of the tuition costs poor families faced. Tax dollars raised at the state and local level played an equally vital role, most spectacularly in New York and California, the two great continental bookends of the postwar middle class.

New York City was already operating four tuition-free colleges when World War II ended. By 1960, the city's higher education network boasted four new two-year schools and two more four-year divisions. The total enrollment: ninety-three thousand full- and part-time students. At the state level, the rapidly growing State University of New York system did charge tuition, but only $400 a semester. Students who scored well on state subject matter tests received "regents scholarships" that covered that cost. Other students could handle tuition costs with part-time campus jobs.[17]

California would do even more to expand access to higher education. In 1959, Assemblywoman Dorothy Donohue, a former high school educator, and Senate leader George Miller started the ball rolling on a daring "master plan" for a new statewide higher education system. Under the plan, presented early the next year and adopted soon afterward, the state's top-ranking eighth of high school seniors would be eligible to matriculate in the state's public university system, the top third in a broader network of four-year state public colleges. All other students would have a right to a seat in one of California's eighty-two local community colleges, where they could obtain— tuition free—vocational training or academic credits they could transfer into a California four-year school. These two-year community colleges, notes historian Kevin Starr, offered "a safety valve for late starters, even high school dropouts, who could use these local institutions to complete the first half of their educations."[18]

For the parents of the postwar student generation, the new middle-class America offered escape from cramped quarters. Low-cost, federally insured mortgage loans made home ownership invitingly affordable. An ex-GI, as *Time* magazine noted in 1950, could buy a modest suburban home with no down payment and a fifty-six-dollar monthly mortgage. "No longer must young married couples plan to start living in an apartment, saving for the distant day when they can buy a house," *Time* proclaimed. "Now they can do it more easily than they can buy a $2,000 car on the installment plan."[19]

In 1940, less than half the nation's families, 44 percent, owned their own homes. By 1960, closer to two-thirds of Americans, 62 percent, lived in homes they owned.[20] But these numbers only hint at the scope of the postwar housing transformation. Working families weren't just becoming owners. They were moving from city grime to suburban green. They had yards. They had space. They were living what seemed a new adventure.

The exodus from America's urban cores would be massive. Nassau County, the jurisdiction just east of New York City on Long Island, nearly doubled in population between 1950 and 1960 to 1.3 million. In 1940, New York City held within its borders two-thirds of the New York metro area population. By 1970, under half.[21] Northwest of downtown Los Angeles, only 230,000 people lived in the agricultural San Fernando Valley in 1945. Over the next five years, the Valley's population doubled. Over the next ten, the Valley doubled again.[22]

New suburban bedroom communities. Young couples. And babies everywhere. By 1960 a third of the nation resided in the new suburban promised land, sixty million people who represented, as *Time* put it, "every patch of democracy's hand-stitched quilt, every economic layer, every laboring and professional pursuit in the country."

"Suburbia," exulted the magazine, "is the nation's broadening young middle class, staking out its claim across the landscape, prospecting on a trial-and-error basis for the good way of life for itself and for the children that it produces with such rapidity."[23]

Federal aid for homeowners provided one impetus for the new middle-class suburban building boom, federal aid for homebuilders another. Lawmakers from both major parties had realized right after World War II that the federal government had to do something about housing. Millions of soldiers were returning home to a nation that had added relatively little new housing stock over the long years of Great Depression and war. Progressive lawmakers advocated a broad housing program that would encourage the construction of more publically funded options. But conservative majorities in Congress kept those options off the table. Lawmakers would eventually opt to take an indirect approach. The federal government wouldn't build housing, or help local governments build it. Instead, the feds would help private contractors do the building. The Federal Housing Administration spent the postwar years insuring bank loans to homebuilders for up to 95 percent of the value of the homes they built.[24] That subsidy made billions in low-cost building loans available.

The Levitts, father Abraham and sons William and Alfred, took full advantage. During the war, the Levitts had successfully mass-produced low-cost housing for the navy in Norfolk. After the war, they figured they could apply similar assembly-line construction techniques to residential housing.

"We had known all along we could mass-produce houses if there was a market for them and credit for builders," William Levitt noted in a 1950 interview. "Now the market was there and the government was ready with the backing. How could we lose?"[25]

The landmark Levitt project—Levittown—went up on twelve hundred acres of what had been potato field in the middle of Long Island's Nassau County. Local homebuilders on Long Island had traditionally started and completed just three or four new homes a year. The Levitts had a somewhat more ambitious goal in mind: thirty or forty houses a day.

Levitt & Sons broke ground on their new Levittown on July 1, 1947, in an assault on the flat Long Island countryside almost as meticulously planned as D-Day. First the trucks arrived, depositing lumber and brick and pipes, in identical bundles, every hundred feet along newly paved roads. Then the heavy machinery moved in for digging foundation trenches. Next cement crews came by to lay the home base, a four-inch-thick slab. Nearly two dozen other subcontractors would follow, each a specialist in a single construction task, one subcontractor for tiling, another for roofs, one to paint only in red, another only in white.[26] Lot by lot, the subcontractors worked their way down every Levittown street. At the height of construction, Levitt & Sons was completing one new home every fifteen minutes.[27] Between 1947 and 1951, the company filled in Levittown with an amazing 17,450 new single-family houses.[28]

By midway through 1950, Levittown had forty thousand residents, almost all of them under thirty-five years old. They averaged $3,800 in annual income, about $36,000 today, and few of them ever had hopes of owning a home of their own, anytime soon, before Levittown came around.[29]

William Levitt would call his firm's handiwork "the best house in the U.S."[30] Best house? Hardly. Best value? Unquestionably. For $7,990, the price of a Levittown Cape Cod, a young couple could have a twelve-by-sixteen living room and a picture window, a kitchen, bath, and two bedrooms, all on the first floor, and an attic that could convert into two more bedrooms and a bath. Refrigerator, stove, washing machine, even a built-in, eight-inch television all came included.[31]

New York sophisticates alternated between gagging at the plebeian pleasures the Levitt homes offered and gawking at the sight of young workers in their own homes. *Time* magazine reported that one "elderly dowager" liked to take her friends on chauffeur-driven tours through Levittown to show "what Levitt has done for the poor people." That condescension would not be rare.

"Whenever I tell people outside where I live, I get the same old freeze," one early Levittown resident told *Time*. "Some of them think that everyone who lives in Levittown is on relief. But the only people who criticize the place are the ones who don't live here."[32]

More Levitt developments followed elsewhere. In 1952, five thousand acres of woodlot and farmland north of Philadelphia became home to a community planned for sixty thousand people.[33] Other builders from Chicago in the Midwest to Portland on the Pacific Coast also copied the Levitt construction recipe. Affordable suburban homes would soon be for sale outside nearly every major US city. California's version of Levittown, Lakewood, sat on thirty-five hundred acres of sugar beet fields next to Long Beach. The Lakewood Park Company operated at even a faster pace than Levitt & Sons. The firm could build fifty new houses a day. By 1954, Lakewood boasted seventy thousand residents.

Lakewood and other Southern California suburbs soon eclipsed Levittown and Long Island as the ultimate expression of America's new middle-class ideal. In January 1960, *Changing Times* magazine spotlighted a typical family living this California dream, a couple from Chicago that had moved into a new six-room home in the San Fernando Valley. The husband, an industrial designer, had an $11,000 income, the equivalent of $85,000 today. That income would be quite enough to support the entire family in Californian middle-class comfort. The wife, notes historian Kevin Starr, "could devote her time to home-making and child care" and on most days "also find time to sunbathe on a chaise lounge in her backyard." The couple didn't have a pool in that backyard. But their next-door neighbors had one in theirs and shared their good fortune. The couple did have a patio, and they dined outdoors on it several nights a week for at least half the year. They also hosted at least one neighborhood dinner party or barbecue a month and lots of smaller weekend afternoon gatherings of friends and neighbors.[34]

The good life. Over the midcentury years, most Americans could reasonably aspire to live something close to it.

America's suburbs made headlines, but life was changing for the better in America's cities as well. New York City led the way, but middle-class security in the city would follow a unique trajectory. In the nation as a whole, progressives didn't have the strength to get the government directly involved in building affordable new housing. In New York, they did.

New York had opened the nation's first major public housing in 1935. By the end of World War II, over fifty-eight thousand New Yorkers were living in city housing authority projects. Over the next decade, the city added over seventy-five thousand more public units, providing housing for a wide economic cross section of New Yorkers, not just the city's poorest.[35] Middle-income New Yorkers wanted this housing. They demanded it. In 1946, a broad coalition of groups—from left-led trade unions to the American Legion—staged a one-day occupation of the state Senate chamber in Albany to press the case for housing action. Their continuing pressure eventually exacted from New York mayor William O'Dwyer "a sweeping program of public housing construction aimed at veterans and middle-income families."[36]

The city also provided tax breaks and other assistance for housing cooperatives that enabled tenants to jointly own the buildings where they lived. By the mid-1960s, these new co-ops, combined with new public housing and other forms of government-assisted housing development, had "considerably upgraded" the city's housing stock. Average New Yorkers, notes historian Josh Freeman, would have "significantly more living space" for their families, as measured by rooms per person.[37]

The postwar difference would be particularly pronounced, Freeman adds, for the workers who kept New York running. In 1945, the city's garbagemen, bus drivers, and hospital aides "could afford to live only the most constrained lives—cramped apartments, few possessions, old ages in poverty." By the 1970s, after years of municipal union advocacy, city workers "had acquired elements of what was once considered a middle-class way of life: car and perhaps home ownership, vacations and sometimes vacation homes, comfortable retirements."[38]

City workers could even enjoy affordable, high-quality entertainment. During the war, the city had taken over a huge Shriners temple in a tax default. Mayor Fiorello LaGuardia turned the hulking structure into a nonprofit City Center for the arts that offered top-notch, low-cost symphony, theater, opera, and ballet. The venerable New York Metropolitan Opera—where the ghosts of Gilded Age dandies still danced—charged $6.05 for an orchestra seat. Any New Yorker could see a performance of the City Center's world-class New York City Opera Company for less than a third that price.[39]

Levittown, Lakewood, the City Center in New York: the iconic landmarks of a new middle-class America. In this new nation, the chattering class—the syndicated columnists, the radio hosts, the television personalities—no longer fawned over the lifestyles of the rich and famous. They explored instead the interests and exploits of average-income men and women. The rich had lost their role as cultural pacesetters.

The behavioral economist George Katona, the founder of modern consumer confidence research, documented this remarkable development in his postwar work at the University of Michigan Survey Research Center. Families in the nation's middle-income brackets, Katona's research found, had become the nation's style leaders. Their consumption drove lifestyle trends. Over recent years, Katona observed in a 1960 book, "many new and generally accepted ways of living have started outside upper-class homes."[40] The cultural innovators—on everything from labor-saving household devices to camping trips—were coming from households with incomes between $4,000 and $10,000 a year.[41]

Most Americans of ample means adapted to this new environment. They became, as *Fortune* magazine would note in 1952, "inconspicuous consumers" and lived "no fancier" than the $12,000-a-year set.[42] In this new atmosphere, trades that had traditionally serviced the rich faded away. Custom-tailored suits no longer carried any special cachet. Nearly everyone seemed to be buying off the rack.[43]

Those still wealthy in the postwar years no longer felt themselves standing on the nation's center stage. Grand accumulations of private wealth, tobacco fortune heir Louis Lorillard observed in a 1960 book, used to be passed down from generation to generation "like a good after-dinner liqueur." Now great wealth had come to seem "more like a hot potato."

"A lot of people have it, sure, in oil and in stocks, and in tankers and Black Angus and even in expense accounts," Lorillard explained. "But it's not the uncommon denominator it once was. People just don't look up to it the way they used to."[44]

Those people not looking up included the nation's politicians. In the new middle-class America, politics also centered on the middle class, and not just rhetorically. Over the entire quarter century after World War II, the direct heirs to New Deal progressivism never once controlled all the levers of congressional and White House power. But that didn't matter. By the Eisenhower years, the leadership of both parties had come to accept the basic outlines of the New Deal fiscal state, as World War II had defined that state: high taxes on the incomes of corporations and the wealthy, modest taxes broadly levied on everyone else. The resulting revenue gave government the wherewithal to fund programs that eased working Americans into the new middle class.

These programs would still face conservative opposition. In the new red-scare years of the late 1940s and the "McCarthy Era" of the early 1950s, watchdogs of the right quickly pounced on any social spending initiative that smacked of fellow-traveling social engineering. But advocates for the new middle class found they could deftly spin Cold War hysteria to their own advantage. "To win Republican support," as political analyst Robert Kuttner notes, these advocates disguised legislation that promoted social objectives "with an ostensible Cold War rationale." The National Defense Education Act boosted aid for

colleges, "the better to combat the Soviets." The National Interstate and Defense Highway Act "built roads for motorists on the premise they might be needed for tanks."[45]

The men and women of America's new middle class wanted government at all levels to help them bring their families to ever better lives. Politicians, they insisted, had better listen or get out of the way. In Montgomery County, the biggest Maryland suburb of Washington, DC, the nation's leaders would see a stark demonstration of what wags had begun to call the new American "pedocracy," rule by the champions of kids. The county manager had been foolish enough to slash $11 million from the local Montgomery County 1961 school budget. A thousand angry PTA activists showed up at the next county council meeting to protest. The county council, news reports related, "scrambled to retreat, not only restored the cuts, but added a few projects of its own for good measure." The local property rate rose five cents per hundred dollars in the new budget. "Scarcely a whimper" of protest met that increase.[46]

Politicians who understood this middle-class demand for improved public services, Democrats and Republicans alike, prospered in the new postwar environment. In California, Republican Governor Earl Warren worked with Democrats to improve and expand workmen's compensation and unemployment insurance. He even pushed proposals for statewide health insurance that some years later helped shape the federal Medicare legislation that passed Congress in 1965. Warren, the GOP vice-presidential candidate in 1948, walked the middle-class walk. He would be, notes historian Kevin Starr, "devoid of personal wealth." He raised a family of six "on the middle-range salary of a public official."[47]

Warren's California Republican rival, Richard Nixon, did his best to exude the same middle-class sensibilities. In 1952, Nixon took the GOP vice-presidential nod that Warren had won four years earlier and quickly ran into crisis over an $18,000 slush fund that supporters had created for him. Nixon would go on national television to defend himself. He introduced himself to the American people, as Kevin Starr notes, as if he were a typical middle-class man "applying for a home loan." Nixon listed his modest assets and debts one by one: the $20,000 he still owed on his mortgage, his 1950 Oldsmobile, the $3,500 personal loan he still owed his parents, his $4,000 life insurance policy, his empty stock portfolio. His wife Pat, Nixon told viewers, had no mink. She did have "a respectable Republican cloth coat."[48]

Nixon's declaration of middle-classness saved his political career. Ike kept him on the GOP national ticket.

Not all political hopefuls in postwar America could credibly deliver a middle-class declaration. Nelson Rockefeller, the grandson of John D. Rockefeller, certainly couldn't. W. Averell Harriman, the son of railroad magnate Edward H. Harriman, couldn't either. In 1908, if someone had told Amos Pinchot—or any other stalwart New York progressive—that New Yorkers fifty years hence would face an Election Day gubernatorial choice between the grandson of John D. Rockefeller and the son of Edward Harriman, absolute, total, immobilizing despair would have been the only possible reaction.

In 1908, Rockefeller and Harriman personified plutocracy as potently as any two individuals in the United States. Old John D. gobbled up oil pipelines and fixed prices on the oil that flowed through them. Harriman gobbled up railroads.[49] They both monopolized what should have been public assets for enormous private gain. They both corrupted democratic politics. If their heirs would be all that New Yorkers could choose from in 1958, Pinchot and other progressives would surely have felt, then plutocracy in America must have won and ordinary people must have lost. Averell Harriman and Nelson Rockefeller *did* face each other in the 1958 gubernatorial election, Harriman as the Democratic incumbent and Rockefeller as the Republican challenger. But their race reflected the midcentury dominance of America's middle class, not the triumph of plutocracy.

Both Rockefeller and Harriman ran as champions of that middle class. The rich in New York faced stiff state and local tax rates. Neither Rockefeller nor Harriman called for cutting these rates. Both pointed proudly to their union support. Both supported government regulation of corporations. Both presented themselves as heirs of New Deal traditions. Both in fact served in the New Deal.

"That old John D's grandson, Nelson Rockefeller, should today be the Republican candidate for governor of New York—and, what is more, a liberal candidate who has a chance to win the support of left of center and minority groups—is one of the political miracles of our time," political pundit Marquis Childs would inform his national audience.[50]

Rockefeller won the 1958 race and, perhaps more miraculously, went on to govern as the middle-class champion he portrayed himself

as during the campaign. As governor, notes historian Josh Freeman, Rockefeller "signed the nation's first state minimum wage law, oversaw a vast expansion of the state university, and greatly enlarged the state's involvement in mass transit."[51]

These achievements did not come easily. The state's budget strained at times under their load. But Republican Nelson Rockefeller would not let that strain become an excuse for abandoning his campaign goal of "a rising standard of living" for all New Yorkers.[52] He pressed ahead, and the resulting political battles would be fought on ideological turf totally unimaginable today.

The battling started with Rockefeller's first budget message to state lawmakers in February 1959, an address telecast statewide. The state couldn't afford all the budget increases that the various state departments of government had requested, Rockefeller explained to New Yorkers. He had pared back some of those requests, Rockefeller continued, but he would not pare back more. The people of New York needed, he declared, "vital" public services to be "maintained, expanded, and improved." Rockefeller went on to detail the contribution the tax dollars that funded those public services were making to the lives of New Yorkers. Revenue from the taxes New Yorkers pay, he related, "provides scholarships for higher education" and dollars for "building modern, safer highways" and "constructing college classrooms, laboratories, and libraries." Tax dollars were also "improving and expanding state park facilities" and taking care of "more than 11,000 patients in our mental hospitals and mental schools."[53]

All these programs, Rockefeller emphasized, reflect the "responsiveness" of elected officials "to the needs and the aspirations of the people." But "we must face our obligation to make difficult decisions, no matter how distasteful they may be." State revenues had simply not kept up with state expenditures. They would have to be increased. State tax rates would have to rise for everybody.

Rockefeller laid out $277 million worth of tax increases, over $2.1 billion in today's dollars. Lower-income New Yorkers would pay more under his budget plan. For taxpayers making under $6,000 a year, the majority of taxpayers in the state, the average increase would be a dollar per month. Richer taxpayers would pay more. The top state income tax rate, 7 percent on all income over $9,000, would jump to 10 percent on income over $15,000, about $115,000 today. The state's estate tax rate would also be raised. Under the Rockefeller budget, the state's wealthiest 0.1 percent—taxpayers making over $60,000, or $460,000 today—would see their share of the state income tax burden rise from 7.8 percent to 8.7 percent. The quarter of the state's taxpayers making under $3,500 would see their share of the state income tax burden drop from 4.9 to 4.1 percent.[54]

Rockefeller's presentation opened what would be a six-week debate on state taxes.[55] The eventual compromise enacted gave Rockefeller most of what he wanted. The total tax package raised the same $277 million he originally proposed, and the top tax rate on income over $15,000 rose from 7 to 10 percent. A national political analyst at the *Washington Post* quickly called the compromise "a spectacular fiscal victory" for Rockefeller that would boost his likely bid for the 1960 GOP presidential nomination.[56]

From an early twenty-first century political perspective, this 1959 tax battle in New York may as well have taken place in an alternate universe. Not one element of it reflects political reality today. Consider the core essence of the 1959 New York budget struggle: A Republican governor facing a budget deficit proposes not one cent of cutback in state expenditures from the current state fiscal year. The governor instead heartily recommends an increase in state expenditures over their current level to build upon already existing public services. To address the deficit, the governor asks all taxpayers to sacrifice, but he asks the state's most affluent to sacrifice appreciably more. The state's conservative Republicans demand a lower tax increase. The state's Democrats demand an even more steeply progressive tax increase. State legislators, after fierce partisan debate, adopt the bulk of the governor's plan, and political pundits see the Republican governor's tax-hike victory as a solid step toward his national political success.

In our time, a little over a half century later, none of this episode seems politically plausible. A contemporary Republican governor faced with a state budget deficit would declare war on "wasteful government spending," propose deep cuts in existing programs that serve low- and middle-income state residents, and vow not to raise taxes one iota. Opposition Democrats, cowed by that avowal, would call for budget cuts less draconian than what the governor had proposed. Some might propose slightly higher taxes on the rich as well. But any increase, even if enacted, wouldn't be enough to avoid real public service cutbacks. Political pundits, in the meantime, would declare the public service–cutting Republican governor a rising national political star.

Two entirely different political cultures, two entirely different political outcomes. A politically ambitious Republican governor sees—fifty-odd years ago—an opportunity to champion the middle class and move up the political ladder. His contemporary counterpart, equally ambitious, chooses instead to squeeze the middle class. The nature of political ambition hasn't changed. The political environment has. In 1959, Nelson Rockefeller plied his political trade in a middle-class America where plutocrats no longer dominated the political process or culture. That America no longer exists.

Political scientists at midcentury had a new label they felt captured the essence of the middle-class nation they saw emerging all around them: pluralism. The rich no longer ruled, the academics postulated. The wealthy constituted merely one of many competing power centers. John D. Rockefeller and J. P. Morgan look-alikes no longer bestrode the American economy or polity. Corporations no longer had magnates at their summit. They had chief executives answerable to boards of directors. Big Business had enormous power, the pluralists maintained, but so did Big Labor and Big Government. In this new pluralistic environment, the wealthy could win, but they also could lose, even on a matter near and dear to their hearts and wallets, a matter like federal price controls on natural gas.

After World War II, natural gas would be a pivotal profit center for the Texas Big Rich oilmen. They aimed to keep it that way. Their political clout had neutralized the Federal Power Commission, the regulatory agency with statutory authority over natural gas, and gas prices had been steadily rising in the years after 1948, from six cents per thousand cubic feet of gas to ten cents in 1955.[57] H. L. Hunt and other Texas Big Rich would enjoy a steady stream of new tax-advantaged windfalls.

States in the Midwest would eventually rise up in revolt against this greed grab. In 1954, Michigan and Wisconsin sued the Federal Power Commission, and their demand for price relief went all the way to the Supreme Court. The high court sided with the protesting states and directed the Federal Power Commission to start getting serious about regulating natural gas prices. But that would not be the last word. The Big Rich had spent large fortunes electing powerful Washington lawmakers like Senate Majority Leader Lyndon Johnson. Now they called in their chips and demanded legislation to nullify the Supreme Court decision. In July 1955 that legislation narrowly passed the House. The Senate vote would come early in 1956, and the stakes would be enormous.

Passage of the nullification bill would raise the value of Big Rich natural gas reserves as much as $30 billion, the equivalent of a quarter-trillion dollars today, and the Big Rich would spare no expense to guarantee a Senate majority. Unfortunately for them, one lobbyist for their cause emptied his pockets in the wrong office. The lobbyist tried to bribe Francis Case, a Republican senator from South Dakota. An angry Case rose late in the Senate debate to announce that the lobbyist had left him an envelope with $2,500 in cash. This bombshell bribery charge cheered the natural gas industry's opposition and sent industry lobbyists scurrying out of Washington and the reach of subpoenas.[58] But the Big Rich still had Lyndon Johnson, and he prevailed. The nullification bill passed the Senate the week after the bribery charge. Victory for the Big Rich, for old-style plutocratic profiteering, now only required Dwight Eisenhower's signature on the final legislative language. That would not come. The public uproar against Big Oil and the Big Rich would be too intense for Ike to ignore, and he vetoed the legislation.[59]

Middle-class America had won. The nation's middle class, sociologist David Riesman would crow, was winning in midcentury America on a regular basis. The nation had shifted from "the power hierarchy of a ruling class" to the "power dispersal" of many groups with veto power—"only another way," Riesman would add, "of saying that America is a middle-class country." Maybe someday, Riesman mused, Americans would "wake up to the fact that there is no longer a 'we' who run things and a 'they' who don't or a 'we' who don't run things and a 'they' who do, but rather that all 'we's' are 'they's' and all 'they's' are 'we's.'"[60]

The pluralists had reason to be enthusiastic. But they were overreaching in their enthusiasm, and more sober analysts—like Columbia University sociologist C. Wright Mills—would call them on it. "When they write of the upper classes," he wrote, "conservatives of the painless school of liberalism often confuse wishful image with reality."[61] But reality in midcentury America would have enough triumphs over the rich and powerful to give the pluralist vision credibility. The pluralist celebration of the new America would continue.

In the middle-class midcentury, one group of Americans—African Americans—would not feel much like celebrating. The march into the new middle class would be overwhelmingly white.

Black income actually increased at a faster annual pace than white income between 1947 and 1967, a 3.6 percent annual increase for average families of color against a 2.8 percent annual increase for white families. Union wages in Detroit and other industrial centers would help double average black family income from $13,558 in 1947—in 2009 dollars—to $27,373 in 1967. Yet black family income remained far behind average white family income. In 1967, white families averaged $46,234, again in 2009 dollars.[62]

What explains the gap? One fundamental factor: The postwar government initiatives that were giving white working families a leg up into the middle class were offering black families little assistance. Outright, overt, conscious bigotry played a part. So did the more subtle institutional racism built into the New Deal era's most important social legislation.

Social Security exhibited both of these dynamics. The original Social Security legislation enacted in 1935 denied coverage to agricultural workers and domestics. The powerful Southern chairmen of key congressional committees demanded that denial as the price of their support for the rest of the legislation. The lawmakers, note sociologist Rose Brewer and her coauthors of *The Color of Wealth*, "wanted to keep their maids, sharecroppers, and fields hands desperate, without any other options." A Social Security benefit of fifteen dollars a month, the expected initial payout, would have towered over sharecropper incomes that seldom exceeded eighty-seven dollars per person per *year*. And Southern maids took home less than five dollars a week for seventy hours of work.[63]

Before Social Security, average elderly Americans would typically spend down their life savings on living expenses in retirement or become financial burdens on their grown children. With Social Security, average elderly white Americans could hang on to their life savings and pass on nest eggs to their kids to help on home down payments or college expenses. Without Social Security, the black elderly typically did not have that capacity.

Those black families that could put together down payments faced other obstacles. The design of New Deal housing programs actually made home ownership "more difficult," notes Brewer and her colleagues, for African Americans.[64] The New Deal insured mortgage loans to give banks the confidence to lend. The federal government, understandably enough, sought to limit that insurance to economically sound loans. In practice, this emphasis on sound loans would encourage the denial of loans to all families that lived in low-income neighborhoods. Most black families lived in these neighborhoods because realtors and racism kept them out of more economically mixed white neighborhoods. With this "redlining" of low-income neighborhoods in effect, even black families that did have the savings necessary for a down payment still couldn't get mortgages.[65]

The GI Bill operated in a similarly subtle racist fashion. For starters, a smaller proportion of black than white young men served in the armed forces during World War II, in part because Southern states early in the war rejected black volunteers, in part because more blacks than whites didn't meet literacy standards. After the war, blacks who did serve received fewer benefits. White colleges often would not accept black veterans as students. Historically black colleges, even with federal help, did not have nearly enough seats. These black colleges would turn away, for lack of space, just under 60 percent of all black veterans who applied.[66]

Racism in society at large would compound all these obstacles to African American middle-class status. The original Levittown had no homes for African American families. The community's eighty-two thousand residents in 1960 did not include a single African American. William Levitt refused to integrate his development. "We can solve a housing problem, or we can try to solve a racial problem," he rationalized. "But we can't combine the two."[67]

In California's San Fernando Valley, most suburban developments had restrictive covenants that banned people of color. Some did slip through. One great irony, notes historian Kevin Starr, would be the ethnic identity of the Valley's most famous 1959 resident, the seventeen-year-old rock-and-roll singer "Ritchie Valens," a stage name for the Chicano youth Ricardo Valenzuela.[68]

Greater economic equality. Continuing social inequality. The immediate postwar years saw them both. But the pairing would not last. Economic equality, Americans would soon learn, begets social equality. The more equal a society becomes, on any significant economic dimension, the more starkly a society's remaining social inequalities will always stand out—and cry out for redress.

Did the young Martin Luther King Jr. sense this inexorable dynamic? He certainly recognized the inequity of maldistributed income and wealth. In 1951, working on his doctorate in theology at Boston University, the young King would tell his new girlfriend Coretta Scott that no small elite should "control all the wealth."[69]

"A society based on making all the money you can and ignoring people's needs is wrong," King's future life partner would remember him saying.[70]

In an academic paper the next year, King argued that injustice sits rooted in "the concentration of power and resources in the hands of a relatively small wealthy class."[71] A few years later, in 1956, King as a young preacher publicly shared his dream of a world that left "privilege and property widely distributed, a world in which men will no longer take necessities from the masses to give luxuries to the classes."[72]

That same year King helped lead the bus boycott in Montgomery, Alabama that would herald the emergence of a new national civil rights movement. The civil rights struggles of the next decade would, in turn, help reignite the women's movement for gender equality and later the gay rights movement. By the late 1960s, all the nation's core inequalities seemed to be challenged as never before. At every turn, a more economically equal society seemed to be becoming a better society. Even a "Great" one.

The new president who would take office after John Kennedy's assassination in 1963, Lyndon Johnson, pledged a "war on poverty" to help create a "Great Society." Johnson's war on poverty would jump off to a strong start. Between 1958 and 1966, the number of Americans living on less than $3,000 a year dropped from thirty-nine to twenty-six million.[73]

Former Senator Paul Douglas from Illinois, a veteran progressive, called that gain only a good first step toward the ever greater leveling up the nation still needed. In a major 1968 report, Douglas urged a new program of massive federal revenue sharing with state and local governments. To level up, his report suggested, we needed to continue leveling down. Explained the Douglas report: "The federal tax system, with all its faults, is more progressive and equitable than the systems currently used by the state and local governments."[74]

Where would this drive for an ever more equal, ever greater society end? The same year the Douglas report appeared, the aging Stuart Chase, now past eighty, authored a new book he entitled *The Probable World*. Chase envisioned a delightfully sane and rational society. He invited readers to imagine a professor walking outside in the year 2001 to pick up his *New York Times* on a sunny Sunday morning. The sky that Chase saw in America's near future would be "a deep, unpolluted blue." Next to the professor's home would be a "fuel-cell car, small, quiet, easy to park, shockproof, fumeless." The programs on television would have no commercials. In the world at large, "the opposing ideologies of Communism and the radical right" would have "all but withered away."[75]

This vision struck Chase as eminently reasonable, and the nation, he believed, had that future within sight. But the nation would not realize his vision for a reasonable, rational 2001. Communism would indeed wither away. But the radical right would not. The right's basic ideological precepts would more or less triumph.

What happened?

Chapter Twelve

CRACKS IN THE
MIDDLE-CLASS FOUNDATION

At midcentury, America's middle-class essence seemed almost eternal. A comeback for plutocracy? Unthinkable. History didn't work that way, not at least in America. We only moved forward, to ever-greater freedom. We took on the King of England and won. Monarchy never came back. We took on slavery. Involuntary servitude never came back. We extended suffrage. We gave workers rights. No one rational would ever dare try to take those rights away. Sure, we had unfinished business, but we would get to that. With plutocracy out of the way, we now had the space to perfect our democracy. We the people really ruled. The Rockefellers and Morgans no longer told us what to do. If they wanted to count in the new America, they asked respectfully what we wanted. And they paid attention to our answers. They had no choice.

C. Wright Mills, the midcentury Columbia University sociologist, never exulted in this celebration of middle-class victory—or shared in any sense of triumph over plutocracy. Mills challenged both middle-class convention and conviction.

"In that era of cautious professors in gray flannel suits," a student of Mills in the 1950s would fondly remember decades later, "he came roaring into Morningside Heights on his BMW motorcycle, wearing plaid shirts, old jeans, and work boots, carrying his books in a duffel bag strapped across his broad back."[1]

In *The Power Elite*, his most famous book, Mills depicted America's new middle-class self-confidence as little more than a fairytale take on reality: "Once upon a time in America, there were the fabulously rich; now that time is past and everyone is only middle class."[2] Mills scoffed at that notion. "Not quite accurate," he called it.

Mills had grown up in Texas, as had Bill Moyers, a younger contemporary who would go on to become one of America's most respected journalists. Moyers saw what Mills did not, that millions of midcentury Americans actually believed they were living a fairytale come true. His own family would be among the believers.

Neither parent of Bill Moyers had made it past eighth grade. Both were working in the fields as tenant farmers, Moyers would write years later, "when the Great Depression knocked them down and almost out."[3] The day young Bill came into the world, in 1934, his father "was making $2 a day working on the highway to Oklahoma City." But Bill would have a brighter future. His parents hailed from a world where workers never shared in the wealth they created, a world where the needs of the many always took a far backseat to the private pleasures of the few. Bill would grow up in a world where taxes on those private pleasures were financing public services that opened doors into the middle class.

"I was one of the poorest white kids in town, but in many respects I was the equal of my friend who was the daughter of the richest man in town," Moyers reminisced in 2011. "I went to good public schools, had the use of a good public library, played sandlot baseball in a good public park and traveled far on good public roads with good public facilities to a good public university."[4]

And at that university the doctrines that justified plutocracy—the endless faith in unregulated private markets—no longer held sway. The "old-time economics," notes historian Robert McElvaine, would remain "in disfavor" throughout midcentury. In this intellectual and social climate, those who did continue to pound the drums for an "out-and-out" laissez-faire America came across as "slightly disreputable" leftovers from a past the nation had outgrown and finally left behind.[5]

America's "disreputable" shills for free-market orthodoxy might not have public favor in the 1950s and 1960s. They did have patrons. Nationally, the super rich had indeed been routed, but plutocratic fortune still held one powerful redoubt: Texas oil. Outside the oil fields, the rich watched steeply graduated progressive tax rates shrink their fortunes. But the depletion allowance enacted in the 1920s and never repealed had kept dollars pouring into Texas Big Rich pockets.

Those dollars proceeded to pour from those pockets into politics. Some oilmen brought modest goals into the political arena. They wanted protection. They wanted lawmakers and governors and presidents who kept their hands off the good thing the Big Rich had going. They didn't particularly care how the politicians they backed behaved or voted on anything outside tax breaks for Big Oil. Lawmakers like House Speaker Sam Rayburn and Senate Majority Leader Lyndon Johnson understood these terms and prospered by them. They gained power. The oilmen behind them gained security.

But other Big Rich out of Texas had grander political agendas. They saw attacks on their tax breaks as part of a broader attack on their way of life—the "American way of life"—from an un-American horde of Communists and Jews intent on fouling a proud Christian nation with trade unions and integration. These Big Rich first entered onto the national political scene in the 1930s behind John Henry Kirby, the East Texas timber baron who founded the Houston Natural Gas Company—the company that three generations later would win infamy as Enron—in 1925. Kirby hobnobbed with the New Era's movers and shakers. He even advised Harding, Coolidge, and Hoover. But the Great Depression shrank Kirby's fortune and left him with a deep hatred for Franklin Roosevelt and anything connected to the New Deal.[6]

The ultraconservatives around Kirby wouldn't have much immediate impact nationally. But inside Texas they managed to purge out of Congress the lawmakers most deeply committed to New Deal ideals and install a governor willing to do Big Oil's bidding at every turn. The significant national impact of the Big Rich wouldn't come until right after World War II. Those early postwar years would prove the hardest of hard times for the right-wing ideological currents that had in the distant past always been able to sweep away plutocracy's critics. In 1950, as Bryan Burrough notes in his history of the Big Rich, the United States had "not a single leading politician who could be termed conservative by today's standards."[7] Most of America's postwar comfortable seemed willing to accept the basic contours of the New Deal state. Executives at America's biggest corporations wanted labor peace. They were signing treaties with trade unions. Enlightened Wall Streeters wanted world peace. Any return to plutocracy, they feared, would only invite a global instability that could bring down the entire modern "free enterprise" system.

Those ultraconservatives who longed for a return to America's plutocratic heyday would be a dispirited bunch in the early postwar era.

Those who yearned for a nation that placed no meddling restrictions on the marketplace—and no serious taxes on that marketplace's noble winners—had virtually no clout or credibility at the national political level. The anti-communist hysteria of midcentury certainly did reflect basic old-time plutocratic values. But this red scare sported limits that had "true" conservatives constantly grumbling and growling. How could America secure victory over communism if the stalking horses of a red America—unions and progressive taxation—could still roam free? The Democrats accepted this roaming. So did Republicans like Dwight Eisenhower, Earl Warren, and Nelson Rockefeller. They all had to be stopped.

The Texas Big Rich would stop them. Or, to put the matter more precisely, dollars from the Texas Big Rich would allow ultraconservatives to regroup and hold the fort until the reinforcements arrived, until America's corporate movers and shakers "came to their senses" and rejoined the battle against unions, progressive taxes, and all those who swore by them.

Texas oil would actually contribute more than dollars to America's plutocratic restoration. Plutocracy's comeback began with William F. Buckley, the politically precocious son of a Texas oilman. In 1951, at just twenty-five, Buckley authored the book *God and Man at Yale*, the first manifesto of American "movement conservatism." Young Buckley's book decried liberal influence at Yale, plutocracy's historic bastion in higher education, and blamed problems like unemployment on "wage rigidities, burdensome taxes," and other restrictions on private enterprisers. The book gave struggling conservatives an eloquent champion, and oilmen soon gave Buckley a broader forum. Buckley's father and his oil industry friends bankrolled the 1955 founding of the *National Review*, a journal that would help the new conservative movement find a voice and spread the word.[8]

Buckley actually had a difficult time raising money for his effort. Not all the Big Rich warmed immediately to his project. Buckley, as one biographer later noted, struck some oilmen as too Catholic and moderate.[9] Oil giant H. L. Hunt turned Buckley down. But Hunt and other Big Rich would find other outlets for their fistfuls of dollars. Some would be election-related. In 1952 and 1954, oilman Hugh Roy Cullen would be America's largest contributor to political campaigns, spreading his largesse to campaigns across the country.[10] He targeted anyone who dared challenge the red-baiting fulminations of Wisconsin Senator Joseph McCarthy.

By mid decade, the oil industry's electoral cash gusher had become front-page headline news. In 1954, a six-part *Washington Post* series profiled "the fabulous money-men of Texas who have been pouring part of their millions into American politics." That spring, the journalist who later became America's best-read presidential historian, Theodore White, traveled through Texas and filed an alarmed dispatch in the *Reporter* magazine. A "nameless Third Party, obsessed with hate, fear and suspicion," White charged, had captured "the machinery of government" within Texas. This "handful of prodigiously wealthy men, whose new riches give them a clumsy and immeasurable power," White continued, "seek to spread this climate and their control throughout the rest of the United States."[11]

The "Texas political imperialism" that White saw trying to turn elections in other states had little immediate political success. Some high-profile targets of the Big Oil political money—like the moderate Republican senator from Maine, Margaret Chase Smith—survived the cash surge against them. Big Oil's more lasting impact would be institutional. Oil dollars kept conservative periodicals publishing and up-and-coming conservative ideologues gainfully employed.

"Virtually every Radical Right movement of the postwar era," as the *Nation* magazine posited in 1961, "has been propped up by Texas oil millionaires."[12] Texas oil influence, the progressive magazine charged, had become "all-pervasive." The massive Big Rich millions, "piled up thanks to the bounteous depletion allowance," had even infested the New York publishing world, where no one could turn around "without bumping into a Texas oil millionaire who bought himself a share—often a controlling share—of an established periodical or book-publishing firm."[13]

The Big Rich would not be the only benefactors of the new movement conservatism. A wealthy candy manufacturer underwrote much of the original John Birch Society, an ultraconservative group that reserved particular venom for the apostasy of GOP moderates like Dwight Eisenhower. But funding for the John Birch Society would also come from Big Oil. One Birch Society founder, oil refining megamillionaire Fred Koch, went on to instill his fervor in his two sons. Starting in the 1970s, David and Charles Koch would bankroll a more sophisticated new generation of institutions dedicated to proselytizing a plutocrat-friendly, "free market" vision.[14]

The ideological warriors who set out to do battle on behalf of America's rich had more than Big Rich money working in their favor. They also had the luxury of an ideologically feeble opposition. By the 1960s, mainstream American liberalism had almost totally abandoned the New Deal's preoccupation with plutocratic threats.

Part of postwar liberalism's indifference to the rich no doubt reflected the celebratory tenor of the times. For many liberals, the rich—aside from those crazies from Texas—no longer seemed to pose much of a threat to the social order. The tycoons of the auto industry, after all, were no longer unleashing thugs on strikers. But a greater part of that indifference reflected the lingering aftershock of what had become known as "McCarthyism." America's second great red scare had purged outspoken advocates for greater equality from American universities and public life. Anyone who talked about income and wealth distribution in this environment would come across as politically suspect. Basic ideas central to the political discourse of the New Deal now had few vigorous, open advocates. This timidity, notes University of Toronto mathematician Chandler Davis, created an "impoverished" national political discourse.

Chandler Davis lived through this degeneration. Davis had begun his career as a professor at the University of Michigan after earning a doctorate from Harvard in 1950. In 1954, he refused to testify to visiting investigators from the House Committee on Un-American Activities. A long legal battle over that refusal ended in a six-month prison sentence. Once released, Davis found himself unemployable in the United States.

Similar spectacles unfolded in communities all across the country. These repeated confrontations silenced open radicals like Chandler Davis and had a chilling impact on their less outspoken colleagues. Soon virtually no one in influential positions would be openly defending basic economic concepts that only a few years earlier seemed to need no defense. In the 1930s, as Chandler Davis would reflect decades later, everyone "who thought about it" understood that regressive taxes that took "more proportionately from the poor than from the rich" would always dampen economic vitality, since "the poor had to spend what they had and the rich could sit on it." Both economic common sense and justice, most people who thought about public policy during the New Deal era would agree, demand "that we take more from the rich so as to reduce inequality."[15]

The logic behind this analysis always seemed obvious to Davis. But few mainstream liberals in the 1950s would agree. Talking about taking from the rich had become too dicey. Liberals instead professed their undying commitment to fostering ever-greater "economic growth." The nation simply needed, the new liberal metaphor went, to "grow" the economic pie. No need for those distasteful and divisive debates over how to slice the pie up. If we grew the pie, everyone could have a bigger piece. By granting "growth" star billing, notes historian Robert Collins, liberals could ride out the Cold War unpleasantness, "avoiding hard questions and evading tough decisions about the distribution of wealth and power in America."[16]

This retreat from challenging wealth's unequal distribution had actually begun before the red scare took its most ferocious hold after the war. Many mainstream liberals, as historian Alan Brinkley observes, genuinely felt no need "to reform capitalist institutions" and no pressure "to redistribute wealth and economic power."[17] The economy had recovered. The Great Depression had finally ended.

"The industrial economy, most liberals now believed, could take care of itself," Brinkley writes. "Intelligent fiscal policies and a generous welfare state would be sufficient to sustain economic growth and ensure at least minimal levels of social justice."[18]

McCarthyism reinforced this powerful drift away from anything that smacked of class struggle. An entire vocabulary would now disappear from America's political discourse: plutocracy, concentrated wealth, monopoly. For generations, progressives had invoked words like these to resist the rich and their dominance over American life. Now a new conservative movement was beginning to proselytize for a return to the "free market" that would make that dominance once again inevitable. This conservative movement encountered remarkably tepid pushback. Against the new conservatives, mainstream liberalism would not summon up the ghosts of plutocrats past. Liberalism instead bestowed upon America a new classless vocabulary. The free marketers would take full advantage.

The most vivid metaphor for the new growth mantra would come from the dashing new president elected in 1960. John F. Kennedy gave growth an evocative nautical twist: "As they say on my own Cape Cod, a rising tide lifts all the boats."[19]

And nothing would get that tide rising faster, the Kennedy White House eventually concluded, than tax cuts for everybody, rich and poor alike. In 1963, the president's state of the union address proposed a permanent reduction in federal tax rates that would cost the federal government $13.5 billion over the next three years. Under the Kennedy proposal, tax rates would drop for every income bracket. The tax rate on income over $400,000 would drop from 91 to 65 percent.[20]

Kennedy also proposed a variety of measures to close tax loopholes. Two years earlier, loopholes had dominated the new Kennedy administration's tax talking points. In January 1961, the nation's top periodical on taxes was telling its insider readers to expect "a long look into expense account deductions" and "a further study of the depreciation and depletion provisions of the tax law."[21] Now in January 1963 the administration was coupling rate reductions and loophole closings. The "elimination of certain defects and inequities" in the tax code, Kennedy told Congress, "will provide revenue gains to offset the tax reductions offered to stimulate the economy."[22]

Behind the scenes, administration officials split over this coupling. Commerce Secretary Luther Hodges favored "an immediate reduction of federal tax rates" without waiting for congressional action on closing loopholes.[23] The president himself would come to tilt in that direction. Three months after his 1963 state of the union, Kennedy told the American Bankers Association that he would support a tax cut bill with or without reforms that targeted the tax code's "defects and inequities."[24]

Kennedy's backsliding on loopholes would certainly be disturbing to the capital's few remaining unreconstructed advocates of stiff and steep tax rates on taxpayers of excessive means. Even more disturbing to these advocates would be the administration rhetoric that accompanied the basic Kennedy tax cut proposal. Right after World War II, Randolph Paul and other champions of New Deal progressive taxation had seen high rates on high incomes as a pivotal step toward winning the Cold War. Now the Kennedy administration was redefining the relationship between taxes and Cold War victory at home and abroad. Victory over communism now demanded economic growth, and economic growth demanded tax cuts, even for the rich.

Steeply graduated tax rates, the 1963 Kennedy tax message to Congress argued, had become a "heavy drag" on that economic growth, the "largest single barrier to full employment."[25] The "present rates up to 91 percent," the message stressed, "discourage investment" and "encourage the diversion of funds and effort into activities aimed more at the avoidance of taxes than the efficient production of goods."[26]

Lowering that top 91 percent rate to 65 percent would "restore an idea that has helped make our country great—that a person who devotes his efforts to increasing his income, thereby adding to the nation's income and wealth, should be able to retain a reasonable share of the results."[27] The long dead and departed Andrew Mellon, a patron saint of the new movement conservatism, could not have made tax breaks for the rich any more enticing.

The evidence for the Kennedy claim that the 91 percent tax rate had become a "heavy drag" on the economy? The administration had none. That would become clear the day Commerce Department Secretary Luther Hodges testified before Congress on behalf of the Kennedy tax cut proposal. Reducing tax rates for low- and middle-income taxpayers, Hodges told lawmakers, would "serve for the most part to increase consumption expenditures," expand consumer demand, and place unused industrial capacity back into operation. Hodges buttressed this claim with ten different detailed charts and graphs. Reducing tax rates on the upper tax brackets, Hodges continued, would give America's most affluent "the motivation to exploit new opportunities" and encourage productive investment "directly."[28] Hodges offered no detailed tables and graphs to make the case for these upper-bracket tax cuts. Congress would have to take his claim on faith.

The Kennedy administration had essentially handed Andrew Mellon's ideological heirs a liberal freshening up of their worn-out and discredited rationales for kid-glove taxation of America's rich. High taxes reduced consumption and undermined our economic get-up-and-go. Low taxes kept Americans working and investments flowing. Tax cuts, in short, can work economic magic. All tax cuts, especially tax cuts for the rich.

Conservatives immediately took the Kennedy administration's case for tax cuts to the next logical level. If the relatively modest cuts Kennedy proposed could create such magical outcomes, why not have more? After all, hadn't the president himself argued that tax cuts, by generating new economic activity, would grow the tax base, "thus increasing revenue"?[29] If tax cuts in the end paid for themselves, why stop cutting at 65 percent? Why indeed. Republican Senator Howard Baker would sponsor a move in 1963 to cut the tax rate on top-bracket income from 91 to 42 percent.[30]

At this point in the 1963 tax cut debate, the basic principles of progressive taxation desperately needed a passionate defense. Someone with a national platform needed to point out what should have been obvious: that tax cuts for the rich in the 1920s had fueled the speculative fever that crashed the economy, that the American economy had grown enormously over the previous two decades, years of record high taxes on America's highest incomes. Someone needed to make this case. No one did.

What had happened to the great champions of steeply graduated progressive taxes? The postwar era's most prominent elite defenders of taxing the rich had moved on. Randolph Paul had gone back to the private practice of tax law after he left government service in 1944. But he continued writing and speaking out until he suddenly slumped over and died while testifying before a Senate committee in early 1956.[31] Chester Bowles, the advertising executive who gave progressive taxation a sophisticated Madison Avenue gloss right after World War II, would serve as governor of Connecticut and then a term in Congress. Kennedy would appoint Bowles undersecretary of state in 1961. He ended up, in 1963, halfway around the world as ambassador to India.

Organized labor would be quiet as well. The CIO had helped lead the charge for a 100 percent tax rate on income over $25,000 during World War II. In 1955 the CIO had merged into the AFL, and the new AFL-CIO had little of the old CIO fire. Kennedy's proposed tax cuts for corporations made no sense as an economic stimulus to labor economists. They had been pushing instead for a federal initiative to build low-cost housing. But AFL-CIO president George Meany wouldn't push that case. In fact, as historian Paul Buhle notes, Meany vetoed a meeting between AFL-CIO economist Stanley Ruttenberg and the president's advisors set up to encourage Kennedy to drop the corporate tax cuts. Kennedy had been helping labor organize federal workers. Meany didn't want to risk alienating the administration.[32]

Meany himself testified before Congress on the broader Kennedy tax plan. He pointed out the plan's essential inequity—those with incomes under $3,000 would save sixty dollars under the administration's proposals, those over $50,000, an average $2,500—and argued that no cutback on rates at the top "can be justified unless loopholes are effectively closed at the same time." But Meany then took the teeth out of his critique. The administration, he stressed, would face no holy war from labor on the tax cut bill's goodies for the rich and the corporations they ran.

"I want to make it clear," Meany testified, "that the AFL-CIO is not opposed to tax reductions for corporations and upper bracket incomes."[33]

America's left—what remained of it—would not wage holy war over the Kennedy tax rate cuts on top income-earners either. The part of the left that could be linked to the Communist Party, Chandler Davis and his soul mates, had already been silenced. But some personalities on the left, broadly defined, could still if they so chose have raised their voices and cast the Kennedy tax cut as a threat to middle-class triumph and a first step toward a new plutocracy. But this broader left never made this warning, mainly because this left didn't believe plutocracy had ever departed.

Author Ferdinand Lundberg, a former *New York Herald Tribune* reporter on the Wall Street beat, had been decrying the concentration of America's wealth ever since his books became best sellers in the late 1930s. New Dealers widely cited his contention that sixty families of immense wealth dominated America's economic and political landscape. That concentration, Lundberg argued straight through the postwar decades, had never changed. A relative handful of "extravagantly endowed" Americans, he contended, still dominated the nation. Lundberg considered claims that the United States had undergone some sort of fundamental middle-class revolution no more than crude Cold War propaganda.

"A horde if not a majority of Americans," he wrote, "live in shacks, cabins, hovels, shanties, hand-me-down Victorian eyesores, rickety tenements, and flaky apartment buildings—as the newspapers from time to time chortle that new Russian apartment-house construction is falling apart."[34]

Lundberg saw "no process of estate destruction taking place in the United States through taxation, as is commonly suggested by propagandists of the establishment."[35]

Other less colorful, more sober analysts argued the same basic point. In a 1962 book, historian Gabriel Kolko marshaled an array of data to debunk the assumption that "the nation's wealth has been redistributed and prosperity has been extended to the vast majority of the population." On the contrary, Kolko argued, "the basic distribution of income and wealth in the United States is essentially the same now as it was in 1939, or even 1910."[36] Kolko considered Kennedy's tax cut a mere "formalization of the systematic, legal evasion of high theoretical tax rates that has gone on since the beginning of the income tax."[37]

In other words, nothing significant had changed. America remained as unequal as ever. Left analysts and activists in midcentury found this bedrock conviction incredibly difficult to shake. Data that showed otherwise, that presented an America becoming more equal, simply could not be accurate. The troubling data had to have a flaw.

C. Wright Mills would be far too honest a scholar to ignore data that called his perceptions into doubt. He acknowledged that economist Simon Kuznets did indeed rate as "an expert with tax-derived data." And the Kuznets data—the best source, as Mills would put it, of the great "leveling up" and the "decline of the rich" perspective—did show that the after-tax income share of the nation's richest 1 percent had dropped from 19.1 percent in 1928 to 7.4 percent in 1945. But Kuznets, Mills noted, had admitted his research effort "encountered considerable difficulty in contracting estimates with a high degree of reliability." And we only know, Mills added, a "small part" of the "legal and the illegal ways of the heavily taxed." That drop from 19.1 to 7.4 percent, Mills speculated, may be "as much an illustration of how well the corporate rich have learned to keep information about their income from the government than of an 'income revolution.'"[38]

But scholars of our own time every bit as progressive and committed to social justice as Mills and Kolko have documented the same equalizing trend that Kuznets tracked.[39] Something fundamental in America did change over the first half of the twentieth century. The nation did become more equal. America's wealthiest were pulling in both a smaller share of the nation's income and smaller absolute amounts. In 1928, the nation's most affluent 0.01 percent averaged just under $5 million in income, in 2010 dollars. In 1945, that top 0.01 percent inflation-adjusted income averaged just $1.9 million.[40]

In 1961, the holders of the four hundred highest incomes in the United States—a much more elite group than the top 0.01 percent— would have on average after taxes only $8.1 million of income left in their pockets. We don't have figures for the top four hundred back in 1928. We do have figures for 2007, a year when top incomes rivaled their late 1920s peak. In 2007, America's top four hundred would have left in their pockets after taxes—and after adjusting for inflation—an incredible $111.8 billion more in combined income than the top four hundred of 1961.[41]

C. Wright Mills and his fellow midcentury left analysts could not have known, of course, how fantastically rich the rich of the early twenty-first century would become. But they had before them ample evidence that the rich of their day had become far less flush than the rich of pre–Great Depression America. Why did they so resist that evidence? Why did they insist nothing significant had changed? We can't read their minds. We can sense their psychological environment.

If the distribution of America's income and wealth had indeed become more fundamentally equal over the first half of the twentieth century, that would have meant—to C. Wright Mills and his fellows—that the movers and shakers of midcentury America had a legitimate reason to celebrate what the country had become. But how could the left join in that celebration? How could a left celebrate an America that demonized dissent as communist heresy, that denied basic civil rights to millions of families of color, that tolerated wide swatches of poverty amid plenty? Accepting the legitimacy of that celebration would mean accepting the legitimacy of those vile personages who celebrated the loudest, the red-baiting politicians who smugly declared the eternal supremacy of the "American way of life," the Cold War liberals who delivered up victims to the ongoing inquisition. The left that remained could not join in this celebration. Left activists and analysts could not acknowledge any change that would give their tormentors legitimate cause to crow.

This refusal to acknowledge a more equal America would have consequences, but not immediately. In 1963, the left would be far too marginal to have any political impact on Kennedy's tax bill. But the postwar left that saw no significant shift in the distribution of American income and wealth would in a few short years be mentoring a new "New Left" generation. This new generation took Mills and Kolko to heart. Nothing significant about inequality, this new progressive generation believed, had changed. America had witnessed no great triumph over plutocratic privilege and power.

By not acknowledging this triumph, the new progressives who came of age in the 1960s would be ill-prepared to defend it. On their watch, the various threads that made that triumph possible would unravel. Plutocracy would return triumphant before the 1960s generation even realized that it had left.

The Kennedy tax cut became law in February 1964, three months after Kennedy's assassination. Onlookers stood in awe at the size of the tax cuts eventually enacted, some $92 billion in rate reduction, an average of 20 percent, "the largest tax cut of all time," as Philadelphia tax lawyer Brady Bryson noted in the nation's leading tax journal.

"The cut is so big," Bryson would marvel just before the bill's final Senate passage, "that there still hangs over the bill an uncomfortable air of being too good to be true."[42]

For America's super rich, the legislation would actually not be as good as it initially appeared. The top tax rate fell, but not to the 65 percent Kennedy had originally proposed. Under the new tax law, the 91 percent rate on income over $400,000 in effect in 1963 would drop to 77 percent in 1964 and only 70 percent—on income over $200,000—in 1965. The top rate would step up again to 77 percent later in the decade to help fund the war in Vietnam before dropping back down to 70 percent in 1971. The legislation also included some tax loophole-narrowing reform, but much less of it, as tax lawyer Bryson explained to his colleagues, "than one might have expected." Overall, for America's richest, the bill produced a somewhat underwhelming benefit. The top half of the nation's most affluent 0.1 percent—a little over ninety thousand taxpayers in all—would pay an average 38.9 percent of their incomes to Uncle Sam in 1963, after taking advantage of every loophole they could find, then 37.2 percent in 1964 and 37.1 percent in 1965.[43]

A longer postwar horizon would yield a similarly underwhelming tax cut for American households as a whole. In 1976, as former Undersecretary of the Treasury Edwin Cohen would calculate a dozen years after the Kennedy tax bill became law, a married couple with two dependents making $8,000 paid 3.1 percent of its income in federal income tax. A family with the same purchasing power in 1946 paid taxes at an effective rate of 3.2 percent. Families making $100,000 in 1976—about $400,000 today—would see a more substantial yield. They paid at a 36.1 percent rate in 1946, then at a 32.8 percent rate thirty years later.[44]

These relatively modest changes would hardly be enough to restore plutocratic privilege and upset America's middle-class golden age. The Kennedy years would not bring the rich great new wealth. That wealth would come later, after movement conservatives made some new friends—and made the Kennedy tax cut rhetoric their own.

A resurgent right wing. An ideologically cowed liberal mainstream. A left unable to discern or defend real progress against privilege. The midcentury triumph over plutocracy might have survived all these political threats. But that triumph would face another obstacle as well, and this obstacle—a sea change in the global economic order—would prove the ultimate game-changer.

The global economy right after World War II had one basic division: on the one side the United States, on the other everyone else. No nation had invaded the United States during the war. No nation had bombed the US heartland either. America's factories and highways and bridges all survived the war intact. Elsewhere in the developed world, the global conflict's winners and losers all shared the same fate: widespread devastation. These nations entered the postwar years with manufacturing plants in ruins, infrastructure destroyed, tens of millions of people hungry and homeless.

In this devastated world, American corporations had virtually no competition. The world's largest domestic market—the United States—had virtually no rival foreign business presence within it. The rest of the world's domestic markets, meanwhile, eagerly lapped up US products. Their own domestic companies could not meet local needs. US companies could. The United States held 60 percent of the world's "capital stock," the plants and equipment that drove the industrial world. As late as the early 1970s, half the world's entire industrial output was coming from US-based factories.[45]

The foreign products that did start trickling into the United States in the 1950s would be cheap goods—shoddy transistor radios from Japan and toy-like Volkswagen Beetles from Germany—that posed no competitive threat to America's industrial giants. But over time the devastated developed economies of Europe and Asia recovered. Bombed-out factories became new, state-of-the-art plants able to produce quality products at competitive prices. Year by year, foreign firms steadily regained lost market share in their own domestic economies and started building market share in the United States. Some even began building their own US factories.[46]

From the developing world came another set of challenges to US economic dominance. Third World nations were demanding more for their raw materials, even in some cases grabbing back control over them from US corporations. The 1959 victory of the Cuban Revolution gave this trend momentum. In the 1960s, oil-exporting nations created their own organization, the Organization of Petroleum

Exporting Countries. They began aggressively probing how they might become able to rejigger prices in the global oil market.

By the early 1970s, US corporate leaders could see the future and feel the pressure. In the new, much more competitive global marketplace, their profit rates were falling. Net profit margins among American manufacturing corporations averaged a robust 24.6 percent from 1959 to 1969. That rate would fall to 15.5 percent over the next decade, notes economic historian Robert Brenner.[47] Life had suddenly become more complicated for America's corporate elite. In the immediate postwar years, the corporations they ran could afford to buy labor peace. These corporations dominated domestic and global markets. If need be, they could pass on the cost of better wages and benefits to consumers. That strategy had now become problematic. Their new foreign competition had them thinking twice about their arrogant marketplace behavior. Consumers now had choices.

So, of course, did America's corporate executive elite. In the face of stiff new foreign competition, corporate executives could have chosen to double-down on productivity. They could have moved to modernize their plants and reengineer their operations. They could have partnered with their workers to think through new approaches to making products and delivering services more efficiently. They could have questioned the top-down, command-and-control hierarchies that had characterized corporate decision making ever since the industrial age had begun.

Going down this road would certainly have required visionary leadership. But American business after World War II did have its visionaries, analysts like W. Edwards Deming, the New York University statistician who first attracted widespread attention for his quality-control initiatives at World War II defense plants. Deming preached teamwork and two-way workplace communication. He emphasized the importance of worker training and tapping the best every worker has to offer. He called on management to stop exhorting and start helping.

Japan's new postwar corporate leaders listened to what Deming had to say. These leaders had no connection to Japan's prewar command-and-control executive class. The American occupation had thoroughly purged away Japan's prewar top executives. Japan's new corporate leaders, engineers who cared deeply about industrial processes and quality, adopted Deming's philosophical approach. By the 1970s, Japanese industry would have a worldwide reputation for product innovation and quality.

In the United States, Deming would remain a largely unheeded prophet. Command-and-control still suited America's top executives just fine. The problem, they believed, lay elsewhere. By the 1970s they were blaming equality for Corporate America's increasingly shaky competitive status. Workers were making too much money and their bosses not enough. The nation needed unions with less power and executives with more incentives. If the nation would only recast the economy along these lines, if the nation would only free "free enterprise" from government busybodies and the unions that egged them on, America would surely meet every challenge any new world order could throw at it.

Two papers written in the 1970s would express this emerging business worldview, one from a genteel corporate lawyer soon to become a justice of the US Supreme Court, the other from a pair of business school academics writing in an obscure academic journal. The two papers would rally Corporate America to do battle. The battle would end in a stunning defeat for America's middle class.

The postwar United States, historian Nelson Lichtenstein reminds us, always had business leaders who opposed the Treaty of Detroit, sometimes stubbornly so. In Wisconsin, for instance, the principals of the fiercely antiunion Kohler family fought for an entire decade to keep the United Auto Workers from organizing their porcelain works.[48] These sorts of business leaders—and many others who had only swallowed the Treaty of Detroit with great difficulty—could not possibly be happy with what they saw all around them as America began to move through the 1970s.

In Washington, government didn't seem to understand that corporations now faced a much more challenging marketplace. To navigate this marketplace successfully, business needed elbow room, the freedom to do whatever success in the marketplace demanded. But instead of fostering that freedom, government—under a Republican president no less—seemed to be hobbling business at every turn. At the end of December 1970, Republican Richard Nixon had signed into law legislation that created a new federal agency to protect workers from injury and illness. Occupational Safety and Health Administration inspectors were soon nosing into dark corporate corners all across the country. Earlier that same December, the Nixon administration had created the Environmental Protection Agency, and the EPA's first administrator, William D. Ruckelshaus, immediately announced his intention to give polluters no quarter.

"EPA is an independent agency," Ruckelshaus pronounced. "It has no obligation to promote agriculture or commerce; only the critical obligation to protect and enhance the environment."[49]

These new occupational safety and environmental protection initiatives came on top of an earlier Nixon administration move to bulk up the federal government's consumer protection capacity. The president himself had labeled consumerism "a healthy development that is here to stay" and even praised by name that great socialist troublemaker Upton Sinclair.[50]

Things were clearly getting out of hand. Business was taking a shellacking from every side: foreign competitors, new federal agencies, a restless labor movement, campuses full of professors and students who now felt free to ridicule business values. Corporate America clearly had to respond. But how? The US Chamber of Commerce's Eugene Sydnor would put that question to Lewis Powell, a Virginia corporate attorney who represented tobacco giant Philip Morris.

Powell's answer came in a confidential memo dated August 23, 1971, just two months before Powell's nomination to the US Supreme Court. American business, Powell pronounced, stands "plainly in trouble."[51] The corporate "response to the wide range of critics has been ineffective." The time had come "for the wisdom, ingenuity, and resources of American business to be marshalled against those who would destroy it." Business must "recognize that the ultimate issue may be survival—survival of what we call the free enterprise system, and all that this means for the strength and prosperity of America and the freedom of our people."

Powell's lengthy memo continued in this remarkably overheated vein. Business confronts, he contended, critics "seeking insidiously" to "sabotage" free enterprise. Left extremists had become "far more numerous, better financed, and increasingly are more welcomed and encouraged by other elements of society, than ever before in our history." Corporate America had to respond with more than "appeasement, ineptitude, and ignoring the problem." Business leaders had to show more "stomach for hard-nose contest with their critics." CEOs needed to consider counterattacking "a primary responsibility of corporate management."

Yet individual corporate leaders, Powell acknowledged, can only do so much. An individual corporation might be reluctant "to get too far out in front and to make itself too visible a target." The answer?

"Strength lies in organization," Powell would explain, "in careful long-range planning and implementation, in consistency of action over an indefinite period of years, in the scale of financing available only through joint effort, and in the political power available only through united action and national organizations."

The rest of Powell's memo detailed the sorts of steps Corporate America could take—on campuses, with the media, and in politics—to wash away "inequitable" taxes on men of means and tame regulatory agencies "with large authority over the business system they do not believe in."

Powell's musings, notes historian Kim Phillips-Fein, "crystallized a set of concerns shared by business conservatives in the early 1970s," and gave "inspiration" to corporate leaders who would later become familiar names and powerful forces, men like the arch-right-winger from Colorado Joseph Coors.[52] Together, these newly energized corporate leaders would unleash upon America what political scientists Jacob Hacker and Paul Pierson have called "a domestic version of Shock and Awe."[53]

Between 1968 and 1978 the number of corporate public affairs offices in Washington, DC, soared from a hundred to over five hundred. In 1971, only 175 US corporations had registered lobbyists in Washington. The 1982 total: almost 2,500. Corporate leaders also joined together in new national organizations, most notably with the 1972 founding of the Business Roundtable, and bankrolled a series of new militantly "free market" think tanks and action centers: the Heritage Foundation and American Legislative Exchange Council in 1973, the Cato Institute in 1977, the Manhattan Institute in 1978, among many others.[54] The US Chamber of Commerce, for its part, doubled its membership between 1974 and 1980 and tripled its budget.[55]

Corporate political action committees, add analysts Hacker and Pierson, increased their outlays for congressional races "nearly five-fold." In the early 1970s, corporate PACs actually contributed less to congressional candidates than labor PACs. By the mid-1970s, business contributions were matching labor PACs. By the end of the decade, under a quarter of all PAC contributions came from labor, half the labor share in 1974.[56] By the mid-1980s, US senators were getting less than a fifth of their funding from trade union PACs. In the mid-1970s, senators had depended on labor for almost half their funding.[57]

By the 1980s America's corporate leaders had fundamentally altered the political battlefield. The internal corporate world, two academics would argue in 1976, needed a similar alteration.

The *Journal of Financial Economics* had less than a thousand subscribers in the mid-1970s when Michael Jensen, a Harvard business school finance professor, and William Meckling, the dean at the University of Rochester business school, published in it a dry academic treatise that aimed to integrate "elements from the theory of agency, the theory of property rights, and the theory of finance to develop a theory of the ownership structure of the firm."[58]

Jensen and Meckling had first presented their thesis at a conference in June 1974. Theirs would be an ambitious intellectual agenda. They sought to deliver a "theory of the firm," a matter of no small debate in American business and economic circles ever since the typical major corporation had evolved from an enterprise owned and controlled by its founder to an enterprise where ownership and management had split, stockholders on the one side, hired executives on the other.

Jensen and Meckling filled their paper with academic jargon and formulas that would be unintelligible to the typical corporate executive. But the gist of what they had to say would soon be attracting power-suit attention. Too many executives, their basic narrative maintained, had become too comfortable with the status quo. They had become bureaucrats content to collect their paychecks, bureaucrats unwilling to take any risks that might upset their comfortable apple carts. These executives were essentially ignoring the interests of their company's true owners, the shareholders. Shareholders needed to end this sorry state of affairs—and they could if they started paying much closer attention to compensation incentives. Firms needed to offer incentives that aligned the interests of their hired executive help with shareholder interests.

Stock-based compensation could help achieve this alignment. If corporate boards made stock awards central to executive compensation, executives would have much more incentive to do good by shareholders. Executive and shareholder interests, not to mention the free-enterprise stars above, would then all be favorably aligned.[59]

This new theory seemed designed to generate one rather obvious consequence. Lucrative stock-based incentives would encourage executives to focus their attention on company share price above all else. That would be perfectly appropriate—but only if Corporate America assumed that only shareholders had any valid claim on an executive's attention. American business leaders had traditionally not made that assumption. The modern corporation, they had regularly told Americans, had multiple stakeholders. Robert E. Wood, the illustrious midcentury chief executive at Sears Roebuck, identified these stakeholders as "the customer, the employee, and the stockholder."

"The stockholder comes last, not because he is least important," Wood had gone on to explain, "but because, in the larger sense, he cannot obtain his full measure unless he has satisfied customers and satisfied employees."[60]

The Jensen-Meckling thesis represented a direct assault on this multiple stakeholder vision of the modern American corporation. And this new vision would go down well with American executives chafing under the checks and balances of midcentury middle-class America. Maximize shareholder value above all else? Absolutely! America's corporate executives would buy into the Jensen-Meckling thesis immediately and enthusiastically.

The "maximizing shareholder value" mantra would soon provide cover for the greatest corporate greed grab in American history. In 1976, the year the Jensen-Meckling piece appeared, stock-based compensation totaled less than 1 percent of CEO pay at major American companies. In the 1980s and 1990s, that share skyrocketed, so much so that overall CEO compensation per dollar of net corporate income multiplied eight times over.[61]

This fixation on shareholder value also sped the "financialization" of the US economy. Corporations in the public mind remained enterprises that hired workers to make and market products. For Corporate America's movers and shakers, note analysts Thomas Kochan and Frank Levy, the corporation would now become nothing more than a "bundle of assets" that could be endlessly reconfigured in mergers and leveraged buyouts.[62] All that mattered at the end of the day would be a share price on Wall Street. Those who could raise that share price—by whatever means—would be richly rewarded.

The contrast with the economy of midcentury America could not have been any more fundamental. At midcentury, notes economist

Robert Kuttner, banks and other financial institutions had operated under sets of government regulations that limited Wall Street
to "providing capital to the 'real' part of the economy that produced
goods and services." Mergers did sometimes occur, "but not hostile
takeovers arranged with borrowed money."[63] In the emerging new
economy of the 1970s, wheeling and dealing mergers and acquisitions
would be the only game worth playing. The rewards would be awesome.

Thomas Kochan and Frank Levy have come across some private
correspondence from a former Wall Street banking partner that offers
a bird's-eye view of the enormity of America's economic transformation and the new wealth this transformation created.

"In 1974 as a successful young investment banker with 8 years experience, I was paid less than my peers in the large industrial companies
or utilities and had no benefits of significance," this former partner
wrote. "Everyone left the office at 5:00 o'clock and it was resented if
you tried to come into the office on weekends (doors locked, no staff,
no lights, a/c almost off). By 1985 I was a mid-level partner earning $4
million a year, working 12–14 hour days and frequent weekends, and
the busiest parts of the firm had second shifts of support staff every
day and all weekend."[64]

The same dynamic that made this former partner fabulously rich
would depress the life chances of average workers. Corporations would
merge and then spin off divisions to concentrate on "core competen-
cies" that fetched a stock market premium. Large employers, note
Kochan and Levy, would become smaller employers. Manufacturers
that had offered "stable jobs with high wages" began outsourcing and
creating "second- and third-tier jobs offering lower wages and benefits in supplier firms."[65]

The Jensen-Meckling paper did not cause this surge of "financial
engineering." The first private equity leveraged buyout had taken
place in 1970, six years before their paper appeared.[66] But Jensen and
Meckling's work did give American business a new rallying cry, a
corporate call to arms. Maximize shareholder value. Nothing else
mattered.

The foundation of middle-class America was now cracking. That
foundation rested on progressive taxes and a vital labor presence.
Enlightened elites had supported those taxes in the early postwar

years. They considered high taxes on high incomes crucial to Cold War victory and the nation's continued economic success. By 1970, that enlightened elite consensus on taxes had largely evaporated. Corporate America's commanding heights had also accepted a vital labor presence in those same postwar years. Corporate leaders needed labor peace to be able to produce and prosper. But the Treaty of Detroit now no longer served their interests. Labor had become an albatross. For some strange reason, labor could not seem to understand that only maximizing shareholder value mattered. Labor had to be moved out of the way.

But labor had allies, various enlightened elite leaders who still regarded unions an important and necessary player in America's future. No drive against labor could succeed so long as these enlightened elites stood shoulder to shoulder with labor. But in October 1975 a foundational crack in this alliance suddenly appeared, right under the noses of the national political and chattering classes, at the bastion of everything that seemed good and noble in American liberalism, the celebrated *Washington Post*.

No major media outlet in 1975 enjoyed anything close to the acclaim and respect that liberals held for the *Washington Post*. The paper's relentless crusading had toppled a crooked president only the year before and helped expose a crooked war three years before that with the publication of the Pentagon Papers. Hollywood's brightest stars, Robert Redford and Dustin Hoffman, were even about to portray the *Post*'s Watergate heroics in a major motion picture, *All the President's Men*. On October 1, 1975, the union that represented the paper's two hundred press operators would spoil the paper's party. Members of Pressmen's Local 6 walked out on strike in a job action that almost immediately attracted national attention. The strikers hadn't just walked off the job. They had vandalized, the *Post* charged, millions of dollars of pressroom equipment.

The charge played into the darkest antilabor stereotype imaginable: union thugs on the rampage! The story would remain headline fodder for months. A grand jury investigation, begun two weeks after the strike started, called over one hundred pressmen strikers and wasted away union resources and energy. Nine months later, the grand jury returned fifteen indictments, some on felony charges. Strikers faced as many as forty years in jail.

Few noticed nine additional months later when prosecutors dropped all the felony charges in exchange for guilty pleas on minor misdemeanors. The "millions of dollars" in pressroom vandalism, notes labor journalist Fred Solowey, may have actually been as little as $13,000 in damages.[67] No union rampage had ever taken place, just some isolated outbursts of worker frustration.

And pressmen at the *Post* had plenty to feel frustrated about. The *Post* had once been a model employer, and its owner, Eugene Meyer, had been enormously popular with the paper's unions. In 1951, Pressmen's Local 6 had even inducted him as an honorary member. Meyer had established a profit-sharing plan for *Post* workers, and his son-in-law, Philip Graham, followed in his footsteps. But Meyer's daughter, Katharine Graham, inherited the paper after her husband's death and then took it public in a 1971 Wall Street stock offering. Labor relations at the *Post* would never be the same.

"The first order of business at the *Washington Post*," as Katharine Graham told securities analysts in 1972, "is to maximize profits from our existing operations."

Graham hired a hard-edged labor relations manager, killed the paper's profit-sharing plan, and began to take on the paper's unions, the printers in 1973, the white-collar Newspaper Guild journalists and ad salespeople in 1974. But the big showdown would come in 1975 with the pressmen. The pressmen had always been the paper's labor pacesetter, the first union at the paper, for instance, to win a cost-of-living wage clause. Now Katharine Graham's *Post* moved to set the pace in the opposite direction. With the pressmen's contract deadline approaching, *Post* management made secret arrangements to train strikebreaking workers to replace the union pressmen and keep the presses rolling. Helicopters would ferry these strikebreakers to the *Post* once the strike started.

Management now had no incentive to bargain in good faith. The strikers had no leverage and, after the vandalism episode, no public sympathy. *Post* management made sure of that, hiring the J. Walter Thompson advertising agency to keep the union "vandalism" in the news.

By May 1977, the month all court proceedings finally ended against the indicted pressmen, the proud pressmen's union at the *Post* no longer existed. Three distraught pressmen had attempted suicide. Two survived. One did not. The *Washington Post* had done the unthinkable. The paper had plotted to replace strikers with strikebreakers and successfully busted a striking union. In midcentury middle-class America, responsible employers simply did not replace striking workers. They negotiated with them. The great liberal *Washington Post* had, in effect, redefined "responsible" employer behavior to include union busting.

In August 1981, President Ronald Reagan applied that same definition to striking federal air traffic control operators, members of a conservative union that had, ironically, endorsed his 1980 presidential bid. Reagan gave thirteen thousand striking PATCO air traffic controllers forty-eight hours to end their strike, a walkout that violated a statute against federal worker walkouts that hadn't been enforced in several previous federal worker strike situations. Most strikers ignored Reagan's ultimatum. He fired them.

Two major private sector employers, Phelps Dodge and International Paper, soon followed Reagan's example with their own striking unions, and other employers would take the same union-busting approach. This willingness to replace striking workers, historian Joseph McCartin notes, would reshape "the world of the modern workplace."[68] Strikes would now almost totally disappear from American labor relations. With the loss of "the leverage that strikes once provided," adds McCartin, unions would now be "unable to pressure employers to increase wages as productivity rises."

Organized labor would rail against the PATCO firings. But many of labor's traditional liberal allies would not object. How could they? If the great liberal *Washington Post* could replace strikers, why couldn't Ronald Reagan?

The deterioration of labor's bargaining position in the 1970s reflected more than employer willingness to end run the right to strike. By the 1970s, the long-term consequences of the 1947 antilabor Taft-Hartley Act had also worked a profound transformation. The nation had essentially been split into two, a Northern tier of states where all workers who enjoyed the benefits that union representation provided had to either join their workplace union or pay a service fee and a Southern tier where state lawmakers had taken advantage of the Taft-Hartley provision that enabled states to ban such "union security" agreements.

Conservatives had tried and failed to ban union security arrangements in Northern and West Coast states. But their "right-to-work" victories in the South undercut unions and workers in the North and West almost just as surely. Northern unions now faced a powerful and credible "threat of exit." Either accept wage and benefit concessions at the bargaining table, employers would warn, or lose your union jobs to the nonunion South. Many employers didn't even bother with threats. They just moved South. In the process, the manufacturing base of cities like New York gradually withered away. This base had supported the wide array of quality public services that New York had offered, services that had enabled millions of New Yorkers to lead comfortable middle-class lives. Without this manufacturing base, New York—and other Northern industrial centers—fell into chronic fiscal crisis.

In New York, conservatives blamed the crisis on overpaid public employees and demanded that the city slash public services. Wall Street then piled on. Bankers refused to underwrite the city's debt, and New York slid to the brink of bankruptcy in 1975. City and state political leaders appealed to Washington for short-term federal loan guarantees. Secretary of Treasury William Simon and President Gerald Ford refused. Simon, notes historian Josh Freeman, would put the fault for the city's fiscal predicament on "absurd" public employee salaries and "appalling" pensions. He also objected to city subsidies for "what he termed the middle class: the City University, middle-income housing, rent control, and the like."[69]

In the end, the Ford administration relented on its "drop dead" stance and agreed to $2.3 billion in short-term loans. But the aid package, notes Freeman, stripped "the city government, the municipal labor movement, and working-class New Yorkers of much of the power they had accumulated over the previous three decades."[70] Between 1975 and 1980, the city shed a quarter of its jobs—sixty-three thousand in all—to layoffs and attrition. Public services shriveled. In public schools, class sizes shot up to forty students and more. New York as a middle-class haven would no longer exist.

"Subways and buses not only cost more than before the fiscal crisis, they came less frequently, suffered more service breakdowns, arrived late more frequently, and caused more injuries," writes Freeman. "Service deterioration and fear led riders to switch to automobiles, adding to traffic congestion. On Manhattan side streets, the average speed bogged down to just 4.4 miles an hour. With street resurfacing all but ended, potholes bloomed like flowers in the spring."[71]

The damage would devastate the notion of shared community. The more that public services deteriorated, the more that those who could afford private service alternatives chose them. The public institutions once so "attractive to all sorts of New Yorkers," observes Freeman, "became subnormal institutions of last resort."[72]

By the mid-1970s, average Americans would no longer feel the economic security they had enjoyed in earlier postwar years. Good jobs were vanishing, turning into low-wage positions in the South or even lower-wage jobs abroad. The OPEC oil embargo in 1973 and subsequent oil shocks would send gasoline and other consumer prices on unnerving roller coasters. The nation was now moving in a new direction, back toward the deep economic divides of the plutocratic past.

A desperate labor movement would regroup and try to fight back. The corporate onslaught against unions had stalled new organizing almost totally. Labor leaders now made a stand for the right to organize. They had union-friendly lawmakers put before Congress a package of reforms designed to modernize the National Labor Relations Board and prevent the corporate stonewalls and intimidation tactics that made successful organizing drives so impossibly difficult. The NLRB's own figures told the story. In 1957, the NLRB had ordered employers to reinstate 922 union organizers who had been illegally fired. By the late 1970s, that total had increased tenfold.[73] The labor law reform bill before Congress, labor believed, would reduce that intimidation by increasing penalties for corporate labor law violators.

"We are going to fight harder for this bill," AFL-CIO President George Meany promised, "than any bill since the passage of the Wagner Act."[74]

Labor did fight hard, and the labor law reform legislation flew through the House by a wide margin. But the new, more aggressive business political networks that Lewis Powell had helped inspire earlier in the decade stopped the legislation dead in the Senate. Labor had a majority in the Senate, but not one large enough to break a conservative filibuster. The bill fell two votes short. In June 1978, Democratic supporters of the legislation finally surrendered and let the labor law reform bill fade off to die back in committee. Corporate America had scored a phenomenal victory. Business historian Kim McQuaid would later call 1978 a "Waterloo" for labor.[75]

The description would be apt for more than the outcome of labor law reform. In California just a few weeks before the Senate vote failure, labor had suffered what would be a political defeat perhaps even more crushing. The labor law reform defeat had been an inside job, a sneak attack of sorts by Corporate America that parlayed corporate cash into just enough votes to frustrate the will of a prolabor congressional majority. The forces of resurgent plutocracy had not yet demonstrated any new capacity to score a knockout against labor at the ballot box. In California they would.

Conservatives had already shown they could win state office in California. Ronald Reagan had exploited his celebrity—and public anger at student antiwar demonstrators—to get himself elected governor in 1966. Along the way, Reagan had exploited America's racial divide as well. He campaigned with a pledge to repeal the state's fair housing act. As Reagan told voters: "If an individual wants to discriminate against Negroes or others in selling or renting his house, he has a right to do so."[76]

Reagan later became a more sophisticated player of the race card. "Welfare queens" would replace rationalizations for discrimination. But the conservative cause dearest to Reagan would always be opposition to progressive taxation. As a Hollywood star during World War II, Reagan had faced the 94 percent top marginal rate on income over $200,000. He didn't like it. He would spend the postwar years denouncing high taxes on the rich as a Communist plot.

"The originator of this system of taxation, Karl Marx, said you should use progressive taxation to tax the middle class out of existence," Reagan charged in the early 1960s, "because you can't have socialism where you have a strong middle class."[77]

Claptrap like this would have movement conservatives in California swooning, but failed to connect at all with California's vast middle class. If conservatives were going to advance on the tax front, they would need a pitch that could resonate far more reasonably with their middle-class targets. The "stagflation" of the 1970s gave conservatives an opportunity to make this new pitch. Average Californians, just like average Americans, were watching their paychecks stagnate after years of regular pay hikes. At the same time, rising inflation was pushing them into ever higher tax brackets. The conservative answer, Proposition 13, promised relief. Need more spending money to get your family by? Get the taxman out of your pocket, conservatives urged. Limit the government's ability to raise your taxes.

The Prop 13 ballot initiative that went before voters in 1978 aimed to roll back and freeze property taxes. That sounded good to the vast majority of Californians. They passed Prop 13 by a two-to-one margin. Prop 13's biggest beneficiaries would prove to be large corporate property owners like Standard Oil of California. Average homeowners would see some savings but far more losses in public services. California's public school system rated near the nation's top before Prop 13. After Prop 13, the state's schools plummeted almost to the bottom.[78]

But that didn't matter to movement conservatives like the young Grover Norquist, who tasted sweet victory in the Prop 13 campaign.[79] In an emerging new America where employers weren't putting particularly much into the pockets of average Americans, railing against government for pulling too much out could be a potent political strategy.

Norquist and his fellow movement conservatives watched Prop 13 ignite a "tax revolt" all across the United States. Over the next two years, states and cities would enact a variety of "tax limitations" and tax cuts. In Washington, a Carter administration legislative package originally designed to simplify the tax code and end egregious tax loopholes that benefited the rich would be turned by late 1978 into an expansion of the preferential treatment for capital gains. Republicans suddenly felt "emboldened," Republican staff aide Bruce Bartlett would later write, "by their ability to force a Democratic president and Congress to enact what was essentially a conservative tax bill." Suitably encouraged, Republicans would "press on with more radical tax reduction efforts," namely a bill introduced the year before to chop income tax rates across the board, including a cut in the top tax rate from 70 to 50 percent.[80]

With their victories on the tax-cut front, movement conservatives had demonstrated that they could collect votes in a stagnant America. Corporate America had demonstrated a powerful inside-the-Beltway game in the labor law reform battle. These two forces would unite behind Ronald Reagan in the 1980 presidential election and score a blowout victory, the first of many over the next three decades.

In 1981 Congress would give the newly elected Reagan a tax bill that cut the top rate on America's wealthy from 70 to 50 percent. In 1986, Congress would lower the top rate to 28 percent, only three points higher than the top rate Andrew Mellon had celebrated in the 1920s.

"With the tax cuts of 1981 and 1986," Ronald Reagan would later write, "I'd accomplished a lot of what I'd come to Washington to do."[81]

Chapter Thirteen

WHAT IF THE RICH NEVER STOP GETTING RICHER?

Ronald Reagan may have thought his work complete after the top income-bracket tax rate shriveled to 28 percent in 1986. But his cheer-leaders from America's corporate executive suites and the ranks of movement conservatives most definitely felt otherwise. They had estate taxes to repeal and capital gains taxes to eliminate. They had IRS auditors and federal workplace safety inspectors to ax away. They had New Deal financial regulations to dismantle. They had a labor movement to marginalize. They had, in short, a plutocracy to restore.

Over the next quarter century, these drum majors for grand fortune would complete this plutocratic restoration. The early twenty-first century would begin just as the previous century had begun, with astounding quantities of wealth and power concentrated at America's economic summit. Indeed, by some yardsticks the ultra rich of the early twenty-first century had outpaced their predecessors. In 1913, the year the modern federal income tax kicked in, the nation's richest 0.1 percent of households collected 8.6 percent of the nation's income. In 2007, the year the US economy began to crumble, this super rich sliver totaled half again as much, a 12.3 percent share.[1]

The even more striking contrast: In 1970—at the depth of plutoc-racy's slumber during the middle-class golden age—this same top 0.1 percent had grabbed only 2.8 percent of the nation's personal income. America's richest had essentially quadrupled their share of the nation's income over the last third of the twentieth century. Those who led the corporate empires of midcentury had been comfortably affluent. Those who led the same empires at century's end would be fantastically rich.

Hints of this plutocratic restoration would sometimes surface in the unlikeliest of places. In 2011, for instance, the game show *Jeopardy!* would draw record ratings as two former human champs on the program squared off against an IBM computer named "Watson" that had been engineered to understand and answer natural-language questions.

Why name the computer Watson? The machine's namesake, Thomas Watson, had put IBM together in the 1920s. Thomas Jr. took over in 1956. He retired 15 years later, then died in 1993, leaving behind a family fortune worth $127 million.[2] A hefty sum to be sure, but no more than the haul one of the Watson CEO successors at IBM would take home from the company for just one single year of executive labor. In 2001, IBM chief Lou Gerstner pulled in $127 million.[3]

This $127 million "coincidence" could have made an interesting puzzler for Watson the computer: How could the founding family of IBM, after 70 years at the top of the high-tech industry, end up with a fortune no bigger than the compensation IBM CEO Gerstner took home in just one year? Watson the computer probably wouldn't have been able to explain the vast gap between the rewards that the Watsons reaped and the much grander payoff that poured into Gerstner's pockets. We can.

In the mid-twentieth century, the Watsons and other top executives operated in an environment where stiff taxes and strong unions had created an economic and political culture that frowned on vast accumulations of private wealth. That culture kept even the grandest rewards relatively modest and subjected those modest rewards to steep taxes. In 1941, IBM patriarch Thomas Watson ranked as the nation's third-highest-paid corporate executive. He reported $572,746 in total income on his federal tax return, about $8.7 million in today's dollars. His net income after federal taxes: $146,363. Watson's effective tax rate: 74.4 percent.[4]

In the early twenty-first century, Lou Gerstner's generation of corporate and financial executives faced no such economic and political restraints. In 2010, the third-highest-paid corporate executive in the United States, TRW Automotive CEO John Plant, claimed $76.8 million in corporate compensation.[5] We don't know how much of his total income Plant paid in taxes in 2010. We do know from IRS data that taxpayers making over $10 million the year before paid just 24.1 percent of their incomes in federal income tax, less than a third the effective tax rate levied on Thomas Watson.[6]

The rewards and tender tax treatment that top corporate executives today take as a matter of course would no doubt have astounded IBM's Watson father and son. But corporate executives like Lou Gerstner and John Plant often consider themselves undercompensated and overtaxed. They do have cause to feel that way. Their paydays pale against the rewards that routinely cascade into the pockets of America's top financial industry movers and shakers. In 2009, top managers in the hedge fund industry had to make $350 million just to *enter* the ranks of the industry's twenty-five highest-paid superstars. The year's top twenty-five hedge fund managers averaged $1.01 billion. Each.[7] And the bulk of that income faced a mere 15 percent tax rate, the going twenty-first century tax rate for capital gains.

How did the hedge fund industry's top actors ever do so well in the midst of the Great Recession? Many of the year's top hedge fund "performers" had essentially bet that the federal government would bail out the reckless Wall Street bankers who had crashed the nation's economy in 2008. That proved to be a safe bet, given the mammoth sums of campaign cash these same reckless bankers and hedge fund managers had invested in lawmakers and the many alumni and friends of Wall Street who populated the government offices most pivotally positioned to impact federal financial policy.

Plutocracy at work. Plutocracy once again triumphant.

In the 1950s and 1960s, no serious students of American history ever dared imagine a plutocratic restoration. Midcentury historians lived during a middle-class golden age that seemed an irreversible step in America's grand march to an ever more perfect democracy. In the early twenty-first century, students of history reconsidered that vision of democracy on the march. Had America's middle-class golden age, they began asking, been a historical fluke, an exceptionally fortuitous turn of events never likely to be repeated?

Plutocracy, analysts even began speculating, may well be America's default state. Progressives in the 1970s and 1980s, Cornell University historian Jefferson Cowie would note in the early twenty-first century, waited patiently "for a return to what they regarded as the normality of the New Deal order." They never understood that this New Deal–infused order in no way represented industrial America's "normal" state. The middle-class golden age may have actually amounted to no more than a chance "interregnum between Gilded Ages."[8]

A set of unique and unrepeatable historical circumstances, the new historical analysis of mid-twentieth-century America continued, had created the space for a brief middle-class moment. A world war had nurtured an enormous demand for revenue that enabled progressives to realize startlingly high tax rates on high incomes. The Great Depression had almost totally discredited America's rich and their ideologies and opened the door for massive trade union renewal. And only the United States had escaped World War II's massive destruction.

Without these special circumstances, would America's middle-class golden age have even been imaginable? Would America's postwar corporate powers-that-be have been willing to sign the Treaty of Detroit and pay middle-class wages if they faced more challenging global competition? And what if the United States had not faced in the Soviet Union a rival social system that portrayed vast concentrations of wealth and power as inevitable under capitalism? Would elite reformers still have supported high taxes on high incomes?

These what-ifs plausibly suggest that America's middle-class golden age rested on a series of highly unusual shocks to the nation's economic and political system. In the absence of these shocks, America's rich might well have maintained their overriding dominance. Plutocracy might have survived.

But we can also make a plausible case—with a contrasting set of what-ifs—that a middle-class golden age might have emerged even without the striking shocks of war and depression and rival social system. What if World War I had never come along and incited a fierce repression that split apart America's broad and energetic socialist movement? Or what if Henry Wallace had remained vice president after 1944 and succeeded Franklin Roosevelt after FDR's death in 1945? What if Wallace's diplomacy had prevented the Cold War and kept anti-Communist hysteria at bay? What if a united CIO, unhobbled by red-scare purges, had been able to wage a relentless postwar campaign on behalf of FDR's 1944 "economic bill of rights"? Might the midcentury golden age have glowed even brighter—and longer?

We could, of course, go on forever with what-ifs. "Counterfactual" history—the formal label for what-if exercises—can make for engrossing intellectual parlor games. But in the end no string of what-ifs can help us predict with any certainty how America's midcentury future would have played out without war and depression.

What-if questions that look *to the future*, on the other hand, make more sense to ask. What if we here in the United States today continue along on our present economic trajectory? What if our rich continue to grab and keep an ever-larger share of America's wealth? What kind of nation will we have then?

This question we *can* answer with a high degree of certainty. A more unequal America would be more nasty, brutish, and short—by every measure. How can we be so certain? Our certainty comes from a generation of social science research on the impact of inequality on every significant aspect of our modern lives, from our health to our happiness, research surveyed powerfully in *The Spirit Level: Why More Equal Societies Almost Always Do Better*, the widely acclaimed 2010 book by the British epidemiologists Richard Wilkinson and Kate Pickett. Inequality, Wilkinson and Pickett help us understand, melts away the social glue that keeps societies cohesive and civil. "More unequal societies," they write, "are harsher, tougher places."[9]

In such societies, social distances between people widen, attitudes of "us" and "them" become more entrenched, trust withers. Rates of mental illness, Wilkinson and Pickett note, run five times higher in the world's more unequal developed societies. In these societies, they add, people "are five times as likely to be imprisoned, six times as likely to be clinically obese."

"The reason why these differences are so big," the two social scientists go on to explain, "is, quite simply, because the effects of inequality are not confined just to the least well-off; instead, they affect the vast majority of the population."[10]

The United States currently exhibits more inequality than any of its peer developed nations. But other nations outside this circle of privilege—from Southern Africa to South America—tolerate more inequality than does the United States. In these nations, the rich live in private compounds behind high walls. They commute by helicopter and only venture onto roads in armored luxury cars. Some cosmetic surgeons in these hyper unequal societies specialize in ear reconstruction.[11] The reason: Kidnappers include cut-off ears with the ransom notes they send their wealthy victims.

The American people never voted for a return to plutocracy. The vast majority of Americans would prefer to live in a society that shares wealth much more equally than the present-day United States. In fact, most Americans would prefer to live in a society that distributes wealth much more like Sweden, the nation that year after year ranks as one of the world's most equal. Harvard Business School scholar Michael Norton and his Duke University Business School colleague Dan Ariely have documented this preference in recent research.[12] The pair examined what Americans know—and feel—about their nation's wealth and its distribution.

Americans, their research found, *feel* that the nation's richest 20 percent ought to own no more than 32 percent of the nation's wealth. Americans *believe*, the research also found, that this richest 20 percent currently holds about twice that much, a 59 percent share of the nation's wealth. In reality, note Norton and Ariely, America's richest 20 percent actually hold 84 percent of US wealth.

Norton and Ariely gave the broad cross sample of Americans they surveyed a set of wealth distribution pie graphics. One graphic displayed the actual distribution of wealth in the United States, with an 84 percent slice going to the richest 20 percent. Another displayed the Swedish distribution. Sweden's top 20 percent own 36 percent of that nation's wealth. A third graph showed a perfectly equal distribution of wealth, with each 20 percent of the population holding 20 percent of the society's wealth. Norton and Ariely left the US and Swedish pies unidentified by country name and asked the Americans in their research sample to indicate which wealth distribution pie they preferred. A stunning 92 percent of Americans chose the more equal Swedish distribution over the distinctly less equal American distribution. Perhaps even more stunning: Over three-quarters of Americans—77 percent—chose the totally equal distribution pie over the pie that reflected the actual and distinctly unequal US wealth distribution.

Other researchers have found that Americans oppose, by substantial margins, those public policies that would move the United States in an ever more plutocratic direction. Americans clearly want to live in a middle-class society, a society with no extremes, no desperately poor and no excessively wealthy. But they don't have one, and that reality, the nation's most astute pollsters are finding, has left the American people deeply cynical about politics.

How cynical? Veteran Democratic Party pollster Stanley Greenberg surveyed voters on the evening of the November 2010 Republican electoral sweep and found overwhelming opposition to basic conservative policy positions. Americans wanted more investments in public infrastructure, not austerity budget cuts. They opposed across-the-board tax cuts that would lower the taxes rich people pay. Greenberg also found that voters considered Democrats "more likely to champion the middle class."[13]

So how could Republicans sweep to victory? The follow-up focus groups that Greenberg conducted found that voters had come to "tune out" the policy positions they heard Democrats—and Republicans as well, for that matter—espousing. "It's just words," Greenberg heard from voters, just words from both parties.

"We don't have a representative government anymore," American voters told him. "There's just such a control of government by the wealthy that whatever happens, it's not working for all the people; it's working for a few of the people."

A government that works only for the wealthy few. The classic textbook definition of plutocracy.

Plutocracies rest upon cynicism, upon a deep-rooted sense that what we do as average people doesn't matter, that the rich always get richer. Until September 2011 this cynicism seemed to ensure that our plutocracy would continue to prosper at the expense of what remained of America's middle class.

But the Occupy Wall Street movement that began unfolding in September 2011 has begun shattering that cynicism, particularly among younger Americans. Occupy has raised hopes. More and more Americans appear to feel that things *can* change. But what things most need changing? What do we need to do to create a society that works for the 99 percent? We were moving rapidly toward that sort of society in midcentury America. How can we get back on that trajectory? Should we just retrace the footsteps of our egalitarian forebears?

Our predecessors struggled mightily over the first half of the twentieth century—some even perishing in the process—to build a labor movement powerful enough to level up millions of Americans into the middle class. They struggled just as earnestly to put in place progressive tax rates that leveled the super rich down to democratic size. If we renewed their struggles and won, would we have done enough to beat back plutocracy once and for all?

In a broad sense, yes. We have developed nations in the world today considerably more equal economically than we are. Not one of these developed nations has a weaker labor movement than the United States. Not one of these nations has a tax system friendlier to the super rich than the United States. Strong labor unions and progressive taxation provided the foundation for America's midcentury middle-class golden age. Unions and progressive taxes will be no less central to a more egalitarian future.

But that doesn't mean we today need the *same* unions or the *same* progressive tax system that graced the middle-class golden age.

Most unions back in midcentury America, particularly after the Cold War purge of left activists, much too closely mimicked the corporations that employed the workers they represented. Unions too often operated internally as self-perpetuating hierarchies. They made little effort to actively engage, inform, and inspire rank-and-file workers. Nationally and locally, they became hollow shells. Their leaders would seldom put forward visions bold enough to move America forward. Midcentury unions would prove unable to effectively resist those who sought to drive America back.

The future demands unions that won't repeat those mistakes, and many labor leaders today seem to understand that imperative.

The future also demands a bolder approach to progressive taxation. We need to acknowledge that steeply graduated tax rates as traditionally structured have not demonstrated any appreciable staying power. No nation has been able to maintain top-bracket tax rates at 90 or even 70 percent for any sustained period of time. One likely reason: These high rates give the rich no incentive whatever to do anything but seek to avoid taxes by whatever means necessary. They will tunnel loopholes in the tax code. They will conceal income and wealth in overseas shelters. They will buy enough lawmaker votes to rewrite the tax code and lower the top rates.

This reality prompts many policymakers to reject high tax rates altogether. If we lowered the highest tax rates on the rich, the argument goes, the rich would give up their tax-avoiding and tax-evading ways. They would have no need to hatch loophole schemes or corrupt lawmakers. This thesis drove the 1986 tax cut debate and deal. Lawmakers would end up cutting the tax rate on top-bracket income from 50 to 28 percent and abolishing assorted loopholes—most notably the preferential treatment for capital gains income—all in one fell swoop.

This reform turned out to be a disaster for progressive taxation and the campaign against tax evasion. The big loopholes almost all reappeared in the tax code. In 1997, with a Democrat as president, the tax rate on capital gains shrank to what was then an all-time low of 20 percent, then shrank even lower, to 15 percent, under a Republican president in 2003. And more new loopholes would be added. Dividend income would in 2003 get the same preferential treatment as capital gains. In the meantime, the tax rate on income in the nation's top tax bracket remained low, jumping to 39.6 percent under Bill Clinton, but falling back to 35 percent under George W. Bush in 2003.

And tax evasion? The IRS would do one major study on 2001 income and tax returns, then another on 2006 income and tax returns. Between these years, the statutory tax rates on high income fell. But tax evasion between 2001 and 2006 actually increased. In 2001, $290 billion in individual and business taxes due went uncollected. In 2006, $385 billion.[14] The rich, this history helps show, don't like paying taxes when tax rates run high. They don't like paying taxes when rates run low either. To update that old adage. We can count on only three certainties in this life: death, taxes, and resistance by the rich to any taxes, high or low, that our societies expect them to pay.

Can we ever possibly structure a progressive tax system to reduce this resistance? Can we fashion a progressive tax approach that gives the 99 percent a greater incentive to push back against those rich who keep resisting? We can.

We could start where midcentury America left off—with a 91 percent tax rate on income in the top tax bracket. For most of the 1950s this 91 percent rate kicked in at $400,000. The 91 percent rate applied only to the income on joint returns above that level. The rich seethed in response. They cheated on their tax returns. They endeavored to corrupt politicians. They saw no other way to hang on to more of their income. But what if we gave the rich an out, an opportunity to keep more of their income without having to play games to escape a stiff top tax rate? Suppose, for instance, that we set the entry threshold for our new 91 percent *maximum* tax rate as a multiple of our nation's *minimum* wage. For argument's sake, let's place that multiple at twenty-five times, the ratio between CEO and typical worker pay for much of the mid-twentieth century.

The federal minimum wage in 2012 stood at $7.25 an hour. A couple working at minimum wage jobs for an entire year would earn an annual income just over $30,000. Twenty-five times that $30,000 would equal $750,000. If the entry threshold for America's top tax bracket sat linked to the minimum wage, wealthy taxpayers in this new $750,000-and-up tax bracket would have a new incentive. If the nation's minimum wage rose, their tax bill would sink. If the minimum wage rose to ten dollars an hour, a top tax bracket keyed to twenty-five times the minimum wage would begin at just over $1 million, not $750,000.

If our tax code tied our maximum tax rate to the minimum wage, the wealthy would be able to keep ever more money in their pockets so long as the minimum wage kept rising. The wealthiest and most powerful people in society would, in effect, have a vested interest in enhancing the well being of society's poorest and weakest. We would be encouraging, via this linkage, what amounts to a solidarity economy. In our current plutocratic economy, the rich routinely get richer exploiting the poor. In a solidarity economy that tied maximum tax rates to minimum wages, the rich would regularly "get richer"—that is, pay less in taxes—only if they became advocates for society's poorest.

Other approaches could point us toward this same solidarity principle. Hugo Black, the great Supreme Court justice of the mid-twentieth century, suggested one such approach when he served as a US senator in the early years of the Great Depression. In 1932, as these pages earlier detailed, Black sought to limit corporate executive pay by leveraging the power of the public purse. In 1933, he moved successfully through the Senate legislation to deny federal bailout loans to companies that paid their executives over $17,500 a year, about $300,000 today. The New Deal never embraced the Black perspective. We could now. We could deny federal bailouts and contracts and tax breaks to any companies that pay their top executives over a reasonable fixed multiple of what their workers are making.

We already deny our tax dollars to companies with employment practices that discriminate against women and people of color. We have decided, as a society, that our tax dollars must not subsidize greater gender and racial inequality. Why should we let our tax dollars subsidize economic inequality?

Congress has actually already laid in place one building block for this approach to plutocrat busting. The Dodd-Frank financial reform legislation enacted in 2010 requires corporations to annually publish the ratio between the compensation of their top executives and their median workers. Corporate lobbyists asleep at the switch let this precedent-setting provision slip into the Dodd-Frank bill at the eleventh hour. Those same lobbyists have been battling ever since to prevent this pay-ratio disclosure mandate from going into effect. The labor movement has been leading the campaign to save ratio disclosure. "Large pay disparities within a company," AFL-CIO President Richard Trumka told the federal Securities and Exchange Commission in 2011, undermine everything from workplace "morale and productivity" to "teamwork, loyalty, and motivation."[15]

A half century ago, AFL-CIO President George Meany offered virtually no resistance at all when the Kennedy administration labeled tax cuts for the rich an appropriate path to a healthy economy. Labor's current leadership seems intent on not making that same error. Excessive rewards that flow to the top, today's top labor leadership understands, endanger us all.

But has the horse already left the barn? Have we allowed plutocracy to regain too entrenched a foothold? Has our polity been so corrupted by grand concentrations of private wealth that dislodging our contemporary plutocrats from their privileged perches will take a shock to the system too ugly to even imagine? Something comparable to the Great Depression? Or another world war?

Or, as sociologist Michael Schwalbe asks, can we create "cultures of solidarity" in the absence of intense crisis?

If a society rigged to favor privilege is running smoothly enough, Schwalbe acknowledges, those exploited by it will typically adapt themselves. The exploited will lack "the energy and the will to overcome social inertia." Our current rigged society is obviously not running smoothly. But is Great Recession America not running smoothly enough? Do our hard times have to get significantly harder before plutocracy feels any need to tremble? Schwalbe doesn't think so. We can, he believes, "create conditions that help cultures of solidarity to emerge" by helping people gain a better understanding of how "existing social arrangements" actually work. People who gain this new understanding may become "more inclined to see a need to create new arrangements, rather than just complain, when their dissatisfaction rises."[16]

The Occupy movement is endeavoring to build this understanding. That work, to be sure, still remains at the earliest of stages. We have a long way to travel before we reach the level of understanding that stirred so many millions of Americans over the first half of the twentieth century. But we have an easier way to travel. They never knew for sure whether a complex, modern society could topple hierarchies of wealth and privilege and prosper. We today, by contrast, have their history to look back on. And that history teaches a valuable lesson: The rich don't always win. We *can* create a significantly more equal society. We also know we must.

ACKNOWLEDGMENTS

I owe some hearty thanks to a good number of people who helped make this book possible. One person sadly won't be around to get those thanks. Ward Morehouse passed away just as I was completing these pages. Back in 1990 Ward came across a piece I'd done about capping income in an obscure political magazine and asked if I would consider expanding the article into a book for the publishing house he ran. That would be the start of a fruitful partnership that spanned two books on income and wealth maldistribution and the launch of a newsletter devoted to exposing excess and inequality. None of these efforts would likely have materialized if Ward had never reached out and made that initial contact.

In 1992, the first book Ward asked me to write ended up on a bookstore shelf in Massachusetts. A young social justice activist by the name of Chuck Collins saw it and asked if we could talk. Another new relationship. This one is still going strong. Chuck has become one of the wisest observers of all things inequality-related and a master political strategist. I remain inspired by his energy and the depth of his insights.

Through Chuck, I ended up a few years ago hooking up with researchers and activists at the Institute for Policy Studies in Washington, DC. I've learned so much from Sarah Anderson and Scott Klinger and everyone else at the Institute who supports the work of our inequality team. A special thanks to John Cavanagh, the IPS director. John's enthusiasm for the history chapter in the last book on inequality I did, *Greed and Good: Understanding and Overcoming the Inequality that Limits Our Lives*, helped light the fires that led to this book.

John actually read *Greed and Good* before I joined the Institute. He received his copy from Mark Simon, a former social studies teacher extraordinaire who's now a national leader on progressive education policy. Mark and I have been part of a circle of DC-area activists who've supported each other since we all first met in the mid-1970s. At that time, we all thought we'd spend our lives building on the achievements of the sixties. We never dreamed we would spend the next three dozen years playing defense. To all this crew, my deepest appreciation for keeping me focused and refreshed.

I've only known the crew at Seven Stories Press for a much shorter time. They've kept me focused, too, especially on deadlines. I value their suggestions and their nudges.

Finally, family. To Nancy Leibold, the first reader of these pages, thanks so much for going above and beyond. To Nick and Ixchel, thanks for the patience you show and the pleasure you bring. And to Karabelle, my life partner since 1967, all credit goes. Always.

NOTES

Introduction

1. Frederick Lewis Allen, *The Big Change: America Transforms Itself, 1900–1950* (New York: Harper & Brothers, 1952), 27.
2. Stuart Chase, *The Most Probable World* (New York: Harper & Row, 1968), 8.
3. Stuart Chase, *Live and Let Live: A Program for Americans* (New York: Harper & Brothers, 1960), 30.
4. Chase, *Live and Let Live*, 29.
5. Kenneth Lamott, *The Moneymakers: The Great Big New Rich in America* (Boston, MA: Little, Brown and Company, 1969), 294.
6. Lamott, *The Moneymakers*, 306.
7. We follow here the pioneering work of economists Emmanuel Saez and Thomas Piketty. See their "Income Inequality in the United States, 1913–1998," *Quarterly Journal of Economics* 118, no. 1 (2003), 1–39. See also a longer, updated version published in A. B. Atkinson and T. Piketty, eds., *Top Incomes Over the Twentieth Century: A Contrast between European and English-Speaking Countries* (New York: Oxford University Press, 2007). Tables and figures updated to 2010 in Excel format (March 2012), http://elsa.berkeley.edu/~saez/TabFig2010.xls.
8. C. Wright Mills, *The Power Elite* (New York: Oxford University Press, 1956), 148.
9. Simon Kuznets, "Economic Growth and Income Inequality," *American Economic Review*, March 1955.
10. Saez and Piketty, "Income Inequality in the United States."
11. *The 400 Individual Income Tax Returns Reporting the Highest Adjusted Gross Incomes Each Year, 1992–2007* (Washington, DC: Internal Revenue Service), http://www.irs.gov/pub/irs-soi/07intop400.pdf.
12. The IRS has not published official data on the top four hundred for any year before 1992. But a comparable tally, for 1955's top 427, appears in Janet McCubbin and Fritz Scheuren, "Individual Income Tax Shares and Average Tax Rates, 1951–1986," *Statistics of Income Bulletin* (Spring 1989).
13. David Leonhardt, "2 Candidates, 2 Fortunes, 2 Views of Wealth," *New York Times*, December 23, 2007.
14. Leonhardt, "2 Candidates, 2 Fortunes, 2 Views of Wealth."
15. "'Soaking Rich' Opposed," *Los Angeles Times*, November 21, 1925.
16. Edward Folliard, "Robinson Raps Higher Levy on Large Incomes," *Washington Post*, November 22, 1931.
17. "Historical Individual Income Tax Parameters," Tax Policy Center, January 19, 2011, http://www.taxpolicycenter.org/taxfacts/displayafact.cfm?DocID=543&Topic2id=30&Topic3id=38.
18. These figures, to be exact, cover 1961's top 398. See McCubbin and Scheuren, "Individual Income Tax Shares and Average Tax Rates."

19. *The 400 Individual Income Tax Returns Reporting the Highest Adjusted Gross Incomes Each Year,* 1992–2009 (Washington, DC: Internal Revenue Service, June 6, 2012), http://www.irs.gov/pub/irs-soi/09intop400.pdf.
20. Herbert Pell, "A Contented Bourgeois," *North American Review* (Summer 1938).
21. Denis Brian, *Pulitzer: A Life* (New York: John Wiley & Sons, 2001), 1.
22. Robert Kuttner, *The Squandering of America: How the Failure of Our Politics Undermine Our Prosperity* (New York: Alfred A. Knopf, 2007), 47.
23. Steven Hill, *Europe's Promise: Why the European Way Is the Best Hope in an Insecure Age* (Berkeley: University of California Press, 2010), 92.
24. Hill, *Europe's Promise,* 365.
25. Kuttner, *The Squandering of America,* 4.
26. Michael Perelman, *The Confiscation of American Prosperity: From Right-Wing Extremism and Economic Ideology to the Next Great Depression* (New York: Palgrave Macmillan, 2007), 120.
27. Nicholas Kristof, "Pay Teachers More," *New York Times,* March 12, 2011.
28. "America's Billion-Dollar-a-Year Men," *Too Much,* Institute for Policy Studies (April 2, 2011), http://toomuchonline.org/americas-billion-dollar-a-year-men/.
29. Sylvia Allegretto, "The State of Working America's Wealth, 2011," Economic Policy Institute (March 23, 2011), http://www.epi.org/publications/entry/the_state_of_working_americas_wealth_2011.
30. Jim Hightower, "Rich Lawmakers Take Country Back by Making Wealthy Even Wealthier," *Lubbock Avalanche-Journal,* March 26, 2011, http://lubbockonline.com/columnists/2011-03-26/hightower-rich-lawmakers-take-country-back-making-wealthy-even-wealthier.
31. Peter Whoriskey and Michael Fletcher, "Michigan First to Act as States Weigh Reductions in Unemployment Benefits," *Washington Post,* March 24, 2011.
32. Michael Fletcher, "GOP Revamps State, Local Agendas," *Washington Post,* March 25, 2011.
33. "Compromise Agreement on Taxes," Tax Policy Center, http://www.taxpolicycenter.org/taxtopics/Compromise_Agreement_Taxes.cfm.
34. William Greider, "The End of New Deal Liberalism," *Nation,* January 24, 2011.

Chapter 1

1. John Hay, "Hay to Adams, Cleveland, October 20, 1896," in *Letters of John Hay and Extracts from Diary, Volume III,* ed. Alexander Goldstein (Washington, DC, 1908), http://www.archive.org/stream/extractsjohnhay03jhayrich/extractsjohnhay03jhayrich_djvu.txt.
2. Ezra Klein, "The Most Expensive Election Ever," *Washington Post,* March 12, 2012, http://www.washingtonpost.com/blogs/ezra-klein/post/the-most-expensive-election-ever/2011/08/25/gIQA9rtZsR_blog.html. The piece cites the work of political scientist Seth Masket.
3. R. F. Pettigrew, *Triumphant Plutocracy: The Story of American Public Life from 1870 to 1920* (New York: The Academy Press, 1922), 251.
4. William F. Warde [George Novack], "A Forgotten Fighter Against Plutocracy," *Fourth International* (February 1949), http://www.marxists.org/archive/novack/works/1949/feb/x01.htm.
5. Pettigrew, *Triumphant Plutocracy,* 78.
6. Pettigrew, *Triumphant Plutocracy,* 23.
7. Pettigrew, *Triumphant Plutocracy,* 118.
8. Pettigrew, *Triumphant Plutocracy,* 301–305.
9. Milford Wriarson Howard, *The American Plutocracy* (New York: Holland Publishing Company, 1895).
10. John C. Reed, *The New Plutocracy* (New York: Abbey Press, 1903), 365.
11. Henry George, *Progress and Poverty* (Library of Economics and Liberty, 1879; repr. Garden City, NY: Doubleday, 1912), http://www.econlib.org/library/YPDBooks/George/grgPP.html.
12. Alanna Hartzok, "In the History of Thought: Henry George's Single Tax," Earth Rights Institute, 2003, http://www.earthrights.net/docs/singletax.html.

13. Reed, *The New Plutocracy*, 365.
14. *The Prosperity Paradox: The Economic Wisdom of Henry George—Rediscovered*, ed. Mark Hassed (Canterbury, Victoria: Chatsworth Village, 2000), 160–161.
15. Alan Dawley, *Struggles for Justice: Social Responsibility and the Liberal State* (Cambridge, MA: Harvard University Press, 1991), 43.
16. Joseph Thorndike, "A Century of Soaking the Rich: The Origins of the Federal Estate Tax," Tax Analysts Tax History Project, July 10, 2006, http://goo.gl/6JzNR/.
17. M. Susan Murnane, "Andrew Mellon's Unsuccessful Attempt to Repeal Estate Taxes," Tax Analysts Tax History Project, August 22, 2005, http://goo.gl/jHAq5.
18. C. Wright Mills, *The Power Elite* (New York: Oxford University Press, 1956), 101.
19. Jack Beatty, *Age of Betrayal: The Triumph of Money in America, 1865–1900* (New York: Alfred A. Knopf, 2007), 7.
20. Otis Pease, ed., *The Progressive Years: The Spirit and Achievement of American Reform* (New York: George Braziller, 1962), 13.
21. Kevin Phillips, "How Wealth Defines Power," *American Prospect*, May 1, 2003.
22. Pease, *The Progressive Years*, 4.
23. Pease, *The Progressive Years*, 37.
24. Pease, *The Progressive Years*, 40.
25. Estes Kefauver, *In a Few Hands: Monopoly Power in America* (New York: Pantheon Books, 1965), 160–161.
26. Melvin Urofsky, *Louis D. Brandeis: A Life* (New York: Pantheon Books, 2009), 158.
27. Urofsky, *Louis D. Brandeis*, 157–161.
28. William Vickroy Marshall, *A Curb to Predatory Wealth* (New York: R. F. Fenno & Company, 1909), 53.
29. Marshall, *A Curb to Predatory Wealth*, 54.
30. Gustavus Myers, *History of the Great American Fortunes, Volume I* (Chicago: Charles H. Kerr & Company, 1910), iii.
31. Lawrence Mitchell, *The Speculation Economy: How Finance Triumphed Over Industry* (San Francisco: Berrett-Koehler Publishers, Inc., 2007), 9.
32. Mitchell, *The Speculation Economy*, 2.
33. Mitchell, *The Speculation Economy*, 9.
34. Mitchell, *The Speculation Economy*, 47.
35. Mitchell, *The Speculation Economy*, 90–91.
36. Mills, *The Power Elite*, 112.
37. Urofsky, *Louis D. Brandeis*, 302.
38. Louis Dembitz Brandeis, *Other People's Money: And How the Bankers Use It* (New York: Frederick A. Stokes, 1914), 23.
39. Dawley, *Struggles for Justice*, 144.
40. Mitchell, *The Speculation Economy*, 105.
41. Urofsky, *Louis D. Brandeis*, 302.
42. David Nasaw, *Andrew Carnegie* (New York: Penguin Press, 2006), 587. Nasaw, using gross national product as an inflation-adjusting measure, actually puts the value today at nearly $140 billion. We use a consumer price index extrapolation here. See http://www.measuringworth.com/index.php.
43. Howard, *The American Plutocracy*, 59.
44. *Final Report of The Commission on Industrial Relations* (Washington, DC, August 23, 1915), http://goo.gl/MKXkH.
45. *Final Report of The Commission on Industrial Relations*.
46. "Setting the Stage," ParkNet, National Park Service, http://www.nps.gov/nr/twhp/wwwlps/lessons/78vanderbilt/78setting.htm.
47. Frederick Lewis Allen, *The Big Change: America Transforms Itself, 1900–1950* (New York: Harper & Brothers, 1952), 36.
48. Larry Samuel, *Rich: The Rise and Fall of American Wealth Culture* (New York: Amacom, 2009), 54.
49. Mark Stevens, "The Rich Were Different a Century Ago, They Really Knew How to Spend Money," *New York Magazine*, January 15, 2007.
50. Diana Shaman, "Next Role for Otto Kahn's 126-Room Mansion: A Spa," *New York Times*, January 4, 1998.

51. Edward Moss, "In the Ring for a Million: The Enormous Sums Involved in the Coming Jeffries-Johnson Fight for the World's Championship," *Harper's Weekly*, May 14, 1910.

52. Thorstein Veblen, *The Theory of the Leisure Class*, 1899 (Project Gutenberg edition, http://www.gutenberg.org/files/833/833-h/833-h.htm#2HCH0004).

53. Sophy Burnham, *The Landed Gentry: Passions and Personalities Inside America's Propertied Class* (New York: G. P. Putnam's Sons, 1978), 106.

54. Chuck Anesi, "The Titanic Casualty Figures," http://www.anesi.com/titanic.htm.

55. John Graham, ed., *Yours for the Revolution: The Appeal to Reason, 1895–1922* (Lincoln: University of Nebraska Press, 1990), 100.

56. Henry Laurens Call, *The Concentration of Wealth: Read Before the American Association for the Advancement of Science at Columbia College, New York, December 27, 1906* (Boston: The Chandler Publishing Company, 1907).

57. Osmond K. Fraenkel, ed., *The Curse of Bigness: Miscellaneous Papers of Louis Brandeis* (New York: The Viking Press, 1934), 38.

58. Amos Pinchot, *What's the Matter with America: The Meaning of the Progressive Movement and the Rise of the New Party*, 1912, 32, http://hdl.loc.gov/loc.gdc/scd0001.00137885141.

59. Lewis Gould, *Four Hats in the Ring: The 1912 Election and the Birth of Modern American Politics* (Lawrence: University Press of Kansas, 2008), 27.

60. *Final Report of The Commission on Industrial Relations.*

61. Pinchot, *What's the Matter with America*, 34.

62. Pease, *The Progressive Years*, 105–106.

63. Glenn Altschuler, "Conquering Gotham," Baltimore Sun, April 29, 2007.

64. Norman Hapgood, *Industry and Progress* (New Haven, CT: Yale University Press, 1911), 65.

65. Nathan Ward, "Take Me to the River. Finally," *New York Times*, July 2, 2010.

66. Dawley, *Struggles for Justice*, 74.

67. Pinchot, *What's the Matter with America*, 32.

68. Beatty, *Age of Betrayal*, 17.

69. Reed, *The New Plutocracy*, 270.

70. Washington Gladden, *Christianity and Socialism* (New York: Eaton & Mains, 1905), 65.

71. Jacob Hacker and Paul Pierson, *Winner-Take-All Politics: How Washington Made the Rich Richer—and Turned Its Back on the Middle Class* (New York: Simon & Schuster, 2010), 79.

72. Dawley, *Struggles for Justice*, 161.

73. Paul Krugman, *The Conscience of a Liberal* (New York: W. W. Norton & Co., 2007), 22.

74. *Final Report of The Commission on Industrial Relations.*

75. Dawley, *Struggles for Justice*, 26.

76. Urofsky, *Louis D. Brandeis*, 229.

77. Dawley, *Struggles for Justice*, 148.

78. Urofsky, *Louis D. Brandeis*, 317.

79. Pettigrew, *Triumphant Plutocracy*, 121.

80. Pettigrew, *Triumphant Plutocracy*, 127–128.

81. Call, *The Concentration of Wealth*, 5.

82. Call, *The Concentration of Wealth*, 7.

83. "The Country's Wealth; Is 99 Per Cent of It In the Hands of 1 Per Cent of the People—Statement Made by Prof. Call Arouses Alarm and Provokes Denial—Eminent Sociologists Doubt Its Truth," *New York Times*, January 6, 1907.

84. "The Country's Wealth," *New York Times.*

85. John Spargo, *Socialism: A Summary and Interpretation of Socialist Principles* (New York: The Macmillan Company, 1916), 145.

86. *Final Report of The Commission on Industrial Relations.*

87. *Final Report of The Commission on Industrial Relations.*

88. Gould, *Four Hats in the Ring*, 194.

89. *Final Report of The Commission on Industrial Relations.*

90. Urofsky, *Louis D. Brandeis*, 302.

91. Norman Hapgood, *The Advancing Hour* (New York: Boni & Liveright, 1920), 219.

92. "Conserve Capital, Is Hill's Advice; Great Northern Head Tells Minnesota Conservators That Is Nation's Great Need. Scores Our Wastefulness, Explains High Prices as Result with High Wages as Not Least Contributing Cause," *New York Times*, March 18, 1910.
93. Pinchot, *What's the Matter with America*, 28.
94. Pinchot, *What's the Matter with America*, 29.

Chapter 2

1. Seymour Martin Lipset and Gary Marks, *It Didn't Happen Here: Why Socialism Failed in the United States* (New York, W. W. Norton & Company, 2000), 177.
2. James Weinstein, *The Decline of Socialism in America, 1912–1925* (New York: Vintage Books, 1969), 109.
3. Charles M. Howell, *The Howell System. A Proposed System—Not a Mere Theory—of National Laws Equally Opposed to the Illusive Dreams of Socialists and the Lawless Methods of Predatory Wealth for the Inauguration, Enforcement and Perpetuity of Economic Liberty* (New York: Isaac H. Blanchard Company, 1911), 70.
4. James J. Hill, "A Warning to the Nation," *New York Times*, November 21, 1909.
5. Philippa Strum, *Brandeis on Democracy* (Lawrence: University Press of Kansas, 1995), 3.
6. Melvin Urofsky, *Louis D. Brandeis: A Life* (New York: Pantheon Books, 2009), 73.
7. Urofsky, *Louis D. Brandeis*, 83–95.
8. Urofsky, *Louis D. Brandeis*, 168.
9. Urofsky, *Louis D. Brandeis*, 83.
10. Urofsky, *Louis D. Brandeis*, 130–134.
11. Louis Dembitz Brandeis, *Business: A Profession* (Boston: Small, Maynard, 1914), ix.
12. Lawrence Mitchell, *The Speculation Economy: How Finance Triumphed Over Industry* (San Francisco: Berrett-Koehler Publishers, Inc., 2007), 50.
13. John C. Reed, *The New Plutocracy* (New York: Abbey Press, 1903), 478.
14. Washington Gladden, *Christianity and Socialism* (New York: Eaton & Mains, 1905), 231.
15. Osmond K. Fraenkel, ed., *The Curse of Bigness: Miscellaneous Papers of Louis Brandeis* (New York: The Viking Press, 1934), 118.
16. Otis Pease, ed., *The Progressive Years: The Spirit and Achievement of American Reform* (New York: George Braziller, 1962), 87.
17. Pease, *The Progressive Years*, 30.
18. Lewis Gould, *Four Hats in the Ring: The 1912 Election and the Birth of Modern American Politics* (Lawrence: University Press of Kansas, 2008), 64.
19. "Adler On Surplus Wealth; Evils of Child Labor Also," *New York Times*, January 14, 1907.
20. Reverend Rodney Romney, "The Little Gate to God: A Reflection on the Legacy of Walter Rauschenbusch," (Seattle, WA: University Baptist Church, March 3, 2002), http://www.rauschenbusch.org/documents/littlegate.htm.
21. Lew Daly, "The Catholic Roots of American Liberalism," *Boston Review*, May–June 2007.
22. Daly, "The Catholic Roots of American Liberalism."
23. Frank Cocozzelli, "Saving Monsignor Ryan," *New Deal 2.0*, December 18, 2010, http://www.newdeal20.org/2010/12/17/saving-monsignor-ryan-30302/.
24. Paul Buhle, *Taking Care of Business: Samuel Gompers, George Meany, Lane Kirkland, and the Tragedy of American Labor* (New York: Monthly Review Press, 1999), 67.
25. Lipset and Marks, *It Didn't Happen Here*, 239.
26. *Final Report of The Commission on Industrial Relations* (Washington, DC, August 23, 1915), http://goo.gl/MKXkH.
27. Alan Dawley, *Struggles for Justice: Social Responsibility and the Liberal State* (Cambridge, MA: Harvard University Press, 1991), 84.
28. Lipset and Marks, *It Didn't Happen Here*, 127–130.
29. Pease, *The Progressive Years*, 70.
30. Sam Roberts, "Triangle Fire: New Leaders Emerge," *New York Times*, March 24, 2011.

31. This account of the Lawrence struggle draws mainly from Joyce Kornbluh, *Rebel Voices: An IWW Anthology* (Chicago: Charles H. Kerr Publishing, 1988), http://www.lucyparsonsproject.org/iww/kornbluh_bread_roses.html.
32. Saul Schniderman, "Mother Jones in 2010," Labor Heritage Foundation, www.laborheritage.org.
33. Strum, *Brandeis on Democracy*, 6.
34. Lipset and Marks, *It Didn't Happen Here*, 138.
35. Weinstein, *The Decline of Socialism in America*, 11.
36. Gould, *Four Hats in the Ring*, 107.
37. Reginald Wright Kauffman, *What Is Socialism* (New York: Moffat, Yard and Company, 1910), 102.
38. Hal Crowther, "Prince George and the Return of the Sheriff of Nottingham," *Indy-Week*, October 4, 2006.
39. John Graham, ed., *Yours for the Revolution: The Appeal to Reason, 1895–1922* (Lincoln: University of Nebraska Press, 1990), 62–64.
40. Lipset and Marks, *It Didn't Happen Here*, 17.
41. Graham, *Yours for the Revolution*, 174.
42. Lipset and Marks, *It Didn't Happen Here*, 155.
43. Lipset and Marks, *It Didn't Happen Here*, 172.
44. Dawley, *Struggles for Justice*, 99.
45. Weinstein, *The Decline of Socialism in America*, 24.
46. Graham, *Yours for the Revolution*, 174.
47. Graham, *Yours for the Revolution*, 11.
48. Reed, *The New Plutocracy*, 370
49. Graham, *Yours for the Revolution*, x–xi.
50. Graham, *Yours for the Revolution*, 174.
51. Weinstein, *The Decline of Socialism in America*, 85.
52. Weinstein, *The Decline of Socialism in America*, 90.
53. Pease, *The Progressive Years*, 234.
54. Pease, *The Progressive Years*, 231.
55. Pease, *The Progressive Years*, 216–217.
56. Weinstein, *The Decline of Socialism in America*, 55.
57. Norman Hapgood, *The Advancing Hour* (New York: Boni & Liveright, 1920), 166–167.
58. Gould, *Four Hats in the Ring*, 102.
59. Randolph Paul, *Taxation in the United States* (Boston: Little, Brown, and Company, 1954), 87–88.
60. Herbert Croly, *The Promise of American Life* (New York: The Macmillan Company, 1909), 23.
61. Gladden, *Christianity and Socialism*, 28.
62. Gladden, *Christianity and Socialism*, 102–103.
63. Lipset and Marks, *It Didn't Happen Here*, 151.
64. Norman Hapgood, *Industry and Progress* (New Haven, CT: Yale University Press, 1911), 28–29.
65. "Louis D. Brandeis Quotes," Louis D. Brandeis Legacy Fund for Social Justice (Waltham, MA: Brandeis University), http://www.brandeis.edu/legacyfund/bio.html.
66. William Van Til, *Economic Roads for American Democracy* (New York: McGraw-Hill Book Company, 1947), 87.
67. Theodore Roosevelt, "The New Nationalism," August 31, 1910, http://www.presidentialrhetoric.com/historicspeeches/roosevelt_theodore/newnationalism.html.
68. Roosevelt, "The New Nationalism."
69. Urofsky, *Louis D. Brandeis*, 319.
70. Weinstein, *The Decline of Socialism in America*, 8.
71. John Spargo, *Socialism: A Summary and Interpretation of Socialist Principles* (New York: The Macmillan Company, 1916), 335.
72. Dawley, *Struggles for Justice*, 105.
73. Dawley, *Struggles for Justice*, 105.
74. Sanford Jacoby, *Modern Manors: Welfare Capitalism Since the New Deal* (Princeton, NJ: Princeton University Press, 1997), 97.
75. Urofsky, *Louis D. Brandeis*, 168.

76. Paul, *Taxation in the United States*, 30.
77. Ajay Mehrotra, "Edwin R. A. Seligman and the Beginnings of the US Income Tax," Tax Analysts Tax History Project, October 31, 2005, http://www.taxhistory.org/thp/readings.nsf/ArtWeb/EB941FE0419B0DDC852570BA0048848C?OpenDocument.
78. Weinstein, *The Decline of Socialism in America*, 57.
79. Weinstein, *The Decline of Socialism in America*, 82.
80. Roberts, "Triangle Fire: New Leaders Emerge."
81. John C. Culver and John Hyde, *American Dreamer: A Life of Henry Wallace* (New York: W. W. Norton & Company, 2000), 43.
82. *Final Report of The Commission on Industrial Relations.*
83. *Final Report of The Commission on Industrial Relations.*
84. Gladden, *Christianity and Socialism*, 129.
85. Todd Venezia, "104-Year-Old Heiress Huguette Clark's Sad, Secret life," *New York Post*, August 27, 2010.
86. Michael Malone, Richard Roeder, and William Lang, *Montana: A History of Two Centuries* (Seattle: University of Washington Press, 1991), 218–223.
87. Richard Little, "Roosevelt Gives a Radical Creed in Kansas Speech," *Chicago Daily Tribune*, September 1, 2010.
88. Ronald Mulder, *The Insurgent Progressives in the United States Senate and the New Deal*, 1933–1939 (New York: Garland Publishing, Inc., 1979), 68.
89. M. Susan Murnane, "Andrew Mellon's Unsuccessful Attempt to Repeal Estate Taxes," Tax Analysts Tax History Project, August 22, 2005.
90. Howell, *The Howell System*, 32.
91. William Vickroy Marshall, *A Curb to Predatory Wealth* (New York: R. F. Fenno & Company, 1909), 9–11.
92. Murnane, "Andrew Mellon's Unsuccessful Attempt to Repeal Estate Taxes."
93. "Incomes Now Taxed in Many Countries," *New York Times*, January 11, 1914.
94. Mehrotra, "Edwin R. A. Seligman and the Beginnings of the US Income Tax."
95. Randolph Paul, *Taxation for Prosperity* (Indianapolis, IN: The Bobbs-Merrill Company, 1947), 14.
96. "Theodore Roosevelt on Estate and Inheritance Taxes: Excerpt from the President's Annual Message to Congress," 1906, http://www.taxhistory.org/TR/1906.htm.
97. Croly, *The Promise of American Life*, 382–384.
98. Ben Jackson, "How to Talk about Redistribution: A Historical Perspective," *History & Policy* (September 2008).
99. Mehrotra, "Edwin R. A. Seligman and the Beginnings of the US Income Tax."
100. "Leaders Like Hughes's Stand; Republicans in Legislature As a Rule Approve Income Tax Message," *New York Times*, January 6, 1910.
101. Ajay Mehrotra, "'More Mighty than the Waves of the Sea': Toilers, Tariffs, and the Income Tax Movement, 1880–1913," *Labor History* (May 2004).
102. Sidney Ratner, *American Taxation: Its History As a Social Force in Democracy* (New York: W. W. Norton & Company, Inc., 1942), 309.
103. Urofsky, *Louis D. Brandeis*, 261.
104. Urofsky, *Louis D. Brandeis*, 342.
105. James Chace, 1912: *Wilson, Roosevelt, Taft & Debs: The Election that Changed the Country* (New York: Simon & Schuster, 2004), 213.
106. Chace, 1912, 135–136.
107. Gould, *Four Hats in the Ring*, 32.
108. Louis Dembitz Brandeis, *Other People's Money: And How the Bankers Use It* (New York: Frederick A. Stokes, 1914), 1.
109. Joseph Gardner, *Departing Glory: Theodore Roosevelt as Ex-President* (New York: Charles Scribner's Sons, 1973), 127.
110. Robert La Forte, "Theodore Roosevelt's Osawatomie Speech," *Kansas Historical Quarterlies* (Summer 1966), http://www.kancoll.org/khq/1966/66_2_laforte.htm.
111. Gardner, *Departing Glory*, 186–187.
112. La Forte, "Theodore Roosevelt's Osawatomie Speech."
113. La Forte, "Theodore Roosevelt's Osawatomie Speech."
114. Gardner, *Departing Glory*, 212–213.

115. Theodore Roosevelt, "The Right of the People to Rule," in Amos Pinchot, *What's the Matter with America: The Meaning of the Progressive Movement and The Meaning of the New Party*, 1912, 3–4.
116. Gould, *Four Hats in the Ring*, 63
117. Pinchot, *What's the Matter with America*, 5.
118. Pinchot, *What's the Matter with America*, 12.
119. Pinchot, *What's the Matter with America*, 37.
120. "Democratic Party Platform of 1912," from Gerhard Peters and John T. Woolley, American Presidency Project, http://www.presidency.ucsb.edu/ws/index.php?pid=29590#axzz1PHmhBWQR.
121. Urofsky, *Louis D. Brandeis*, 345.
122. Pease, *The Progressive Years*, 377.
123. Pease, *The Progressive Years*, 344.
124. Chace, 1912, 223.
125. Bernard Brommel, *Eugene V. Debs: Spokesman for Labor and Socialism* (Chicago: Charles H. Kerr Publishing Company, 1978), 136.
126. Chace, 1912, 220.
127. Brommel, *Eugene V. Debs*, 134.
128. Mehrotra, "'More Mighty than the Waves of the Sea.'"
129. Dawley, *Struggles for Justice*, 147.
130. Dawley, *Struggles for Justice*, 148.
131. Urofsky, *Louis D. Brandeis*, 398.
132. Mitchell, *The Speculation Economy*, 137–138.
133. Emmanuel Saez and Thomas Piketty, "Income Inequality in the United States, 1913–1998," *Quarterly Journal of Economics* (March 2012), http://elsa.berkeley.edu/~saez/TabFig2010.xls.
134. Urofsky, *Louis D. Brandeis*, 435.
135. Urofsky, *Louis D. Brandeis*, 435.
136. Urofsky, *Louis D. Brandeis*, 438.
137. Strum, *Brandeis on Democracy*, 15.
138. Amos Pinchot Papers, container no. 139, Manuscript Division, Library of Congress, Washington, DC, OV 1 (scrapbook).
139. Lipset and Marks, *It Didn't Happen Here*, 180.

Chapter 3

1. "Diners, Angered, Rebuke Pinchot: 'No! No!' Greets His Suggestion That the Rich Are Unwilling to Fight," *New York Times*, June 6, 1917.
2. Joseph Gardner, *Departing Glory: Theodore Roosevelt as Ex-President* (New York: Charles Scribner's Sons, 1973), 339.
3. Gardner, *Departing Glory*, 352.
4. John Mason Hart, "The Rise of the American Empire," Historians Against the War Conference, Austin, Texas (February 17–19, 2006).
5. Alan Dawley, *Struggles for Justice: Social Responsibility and the Liberal State* (Cambridge, MA: Harvard University Press, 1991), 181.
6. Randolph Paul, *Taxation for Prosperity* (Indianapolis, IN: The Bobbs-Merrill Company, 1947), 23.
7. Joseph Thorndike, "A Century of Soaking the Rich: The Origins of the Federal Estate Tax," Tax Analysts Tax History Project, July 10, 2006.
8. W. Elliot Brownlee, "Wilson and Financing the Modern State: The Revenue Act of 1916," Proceedings of the American Philosophical Society, vol. 129, no. 2, 1985, http://www.jstor.org/pss/986988.
9. Nancy Unger, "'The Economic Crime of All Ages,'" *Fighting Bob*, February 21, 2006, http://www.fightingbob.com/article.cfm?articleID=496.
10. Thorndike, "A Century of Soaking the Rich."
11. Thorndike, "A Century of Soaking the Rich."
12. David Joulfaian, "The Federal Estate Tax: History, Law, and Economics," July 27, 2010, http://ssrn.com/abstract=1579829.

13. M. Susan Murnane, "Andrew Mellon's Unsuccessful Attempt to Repeal Estate Taxes," *Tax Analysts Tax History Project*, August 22, 2005.
14. Thorndike, "A Century of Soaking the Rich."
15. Paul, *Taxation for Prosperity*, 24.
16. "Pacifists Urge Taxing Wealth To Pay For War," *Chicago Daily Tribune*, April 1, 1917.
17. Letter from E. W. Scripps to Amos Pinchot, Ohio University Department of Archives and Special Collections, April 1, 1917, http://worlddmc.ohiolink.edu/History/Previews?p=1&oid=500240&viewno=4&format=list&result=12&sort=creator&hits=0&count=0.
18. The source for all the American Committee on War Finance literature and internal communications discussed in these pages: Amos Pinchot Papers, container no. 74, Manuscript Division, Library of Congress, Washington, DC.
19. "Who Shall Pay for the War?" pamphlet, Amos Pinchot Papers, container no. 74.
20. John Flynn, "An Approach to the Problem of War," *Annals of the American Academy of Political and Social Science* (January 1936), 220.
21. Editorial, "War Finance," *New York Evening Sun*, April 16, 1917.
22. *Brotherhood of Locomotive Firemen and Enginemen's* magazine, October 1, 1917, 16–17.
23. Letter from Otto H. Kahn, New York, *Philadelphia Public Ledger*, June 9, 1917.
24. "Statement of Amos Pinchot Before Senate Finance Committee," May 15, 1917, Amos Pinchot Papers, container no. 74.
25. Belle Case La Follette and Fola La Follette, *Robert M. La Follette: June 14, 1855–June 18, 1925* (New York: Hafner Publishing Company, 1971), 742.
26. *Let Their Dollars Die for Their Country Too, Speeches of Col. Edward C. Little of Kansas in the House of Representatives, Made on the Floor, May 14, 17, 18, 19, 29; June 28, 29, 31* (1917). *Conscript Incomes in Excess of $100,000* (Washington, DC: Government Printing Office, 1917), 1242, 17694.
27. "Higher Tax Is Asked for Rich: Amos Pinchot Would Have Those Who Can Afford It Pay More Toward National Cost of Carrying on the War," *Christian Science Monitor*, May 15, 1917.
28. *Machinists' Monthly Journal*, October 1917, 859–861.
29. "News of the Week," *The Public: An International Journal of Fundamental Democracy*, September 28, 1917.
30. Arthur Mann, *La Guardia: A Fighter Against His Times, 1882–1933* (Chicago: The University Of Chicago Press, 1959), 79.
31. "Editorial: Patriots and Profits," *The Public: An International Journal of Fundamental Democracy* (September 28, 1917).
32. W. Elliot Brownlee, *Federal Taxation in America: A Short History* (New York: Cambridge University Press, 2004), 64.
33. Steven Bank, Kirk Stark, and Joseph Thorndike, *War and Taxes* (Washington, DC: The Urban Institute Press, 2008), 65.
34. John Graham, ed., *Yours for the Revolution: The Appeal to Reason, 1895–1922* (Lincoln: University of Nebraska Press, 1990), 284.
35. Graham, *Yours for the Revolution*, 284.
36. James Weinstein, *The Decline Of Socialism in America, 1912–1925* (New York: Vintage Books, 1969), 90.
37. Weinstein, *The Decline Of Socialism in America*, 90.
38. Graham, *Yours for the Revolution*, xi.
39. Graham, *Yours for the Revolution*, 285.
40. Seymour Martin Lipset and Gary Marks, *It Didn't Happen Here: Why Socialism Failed in the United States* (New York, W. W. Norton & Company, 2000), 255.
41. Graham, *Yours for the Revolution*, 284.
42. Dawley, *Struggles for Justice*, 187.
43. Graham, *Yours for the Revolution*, 284.
44. Lipset and Marks, *It Didn't Happen Here*, 251.
45. Robert McElvaine, *The Great Depression: America, 1929–1941* (New York: Times Books, 1993), 11.
46. Louis Post, "War Patriotism," *The Public: An International Journal of Fundamental Democracy* (October 19, 1917).
47. Dawley, *Struggles for Justice*, 196.

48. Paul, *Taxation for Prosperity*, 25.
49. "US Federal Individual Income Tax Rates History, 1913-2011," Tax Foundation, http://www.taxfoundation.org/publications/show/151.html.
50. W. Elliot Brownlee, *Federal Taxation in America: A Short History* (New York: Cambridge University Press; 2nd edition, 2004), 68.
51. Dawley, *Struggles for Justice*, 199.
52. Lew Daly, "The Catholic Roots of American Liberalism," *Boston Review*, May–June 2007.
53. "Bishops' Program of Social Reconstruction: A General Review of the Problems and Survey of Remedies," Catholic Welfare Conference, Washington, DC, 1919, http://archives.lib.cua.edu/education/bishops/1919-wel.cfm.
54. Dawley, *Struggles for Justice*, 229.
55. Dawley, *Struggles for Justice*, 234.
56. Dawley, *Struggles for Justice*, 73.
57. Dawley, *Struggles for Justice*, 235.
58. Edward Keating, *The Gentleman from Colorado: A Memoir* (Denver: Sage Books, 1964), 477.
59. Dawley, *Struggles for Justice*, 234.
60. Dick Meister, "The Day Seattle Stood Still," *Portside*, January 26, 2007.
61. Weinstein, *The Decline Of Socialism in America*, 199.
62. Dawley, *Struggles for Justice*, 233.
63. *Profiteering: Letter from the Chairman of the Federal Trade Commission in Response to a Senate Resolution of June 10, 1918* (Washington, DC: Government Printing Office, June 29, 1918).
64. *Profiteering*, 13.
65. Dawley, *Struggles for Justice*, 195.
66. Keating, *The Gentleman from Colorado*, 480.
67. Paul, *Taxation for Prosperity*, 29.
68. Mills, *The Power Elite*, 151.
69. John Womack Jr. and Roxanne Dunbar-Ortiz, "Dreams of Revolution: Oklahoma, 1917," *Monthly Review*, November 2010.
70. Dawley, *Struggles for Justice*, 235.
71. Graham, *Yours for the Revolution*, 285.
72. Dawley, *Struggles for Justice*, 248.
73. Dawley, *Struggles for Justice*, 236.
74. Robert K. Murray, *Red Scare: A Study in National Hysteria, 1919–1920* (New York: McGraw-Hill, 1964), 121.
75. Murray, *Red Scare*, 9.
76. Keating, *The Gentleman from Colorado*, 480.
77. Graham, *Yours for the Revolution*, 285.
78. Murray, *Red Scare*, 240.
79. Murray, *Red Scare*, 240.
80. Graham, *Yours for the Revolution*, 287.
81. Sidney Ratner, *American Taxation: Its History As a Social Force in Democracy* (New York: W. W. Norton & Company, 1942), 16.
82. Scott Nearing, *A Nation Divided, or Plutocracy Versus Democracy* (Chicago: Socialist Party of the United States, 1920), 7.
83. Norman Hapgood, *The Advancing Hour* (New York: Boni & Liveright, 1920), 4.
84. Hapgood, *The Advancing Hour*, 165.

Chapter 4

1. Lynn Parramore, "When Unions Go Bust, We All Do," *Naked Capitalism*, February 28, 2011.
2. Melvin Urofsky, *Louis D. Brandeis: A Life* (New York: Pantheon Books, 2009), 632.
3. Parramore, "When Unions Go Bust."
4. Parramore, "When Unions Go Bust."
5. Nancy C. Unger, *Fighting Bob La Follette: The Righteous Reformer* (Chapel Hill: The University of North Carolina Press, 2000), 277.
6. Arthur Mann, *La Guardia: A Fighter Against His Times, 1882–1933* (Chicago: The University Of Chicago Press, 1959), 208.

7. David Cannadine, *Mellon: An American Life* (New York: Knopf, 2006), 267.
8. John Graham, ed., *Yours for the Revolution: The Appeal to Reason, 1895–1922* (Lincoln: University of Nebraska Press, 1990), 176.
9. Dale Wetzel, "California Recall Drive Puts Former ND Gov. Lynn Frazier in Spotlight," *Bismarck Tribune*, July 5, 2003.
10. Amos Pinchot Papers, container no. 139, Manuscript Division, Library of Congress, Washington, DC.
11. R. F. Pettigrew, *Triumphant Plutocracy: The Story of American Public Life from 1870 to 1920* (New York: The Academy Press, 1922), 7.
12. Pettigrew, *Triumphant Plutocracy*, 119.
13. Pettigrew, *Triumphant Plutocracy*, 130.
14. Amos Pinchot Papers, Library of Congress.
15. Amos Pinchot Papers, Library of Congress.
16. Amos Pinchot Papers, Library of Congress.
17. Alan Dawley, *Struggles for Justice: Social Responsibility and the Liberal State* (Cambridge, MA: Harvard University Press, 1991), 158.
18. Paul Buhle, *Taking Care of Business: Samuel Gompers, George Meany, Lane Kirkland, and the Tragedy of American Labor* (New York: Monthly Review Press, 1999), 88.
19. Irving Bernstein, *The Lean Years: A History of the American Worker, 1920–1933* (Baltimore: Penguin Books, 1966), 147.
20. Bernstein, *The Lean Years*, 153.
21. Nelson Lichtenstein, "The Long History of Labor Bashing," *The Chronicle of Higher Education*, March 6, 2011.
22. Buhle, *Taking Care of Business*, 88.
23. Buhle, *Taking Care of Business*, 82.
24. Buhle, *Taking Care of Business*, 107.
25. Bernstein, *The Lean Years*, 144.
26. Amos Pinchot Papers, Library of Congress. This discussion of power industry policy struggles in the 1920s draws from research Pinchot conducted for a book about wealth concentration.
27. Amos Pinchot Papers, Library of Congress.
28. Mann, *La Guardia*, 217.
29. Amos Pinchot Papers, Library of Congress.
30. Amos Pinchot Papers, Library of Congress.
31. Amos Pinchot Papers, Library of Congress.
32. Joseph Thorndike, "The Republican Roots of New Deal Tax Policy, Tax Reform Debate," Tax Analysts Tax History Project, August 28, 2003.
33. Thorndike, "The Republican Roots of New Deal Tax Policy."
34. M. Susan Murnane, "Andrew Mellon's Unsuccessful Attempt to Repeal Estate Taxes," Tax Analysts Tax History Project, August 22, 2005.
35. Randolph Paul, *Taxation for Prosperity* (Indianapolis, IN: The Bobbs-Merrill Company, 1947), 31.
36. "House Minority Report Attacking Tax Bill," *New York Times*, July 31, 1935.
37. Thorndike, "The Republican Roots of New Deal Tax Policy."
38. Tax Foundation, "Statistics of Income, Federal Individual Income Tax Rates History: Income Years 1913–2010," http://www.taxfoundation.org/files/fed_individual_rate_history-june2010.xls.
39. Paul, *Taxation for Prosperity*, 31.
40. Thorndike, "The Republican Roots of New Deal Tax Policy."
41. Marjorie Kornhauser, "Shaping Public Opinion and the Law: How a 'Common Man' Campaign Ended a Rich Man's Law," *Law and Contemporary Problems*, vol. 73, no. 1 (2009), http://papers.ssrn.com/sol3/papers.cfm?abstract_id=880383.
42. Murnane, "Andrew Mellon's Unsuccessful Attempt to Repeal Estate Taxes."
43. Murnane, "Andrew Mellon's Unsuccessful Attempt to Repeal Estate Taxes."
44. Kornhauser, "Shaping Public Opinion and the Law."
45. Gerhard Peters and John T. Woolley, American Presidency Project, http://www.presidency.ucsb.edu/ws/?pid=29618.
46. Stan Phipps, "La Follette's 'One-Man Show' in the 1924 Presidential Election," *Socialist Organizer*, http://www2.socialistorganizer.org/index.php?option=com_content&task=view&id=51&Itemid=33.

47. Nathan Fine, *Labor and Farmer Parties in the United States, 1828–1928* (New York: Rand School of Social Science, 1928), 412.
48. Fine, *Labor And Farmer Parties*, 412.
49. "'Soaking Rich' Opposed," *Los Angeles Times*, November 21, 1925.
50. Isaac William Martin, "Bankers into Populists: The Texas Tax Clubs and the Mellon Plan," *Journal of Policy History* (October 2009).
51. Mann, *La Guardia*, 209.
52. Thorndike, "The Republican Roots of New Deal Tax Policy."
53. Robert McElvaine, *The Great Depression: America, 1929–1941* (New York: Times Books, 1993), 23.
54. McElvaine, *The Great Depression*, 23.
55. Cannadine, *Mellon*, 366.
56. Linda McQuaig and Neil Brooks, *The Trouble with Billionaires* (Toronto: Viking Canada, 2010), 43.
57. Mann, *La Guardia*, 208.
58. Dawley, *Struggles for Justice*, 328.
59. Larry Samuel, *Rich: The Rise and Fall of American Wealth Culture* (New York: Amacom, 2009), 41.
60. McElvaine, *The Great Depression*, 17.
61. Samuel, *Rich*, 41.
62. Timothy Noah, "The Great Divergence: Computer Exceptionalism," *Slate*, September 8, 2010, http://www.slate.com/id/2266025/entry/2266508/.
63. Matthew Josephson, *Infidel in the Temple: A Memoir of the Nineteen Thirties* (New York: Alfred Knopf, 1967), 62.
64. McElvaine, *The Great Depression*, 39.
65. Dawley, *Struggles for Justice*, 328.
66. McElvaine, *The Great Depression*, 17.
67. McElvaine, *The Great Depression*, 40.
68. Chester Bowles, *Tomorrow Without Fear* (New York: Simon and Schuster, 1946), 21.
69. Samuel, *Rich*, 42.
70. Samuel, *Rich*, 12.
71. C. Wright Mills, *The Power Elite* (New York: Oxford University Press, 1956), 151.
72. William Van Til, *Economic Roads for American Democracy* (New York: McGraw-Hill Book Company, Inc., 1947), 207.
73. Van Til, *Economic Roads for American Democracy*, 16.
74. Emmanuel Saez and Thomas Piketty, "Income Inequality in the United States, 1913–1998," *Quarterly Journal of Economics* (March 2012), http://elsa.berkeley.edu/~saez/TabFig2010.xls.
75. Samuel, *Rich*, 45
76. Amos Pinchot Papers, Library of Congress.
77. Samuel, *Rich*, 47
78. Marriner S. Eccles, *Beckoning Frontiers: Public and Personal Recollections*, ed. by Sidney Hyman (New York: Alfred A. Knopf, 1951), 76–77.
79. McElvaine, *The Great Depression*, 38.
80. Polly Cleveland, "The Great Real Estate Bubble of the Roaring Twenties," *Econamici*, February 16, 2009, http://mcleveland.org/blog/index.php/2009/02/the-great-real-estate-bubble-of-the-roaring-twenties/.
81. Dean Calbreath, "Run-up to Great Depression and Today's Recession Have Some Eerie Similarities, But Many Important Differences," *San Diego Union-Tribune*, October 5, 2008.
82. "Florida in the 1920s, The Great Florida Land Boom," http://floridahistory.org/land-boom.htm.
83. Harold Bubil, "Secret Bank Records Shine Light on 1920s Boom and Bust," *Sarasota Herald-Tribune*, January 27, 2008.
84. Lawrence Mitchell, *The Speculation Economy: How Finance Triumphed Over Industry* (San Francisco: Berrett-Koehler Publishers, Inc., 2007), 206.
85. Ron Chernow, "Everyman's Financial Meltdown," *New York Times*, October 23, 2009.
86. McQuaig and Brooks, *The Trouble with Billionaires*, 46.

87. Robert Kuttner, *The Squandering of America: How the Failure of Our Politics Undermine Our Prosperity* (New York: Alfred A. Knopf, 2007), 83.
88. McQuaig and Brooks, *The Trouble with Billionaires*, 47.
89. McElvaine, *The Great Depression*, 5.
90. McElvaine, *The Great Depression*, 23.
91. McElvaine, *The Great Depression*, 65.
92. McQuaig and Brooks, *The Trouble with Billionaires*, 45.
93. Samuel, *Rich*, 44.
94. Mills, *The Power Elite*, 103.
95. Bowles, *Tomorrow Without Fear*, 23.

Chapter 5

1. C. Wright Mills, *The Power Elite* (New York: Oxford University Press, 1956), 151.
2. Matthew Josephson, *Infidel in the Temple: A Memoir of the Nineteen Thirties* (New York: Alfred Knopf, 1967), 69.
3. Jean Edward Smith, *FDR* (New York: Random House, 2008), 241.
4. Alan Brinkley, *Voices of Protest: Huey Long, Father Coughlin & the Great Depression* (New York: Vintage Books, 1983), 93.
5. Robert McElvaine, *The Great Depression: America, 1929–1941* (New York: Times Books, 1993), 74.
6. Gerald Johnson, *Incredible Tale: The Odyssey Of The Average American in the Last Half Century* (New York: Harper & Brothers, 1950), 165.
7. Paul Buhle, *Taking Care of Business: Samuel Gompers, George Meany, Lane Kirkland, and the Tragedy of American Labor* (New York: Monthly Review Press, 1999), 98.
8. Alan Dawley, *Struggles for Justice: Social Responsibility and the Liberal State* (Cambridge, MA: Harvard University Press, 1991), 72.
9. Josephson, *Infidel in the Temple*, 74.
10. Stuart Chase, *The Road We Are Traveling, 1914–1942* (New York: Twentieth Century Fund, 1942), 38.
11. Larry Samuel, *Rich: The Rise and Fall of American Wealth Culture* (New York: Amacom, 2009), 34.
12. Josephson, *Infidel in the Temple*, 121.
13. Johnson, *Incredible Tale*, 166.
14. Dawley, *Struggles for Justice*, 402.
15. Josephson, *Infidel in the Temple*, 26.
16. McElvaine, *The Great Depression*, 92.
17. McElvaine, *The Great Depression*, 92.
18. McElvaine, *The Great Depression*, 93.
19. Brinkley, *Voices of Protest*, 120.
20. Chase, *The Road We Are Traveling*, 37.
21. Arthur Mann, *La Guardia: A Fighter Against His Times, 1882–1933* (Chicago: The University Of Chicago Press, 1959), 299.
22. Edward Folliard, "Robinson Raps Higher Levy on Large Incomes," *Washington Post*, November 22, 1931.
23. Laurence Benedict, "Garner Spanks Tax Gossipers," *Los Angeles Times*, December 31, 1931.
24. "Warns Taxpayers Of Huge Sacrifice," *Baltimore Sun*, February 12, 1932.
25. Joseph Thorndike, "The Republican Roots of New Deal Tax Policy, Tax Reform Debate," Tax Analysts Tax History Project, August 28, 2003.
26. Thorndike, "The Republican Roots of New Deal Tax Policy."
27. McElvaine, *The Great Depression*, 87.
28. Joseph Thorndike, "New Deal Taxes: Four Things Everyone Should Know," Tax Analysts Tax History Project, November 20, 2008.
29. Thorndike, "The Republican Roots of New Deal Tax Policy."
30. "Balanced Budget Sure, Rainey Says," *New York Times*, March 25, 1932.
31. Thorndike, "The Republican Roots of New Deal Tax Policy."

32. Franklin D. Roosevelt, "Radio Address From Albany, New York: The 'Forgotten Man' Speech," April 7, 1932, from Gerhard Peters and John T. Woolley, American Presidency Project, http://www.presidency.ucsb.edu/ws/?pid=88408.

33. Franklin D. Roosevelt, "Address at Jefferson Day Dinner in St. Paul, Minnesota," April 18, 1932, from Gerhard Peters and John T. Woolley, American Presidency Project, http://www.presidency.ucsb.edu/ws/?pid=88409.

34. Franklin D. Roosevelt, "Oglethorpe University Commencement Address," May 22, 1932, Digital Library of Georgia, http://georgiainfo.galileo.usg.edu/FDRspeeches/FDRspeech32-1.htm.

35. Smith, *FDR*, 56.

36. Smith, *FDR*, 80.

37. Smith, *FDR*, 185.

38. McElvaine, *The Great Depression*, 96.

39. Smith, *FDR*, 218.

40. Smith, *FDR*, 239.

41. Smith, *FDR*, 242.

42. Smith, *FDR*, 251.

43. Joseph Thorndike, "The Depression and Reform: FDR's Search for Tax Revision in NY," Tax Analysts, November 26, 2003, http://goo.gl/eeiDA.

44. Thorndike, "The Depression and Reform."

45. Smith, *FDR*, 272.

46. Franklin D. Roosevelt, "Campaign Address on Progressive Government at the Commonwealth Club in San Francisco, California," September 23, 1932, Heritage Foundation, First Principles Series, http://www.heritage.org/initiatives/first-principles/primary-sources/fdrs-commonwealth-club-address.

47. Franklin D. Roosevelt: "Campaign Address at Detroit, Michigan," October 2, 1932, from Gerhard Peters and John T. Woolley, American Presidency Project, http://www.presidency.ucsb.edu/ws/?pid=88393.

48. Smith, *FDR*, 297.

49. Brinkley, *Voices of Protest*, 49–51.

50. Carleton Beals, *The Story of Huey P. Long* (Westport, CT: Greenwood Press, 1935; repr. 1971), 244–245.

51. Robert Bendiner, *Just Around the Corner: A Highly Selective History of the Thirties* (New York: E. P. Dutton, 1967), 26.

52. Stuart Chase, *The Most Probable World* (New York: Harper & Row, 1968), 102.

53. Josephson, *Infidel in the Temple*, 186.

54. Randolph Paul, *Taxation for Prosperity* (Indianapolis, IN: The Bobbs-Merrill Company, 1947), 39.

55. Melvin Urofsky, "The Value of 'Other People's Money,'" *New York Times*, February 6, 2009.

56. Osmond Fraenkel, ed., *The Curse of Bigness: Miscellaneous Papers of Louis Brandeis* (New York: The Viking Press, 1934), 171.

57. Alan Brinkley, *The End of Reform: New Deal Liberalism in Recession and War* (New York: Vintage Books, 1995), 80.

58. Marriner S. Eccles, *Beckoning Frontiers: Public and Personal Recollections*, ed. Sidney Hyman (New York: Alfred A. Knopf, 1951), 81.

59. Brinkley, *The End of Reform*, 80.

60. McElvaine, *The Great Depression*, 127.

61. McElvaine, *The Great Depression*, 136.

62. Joseph Thorndike, "Historical Perspective: Pecora Hearings Spark Tax Morality, Tax Reform Debate," Tax Analysts Tax History Project, November 10, 2003.

63. Melvin Urofsky, *Louis D. Brandeis: A Life* (New York: Pantheon Books, 2009), 710.

64. Brinkley, *Voices of Protest*, 60.

65. Robert Kuttner, *The Squandering of America: How the Failure of Our Politics Undermine Our Prosperity* (New York: Alfred A. Knopf, 2007), 90.

66. Benjamin Kline Hunnicutt, "The End of Shorter Hours," *Labor History* (Summer 1984), http://www.uiowa.edu/~lsa/bkh/lla/eosh.htm.

67. Brinkley, *Voices of Protest*, 59.

68. Matthew Josephson, *Sidney Hillman: Statesman of American Labor* (Garden City, NY: Doubleday & Company, 1952), 367.

69. Josephson, *Infidel in the Temple*, 286.

70. McElvaine, *The Great Depression*, 168.
71. Smith, *FDR*, 315.
72. Robert Reich, *Aftershock: The Next Economy and America's Future* (New York: Alfred A. Knopf, 2010), 15.
73. Linda McQuaig and Neil Brooks, *The Trouble with Billionaires* (Toronto: Viking Canada, 2010), 51.

Chapter 6

1. Scott Myers-Lipton, *Social Solutions to Poverty: America's Struggle to Build a Just Society* (Boulder, CO: Paradigm Publishers, 2007), 165–166.
2. Alan Dawley, *Struggles for Justice: Social Responsibility and the Liberal State* (Cambridge, MA: Harvard University Press, 1991), 376.
3. Mark Leff, *The Limits of Symbolic Reform: The New Deal and Taxation, 1933–1939* (Cambridge: Cambridge University Press, 2003), 68.
4. Marjorie Kornhauser, "Shaping Public Opinion and the Law: How a 'Common Man' Campaign Ended a Rich Man's Law," *Law and Contemporary Problems*, vol. 73, no. 1 (2009), http://papers.ssrn.com/sol3/papers.cfm?abstract_id=880383.
5. Kornhauser, "Shaping Public Opinion."
6. Leff, *The Limits of Symbolic Reform*, 76–77.
7. Joseph Thorndike, "Too Much: The Historical Link Between Bailouts and Pay Caps," Tax Analysts Tax History Project, October 6, 2008.
8. Leff, *The Limits of Symbolic Reform*, 78. The mandate would come under intense repeal pressure in 1937, amid widespread labor strikes. The mandate, repealers argued, was contributing to "ill feeling between employers and employees."
9. Leff, *The Limits of Symbolic Reform*, 81.
10. Leff, *The Limits of Symbolic Reform*, 82.
11. Leff, *The Limits of Symbolic Reform*, 84.
12. Leff, *The Limits of Symbolic Reform*, 87.
13. Leff, *The Limits of Symbolic Reform*, 64–65.
14. Robert McElvaine, *The Great Depression: America, 1929–1941* (New York: Times Books, 1993), 225.
15. Matthew Josephson, *Infidel in the Temple: A Memoir of the Nineteen Thirties* (New York: Alfred Knopf, 1967), 264.
16. Paul Buhle, *Taking Care of Business: Samuel Gompers, George Meany, Lane Kirkland, and the Tragedy of American Labor* (New York: Monthly Review Press, 1999), 108.
17. McElvaine, *The Great Depression*, 225.
18. Irving Bernstein, *The Turbulent Years: A History of the American Worker 1933–1941* (Boston: Houghton Mifflin Company, 1970), 218–227.
19. Bernstein, *The Turbulent Years*, 229–252.
20. McElvaine, *The Great Depression*, 228.
21. Bernstein, *The Turbulent Years*, 288.
22. Alan Brinkley, *Voices of Protest: Huey Long, Father Coughlin & the Great Depression* (New York: Vintage Books, 1983), 228.
23. McElvaine, *The Great Depression*, 230.
24. Steven Gillon, *The Democrats' Dilemma: Walter F. Mondale and the Liberal Legacy* (New York: Columbia University Press, 1992), 7.
25. Russell Fridley, "What Would Floyd B. Do?" *Minnesota Law & Politics*, http://www.lawandpolitics.com/minnesota/What-Would-Floyd-B.-Do/ab2507f1-2f50-4782-8c89-791009bfd9c5.html.
26. Brinkley, *Voices of Protest*, 227.
27. Seymour Martin Lipset and Gary Marks, *It Didn't Happen Here: Why Socialism Failed in the United States* (New York: W. W. Norton & Company, 2000), 72.
28. McElvaine, *The Great Depression*, 229.
29. Greg Mitchell, *The Campaign of the Century: Upton Sinclair's Race for Governor of California and the Birth of Media Politics* (New York: Random House, 1992), 6.
30. Upton Sinclair, *I, Governor of California, And How I Ended Poverty: A True Story* (New York: Farrar & Rinehart, 1933), 22.
31. Sinclair, *I, Governor of California*, 59.
32. McElvaine, *The Great Depression*, 235.
33. Mitchell, *The Campaign of the Century*, 340.

34. McElvaine, *The Great Depression*, 236.
35. McElvaine, *The Great Depression*, 252.
36. Bryan Burrough, *The Big Rich: The Rise and Fall of the Greatest Texas Oil Fortunes* (New York: The Penguin Press, 2009), 127–129.
37. Leff, *The Limits of Symbolic Reform*, 14.
38. McElvaine, *The Great Depression*, 203.
39. Josephson, *Infidel in the Temple*, 274.
40. Larry Samuel, *Rich: The Rise and Fall of American Wealth Culture* (New York: Amacom, 2009), 69.
41. McElvaine, *The Great Depression*, 229.
42. Brinkley, *Voices of Protest*, 223.
43. McElvaine, *The Great Depression*, 241.
44. Justin Nystrom, "Bourbon Louisiana," KnowLA: Encyclopedia of Louisiana, Louisiana Endowment for the Humanities (August 18, 2011), http://www.www.knowla.org/entry.php?rec=841.
45. William Ivy Hair, *Bourbonism and Agrarian Protest: Louisiana Politics 1877–1900* (Baton Rouge: Louisiana State University Press, 1969), 234.
46. Hair, *Bourbonism and Agrarian Protest*, 235.
47. Hair, *Bourbonism and Agrarian Protest*, 262.
48. Hair, *Bourbonism and Agrarian Protest*, 279.
49. Hair, *Bourbonism and Agrarian Protest*, 279.
50. McElvaine, *The Great Depression*, 243.
51. Brinkley, *Voices of Protest*, 79.
52. Brinkley, *Voices of Protest*, 27.
53. McElvaine, *The Great Depression*, 243.
54. Brinkley, *Voices of Protest*, 18.
55. Bob Anderson, "Seminar Explores Huey Long's History," *Advocate* (Baton Rouge, LA), August 29, 2010.
56. Brinkley, *Voices of Protest*, 30–31.
57. Anderson, "Seminar Explores Huey Long's History."
58. Brinkley, *Voices of Protest*, 34.
59. Brinkley, *Voices of Protest*, 40.
60. Huey P. Long, *Every Man a King: The Autobiography of Huey P. Long* (New Orleans: National Book Co., Inc., 1935), 290.
61. Forrest Davis, *Huey Long: A Candid Biography* (New York: Dodge Publishing Company, 1935), 42.
62. Davis, *Huey Long*, 155.
63. Brinkley, *Voices of Protest*, 54.
64. Brinkley, *Voices of Protest*, 61.
65. Brinkley, *Voices of Protest*, 61.
66. "Huey Long's Share Our Wealth Speech," February 23, 1934, Huey Long: The Man, His Mission, and Legacy. http://www.hueylong.com/programs/share-our-wealth-speech.php.
67. Brinkley, *Voices of Protest*, 70.
68. Brinkley, *Voices of Protest*, 71.
69. McElvaine, *The Great Depression*, 244.
70. McElvaine, *The Great Depression*, 246.
71. Brinkley, *Voices of Protest*, 72.
72. Brinkley, *Voices of Protest*, 237.
73. Brinkley, *Voices of Protest*, 238.
74. Carleton Beals, *The Story of Huey P. Long* (Westport, CT: Greenwood Press, 1935; repr. 1971), 25–26.
75. Beals, *The Story of Huey P. Long*, 312.
76. McElvaine, *The Great Depression*, 239.
77. Brinkley, *Voices of Protest*, 119.
78. Brinkley, *Voices of Protest*, 287.
79. Brinkley, *Voices of Protest*, 164.
80. Brinkley, *Voices of Protest*, 261.
81. Brinkley, *Voices of Protest*, 207.

82. Brinkley, *Voices of Protest*, 247.
83. Joseph Thorndike, "New Deal Taxes: Four Things Everyone Should Know," Tax Analysts Tax History Project, November 20, 2008.
84. Thorndike, "New Deal Taxes."
85. Leff, *The Limits of Symbolic Reform*, 104.
86. Leff, *The Limits of Symbolic Reform*, 127.
87. Leff, *The Limits of Symbolic Reform*, 130.
88. McElvaine, *The Great Depression*, 259.
89. Franklin D. Roosevelt, "Message to Congress on Tax Revision," June 19, 1935, from Gerhard Peters and John Woolley, American Presidency Project, http://www.presidency.ucsb.edu/ws/?pid=15088.
90. C. P. Trusell, "Dual Attack Is Opened Upon Tax Measure," *Baltimore Sun*, July 31, 1935.
91. Darien Jacobson, Brian Raub, and Barry Johnson, "The Estate Tax: Ninety Years and Counting," *Statistics of Income Bulletin* (Summer 2007).
92. Leff, *The Limits of Symbolic Reform*, 152.
93. "Who Favors the Tax Bill?" *Washington Post*, August 12, 1935.
94. "House Minority Report Attacking Tax Bill," *New York Times*, July 31, 1935.
95. "Who Favors the Tax Bill?" *Washington Post*.
96. "Address of Snell in Reply to Roosevelt," *New York Times*, August 26, 1935.
97. Franklin D. Roosevelt, "Jackson Day Dinner Address, Washington, DC," January 8, 1936, from Gerhard Peters and John T. Woolley, American Presidency Project, http://www.presidency.ucsb.edu/ws/?pid=15256.
98. McElvaine, *The Great Depression*, 275.
99. McElvaine, *The Great Depression*, 265.
100. Randolph Paul, *Taxation in the United States* (Boston: Little, Brown, and Company, 1954).
101. "Democratic Party Platform of 1936," June 23, 1936, from Gerhard Peters and John T. Woolley, American Presidency Project, http://www.presidency.ucsb.edu/ws/?pid=29596.
102. Franklin Roosevelt, "A Rendezvous With Destiny, Speech Before the 1936 Democratic National Convention," Philadelphia, Pennsylvania, June 27, 1936, http://www.austincc.edu/lpatrick/his2341/fdr36acceptancespeech.htm.
103. McElvaine, *The Great Depression*, 280.
104. Lipset and Marks, *It Didn't Happen Here*, 75.
105. Lipset and Marks, *It Didn't Happen Here*, 209.
106. Jean Edward Smith, *FDR* (New York: Random House, 2008), 374.
107. McElvaine, *The Great Depression*, 275–276.
108. McElvaine, *The Great Depression*, 279.
109. McElvaine, *The Great Depression*, 281.
110. William Van Til, *Economic Roads for American Democracy* (New York: McGraw-Hill Book Company, Inc., 1947), 207.
111. Charles Merriam, *On the Agenda of Democracy* (Cambridge, MA: Harvard University Press, 1941), 103.
112. Smith, *FDR*, 376.
113. McElvaine, *The Great Depression*, 283.
114. Jim Pope, "Worker Lawmaking, Sit-Down Strikes, and the Shaping of American Industrial Relations, 1935–1958," *Law and History Review* (Spring 2006), http://www.historycooperative.org/journals/lhr/24.1/pope.html.
115. McElvaine, *The Great Depression*, 286.
116. Thorndike, "New Deal Taxes."
117. Alan Brinkley, *The End of Reform: New Deal Liberalism in Recession and War* (New York: Vintage Books, 1995), 28.
118. Brinkley, *The End of Reform*, 140.
119. Clinton Rossiter and James Lare, eds., *The Essential Lippmann: A Political Philosophy for Liberal Democracy* (New York: Random House, 1963), 436.
120. Thorndike, "New Deal Taxes."
121. Steve Fraser, "The Genealogy of Wall Street Crime," *Los Angeles Times*, January 30, 2005.
122. Samuel, *Rich*, 85.

123. Samuel, *Rich*, 91.
124. C. Wright Mills, *The Power Elite* (New York: Oxford University Press, 1956), 79.
125. Mills, *The Power Elite*, 151.
126. McElvaine, *The Great Depression*, 321.
127. Brinkley, *The End of Reform*, 201.
128. Eric Hoyt, "Hollywood and the Income Tax, 1929–1955," *Film History*, vol. 22 (2010).

Chapter 7

1. Robert McElvaine, *The Great Depression: America, 1929–1941* (New York: Times Books, 1993), 295.
2. Alan Brinkley, *The End of Reform: New Deal Liberalism in Recession and War* (New York: Vintage Books, 1995), 58.
3. Linda McQuaig and Neil Brooks, *The Trouble with Billionaires* (Toronto: Viking Canada, 2010), 53.
4. Steven Bank, Kirk Stark, and Joseph Thorndike, *War and Taxes* (Washington, DC: The Urban Institute Press, 2008), 86.
5. Sidney Ratner, *American Taxation: Its History As a Social Force in Democracy* (New York: W. W. Norton & Company, Inc., 1942), 495.
6. Matthew Josephson, *Sidney Hillman: Statesman of American Labor* (Garden City, NY: Doubleday & Co., 1952), 516.
7. Bank, Stark, and Thorndike, *War and Taxes*, 88.
8. Bank, Stark, and Thorndike, *War and Taxes*, 87.
9. Randolph Paul, *Taxation for Prosperity* (Indianapolis, IN: The Bobbs-Merrill Company, 1947), 75.
10. Bank, Stark, and Thorndike, *War and Taxes*, 88.
11. Bank, Stark, and Thorndike, *War and Taxes*, 91.
12. W. Elliot Brownlee, *Federal Taxation in America: A Short History* (New York: Cambridge University Press, 2nd ed., 2004), 108.
13. Bank, Stark, and Thorndike, *War and Taxes*, 92.
14. Josephson, *Sidney Hillman*, 558.
15. Paul, *Taxation for Prosperity*, 97.
16. Paul, *Taxation for Prosperity*, 99.
17. Paul, *Taxation for Prosperity*, 110.
18. Joseph Thorndike, "The Tax That Wasn't: Mid-Century Proposals for a National Sales Tax," Tax Analysts Tax History Project, March 19, 1996.
19. Randolph Paul, *Taxation in the United States* (Boston: Little, Brown, and Company), 1954, 301.
20. Paul, *Taxation in the United States*, 301.
21. Frank Kluckhohn, "$25,000 Income Limit, Ceilings on Prices, Stable Wages, Taxes, Asked by President," *New York Times*, April 28, 1942.
22. Marriner S. Eccles, *Beckoning Frontiers: Public and Personal Recollections*, ed. Sidney Hyman (New York: Alfred A. Knopf, 1951), 372.
23. Ratner, *American Taxation*, 502.
24. John Flynn, "An Approach to the Problem of War," *Annals of the American Academy of Political and Social Science* (January 1936), 221.
25. Paul, *Taxation for Prosperity*, 87.
26. Paul, *Taxation for Prosperity*, 88.
27. "Hawkes Skeptical On Income Ceiling," *New York Times*, April 28, 1942.
28. Associated Press, "First Reaction Is Divided on Income Limit," *Washington Post*, April 28, 1942.
29. Associated Press, "First Reaction Is Divided on Income Limit."
30. Associated Press, "Income Curb Opinions Vary," *Los Angeles Times*, April 28, 1942.
31. Associated Press, "First Reaction Is Divided on Income Limit."
32. Associated Press, "First Reaction Is Divided on Income Limit."
33. "Press Comment on President's Plan," *New York Times*, April 28, 1942.
34. Paul, *Taxation for Prosperity*, 100.
35. Robert Albright, "Tax Asked to Hold Incomes at $25,000," *Washington Post*, June 16, 1942.

36. Warren Francis, "Income Limit Plan Shelved," *Los Angeles Times*, June 17, 1942.
37. "Radio: Roosevelt's Rating," *Time*, September 21, 1942.
38. Paul, *Taxation for Prosperity*, 104.
39. Robert De Vore, "WPB Action Hints $25,000 Salary Limit," *Washington Post*, June 20, 1942.
40. "$25,000 A Year," *Chicago Daily Tribune*, October 8, 1942.
41. "$25,000 A Year," *Chicago Daily Tribune*.
42. "Editorial: Is The Income Tax Just?" *Life*, April 16, 1956.
43. Paul, *Taxation for Prosperity*, 106.
44. Paul, *Taxation for Prosperity*, 107.
45. Bank, Stark, and Thorndike, *War and Taxes*, 97–98.
46. "Disastrous and Dishonest Tax Bill," advertisement from Basil Brewer, publisher, the New Bedford (MA) *Standard-Times*, in *Washington Post*, October 19, 1942.
47. Brinkley, *The End of Reform*, 140.
48. Don Inbody, "Voting and the American Military," *Civil Military Relations*, March 9, 2010.
49. Josephson, *Sidney Hillman*, 590.
50. Paul, *Taxation for Prosperity*, 105.
51. Paul, *Taxation for Prosperity*, 102.
52. "Predict FDR Will Ask Wider Income Ceiling," *Chicago Daily Tribune*, December 2, 1942.
53. W. H. Lawrence, "$25,000 Maximum Set For Salaries In Byrnes Ruling," *New York Times*, October 28, 1942.
54. John Fisher, "FDR Policies Linked to Reds' 1928 Platform," *Chicago Daily Tribune*, November 21, 1942.
55. W. H. Lawrence, "Pay Controls Stir Congress," *New York Times*, December 6, 1942.
56. W. H. Lawrence, "A 210 Billion Debt," *New York Times*, January 12, 1943.
57. Lawrence, "Pay Controls Stir Congress."
58. "Action to Void Salary Ceiling Delayed a Week by House Group to Hear Roosevelt," *Wall Street Journal*, January 30, 1943.
59. "President Asks 100 PC Tax on Net Income Over $25,000," *Christian Science Monitor*, February 17, 1943.
60. John Crider, "Kills Move To Let Salary Fight Wait," *New York Times*, March 12, 2011.
61. William Strand, "Riotous Debate Rages in House on Salary Curb," *Chicago Daily Tribune*, March 12, 1943.
62. "Senate Gets Bill To Void Salary Top," *New York Times*, March 20, 1943.
63. John Fisher, "Repeal of FDR Limit On Salary Voted By Senate," *Chicago Daily Tribune*, March 24, 1943.
64. John MacCormac, "$25,000 Pay Limit Repealed Minus Roosevelt Signature; He Assails Congress," *New York Times*, April 12, 1943.
65. MacCormac, "$25,000 Pay Limit Repealed Minus Roosevelt Signature."
66. Dennis Ventry Jr. and Joseph Thorndike, "The Plan That Slogans Built: The Revenue Act of 1943," Tax Analysts Tax History Project, September 1, 1997.
67. Paul, *Taxation for Prosperity*, 137.
68. Associated Press, "President's Tax Letter," *New York Times*, May 18, 1943.
69. Ventry and Thorndike, "The Plan That Slogans Built."
70. Samuel Bledsoe, "Doughton Rebuffs Treasury Tax Rise of $10,560,000,000," *New York Times*, October 5, 1943.
71. Paul, *Taxation for Prosperity*, 147.
72. "Deny Tax Will Top Income," *New York Times*, October 6, 1943.
73. Paul, *Taxation for Prosperity*, 152.
74. Bank, Stark, and Thorndike, *War and Taxes*, 106.
75. Brownlee, *Federal Taxation in America*, 114–115.
76. "Paul Quits Treasury Post Still Urging Higher Taxes," *Washington Post*, March 23, 1944.
77. Brownlee, *Federal Taxation in America*, 115.
78. Fritz Scheuren and Janet McCubbin, "Individual Income Tax Shares and Average Tax Rates, Tax Years 1916–1950," *Statistics of Income Bulletin* (Winter 1988–1989).
79. "Forum to Debate Salary Mandate," *Washington Post*, January 10, 1943.
80. "Murray Revives Idea of $25,000 Income Ceiling," *Los Angeles Times*, August 22, 1943.

81. "National Groups Press Each Congressman on Tax Program," *Baltimore Sun*, November 11, 1943.
82. Joseph Gaer, *The First Round: The Story of the CIO Political Action Committee* (New York: Duell, Sloan, and Pearce, 1944), 55.
83. Gaer, *The First Round*, 67.
84. Gaer, *The First Round*, 67–68.
85. C. Wright Mills, The Power Elite (New York: Oxford University Press, 1956), 101.
86. Norman Markowitz, *The Rise and Fall of the People's Century: Henry A. Wallace and American Liberalism, 1941–1948* (New York: The Free Press, 1973), 58.
87. Clayton Knowles, "Says Republicans Still Help The Few," *New York Times*, October 28, 1944.
88. Charles Merriam, *On the Agenda of Democracy* (Cambridge, MA: Harvard University Press, 1941), 73.
89. Merriam, *On the Agenda of Democracy*, 100.
90. Joseph Gaer, The First Round: The Story of the CIO Political Action Committee. New York: Duell, Sloan, and Pearce, 1944, p. 57.
91. Henry Wallace, *Democracy Reborn*, ed. Russell Lord (New York: Reynal & Hitchcock, 1944), 35.
92. Henry Wallace, *The Century of the Common Man*, ed. by Russell Lord (New York: Reynal & Hitchcock, 1943), 16.
93. Josephson, *Sidney Hillman*, 526–528.
94. Gaer, *The First Round*, 396.
95. William Van Til, *Economic Roads for American Democracy* (New York: McGraw-Hill Book Company, Inc., 1947), 222.
96. David Brody, *In Labor's Cause: Main Themes on the History of the American Worker* (New York: Oxford University Press, 1993), 185.
97. Joshua Freeman, *Working-Class New York: Life And Labor Since World War II* (New York: The New Press, 2000), 128.
98. Paul Krugman, *The Conscience of a Liberal* (New York: W. W. Norton & Co., 2007), 7.
99. Stuart Chase, *The Road We Are Traveling, 1914–1942* (New York: Twentieth Century Fund, 1942), 58.
100. Chase, *The Road We Are Traveling*, 98.
101. Chase, *The Road We Are Traveling*, 98.
102. W. H. Lawrence, "A 210 Billion Debt," *New York Times*, January 12, 1943.
103. Markowitz, *The Rise and Fall of the People's Century*, 50.
104. Wallace, *The Century of the Common Man*, 56.
105. Wallace, *Democracy Reborn*, 38.
106. Van Til, *Economic Roads for American Democracy*, 209.
107. Van Til, *Economic Roads for American Democracy*, 171.
108. Brinkley, *The End of Reform*, 141.
109. "Republicans Urge Post-War Tax Cut," *New York Times*, May 18, 1944.
110. "Mid-West Businessmen Formulate Post-War Tax Plan Designed to Stimulate Flow of Venture Capital," *Wall Street Journal*, July 10, 1944.
111. George Tagge, "25% Post-War Top on Income Taxes Sought," *Chicago Daily Tribune*, April 14, 1943.
112. "Urges End Of Income Tax," *New York Times*, April 13, 1944.
113. Donald Bailey Marsh, *Taxes Without Tears* (Lancaster, PA: The Jaques Cattell Press, 1945), 177.
114. Gaer, *The First Round*, 305.
115. Inbody, "Voting and the American Military."
116. Gaer, *The First Round*, 181–182.
117. Brinkley, *The End of Reform*, 263.
118. Markowitz, *The Rise and Fall of the People's Century*, 127.
119. Jacob Hacker and Paul Pierson, *Winner-Take-All Politics: How Washington Made the Rich Richer—and Turned Its Back on the Middle Class* (New York: Simon & Schuster, 2010), 137.
120. Brinkley, *The End of Reform*, 257.
121. Jean Edward Smith, *FDR* (New York: Random House, 2008), 585.
122. Brinkley, *The End of Reform*, 263.

123. Larry Samuel, *Rich: The Rise and Fall of American Wealth Culture* (New York: Amacom, 2009), 97.

Chapter 8

1. William Van Til, *Economic Roads for American Democracy* (New York: McGraw-Hill Book Company, Inc., 1947), 15.
2. Van Til, *Economic Roads for American Democracy*, 15.
3. Frank Levy and Peter Temlin, "Inequality and Institutions in 20th Century America," Massachusetts Institute of Technology Working Paper Series, June 27, 2007, http://www.nber.org/papers/w13106.
4. Randolph Paul, *Taxation for Prosperity* (Indianapolis, IN: The Bobbs-Merrill Company, 1947), 182.
5. Joshua Freeman, *Working-Class New York: Life And Labor Since World War II* (New York: The New Press, 2000), 5.
6. Freeman, *Working-Class New York*, 3.
7. Paul Buhle, *Taking Care of Business: Samuel Gompers, George Meany, Lane Kirkland, and the Tragedy of American Labor* (New York: Monthly Review Press, 1999), 125.
8. Freeman, *Working-Class New York*, 3.
9. Jon Garlock, "The 1946 General Strike of Rochester, New York," RochesterLabor.org, 2007, http://www.rochesterlabor.org/strike/index.html.
10. "Oakland General Strike, Part II," *Bay Radical*, June 12, 2007, http://bayradical.blogspot.com/2007/06/this-is-strike-support-our-cause-part.html.
11. "Oakland General Strike Part II."
12. Joseph Gaer, *The First Round: The Story of the CIO Political Action Committee* (New York: Duell, Sloan, and Pearce, 1944), 152.
13. Gaer, *The First Round*, 171.
14. "Oakland General Strike Part II."
15. Freeman, *Working-Class New York*, 74.
16. John Witte, *The Politics and Development of the Federal Income Tax* (Madison: University of Wisconsin Press, 1985), 132.
17. Joseph Thorndike, "Out of (Re)alignment: Taxes and the Election of 1946," Tax Analysts Tax History Project, December 14, 2006.
18. Paul, *Taxation for Prosperity*, 189.
19. Alan Brinkley, *The End of Reform: New Deal Liberalism in Recession and War* (New York: Vintage Books, 1995), 263.
20. Norman Markowitz, *The Rise and Fall of the People's Century: Henry A. Wallace and American Liberalism, 1941–1948* (New York: The Free Press, 1973), 125.
21. Markowitz, *The Rise and Fall of the People's Century*, 146.
22. Markowitz, *The Rise and Fall of the People's Century*, 150.
23. Markowitz, *The Rise and Fall of the People's Century*, 150.
24. Markowitz, *The Rise and Fall of the People's Century*, 139.
25. Joseph Thorndike, "Out of (Re)alignment."
26. Matthew Josephson, *Sidney Hillman: Statesman of American Labor* (Garden City, NY: Doubleday & Company, 1952), 667–668.
27. Randolph Paul, *Taxation in the United States* (Boston: Little, Brown, and Company, 1954), 415.
28. Freeman, *Working-Class New York*, 75.
29. "Pamphlets in the Fight Against Taft-Hartley, 1947–1948," Holt Labor Library, http://www.holtlaborlibrary.org/tafthartley.html.
30. Buhle, *Taking Care of Business*, 128.
31. Markowitz, *The Rise and Fall of the People's Century*, 221.
32. Ethan Kapstein, *Sharing The Wealth: Workers and the World Economy* (New York: W. W. Norton & Company, 1999), 24.
33. John Maynard Keynes, *The General Theory of Employment, Interest, and Money* (New York: Harcourt Brace, 1964; orig. 1936), 372.
34. Kapstein, *Sharing The Wealth*, 37.
35. James Allen Smith, *The Idea Brokers: Think Tanks and the Rise of the New Policy Elite* (New York: The Free Press, 1991), 107.

36. Van Til, *Economic Roads for American Democracy*, 139.
37. Van Til, *Economic Roads for American Democracy*, 137.
38. Van Til, *Economic Roads for American Democracy*, 138.
39. Smith, *The Idea Brokers*, 108.
40. Brinkley, *The End of Reform*, 174.
41. Chester Bowles, *Tomorrow Without Fear* (New York: Simon and Schuster, 1946), 52.
42. Bowles, *Tomorrow Without Fear*, 74.
43. Joseph Thorndike, "Profiles in Tax History: Randolph E. Paul," Tax Analysts Tax History Project, October 6, 2004.
44. "Mr. Paul's Ideas," *Time*, December 29, 1941.
45. Paul, *Taxation for Prosperity*, 253.
46. Paul, *Taxation for Prosperity*, 253.
47. Paul, *Taxation for Prosperity*, 253, 217.
48. Paul, *Taxation for Prosperity*, 253, 413.
49. Paul, *Taxation for Prosperity*, 253, 258.
50. Paul, *Taxation for Prosperity*, 253, 258.
51. Paul, *Taxation for Prosperity*, 253, 414.
52. Thorndike, "Out of (Re)alignment."
53. Markowitz, *The Rise and Fall of the People's Century*, 276.
54. Markowitz, *The Rise and Fall of the People's Century*, 291.
55. "President's Acceptance Speech," July 15, 1948, Harry S. Truman Library and Museum, http://www.trumanlibrary.org/whistlestop/study_collections/1948campaign/large/docs/documents/pdfs/11-4.pdf#zoom=100.
56. "Rear Platform Remarks of the President at Toledo, Ohio, September 6, 1948," Harry S. Truman Library and Museum, http://www.trumanlibrary.org/whistlestop/study_collections/1948campaign/large/docs/documents/pdfs/10-2.pdf#zoom=100.
57. "Campaign Speech, Indianapolis, Indiana, October 15, 1948," Harry S. Truman Library and Museum, http://www.trumanlibrary.org/whistlestop/study_collections/1948campaign/large/docs/documents/pdfs/7-7.pdf#zoom=100.
58. Markowitz, *The Rise and Fall of the People's Century*, 296.

Chapter 9

1. Peter Kihss, "114,699 Unionists Salute Labor Here in 8-Hour Parade," *New York Times*, September 8, 1959.
2. Joshua Freeman, *Working-Class New York: Life And Labor Since World War II* (New York: The New Press, 2000), 99.
3. Jacob Hacker and Paul Pierson, *Winner-Take-All Politics: How Washington Made the Rich Richer—and Turned Its Back on the Middle Class* (New York: Simon & Schuster, 2010), 140.
4. Victor Reuther, *The Brothers Reuther and the Story of the UAW* (Boston: Houghton Mifflin Company, 1976), 12.
5. Reuther, *The Brothers Reuther*, 44.
6. Reuther, *The Brothers Reuther*, 49.
7. Reuther, *The Brothers Reuther*, 1.
8. Reuther, *The Brothers Reuther*, 248.
9. Reuther, *The Brothers Reuther*, 251.
10. Reuther, *The Brothers Reuther*, 251–252.
11. Reuther, *The Brothers Reuther*, 255.
12. Reuther, *The Brothers Reuther*, 276.
13. Kim Scipes, "Neo-Liberal Economic Policies in the United States: The Impact on American Workers," *Z*, February 2, 2007.
14. Frank Levy and Peter Temlin, "Inequality and Institutions in 20th Century America," Massachusetts Institute of Technology Working Paper Series, June 27, 2007, http://www.nber.org/papers/w13106.
15. Nelson Lichtenstein, *Walter Reuther: The Most Dangerous Man in Detroit* (Champaign: University of Illinois Press, 1997), 278–279.
16. Levy and Temlin, "Inequality and Institutions."
17. Lichtenstein, *Walter Reuther*, 282.
18. Reuther, *The Brothers Reuther*, 309.
19. Reuther, *The Brothers Reuther*, 310.

20. Lichtenstein, *Walter Reuther*, 280.
21. Reuther, *The Brothers Reuther*, 311.
22. Reuther, *The Brothers Reuther*, 317.
23. Lichtenstein, *Walter Reuther*, 288.
24. Lichtenstein, *Walter Reuther*, 288.
25. Jim Pope, "Worker Lawmaking, Sit-Down Strikes, and the Shaping of American Industrial Relations, 1935–1958," *Law and History Review* (Spring 2006), http://www.historycooperative.org/journals/lhr/24.1/pope.html.
26. Freeman, *Working-Class New York*, 8.
27. Freeman, *Working-Class New York*, 130.
28. Freeman, *Working-Class New York*, 130.
29. Freeman, *Working-Class New York*, 128.
30. Freeman, *Working-Class New York*, 141.
31. Freeman, *Working-Class New York*, 113.
32. Freeman, *Working-Class New York*, 65.
33. Freeman, *Working-Class New York*, 62.
34. Nelson Lichtenstein, "Taking Unions Out of the Workplace," *Alternet*, November 29, 2007, http://www.alternet.org/story/69198/.
35. Levy and Temlin, "Inequality and Institutions."
36. Lichtenstein, *Walter Reuther*, 295.
37. A. H. Raskin, "Diverse Issues At Stake Today," *New York Times*, November 4, 1958.
38. Levy and Temlin, "Inequality and Institutions."
39. Chester Bowles, *Tomorrow Without Fear* (New York: Simon and Schuster, 1946), 5.
40. Malcolm Gladwell, "Talent Grab: Why Do We Pay Our Stars So Much Money?" *New Yorker*, October 8, 2010.
41. Reuther, *The Brothers Reuther*, 311.
42. John N. Ingham, *Biographical Dictionary of American Business Leaders* (Westport, CT: Greenwood Press, 1983), 1666.
43. Sanford Jacoby, *Modern Manors: Welfare Capitalism Since the New Deal* (Princeton, NJ: Princeton University Press, 1997), 128.
44. James C. Worthy, *Shaping an American Institution: Robert E. Wood and Sears, Roebuck* (Urbana: University of Illinois Press, 1984), 153.
45. Jacoby, *Modern Manors*, 109.
46. Jacoby, *Modern Manors*, 110.
47. Jacoby, *Modern Manors*, 110.
48. Jacoby, *Modern Manors*, 128.
49. Levy and Temin, "Inequality and Institutions."
50. Emmanuel Saez and Thomas Piketty, "Income Inequality in the United States, 1913–1998," *Quarterly Journal of Economics* (March 2012), http://elsa.berkeley.edu/~saez/TabFig2010.xls.
51. Thomas Kochan and Frank Levy, "Addressing the Problem of Stagnant Wages," Employment Policy Research Network, May 20, 2011, http://www.employmentpolicy.org/topic/12/research/addressing-problem-stagnant-wages.
52. Hacker and Pierson, *Winner-Take-All Politics*, 140.
53. Dwight Eisenhower, "Special Message to the Congress on Old Age and Survivors Insurance and on Federal Grants-In-Aid for Public Assistance Programs," January 14, 1954, Social Security Online, http://www.ssa.gov/history/ikestmts.html#1954A.
54. Carola Frydman and Dirk Jenter, "CEO Compensation," Rock Center for Corporate Governance at Stanford University, Working Paper no. 77, March 2010, http://ssrn.com/abstract=1582232.
55. Carola Frydman and Raven Saks, "Executive Compensation: A New View from a Long-Term Perspective, 1936–2005," NBER Working Paper no. 14145, June 2008, http://www.nber.org/papers/w14145.
56. Gladwell, "Talent Grab."
57. David Leonhardt, "2 Candidates, 2 Fortunes, 2 Views of Wealth," *New York Times*, December 23, 2007.

Chapter 10

1. Malcolm Gladwell, "The Risk Pool," *New Yorker*, August 28, 2006.

2. Isaac William Martin, Ajay Mehrotra, and Monica Prasad, "The Thunder of History: The Origins and Development of the New Fiscal Sociology," Indiana University Maurer School of Law, Bloomington, Legal Studies Research Paper Series, Research Paper no. 147, August 2009.

3. Larry Samuel, Rich: The Rise and Fall of American Wealth Culture (New York: Amacom, 2009), 137.

4. Dwight D. Eisenhower, "First State of the Union," February 2, 1953, http://www.presidency.ucsb.edu/ws/index.php?pid=9829&st=&st1=.

5. Dwight D. Eisenhower, "Third State of the Union," January 6, 1955, http://www.presidency.ucsb.edu/ws/index.php?pid=10416&st=&st1=.

6. Dwight D. Eisenhower, "Address in Detroit at the National Automobile Show Industry Dinner," October 17, 1960, http://www.presidency.ucsb.edu/ws/index.php?pid=11982&st=distribution&st1=wealth.

7. P. J. Redford, "Should We Keep the Income Tax?" Taxes: The Tax Magazine, April 1957.

8. Redford, "Should We Keep the Income Tax?"

9. Cleveland Amory, "About Millionaires: Past, Present, Future," New York Times Magazine, March 22, 1959.

10. "Tax Rebellion Leader Thomas Coleman Andrews," New York Times, October 16, 1956.

11. "Tax Bureau Reform Seen," New York Times, August 31, 1953.

12. "Tax Men to Weigh Expense Accounts," New York Times, November 10, 1953.

13. "Honeymoon Is Over Now, But Only on Tax Forms," New York Times, July 30, 1954.

14. "Andrews Resigns As Revenue Chief," New York Times, October 16, 1955.

15. "Why the Income Tax Is Bad: Exclusive Interview with T. Coleman Andrews," US News & World Report, May 25, 1956.

16. "Why the Income Tax Is Bad," US News & World Report.

17. "Tax Rebellion Leader Thomas Coleman Andrews," New York Times.

18. Jonathan Schoenwald, A Time for Choosing: The Rise of Modern American Conservatism (New York: Oxford University Press, 2002), 62.

19. Isaac William Martin, "Redistributing Toward the Rich: Strategic Policy Crafting in the Campaign to Repeal the Sixteenth Amendment, 1938–1958," American Journal of Sociology (July 2010).

20. Martin, "Redistributing Toward the Rich."

21. George H. Gallup, The Gallup Poll: Public Opinion 1935–1971, Volume Two, 1949–1958 (New York: Random House, 1972), 1499.

22. Joseph Thorndike, "New Deal Taxes: Four Things Everyone Should Know," Tax Analysts Tax History Project, November 20, 2008.

23. Bruce Bartlett, "The Roots of Tax Reform, Part I," Tax Notes, December 20, 2010.

24. John Bainbridge, "The Super-American State II—Oil," New Yorker, March 18, 1961.

25. Bryan Burrough, The Big Rich: The Rise and Fall of the Greatest Texas Oil Fortunes (New York: The Penguin Press, 2009), 6.

26. Randolph Paul, Taxation for Prosperity (Indianapolis, IN: The Bobbs-Merrill Company, 1947), 306.

27. Bainbridge, "The Super-American State."

28. C. Wright Mills, The Power Elite (New York: Oxford University Press, 1956), 153.

29. Paul, Taxation for Prosperity, 306.

30. Kenneth Lamott, The Moneymakers: The Great Big New Rich in America (Boston: Little, Brown and Company, 1969), 272.

31. Bainbridge, "The Super-American State."

32. Burrough, The Big Rich, 164.

33. Burrough, The Big Rich, 166.

34. Burrough, The Big Rich, 251.

35. Samuel, Rich, 106.

36. Burrough, The Big Rich, 101.

37. Samuel, Rich, 107.

38. Paul, Taxation for Prosperity, 304.

39. Bainbridge, "The Super-American State."

40. Robert Caro, The Years of Lyndon Johnson: Means of Ascent (New York: Alfred A. Knopf, 1990), 209, 317.

41. Bainbridge, "The Super-American State."

42. Julian Zelizer, "Learning the Ways and Means: Wilbur Mills and a Fiscal Community, 1954–1964," in W. Elliot Brownlee, *Funding the Modern American State, 1941–1995* (Cambridge: Cambridge University Press, 1996), 294.
43. Lamott, *The Moneymakers*, 276.
44. Lamott, *The Moneymakers*, 277.
45. Mills, *The Power Elite*, 153.
46. Lamott, *The Moneymakers*, 272.
47. Eric Hoyt, "Hollywood and the Income Tax, 1929–1955," *Film History*, vol. 22 (2010).
48. Hoyt, "Hollywood and the Income Tax."
49. Hoyt, "Hollywood and the Income Tax."
50. Hoyt, "Hollywood and the Income Tax."
51. "President John F. Kennedy's Special Message to the Congress on Taxation, April 20, 1961," Tax Analysts Tax History Project, http://www.taxhistory.org/thp/readings.nsf/Ar tWeb/2B727964C0A28BE5852571690051FD23?OpenDocument.
52. Paul Krugman, *The Conscience of a Liberal* (New York: W. W. Norton & Co., 2007), 41.
53. Krugman, *The Conscience of a Liberal*, 48.
54. Michael Trotter, "Higher Marginal Rates Revisited," *Daily Report*, October 18, 2007.
55. Mills, *The Power Elite*, 112.
56. Malcolm Gladwell, "Talent Grab: Why Do We Pay Our Stars So Much Money?" *New Yorker*, October 8, 2010.
57. Gladwell, "Talent Grab."
58. Gladwell, "Talent Grab."
59. "Ernest, Holdeman & Collet Inc. v. Commissioner of Internal Revenue," *Open Jurist*, http://openjurist.org/290/f2d/3/ernest-holdeman-collet-inc-v-commissioner-of-inter nal-revenue.
60. Lamott, *The Moneymakers*, 288.
61. "America's Biggest Fortunes," *Fortune*, November 1957. The list appears online at http:// wikipediamaze.com/wiki/Wealthiest_Americans_%281957%29.
62. David Cannadine, *Mellon: An American Life* (New York: Knopf, 2006), 615.
63. Darien Jacobson, Brian Raub, and Barry Johnson, "The Estate Tax: Ninety Years and Counting," *Statistics of Income Bulletin* (Summer 2007).
64. Samuel, *Rich*, 133.
65. "Essay: On Being Very, Very Rich," *Time*, July 12, 1968.
66. Amory, "About Millionaires."
67. Samuel, *Rich*, 135.
68. Eve Pell, *We Used to Own the Bronx: Memoirs of a Former Debutante* (Albany: State University of New York Press, 2009), 21.
69. Pell, *We Used to Own the Bronx*, 63–64.
70. Mark Stevens, "The Rich Were Different a Century Ago, They Really Knew How to Spend Money," *New York Magazine*, January 15, 2007.
71. Diana Shaman, "Next Role for Otto Kahn's 126-Room Mansion: A Spa," *New York Times*, January 4, 1998.
72. Samuel, *Rich*, 16.
73. Samuel, *Rich*, 16.
74. Mills, *The Power Elite*, 148.
75. Mills, *The Power Elite*, 84.
76. Mills, *The Power Elite*, 84.
77. Debby Applegate, "The Clarks of Cooperstown," *New York Times*, May 20, 2007.
78. Applegate, "The Clarks of Cooperstown."
79. Sophy Burnham, *The Landed Gentry: Passions and Personalities Inside America's Prop ertied Class* (New York: G. P. Putnam's Sons, 1978), 217.
80. John Pearson, *Painfully Rich: The Outrageous Fortune and Misfortunes of the Heirs of J. Paul Getty* (New York, St. Martin's Press, 1995), 7.
81. Pearson, *Painfully Rich*, 7.
82. Dwight D. Eisenhower, "Personal and Confidential to Edgar Newton Eisenhower," November 8, 1954, in the Papers of Dwight David Eisenhower, eds. L. Galambos and D. van Ee, doc. 1147, http://www.eisenhowermemorial.org/presidential-papers/first term/documents/1147.cfm.

83. Reuven S. Avi-Yonah, "Why Tax the Rich? Efficiency, Equity, and Progressive Taxation," *Yale Law Journal*, (February 26, 2002).
84. Godfrey N. Nelson, "Income Tax Facing Diminishing Yield," *New York Times*, August 26, 1951.
85. Larry Ramey and Daniel Haley, *Tackling Giants: The Life Story of Berkley Bedell* (Winfield, KS: National Foundation for Alternative Medicine, 2005), xiii.
86. Ramey and Haley, *Tackling Giants*, 39.
87. Ramey and Haley, *Tackling Giants*, 56.
88. Ramey and Haley, *Tackling Giants*, 95.
89. Ramey and Haley, *Tackling Giants*, 98.
90. Ramey and Haley, *Tackling Giants*, 123.
91. Ramey and Haley, *Tackling Giants*, 124.
92. Ramey and Haley, *Tackling Giants*, 132.
93. Ramey and Haley, *Tackling Giants*, 305.
94. Ramey and Haley, *Tackling Giants*, 281.

Chapter 11

1. "Edward Keating, Ex-Congressman," *New York Times*, March 20, 1965.
2. Edward Keating, *The Gentleman from Colorado: A Memoir* (Denver: Sage Books, 1964), 341.
3. Bill Moyers, "For America's Sake," *Nation*, January 5, 2007.
4. Larry Samuel, *Rich: The Rise and Fall of American Wealth Culture* (New York: Amacom, 2009), 126.
5. "Increase in Housing Quality and Its Effect on Home Values: 1940–2010," *Visualizing Economics*, March 31, 2011, http://goo.gl/vU4kk.
6. "Historical Census of Housing Tables: Plumbing Facilities," US Census Bureau, Housing and Household Economic Statistics Division, October 31, 2011, http://www.census.gov/hhes/www/housing/census/historic/plumbing.html.
7. Dwight Macdonald, "Our Invisible Poor," *New Yorker*, January 19, 1963.
8. Stuart Chase, *Live and Let Live: A Program for Americans* (New York: Harper & Brothers, 1960), 103.
9. Chase, *Live and Let Live*, 44.
10. Samuel, *Rich*, 24.
11. Samuel, *Rich*, 126.
12. Dwight Eisenhower, *In Review: Pictures I've Kept, A Concise Pictorial Autobiography* (Garden City, NY: Doubleday & Company, 1969), 153.
13. Kevin Starr, *Golden Dreams: California in an Age of Abundance, 1950–1963* (New York: Oxford University Press, 2009), 4.
14. Samuel, *Rich*, 24.
15. Samuel, *Rich*, 126.
16. Claude Fischer, "Degree Inequality," *Berkeley Blog*, February 7, 2011, http://blogs.berkeley.edu/2011/02/07/degree-inequality/.
17. Larry Beinhart, "Is America Becoming a Third-World Country?" *Hartford Advocate*, January 31, 2011.
18. Starr, *Golden Dreams*, 234–235.
19. "Housing: Up from the Potato Fields," *Time*, July 3, 1950.
20. Robert Kuttner, *The Squandering of America: How the Failure of Our Politics Undermine Our Prosperity* (New York: Alfred A. Knopf, 2007), 27.
21. Joshua Freeman, *Working-Class New York: Life And Labor Since World War II* (New York: The New Press, 2000), 172.
22. Starr, *Golden Dreams*, 5.
23. "Americana: The Roots of Home," *Time*, June 20, 1960.
24. "Housing: Up from the Potato Fields," *Time*.
25. "Housing: Up from the Potato Fields," *Time*.
26. Richard Lacayo, "Suburban Legend William Levitt," *Time*, December 7, 1998.
27. "Housing: Up from the Potato Fields," *Time*.
28. Freeman, *Working-Class New York*, 106.
29. "Housing: Up from the Potato Fields," *Time*.

30. "Housing: Up from the Potato Fields," *Time*.
31. "Housing: Up from the Potato Fields," *Time*.
32. "Housing: Up from the Potato Fields," *Time*.
33. "Cities: For 60,000 People," *Time*, December 22, 1952.
34. Starr, *Golden Dreams*, 12.
35. Freeman, *Working-Class New York*, 66.
36. Freeman, *Working-Class New York*, 108.
37. Freeman, *Working-Class New York*, 124.
38. Freeman, *Working-Class New York*, 214.
39. Freeman, *Working-Class New York*, 67.
40. Stuart Chase, *American Credos* (New York: Harper & Brothers, 1962), 86.
41. "US Families Are Integrated Buying Units," *Milwaukee Journal*, March 23, 1960.
42. Samuel, *Rich*, 126.
43. Samuel, *Rich*, 126.
44. Cleveland Amory, *Who Killed Society?* (New York: Harper & Brothers, 1960), 523.
45. Kuttner, *The Squandering of America*, 50.
46. "Americana: The Roots of Home," *Time*.
47. Starr, *Golden Dreams*, 206–207.
48. Starr, *Golden Dreams*, 205.
49. Drew Pearson, "Grooming Rockefeller," *Gadsden Times*, August 22, 1958.
50. Marquis Childs, "Washington Calling," *Reading Eagle*, August 25, 1958.
51. Freeman, *Working-Class New York*, 102.
52. Roscoe Drummond, "Nelson Rockefeller Gives His Views," *Herald-Journal*, October 7, 1958.
53. "Text of Rockefeller Television Talk," *New York Times*, February 3, 1959.
54. "Excerpts From Rockefeller's Record 2-Billion Budget Presented to the Legislature," *New York Times*, February 3, 1959.
55. Leo Egan, "State GOP Nears Pact to Ease Tax and Trim Budget," *New York Times*, March 3, 1959.
56. "Review Of The Week Editorials," *New York Times*, March 15, 1959.
57. Bryan Burrough, *The Big Rich: The Rise and Fall of the Greatest Texas Oil Fortunes* (New York: The Penguin Press, 2009), 246.
58. Burrough, *The Big Rich*, 246–247.
59. Burrough, *The Big Rich*, 247.
60. C. Wright Mills, *The Power Elite* (New York: Oxford University Press, 1956), 243.
61. Mills, *The Power Elite*, 332.
62. "The State of Working America, Minority Families," Economic Policy Institute, January 26, 2011, http://stateofworkingamerica.org/charts/median-family-income-2009-dollars-by-raceethnic-group-1947-2009/.
63. Meizhu Lui, Barbara Robles, Betsy Leondar-Wright, Roe Brewer, and Rebecca Adamson, *The Color of Wealth: The Story Behind the US Racial Wealth Divide* (New York: The New Press, 2006), 92.
64. Lui et al., *The Color of Wealth*, 95.
65. Lui et al., *The Color of Wealth*, 95.
66. Lui et al., *The Color of Wealth*, 96.
67. Lacayo, "Suburban Legend."
68. Starr, *Golden Dreams*, 5.
69. Thomas F. Jackson, *From Civil Rights to Human Rights: Martin Luther King Jr., and the Struggle for Economic Justice* (Philadelphia: University of Pennsylvania Press, 2007), 42.
70. Jackson, *From Civil Rights to Human Rights*, 42.
71. Jackson, *From Civil Rights to Human Rights*, 44.
72. Jackson, *From Civil Rights to Human Rights*, 2.
73. "Cities and Suburbs: More and More, the Same Problems," *Time*, December 27, 1968.
74. "Cities and Suburbs," *Time*.
75. Stuart Chase, *The Most Probable World* (New York: Harper & Row, 1968), 226.

Chapter 12

1. Dan Wakefield, "C. Wright Mills: Before His Time," *Nation*, March 18, 2009.
2. C. Wright Mills, *The Power Elite* (New York: Oxford University Press, 1956), 94.
3. Bill Moyers, "How Wall Street Occupied America," *Nation*, November 2, 2011.
4. Moyers, "How Wall Street Occupied America."
5. Robert McElvaine, *The Great Depression: America, 1929–1941* (New York: Times Books, 1993), 30.
6. Bryan Burrough, *The Big Rich: The Rise and Fall of the Greatest Texas Oil Fortunes* (New York: The Penguin Press, 2009), 129.
7. Burrough, *The Big Rich*, 202.
8. Burrough, *The Big Rich*, 204.
9. Burrough, *The Big Rich*, 249.
10. Burrough, *The Big Rich*, 241.
11. Burrough, *The Big Rich*, 233.
12. Burrough, *The Big Rich*, 305.
13. Burrough, *The Big Rich*, 305.
14. Yasha Levine and Mark Ames, "Charles Koch to Friedrich Hayek: Use Social Security!" *Nation*, October 17, 2011.
15. Chris Hedges, "The Origin of America's Intellectual Vacuum," TruthDig.com, November 15, 2010.
16. Robert Collins, *More: The Politics of Economic Growth in Postwar America* (New York: Oxford University Press, 2000), xi, 240.
17. Alan Brinkley, *The End of Reform: New Deal Liberalism in Recession and War* (New York: Vintage Books, 1995), 7.
18. Brinkley, *The End of Reform*, 271.
19. John F. Kennedy, "Address in the Assembly Hall at the Paulskirche in Frankfurt," Published Papers (June 25, 1963), 519, http://www.presidency.ucsb.edu/ws/index.php?pid=9303&st=&st1=#axzz1 HouLXFcb.
20. "Washington Tax Talk," *Taxes: The Tax Magazine*, February 1963.
21. "Washington Tax Talk," *Taxes: The Tax Magazine*, January 1961.
22. "President John F. Kennedy's Special Message to the Congress on Taxation, April 20, 1961," Tax Analysts Tax History Project, http://www.taxhistory.org/thp/readings.nsf/ArtWeb/2B727964CoA28BE5852571690051FD23?OpenDocument.
23. "Washington Tax Talk," *Taxes: The Tax Magazine*, December 1962.
24. "Washington Tax Talk," *Taxes: The Tax Magazine*, April 1963.
25. "President's 1963 Tax Message." *Hearings Before the Committee on Ways and Means, Eighty-eighth Congress First Session on the Tax Recommendations of the President Contained in His Message Transmitted to the Congress, January 24, 1963; February 6, 7, 8, 1963*, 5.
26. "President's 1963 Tax Message," 9.
27. "President's 1963 Tax Message," 9.
28. "President's 1963 Tax Message," 544.
29. "President John F. Kennedy's Special Message to the Congress on Taxation."
30. "President's 1963 Tax Message," 732.
31. Joseph Thorndike, "Profiles in Tax History: Randolph E. Paul," Tax Analysts Tax History Project, October 6, 2004.
32. Paul Buhle, *Taking Care of Business: Samuel Gompers, George Meany, Lane Kirkland, and the Tragedy of American Labor* (New York: Monthly Review Press, 1999), 178.
33. "President's 1963 Tax Message," 1957.
34. Ferdinand Lundberg, *The Rich and the Super Rich: A Study of the Power of Money Today* (New York: Lyle Stuart, Inc., 1968), 1.
35. Sophy Burnham, *The Landed Gentry: Passions and Personalities Inside America's Propertied Class* (New York: G. P. Putnam's Sons, 1978), 201.
36. Gabriel Kolko, *Wealth and Power in America: An Analysis of Social Class and Income Distribution* (New York: Frederick A. Praeger, 1962), 3.
37. Kolko, *Wealth and Power in America*, ix.
38. Mills, *The Power Elite*, 389.
39. Emmanuel Saez and Thomas Piketty, "Income Inequality in the United States, 1913–1998," *Quarterly Journal of Economics*, vol. 118, no.1 (2003), tables and figures

updated to 2008 in Excel format, July 2010, http://elsa.berkeley.edu/~saez/TabFig2008.xls.

40. Emmanuel Saez and Thomas Piketty, "Income Inequality in the United States."
41. Author's calculations comparing top 400 data in the Internal Revenue Service study, "The 400 Individual Income Tax Returns Reporting the Highest Adjusted Gross Incomes Each Year, 1992–2007," available at http://www.irs.gov/pub/irs-soi/07intop400. pdf, with 1961 data for the top 398 that appears in Janet McCubbin and Fritz Scheuren, "Individual Income Tax Shares and Average Tax Rates, 1951–1986," *Statistics of Income Bulletin* (Spring 1989).
42. Brady Bryson, "The Revenue Act of 1963," *Taxes: The Tax Magazine*, January 1964.
43. McCubbin and Scheuren, "Individual Income Tax Shares and Average Tax Rates, 1951–1986." See "Table 6, Part II: Top 50 Returns Per 100,000 Population, Individual Income Tax Shares and Average Tax."
44. Edwin S. Cohen, "Reflections on the US Progressive Income Tax: Its Past and Present," *Virginia Law Review* (December 1976).
45. Rick Perlstein, "That Seventies Show," *Nation*, November 8, 2010.
46. Kim Scipes, "Neo-Liberal Economic Policies in the United States: The Impact on American Workers," *Z*, February 2, 2007.
47. John Judis, "Structural Flaw: How Liberalism Came to the US," *New Republic*, February 28, 2005.
48. Nelson Lichtenstein, "The Long History of Labor Bashing," *Chronicle of Higher Education*, March 6, 2011.
49. "William D. Ruckelshaus, First Administrator on Establishment of EPA," Environmental Protection Agency press release, December 16, 1970, http://www.epa.gov/aboutepa/history/org/origins/first.html.
50. Richard Nixon, "Special Message to the Congress on Consumer Protection, October 30, 1969," from Gerhard Peters and John T. Woolley, American Presidency Project, http://www.presidency.ucsb.edu/ws/?pid=2299.
51. *Supreme Court History, Primary Sources: Attack of American Free Enterprise System*, PBS, http://www.pbs.org/wnet/supremecourt/personality/sources_document13.html.
52. Kim Phillips-Fein, *Invisible Hands: The Making of the Conservative Movement from the New Deal to Reagan* (New York: W. W. Norton & Company, 2009), 162.
53. Jacob Hacker and Paul Pierson, *Winner-Take-All Politics: How Washington Made the Rich Richer—and Turned Its Back on the Middle Class* (New York: Simon & Schuster, 2010), 118.
54. Hacker and Pierson, *Winner-Take-All Politics*, 120.
55. Hacker and Pierson, *Winner-Take-All Politics*, 119.
56. Hacker and Pierson, *Winner-Take-All Politics*, 121.
57. Hacker and Pierson, *Winner-Take-All Politics*, 122.
58. Michael Jensen and William Meckling, "Theory of the Firm: Managerial Behavior, Agency Costs and Ownership Structure," *Journal of Financial Economics* (October 1976).
59. Steve Denning, "Fighting the Kool-Aid of Stock-Based Compensation: Q&A With Roger Martin," *Forbes*, January 3, 2012.
60. James C. Worthy, *Shaping an American Institution: Robert E. Wood and Sears, Roebuck* (Urbana: University of Illinois Press, 1984), 63.
61. Steve Denning, "Fighting The Kool-Aid Of Stock-Based Compensation."
62. Thomas Kochan and Frank Levy, "Addressing the Problem of Stagnant Wages," Employment Policy Research Network, May 20, 2011, http://www.employmentpolicy.org/topic/12/research/addressing-problem-stagnant-wages.
63. Robert Kuttner, *The Squandering of America: How the Failure of Our Politics Undermine Our Prosperity* (New York: Alfred A. Knopf, 2007), 69.
64. Frank Levy and Peter Temlin, "Inequality and Institutions in 20th Century America," Massachusetts Institute of Technology Working Paper Series, June 27, 2007, http://www.nber.org/papers/w13106.
65. Kochan and Levy, "Addressing the Problem of Stagnant Wages."
66. Kevin Phillips, *Bad Money: Reckless Finance, Failed Politics, and the Global Crisis of American Capitalism* (New York: Viking, 2008), 33.

67. Fred Solowey, "Unhappy Anniversary Twenty Years After the *Washington Post* Pressmen's Strike," *Washington City Paper*, September 29, 1995, http://www.washingtoncitypaper.com/articles/7517/unhappy-anniversary.
68. Joseph McCartin, "The Strike That Busted Unions," *New York Times*, August 2, 2011.
69. Joshua Freeman, *Working-Class New York: Life And Labor Since World War II* (New York: The New Press, 2000), 259.
70. Freeman, *Working-Class New York*, 271.
71. Joshua Freeman, *Working-Class New York*, 271.
72. Freeman, *Working-Class New York*, 272.
73. Judis, "Structural Flaw: How Liberalism Came to the US."
74. Hacker and Pierson, *Winner-Take-All Politics*, 129.
75. Kevin Drum, "Plutocracy Now: What Wisconsin Is Really About," *Mother Jones*, March/April 2011.
76. Paul Krugman, *The Conscience of a Liberal* (New York: W. W. Norton & Co., 2007), 86.
77. Ronnie Dugger, *On Reagan: The Man & His Presidency* (New York: McGraw-Hill Book Company, 1983), 102.
78. Polly Cleveland, "Restore the Original Wealth Tax," *Dollars & Sense*, March/April 2011.
79. Michael Perelman, *The Confiscation of American Prosperity: From Right-Wing Extremism and Economic Ideology to the Next Great Depression* (New York: Palgrave Macmillan, 2007), 85.
80. Bruce Bartlett, "The Roots of Tax Reform, Part I," *Tax Notes*, December 20, 2010.
81. Eric Hoyt, "Hollywood and the Income Tax, 1929–1955," *Film History*, vol. 22 (2010).

Chapter 13

1. Sam Roberts, "As the Data Show, There's a Reason the Wall Street Protesters Chose New York," *New York Times*, October 25, 2011.
2. *Too Much*, Institute for Policy Studies, February 21, 2011.
3. "Lou Gerstner Takes the Gloves Off," *BusinessWeek*, November 17, 2002.
4. "Memorandum for the President," US Treasury Department, March 4, 1943, Papers of Eleanor Roosevelt, Franklin D. Roosevelt Library, Hyde Park, New York.
5. Jay Bookman, "This Will Make Your Holiday Brighter: CEO pay up 36.5%," *Atlanta Journal-Constitution*, December 16, 2011.
6. "Income and Tax Items, by Type of Tax Computation, by Size of Adjusted Gross Income, Tax Year 2009," *Statistics of Income* (Washington, DC: Internal Revenue Service), http://www.irs.gov/taxstats/indtaxstats/article/0,,id=96981,00.html.
7. Nelson Schwartz and Louise Story, "Pay of Hedge Fund Managers Roared Back Last Year," *New York Times*, March 31, 2010.
8. Rick Perlstein, "That Seventies Show," *Nation*, November 8, 2010.
9. Richard Wilkinson and Kate Pickett, *The Spirit Level: Why More Equal Societies Almost Always Do Better* (London: The Penguin Group, Allen Lane, 2009), 111.
10. Wilkinson and Pickett, *The Spirit Level*, 180.
11. Anthony Faiola, "Brazil's Elites Fly Above Their Fears," *Washington Post*, June 1, 2002.
12. Michael Norton and Dan Ariely, "Building a Better America—One Wealth Quintile at a Time," *Perspectives on Psychological Science*, January 2011.
13. Stanley Greenberg, "Why Voters Tune Out the Democrats," *New York Times*, July 30, 2011.
14. "IRS Releases 2006 Tax Gap Estimates," (Washington, DC: Internal Revenue Service, January 2012), http://www.irs.gov/newsroom/article/0,,id=252094,00.html.
15. Richard Trumka, "Letter to Elizabeth Murphy, US Securities and Exchange Commission," August 1, 2011, http://www.aflcio.org/corporatewatch/capital/upload/AFL-CIO-Comment-Letter-on-Dodd-Frank-Section-953-b.pdf.
16. Michael Schwalbe, *Rigging the Game: How Inequality Is Reproduced in Everyday Life* (New York: Oxford University Press, 2008), 263.

INDEX

ABOUT THE AUTHOR

A veteran labor journalist, Sam Pizzigati has written widely on economic inequality in publications ranging from the *New York Times* to *Le Monde Diplomatique*. His last book, *Greed and Good: Understanding and Overcoming the Inequality that Limits Our Lives*, explored the price we pay when we tolerate staggeringly huge accumulations of private wealth. He currently serves as an associate fellow at the Institute for Policy Studies in Washington, DC, and edits *Too Much*, an online weekly on excess and inequality.

ABOUT SEVEN STORIES PRESS

Seven Stories Press is an independent book publisher based in New York City. We publish works of the imagination by such writers as Nelson Algren, Russell Banks, Octavia E. Butler, Ani DiFranco, Assia Djebar, Ariel Dorfman, Coco Fusco, Barry Gifford, Martha Long, Luis Negron, Hwang Sok-yong, Lee Stringer, and Kurt Vonnegut, to name a few, together with political titles by voices of conscience, including Subhankar Banerjee, the Boston Women's Health Collective, Noam Chomsky, Angela Y. Davis, Human Rights Watch, Derrick Jensen, Ralph Nader, Loretta Napoleoni, Gary Null, Greg Palast, Project Censored, Barbara Seaman, Alice Walker, Gary Webb, and Howard Zinn, among many others. Seven Stories Press believes publishers have a special responsibility to defend free speech and human rights, and to celebrate the gifts of the human imagination, wherever we can. In 2012 we launched Triangle Square books for young readers with strong social justice and narrative components, telling personal stories of courage and commitment. For additional information, visit www.sevenstories.com.